D0396995

Bloody Roads South

Bloody Roads South

The Wilderness to Cold Harbor
May–June 1864

Noah Andre Trudeau

LITTLE, BROWN AND COMPANY
BOSTON · TORONTO · LONDON

To my mother,
Bridget B. Trudeau,
with love and respect

FIRST EDITION

Acknowledgments of permission to quote previously published
material appear on page 339.

TEXT DESIGN BY JOYCE C. WESTON
MAPS BY MAUREEN TIERNEY CARR

Library of Congress Cataloging-in-Publication Data

Trudeau, Noah Andre, 1949–
    Bloody roads south: the Wilderness to Cold Harbor, May–June 1864/
Noah Andre Trudeau.
        p.   cm.
    Bibliography: p.   Includes index.
    ISBN 0-316-85326-7
        1. Virginia — History — Civil War, 1861–1865 — Campaigns.   2. United
States — History — Civil War, 1861–1865 — Campaigns.   3. Wilderness,
Battle of the, 1864.   4. Spotsylvania, Battle of, 1864.   5. North
Anna River (Va.), Battle of, 1864.   6. Cold Harbor, Battle of,
1864.   I. Title.
E476.52.T78   1989
973.7'36 — dc20   89-32817
                                                                              CIP

10 9 8 7 6 5 4 3 2 1

MV PA

*Published simultaneously in Canada
by Little, Brown & Company (Canada) Limited*

PRINTED IN THE UNITED STATES OF AMERICA

Contents

Preface

By 1864 the glory battles of the Civil War were over. The ornamental latticework of chivalry and righteousness had been seared completely away from the iron machines of war. Battles in which winning or losing seemed to be important were no longer a part of the scheme of things. Men would still fight with personal courage and die clutching for bright banners, but the battles they now fought were the means to an end rather than the end itself.

At the beginning of 1864, North and South stood in weary stalemate. In the wake of Union victories that laid claim to the full course of the Mississippi, lifted the siege of Chattanooga, sealed off coastal seaports, and seriously damaged an already fragile rail supply system, the Confederacy was bowed but not broken. Despite all of this, there were still enough resources available to sustain the Southern armies, and no one doubted that those armies *would* fight.

That, in essence, was what the campaigns of 1864 were about. For the North to end the war, it had to cut even more deeply into the South's resources, both material and psychological. For the South to end the war, it had to stymie the North's plans and count upon a war-weary Northern home front to force the conflict to the peace table.

The campaigns of 1864 were filled with hard-fought, desperate battles whose names have never stuck in the popular consciousness. In the end, the places themselves meant nothing. Ground that was fought over with brutal ferocity one day was abandoned shortly thereafter. Victory was no longer measured by the land held, but rather by the continuation of the will to fight again the next day, and the next.

This is a chronicle of the great 1864 Overland Campaign in Virginia. It pitted the South's best general and its most successful army against the North's best general and, arguably, its least successful army. To win this campaign, Robert E. Lee would have to either beat his enemy decisively or put the price tag of a Northern victory out of reach. For Grant, on the other hand, victory would require that he somehow transfer his own implacable will to the hearts and minds of the men and officers of the Army of the Potomac. Few of the (mostly young) men who shouldered arms and marched into this campaign realized that they were embarking upon the most terrible journey of the Civil War, leaving behind them the last vestiges of a romantic conflict and entering the scarred landscape of total war.

It was curiosity, more than anything else, that first set me on the trail of this largely forgotten campaign. As I walked the battlegrounds and read the words of the men who fought there, I became convinced that here was a tale to be told — an intriguing and important one, about human beings facing the unimaginable. To understand the final cost of the Civil War, one must understand the campaigns of 1864. On the bloody battlefields from the Wilderness to Cold Harbor, Americans of Blue and Gray stumbled out of the nineteenth century and blundered into the twentieth.

This is their story.

Author's Note

The Union Army of the Potomac and the Confederate Army of Northern Virginia were organized along the same lines. Each was first divided into corps, which were then successively subdivided into divisions, brigades, regiments, and companies. I have generally referred to the various corps, divisions, and brigades of both sides by the name of their commanders: for example, Hill's corps, Gibbon's division, and Brooke's brigade. This was a common practice in the Confederate armies, but not so in the Union forces. To differentiate between these "official" unit names and my own unofficial designations, the unit name is capitalized in the former case but not in the latter. When the full name of a unit commander is employed, standard grammatical rules are followed. Some Confederate brigades retained the name of a former commander (Kershaw's Brigade, for instance, was led by Colonel John Henagan), and another, the Stonewall Brigade, enjoyed an officially sanctioned nickname. References to regiments are always by number and state, hence 13th Virginia and 32nd Maine.

The armies marched in long columns, four abreast. When it was time to fight, these columns changed into double-ranked lines of battle. Either end of a line of battle was its flank, while the regimental and national flags were normally carried in the center of the line. Geographic directions are always given from the perspective of the side under discussion.

In order to free the text from numerous uses of the qualifier *sic*, I have adapted a variable rule on spelling. Misspellings that convey a sense of character have been preserved, while those that reflect outdated word usages have been changed. Place names and words that normally appeared in slightly alternate versions (*Spotsylvania* vs. *Spottsylvania; entrench* vs. *intrench*) have also not been altered.

A Note on the Illustrations

The newspapers of the 1860s brought the Civil War into the parlors of America much as television brought Vietnam into its living rooms in the 1960s. There were few communities, North or South, that were not touched by the conflict, and the need to know all about it became a consuming passion for those on the home front. Accurate, timely reportage replaced partisan politicking and dilettantism as the driving force of the American newspaper industry. And as often as not, that coverage was *visual* as well as verbal, for alongside the many hardworking field correspondents toiled a smaller but equally dedicated corps of combat artists, who captured images of the great struggle in ink, charcoal, and paint.

The Special Artists, as they were called, needed special skills besides the daring and enterprise required of all field correspondents. The Special Artists had to be able to sketch quickly and accurately. Out of the inevitable chaos of battle, they had to find the dramatic instant worthy of pictorial record.

When the Army of the Potomac marched into the Wilderness in 1864, it was accompanied by two of the finest Special Artists of the war: Alfred R. Waud and Edwin Forbes. Waud, an Englishman working for *Harper's Weekly*, was described by a fellow correspondent as "blue-eyed, fair-bearded, strapping and stalwart, full of loud cheery laughs and comic songs, armed to the teeth, jack-booted, gauntleted, slouch-hatted." His rival Forbes, of *Frank Leslie's Illustrated Newspaper*, was a New York native who had exhibited at the National Academy of Design before the war.

The drawings included in this book are all original field sketches produced by these artists during the campaign from the Wilderness to Cold Harbor. Some of the images have been reprinted often, a few are less well known, and one is published here for the first time.

The readers of 1864 did not see these drawings. Once the sketches were completed on the spot, they were rushed to the New York offices of the illustrated weeklies, where the artwork was copied onto boxwood blocks by staff engravers. Next, an electrotyped metal impression was made for printing runs that often exceeded a hundred thousand copies. Inevitably, the final product was more polished, posed, and (to my eye, at least) stilted, as any side-by-side comparison reveals. I have elected to return to the sketch work made on the scene by the combat artists. For me, these images have a vitality and a presence that complement perfectly the words of the soldiers themselves.

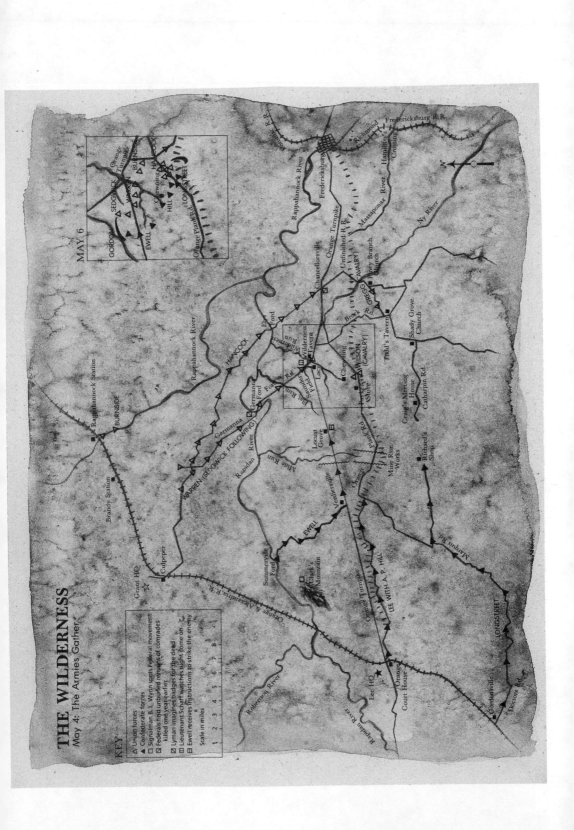

THE WILDERNESS
May 4: The Armies Gather

KEY

- △ Union forces
- ▲ Confederate forces
- ◻ Signalman B. L. Wyon spots Federal movement
- ◻ Federals find unburied remains of comrades killed one year earlier
- ◻ Lyman imagines badges for the dead
- ◻ Lieutenant Scharf watches night come on
- ◼ Ewell receives instructions to strike the enemy

Scale in miles
1 2 3 4 5 6 7 8

MAY 6

GORDON
SEDGWICK
WARREN
BURNSIDE
HANCOCK
Orange Turnpike
Catharpin Rd.
EWELL
HILL
Orange Plank Rd.
LONGSTREET

Fredericksburg R. R.
Richmond
Hamilton's Crossing
Rappahannock River
Massaponax River
Ny River
Orange Turnpike
Unfinished R. R.
Chancellorsville
Ely's Ford
GREGG (CAVALRY)
Piney Branch Church
Germanna Ford
Germanna River
HANCOCK
Rapidan River
WARREN (SEDGWICK FOLLOWING)
Shady Grove Church
Todd's Tavern
Brock Rd.
Wilderness Tavern
Wilderness Run
Saunders Field
Lacy
Chewning
WILSON (CAVALRY)
Stone
Craig's Meeting House
Plank Rd.
Catharpin Rd.
Brandy Station
Rappahannock Station
BURNSIDE
Culpeper
Grant HQ
Locust Grove
Robertson
Mine Run Works
Richard's Shop
Marquis Rd.
Summerville Ford
Raccoon Ford
Orange Turnpike
EWELL
Clark's Mountain
LEE WITH A. P. HILL
Rapidan River
Orange & Alexandria R. R.
Robertson River
Orange Court House
Lee HQ
Gordonsville
Doctor's Rd.
LONGSTREET

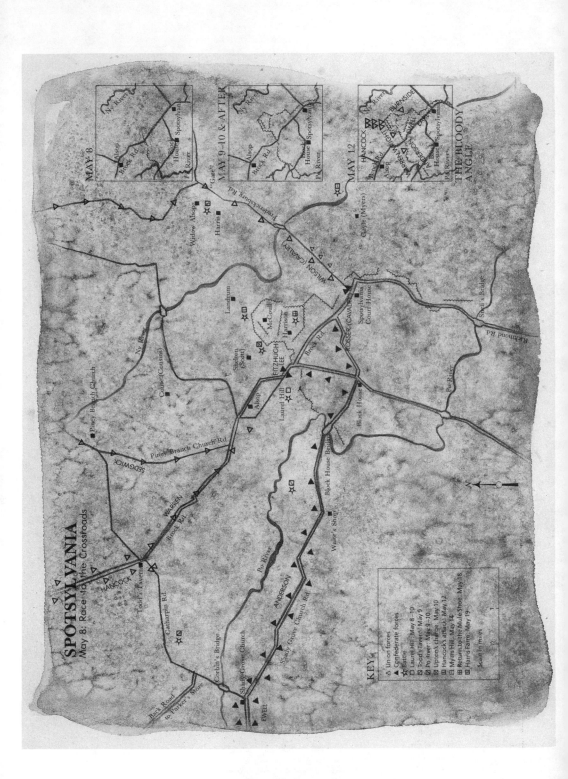

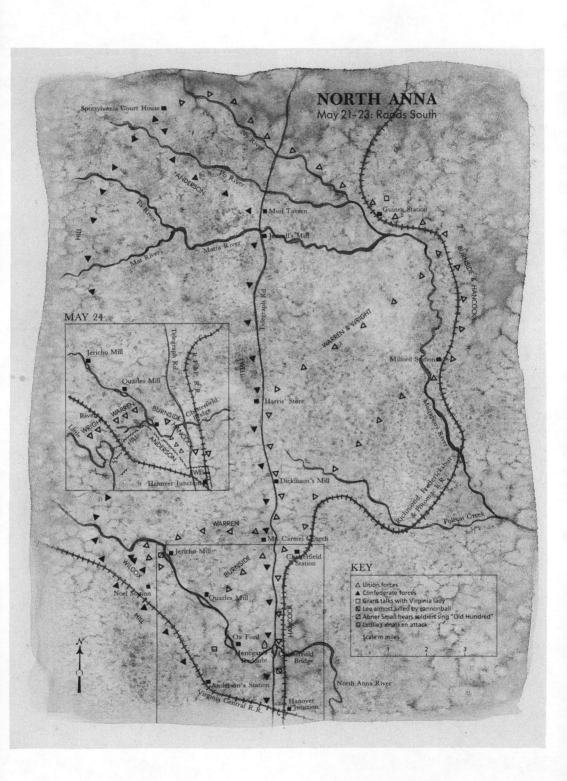

NORTH ANNA
May 21-23: Roads South

Spotsylvania Court House

ANDERSON

Po River

Ta River

Mat River

Matta River

Mud Tavern

Jewell's Mill

HILL

Telegraph Rd.

Guinea Station

BURNSIDE & HANCOCK

WARREN & WRIGHT

Milford Station

Mattapony River

MAY 24

Jericho Mill

Quarles Mill

Telegraph Rd.

R. & P. R.R.

EWELL

Chesterfield Bridge

River

Little WRIGHT

WARREN

BURNSIDE

HANCOCK

HILL

ANDERSON

EWELL

Hanover Junction

Harris' Store

Dickinson's Mill

Richmond, Fredericksburg & Potomac R.R.

Polecat Creek

WARREN

Mt. Carmel Church

Jericho Mill

BURNSIDE

Chesterfield Station

WILCOX

Quarles Mill

HANCOCK

HILL

Noel Station

Ox Ford

Henegan's Redoubt

Chesterfield Bridge

North Anna River

N

Anderson's Station

Virginia Central R.R.

Hanover Junction

KEY

△ Union forces
▲ Confederate forces
▣ Grant talks with Virginia lady
◪ Lee almost killed by cannonball
◨ Abner Small hears soldiers sing "Old Hundred"
⊠ Ledlie's drunken attack

Scale in miles

1   2   3

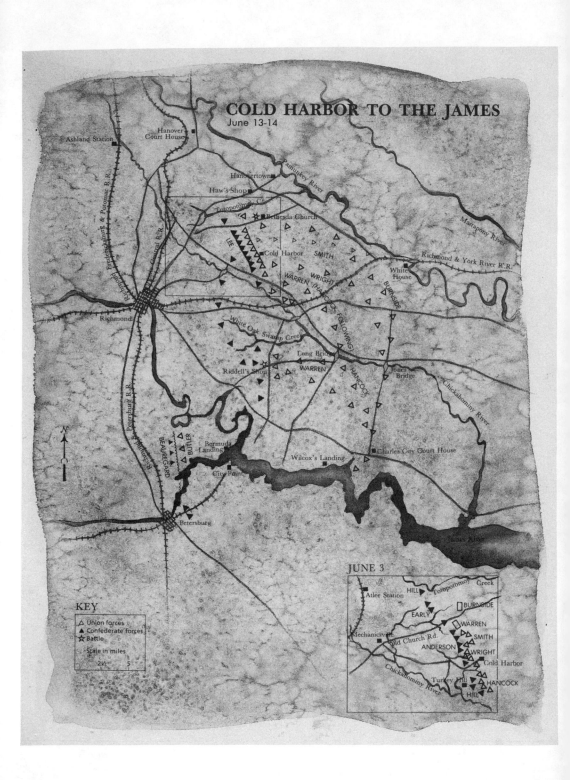

COLD HARBOR TO THE JAMES
June 13-14

Ashland Station

Hanover Court House

Pamunkey River

Hanovertown

Haw's Shop

Totopotomoy Cr.

Bethesda Church

Mattapony River

LEE

Cold Harbor   SMITH

WRIGHT

Richmond & York River R.R.

White House

WARREN (HANCOCK FOLLOWING)

Fredericksburg & Potomac R.R.

Virginia Central R.R.

BURNSIDE

Richmond

White Oak Swamp Creek

Long Bridge

Riddell's Shop   WARREN

Jones Bridge

HANCOCK

Chickahominy River

Richmond & Petersburg R.R.

BEAUREGARD

BUTLER

Bermuda Landing

Wilcox's Landing

Charles City Court House

City Point

James River

Petersburg

KEY

△ Union forces
▲ Confederate forces
☆ Battle
Scale in miles
2½   5

JUNE 3

Atlee Station   HILL   Totopotomoy Creek

BURNSIDE

EARLY   WARREN

Mechanicsville   Old Church Rd.   SMITH

ANDERSON   WRIGHT

Chickahominy River   Cold Harbor

Turkey Hill   HANCOCK

HILL

Bloody Roads South

Prologue

TUESDAY, MARCH 8, 1864

The March wind swept down off the Blue Ridge Mountains, cold, but promising spring. It swirled along the swift-rolling Rapidan River and darted impishly in and out of the winter camps of the two great armies, indifferent to the boundaries established by force of arms.

North along the Rapidan lay the log-and-canvas cities of the Army of the Potomac. A few of the Union soldiers looked forward to the winds that would dry and harden the ground. Then the boredom of winter camp would be broken by various amusements, "such as foot and base-ball playing, gymnastic exercises with the cross-bar and swing, leaping, running and quoits."

South along the Rapidan lay the log-and-canvas settlements of the Army of Northern Virginia. "We never got a square meal that winter," remembered a Confederate artilleryman, William Dame. "We were always hungry." Some responded to their plight with bitter humor, characterizing their enemies and themselves as the "Fed and Cornfed."

Scattered along either side of the river were the outposts of each army, separated by sectional rivalries and ideologies but sharing a common loneliness. Said one Alabama captain, "When encamped on the banks of the Rapidan, often we could hear snatches of songs from the encampments or pickets of the Federal soldiers on the opposite side of the river and our men . . . would sing from our side, and more than once the sweet tones of 'Home, Sweet Home' were sung by the opposing men, and echoed and re-echoed from bank to bank."

It was the 1,062nd day of the war between the states.

Today, as he had done nearly every day since the Confederacy was born, War Clerk John B. Jones dutifully set down in his diary Richmond's street talk. Stories were coming in from Virginia's eastern shore, now under Yankee control. The district was commanded by Benjamin Butler, a fat-faced Federal general whose harsh military rule of New Orleans had brought him the nickname Beast. Virginians who rejected the Union oath of allegiance were being hounded. It was reported to Jones that one family in particular had refused to yield and was paying the price. His pen fairly seethed with indignation as he wrote, "They allege that their father and oldest sister were persecuted to death by the orders of the general, and they *could not* swear allegiance to any government sanctioning such outrages."

Jones remembered an incident that had happened only a week earlier. Two columns of Yankee cavalry had raided Richmond from the north and the south. At the height of the Federal threat, when it was feared that the raiders might free the Union prisoners who were being held at Libby Prison, the city's military commander, John Winder, had ordered that the captives be blown up if the attempt was made. Fortunately War Secretary James Seddon had promptly canceled the order, but it was a clear sign that there was a new desperation in the air in this fourth year of the war.

Even though it was a wet, blustery evening, a larger crowd than usual gathered at the President's White House reception hoping to see the most celebrated Federal officer of the day, Ulysses S. Grant. Secretary of the Navy Gideon Welles, a tall man with a flowing white beard and a huge brown wig, arrived at about half past nine. Welles carefully positioned himself where he could keep an eye on everything. Hardly anyone in the East Room, including Lincoln, had ever seen Grant before this occasion.

One exception was a stern-faced young man named Horace Porter. He had been a volunteer aide on the staff of Major General George H. Thomas when he first met Grant in October 1863. In the succeeding months, Porter's work had put him in daily contact with the Federal general, and now he hoped to serve him directly.

For the moment Porter's attention was fully occupied by the lanky man shaking the hands of well-wishers and favor-seekers. Abraham Lincoln, Porter noticed, "was in evening dress, and wore a turned-down collar a size too large. . . . His form was ungainly, and the movements of his long, angular arms and legs bordered at times upon the grotesque. . . . His face wore a general expression of sadness, the deep lines indicating the sense of responsibility which weighed upon him; but at times his features lighted up with a broad smile, and there was a merry twinkle in his eyes as he greeted an old acquaintance and exchanged a few words with him in a tone of familiarity."

———— ★ ————

Some of the craggy lines in Lincoln's face stemmed from his bitter disappointments over the fortunes of the Army of the Potomac. Lincoln's search for an aggressive military man to direct the fighting in the East had begun in 1861. First there was Irvin McDowell, a rotund professional soldier of no great merit who provided the Union with its first major defeat, at Bull Run. Lincoln replaced McDowell with a dashing, charismatic officer named George B. McClellan. Little Mac, as the soldiers called him, took the fragments of McDowell's army, added the flood of raw recruits who were pouring into Washington, and forged the Army of the Potomac. McClellan did not want to take his army into battle until everything was perfect, and he found endless reasons for delay. Finally, under great pressure from Lincoln, he moved against Richmond. The succeeding campaign, waged on the Virginia Peninsula, revealed only too clearly Little Mac's excessive caution and his eager willingness to believe unsubstantiated reports of greater enemy numbers. His grand army ended its first major offensive huddled behind entrenchments around Harrison's Landing, preparing to withdraw. Instead of sacking McClellan, Lincoln brought in a blustery general from the West named John Pope and set him up with his own eastern command, the Army of Virginia. In short order Pope blundered into a Confederate trap and lost the battle of Second Bull Run. After he was told the news of Pope's defeat a weary Lincoln admitted to his secretary, John Hay, "Well, John, we are whipped again, I am afraid." The Union army was badly shaken and victorious Confederates were invading Maryland when Lincoln swallowed his pride and asked McClellan to pick up the pieces once more.

McClellan saved the day in a bloody battle fought close by Antietam Creek at Sharpsburg in western Maryland, stopping the Confederate invasion. Lincoln and the country rejoiced. Then disturbing rumors came to the capital. McClellan, it was said, had managed the campaign badly, refusing to advance aggressively even after he captured the enemy's battle plans. During the savage combat that ebbed and flowed across pastoral farmland along a four-mile line, he failed to use his overwhelmingly superior numbers and instead fought the battle piecemeal, allowing the hard-pressed Confederate army to blunt his every assault. Then, when the fight was over, McClellan sat and licked his wounds, letting the equally bloodied Southern army draw away. Out went McClellan; in his place came one of the most self-effacing men ever to wear a major general's stars, Ambrose Burnside.

The general, described by one soldier as having a "manly countenance, bald head and unmistakable whiskers," planned his battles well but proved utterly incapable of improvising when the plan needed to be changed. In the cold December of 1862 Burnside tried to sneak the Union army across the Rappahannock at Fredericksburg, but things went terribly awry. Burnside stuck to his plan and watched as Union troops marched out onto open plains in front of Confederate defenders and were slaughtered.

Again Lincoln changed commanders. Burnside's replacement was a debonair, self-promoting man named Joseph Hooker. He talked a great battle, but when pressed he was no better at it than McClellan. At Chancellorsville, in May 1863, Hooker was unnerved into retreat by a Southern army half the size of his. When Lincoln was told of this, his response was an anguished "My God! What will the country say?" With the Confederate Army of Northern Virginia launched on a full-scale raid of Pennsylvania, Lincoln removed Hooker and installed baggy-eyed George Gordon Meade. Meade, a hot-tempered professional soldier, at least kept his nerve. He met the Confederate army at Gettysburg in July 1863 and beat it in a defensive battle. Then, as the battered Rebel army withdrew south, Meade let it go. Lincoln read Meade's victory telegram and choked at the words, "drive from the soil every vestige of the presence of the enemy." "Drive the invader from our soil!" Lincoln exclaimed. "My God! Is that all?" In November 1863 Meade took the Army of the Potomac on a halfhearted offensive that rolled up against strong Confederate entrenchments at Mine Run and then rolled limply back. Lincoln's search for a fighting general was not yet over.

Throughout all of this, the name of one western general stayed in the back of Lincoln's mind. In early 1862 Ulysses S. Grant had led a combined naval and infantry force that captured the river forts Henry and Donelson in Tennessee. Then came Shiloh, where Grant's force was surprised and nearly pushed into the Tennessee River by the Confederates. Grant beat back the Union panic, rallied his men, and counterattacked the next day to regain all the lost ground. In late 1862 Grant began a single-minded campaign to take the Mississippi River fortress city of Vicksburg. He captured it on July 4, 1863, after nearly seven months of trial and error. During the fall of that same year, Grant directed the operations that broke the Confederate siege of Chattanooga. His rise in the Union command was anything but meteoric; ugly rumors of alcoholism dogged him, and there were accusations of incompetence. Lincoln was approached with requests to relieve Grant, but he refused them with the comment, "I rather like the man. I think I'll try him a little longer." Now Ulysses Grant had been called east to accept the recently reactivated rank of lieutenant general and to direct all the Union armies in the field. In the popular mind, he was the man who was going to save the Union.

—— ★ ——

Gideon Welles sensed a change in the mood of the crowd. A "stir and buzz attracted attention, and it was whispered that General Grant had arrived." Welles picked out a group of officers standing at the entrance to the East Room, "one of them, a short, brown, dark-haired man." Abraham Lincoln saw the new arrival and stepped forward with his hand outstretched. Ulysses Grant walked toward him. A White House secretary remembered it as "a long walk for a bashful man, the eyes of the world upon him." Horace Porter was standing near the spot where the two met. He heard Lincoln's greeting: "Why, here is General Grant! Well, this is a great pleasure, I assure you."

THURSDAY, MARCH 10

Robert E. Lee prepared to leave army headquarters near Orange Court House, Virginia, for a visit to Richmond. He carried with him up-to-date field returns showing the sorry condition of the Army of Northern Virginia. Of the powerful seventy-five-thousand-man force that had fought at Gettysburg back in July, something less than two thirds now lay huddled in camps south of the Rapidan. Richard Ewell's Second Corps reported 18,421 present for duty in its encampments scattered around the crossroads village of Verdiersville. A. P. Hill's Third Corps, spread about army headquarters at Orange Court House, added 22,261 more. Further east, near Fredericksburg, the horsemen of "Jeb" Stuart's cavalry corps were wintering. Stuart's tabulations were late in arriving and did not appear on the official March 10 list. Also missing from the total was James Longstreet's First Corps, which had been on detached service in Tennessee since September. Lee wanted Longstreet's men back with him, and he was going to Richmond in response to a number of plans that were being put forward to keep these troops detached. Lee was firm in his resolve to reunite his army, and it was a resolve that was not to be taken

lightly. It was Robert E. Lee who had commanded the Southern army
that stopped McClellan on the Peninsula, ensnared Pope at Second
Bull Run, stood off McClellan along Antietam Creek, upset Burnside's plans at Fredericksburg, outnerved Hooker at Chancellorsville,
and pounded Meade at Gettysburg and then lured him up to the
hidden entrenchments at Mine Run. Now Lee looked forward to
the spring with one certainty: no matter what the Union Army of the
Potomac did, he would somehow attack it. That was his way. Henry
Heth, a brigade commander in A. P. Hill's Third Corps, put it
bluntly: "General Lee, I have always thought, was the most bellig-
erent man in his army."

The rain came down in drenching sheets that rippled relentlessly
across the files of men drawn up outside Brandy Station, Virginia, the
headquarters of the Army of the Potomac. Only the limp folds of regimental flags and the sodden ranks of the 114th Pennsylvania splashed
any color over the otherwise dreary study in mud-brown and gray.
The Pennsylvanians were a Zouave outfit turned out for this occasion
in full regalia, wearing baggy red pants, white leggings, short blue
jackets, and turbans. At last the special train from Washington arrived, and Ulysses Grant stepped out of the passenger car. A medical
man named E. W. Locke, standing among a small crowd of onlookers,
was unimpressed. "His dress is very plain, eyes half closed, he takes
little or no notice of anything. . . . He is the last man we would have
selected for the Commander-in-Chief." Noting that the turnout consisted almost entirely of the headquarters units required for such occasions, Locke estimated that a "small fight between two negroes
would call out twice as many as have come to see General Grant make
his first appearance in the Army of the Potomac!" The smart little
headquarters band launched into a spirited performance of "Hail to
the Chief." Its players tooted away in the driving rain, blissfully unaware that the lieutenant general was tone-deaf and could not tell one
tune from another.

Grant had come to Brandy Station to take the measure of the
man who commanded the Army of the Potomac, George Gordon
Meade. Meade had never coveted command of the army. He had
handled it with competence at Gettysburg, but then failed to deliver
the killing blow. His direction of it since then had been lackluster.

Now, with Grant's arrival at Brandy Station, Meade waited sto-
ically for the ax to fall. Two days earlier, he had poured out his anxiety
in a letter to his wife. "As [Grant] is to be commander in chief,"

Meade wrote, "and responsible for the doings of the Army of the Potomac, he may desire to have his own man in command, particularly as I understand he is indoctrinated with the notion of the superiority of the Western armies, and that the failure of the Army of the Potomac to accomplish anything is due to their commanders."

The meeting between Grant and Meade was brief. Meade began by offering to resign. As Grant remembered it later, "He said to me that I might want an officer who had served with me in the West. . . . He urged that the work before us was of such vast importance to the whole nation that the feeling or wishes of no person should stand in the way of selecting the right men for all positions. For himself, he would serve to the best of his ability wherever placed." Grant came to this meeting seriously considering finding a replacement for Meade. Now he was won over by the officer's candor and willingness to step aside. "It is men who wait to be selected, and not those who seek, from whom we may always expect the most efficient service," Grant thought, and he decided to keep Meade on. Meade, for his part, admitted that Grant "showed much more capacity and character than I had expected."

His trip to Brandy Station helped Grant make another difficult decision. When he left Chattanooga to accept his commission, Grant had fully expected to return west and run the military machine from there. "But when I got to Washington and saw the situation," Grant recalled, "it was plain that here was the point for the commanding general to be." Grant would not allow himself to become deskbound, however. He would exercise his overall direction of all the Union armies from a headquarters in the field, with the Army of the Potomac.

This time it would be Grant against Lee.

Preparation

SUNDAY, MARCH 20

Washington

It was William Stoddard's first day back on the job after a bout with typhoid fever. Stoddard, a member of the White House secretariat this spring, returned to find his boss, Abraham Lincoln, stretched out on a sofa, hands clasped behind his head, "looking as if he did not care two cents for the past, present or future."

Stoddard had missed Grant's visit and was curious to find out how things had gone between the President and his new army commander.

"Stoddard, Grant is the first general I've had! He's a general!" Lincoln exclaimed. "You know how it's been with all the rest. As soon as I put a man in command of the army he'd come to me with a plan of campaign and about as much as say, 'Now, I don't believe I can do it, but if you say so I'll try it on,' and so put the responsibility of success or failure on me. They all wanted me to be the general. It isn't so with Grant. He hasn't told me what his plans are. I don't know, and I don't want to know. I'm glad to find a man who can go ahead without me."

It dawned on Stoddard that Lincoln's "lying there so contentedly on the sofa this Sunday afternoon was due to the fact that the army had been lifted from his shoulders by someone competent to carry it on."

Lincoln continued to talk. "When Grant took hold I was waiting to see what his pet impossibility would be, and I reckoned it would be cavalry as a matter of course, for we hadn't horses enough to mount even what men he had. There were fifteen thousand or thereabouts up near Harper's Ferry, and no horses to put them on. Well, the other day, just as I expected, Grant sent to me about those very men; but what he wanted to know was whether he should disband them or turn 'em into infantry.

"He doesn't ask me to do impossibilities for him, and he's the first general I've had that didn't."

── ★ THE SOLDIERS ★ ──

Virginia private John Casler had spent the winter reasonably well fed and reasonably in love. Casler was a three-year veteran who was determined to survive the war in style.

When the army had first set down in its winter camps, a friend had told John Casler about the Kube family, who lived near Mine Run. Casler paid a visit and was promptly smitten with one of Kube's daughters, Mollie. Throughout the fall and winter Casler visited Mollie often. "I came nearer falling in love than I had during any time of the war," John Casler remembered.

Captain John G. B. Adams waded through the ankle-deep mud and ordered Company A to fall in. There were thirteen men in all, a sad shadow of "the grand company which had left Massachusetts in 1861." Adams got right down to business. Governor John Andrew had written a letter to the colonel of the 19th Massachusetts, asking that the regiment reenlist for three more years, or until the end of the war.

Throughout the Army of the Potomac the coming of spring also meant that the term of service for many veteran soldiers was drawing to an end. But the army could not afford to lose so many trained men, and it offered them inducements to stay: thirty days' furlough along with fat bounty payments. Yet when the veterans' decision was made, it was often made for other reasons.

Adams finished his little speech and looked at the thirteen men of Company A. After a moment of silence, one of them spoke up. "Well, if new men won't finish the job, old men must, and as long as Uncle Sam wants a man, here is Ben Falls." Another, Mike Scannel, added, "I had expected to go home when my time was out and stay there, but we must never give up this fight. . . . I am with you to the end."

Tiny Company A of the 19th Massachusetts Regiment stepped forward and reenlisted to a man.

For others, the decision was made in solitude. A soldier in the 32nd Massachusetts Regiment, Henry B. James, listened to the reenlistment speech and thought hard about it during a lonely stint of outpost duty. "I fought it out alone on picket that cold long night," he remembered. James knew that his father would oppose his reenlisting, but he decided to sign up again. "My country needed me," James declared, "and so I would do my duty and leave the rest to God."

In all, about half of those eligible for discharge chose to fight on. One in two agreed with the Massachusetts veteran who said, "I have no desire to monopolize all the patriotism there is, but am willing to give others a chance."

A similar decision was faced by many soldiers in the camps across the Rapidan. Here the inducements were all of the moral kind. "The Confederate soldier," insisted the Mississippi surgeon LeGrand James Wilson, "was fighting for a 'principle,' the right to be free, for home, for 'Dixie.' He was not fighting for the negro, for bounty, for pay or pension." Some states were planning to make the decision for their soldiers. James Graham pragmatically hoped that the men of his regiment, the 27th North Carolina, would reenlist on their own, "for it will be a great deal better to go in voluntarily before we are kept in by law, or at least, it will sound a great deal better." Even though the men of the 2nd Florida had until July 13 to decide, they met and passed this resolution: "Whereas, we . . . believe, as we did, from the first, that the cause in which we are engaged . . . is just and right, and that our liberties, our honor, and all that makes life dear to us, depend upon our maintaining it . . . *Be it resolved,* That we are determined never to give that cause up . . . we . . . reenlist for the war."

SATURDAY, MARCH 26

Brandy Station, Virginia

On this day Ulysses Grant formally established his headquarters with the Army of the Potomac. The implications of Grant's being at Brandy Station instead of in Washington were not lost on the Union soldiers, one of whom declared, "Boys, the next campaign means business; Uncle U.S. is going to travel with the Army of the Potomac."

FRIDAY, APRIL 8

Richmond

There were no beggars in the Confederate capital, and that bothered John B. Jones. The war clerk's diary catalogued the sad disintegration of civilization as he knew it. On April 1 city papers had carried the story of an infant shot by Yankees — on account of its name, it was said. Two days later Jones noted that it was "generally believed that Grant . . . will concentrate an immense army for the capture of Richmond." Today the subject was starvation. "I cannot afford to have more than an ounce of meat daily for each member of my family of six," Jones complained. To make matters worse, his son's parrot, "which has accompanied the family in all their flights, and, it seems, will *never* die, stole the cook's ounce of fat meat and gobbled it up before it could be taken from him." There were other ominous signs: "The old cat goes staggering about from debility. . . . We see neither rats nor mice about the premises now. . . . Even the pigeons watch the crusts in the hands of the children. *And still*," Jones added with special emphasis, "*there are no beggars.*"

★ THE OFFICERS ★

Since its organization in 1862, the Army of the Potomac had fought Robert E. Lee and the Army of Northern Virginia in a series of major battles. Invariably Union arms lost, or at best managed a bloody draw. The Federal field officers now anticipated defeat: "Our annual Bull Run Flogging," was how one put it. Ulysses Grant knew that this inferiority complex posed as much danger to the success of his spring plans as did the actions of Robert E. Lee. Grant noted ironically that "General Lee . . . filled . . . a very high place in the estimation of the people and press of the Northern states. His praise was sounded throughout the entire North after any action he was engaged in." Grant sent his staff aides — handpicked for the most part from western commands — out to confer with their opposite numbers in this eastern army. They brought back the same disturbing comment from officers throughout the Army of the Potomac: "Well, Grant has never met Bobby Lee yet."

TUESDAY, APRIL 12

Army of the Potomac Headquarters, Brandy Station, Virginia

It had been five days since Army Headquarters issued General Order No. 17, which called for all personal property, all sutlers, and all citizens without passes to be sent to the rear. Today the first group, made up mostly of officers' wives, clustered around Brandy Station, waiting to catch a train to Washington. A New York soldier, F. W. Morse, and a friend rode down to the depot to watch the exodus.

"We sat on a bundle of hay till the most affecting scenes were over, and then attended to our own little business in that line. The remainder of the twenty-five hundred of our guests left on the next day, under circumstances still more heart-rending."

Cornelia Hancock was a slight, pretty girl of twenty-four who had left her comfortable Quaker home in 1863 and never turned back. Cornelia's good looks had proved to be a debit in her account when she applied to Dorothea Dix's fledgling Army Nurse program. Hancock was just too young and too comely, Miss Dix declared, rejecting her application. Moving with a determination that matched Dix's own, Hancock promptly rode toward the sound of the guns and nursed the wounded at Gettysburg.

In February 1864 Cornelia Hancock attached herself to the 3rd Division hospital of the Second Corps and wintered with the army near Brandy Station. There she cared for young recruits with measles and occasional accident victims. On this day Cornelia wrote a long letter to her mother. First there were reassurances: "No soldier would be allowed to come into my house without knocking even in the day time and at night they could not get in without sawing out the logs." Next came declarations of comfort: "I have a stove up in an adjoining shanty, and my front room . . . is a regular army parlor. No one could be more comfortably situated than I am." Then came a little stubbornness: "I think I shall stay around this hospital, orders or no orders, until they stop bringing in 7 or eight sick per day." Finally she took up the subject that was on everyone's mind: "Every one dreads the summer campaign. . . . I want to come home. I dread a battle awfully; somebody that I am attached to must suffer and I can tell you it is easier to see *strange* soldiers suffer than those you have lived with for nearly three months."

From the windows of the Patent Office Building in Washington, Clara Barton looked south with a mixture of revulsion and anticipation. The sight of bodies mangled by shot and shell was no longer shocking to her; the forty-two-year-old Barton had already nursed Union wounded after Antietam and Fredericksburg. Her family wondered how the sensitive Clara could stand to see others in such agony. "You no longer have an identity at such times," she replied. "You are merely a channel through which flows hardest work."

Tending the sick and dying gave Clara Barton purpose and brought meaning to her life. "This conflict," she declared, "is the one thing I've been waiting for. I'm well and strong and young — young enough to go to the front. If I can't be a soldier, I'll help soldiers."

Now Clara Barton toiled at her routine job, waiting impatiently for the guns of 1864 to sound their call.

—— ★ THE COMMANDERS ★ ——

As he prepared his spring plans for all the Federal armies, U. S. Grant was guided by these thoughts:

> [In the past, the] Armies in the East and West acted independently and without concert, like a balky team, no two ever pulling together, enabling the enemy to use to great advantage his interior lines of communication for transporting troops east to west. . . . I therefore determined, first, to use the greatest number of troops practicable against the armed force of the enemy . . . ; second, to hammer continuously against the armed force of the enemy and his resources, until by mere attrition, if in no other way, there should be nothing left to him. . . .

"During the winter of 1863–64," wrote Lee's aide Charles Venable, "General Lee's headquarters were near Orange Court House. They were marked by the same bare simplicity and absence of military form and display which always characterized them. Three or four tents of ordinary size, situated on the steep hillside, made the winter home of himself and his personal staff. It was without sentinels or guards."

The word *duty* meant a great deal to Robert E. Lee. He explained, "I think and work with all my power to bring the troops to the right place at the right time; then I have done my duty. As soon as I order them into battle, I leave my army in the hands of God."

SUNDAY, APRIL 17

Union Camps near Brandy Station, Virginia

The newly delivered recruits stood awkwardly together, feeling as much out of place as they looked. There were 116 of them in all, 116 freshly arrived patriots destined for the ranks of the 20th Massachusetts Regiment. George Bruce stood among the Bay State veterans who eyed the newcomers warily. "Each squad," he insisted, "was looked at and inspected with curious and critical eyes, to form an estimate as to whether or not they were likely to prove reliable in the day of battle. . . . More often than not, this inspection was . . . far from inspiring confidence in the future."

A different breed of soldier was coming into the Army of the Potomac this winter. Previous infusions of new blood had consisted of men who, for one reason or another, *wanted* to be in on the fighting. These fresh batches, however, were made up largely of men who had been forced to come by the draft or paid to come by states anxious to fill Federal quotas. Some were making a business of signing up, collecting a hefty bounty payment, deserting at the earliest opportunity, and then enlisting somewhere else and beginning the process all over again. Cynical veterans crowded near recently arrived recruits for their first roll call, to find out how many would forget the false names they were using.

Still other groups were made up of foreigners who spoke not a single word of English. This was the case for the 116 recruits displayed before the 20th Massachusetts. George Bruce observed, "How and by whom they had been gathered up, or from what motive they had come across the water to take part in the American Civil War was a matter of conjecture and not of knowledge." As night came, the German recruits bedded down together and comforted themselves by singing. Bruce noted, "There were many voices of much sweetness and power among them, and for hours the camp resounded with this unfamiliar music. There was a pathos in the tones of these voices that fitted well with the pathos of their surroundings."

MONDAY, APRIL 18

Army of the Potomac Headquarters, Brandy Station, Virginia

Theodore Lyman was a Massachusetts man with a miniaturist's eye for written portraiture. A colonel on the staff of George Meade, the army's commander, Lyman had ample opportunity to jot down word-sketches of the men who made up the Federal high command. Winfield Scott Hancock, the veteran commander of the Second Corps, was "a tall, soldierly man, with light-brown hair and a military heavy jaw; and has the massive features and the heavy folds round the eye that often mark a man of ability." Cyrus Comstock, a Massachusetts engineer on Grant's staff, "had somewhat the air of a Yankee schoolmaster, buttoned in a military coat." Then there was Grant himself: "He habitually wears an expression as if he had determined to drive his head through a brick wall, and was about to do it."

Today Lyman took note of spring. "I have seen some high-bush blackberries that already had wee leaves, just beginning to open, and the buds of the trees are swelling, and hundreds of little toads sing and whistle all night, to please other hundreds of Misses toads." But thoughts of the coming campaign were never far away, adding a somber close to Lyman's musings: "I suppose we may call this the lull before the hurricane, which little short of a miracle can avert."

―――― ★ **THE SOLDIERS** ★ ――――

In the bleak winter months of 1863–1864, Robert E. Lee's army found its soul. During that time, reported artilleryman William Dame, "there was a deep spiritual interest and strong revival of religion throughout the whole Army of Northern Virginia." It was estimated that more than fifteen thousand men were converted. One Confederate brigadier, John Gordon, felt that the movement strengthened the army: "The religious revivals which occurred in the Southern camps . . . , while banishing from the heart all unworthy passions, prepared the soldiers for more heroic endurance, lifted them, in a measure, above their sufferings, nerved them for the coming battles." Some soldiers viewed their plight in biblical terms. "No army ever had such a leader as General Lee," William Wilson, a Virginian, wrote on April 19. "No General ever had such an army as he — but the God of Battles . . . has suffered us to be sorely tormented and aliens to occupy our lands and strangers our houses. . . . I sincerely hope that many humble fervent petitions of Christians throughout the Confederacy will work out more substantial success for us in the coming summer than an Army with banners."

MONDAY, APRIL 25

Washington

It rained during the night, and morning brought scattered clouds with the possibility of more rain. The long blue columns had been easing their way into Washington from Annapolis since late Sunday. The leading elements of the twisting procession came within sight of the recently completed Capitol dome at about 9:00 A.M.

The Ninth Corps was one of the most peripatetic units of its kind in the Federal army. It fought with McClellan at Antietam, took part in the Fredericksburg debacle, was stationed in southern Virginia near Newport News, served for a while in Kentucky, did mopping-up chores in Vicksburg, Mississippi, spent the winter of 1863–1864 in eastern Tennessee, and was ordered to Annapolis in March to refit. Much of its history was bound up in the personality of the man who had commanded the outfit twice before and was once again in charge: Ambrose Burnside. This was the same Burnside who had been responsible for the fiasco at Fredericksburg. For a while he had served in the West, but now he was back with the Army of the Potomac, and his very presence was causing Grant headaches. According to strict military protocol, Burnside had seniority over Meade. Grant solved the dilemma by joining the Ninth Corps to his own command as an independent unit reporting directly to him. This solution created a new problem, however — an unwieldy dual-command system that could cause dangerous delays when the Army of the Potomac and the Ninth Corps needed to work in close concert.

The corps formed up at about 11:00 A.M. and began a slow march down New York Avenue, toward the heart of the city. A Massachusetts soldier in the 1st Division noticed that "the sidewalks, and even the streets were thronged with people, great interest being manifested to see the troops pass." The front units halted at Fourteenth Street to allow the long column to close up. Then the procession made the turn down Fourteenth Street and marched past Willard's Hotel. Waiting on a second-floor balcony to review the troops was a small crowd of notables, including the bushy-whiskered Burnside and President Abraham Lincoln.

"Right shoulder shift," came the command as the various units passed the hostelry. A New York battery led the way. "The cannoneers sat on the ammunition chests as rigid and erect as English cockney coachmen," Major Jacob Roemer noted proudly, "and acted as if they thoroughly appreciated their dignity and the importance of the occasion." A young drummer in an infantry unit further down the line would write home excitedly this evening, "How I drummed when we passed the President."

Then came the two brigades representing the great experiment. Eight regiments of black soldiers — the first significant body to serve in the Army of the Potomac — came into view. Charles Coffin, a reporter for the *Boston Journal*, noted the moment as one of "sublime spectacle." The troops marched well even though most had been in uniform for barely two weeks. Standing across the street from Willard's, with a clear view of the balcony, was a newspaperman–turned–hospital attendant named Walt Whitman. The forty-four-year-old poet had come down to watch the procession in hopes of seeing his brother George, a soldier in the 51st New York. Lincoln was not wearing a hat, and Whitman thought it looked odd for the President to have his head so uncovered as the black regiments passed. The discipline of two weeks was not enough to hold the former slaves in line as they recognized the man who had signed the Emancipation Proclamation. Reporter Coffin scribbled down this description: "They swing their caps, clap their hands and shout their joy. Long, loud and jubilant are the rejoicings of those redeemed sons of Africa."

Black men were taking a terrible risk in joining the Union army. Just how terrible had been made clear by recent events. Thirteen days earlier a Confederate force commanded by Nathan Bedford Forrest had overrun Union Fort Pillow, located forty miles north of Memphis. About half of the garrison's six hundred defenders were black. Enraged Confederates had gone on a killing rampage, and when it was over some 231 Federals, mostly black, were dead.

As correspondent Coffin watched the solid mass of black regiments approach, he felt the irony of the moment. "And now with full ranks, platoons extending from sidewalk to sidewalk, are brigades which never have been in battle, for the first time shouldering arms for their country; who till a year ago never had a country, who even now are not American citizens, who are disfranchised — yet they are going out to fight for the flag!"

Standing among the thousands who watched the Ninth Corps on parade was at least one Confederate spy. Four days later Robert E. Lee would wire Jefferson Davis, "I received . . . a report from a scout just from the vicinity of Washington that General Burnside, with 23,000 men, 7,000 of which are negroes, marched through that city . . . to Alexandria."

WEDNESDAY, APRIL 27

Union Army Headquarters, Culpeper, Virginia

Ulysses Grant marked his forty-second birthday by writing to his wife, Julia, "Getting old am I not? . . . Don't know exactly the day when I will start, or whether Lee will come here before I am ready to move. Would not tell you if I did know. . . ."

FRIDAY, APRIL 29

In the Fields South of Gordonsville, Virginia

All morning the ragged, proud veterans of James Longstreet's First Corps made ready. Captain D. Augustus Dickert of South Carolina

watched the activity: "Guns were burnished and rubbed up, cartridge boxes and belts polished, and the brass buttons and buckles
made to look as bright as new. Our clothes were patched and brushed
up, so far as was in our power, boots and shoes greased, the tattered
and torn old hats were given here and there 'a lick and a promise,'
and on the whole I must say we presented not a bad-looking body of
soldiers."

The ten thousand men of the Corps marched onto a wide field
and formed double rows. There they waited for Robert E. Lee. The
First Corps had not seen Lee since its transfer to Tennessee in September, about eight months earlier. It was, remarked Lieutenant
Richard Lewis of South Carolina, "a long time since we have been
graced by his noble and majestic appearance."

The artillery units on the flanks of the long review lines boomed
their salutes. Lee came into view. "Hats and caps flew high in the air,
flags dipped and waved to and fro, while the drums and fifes struck
up 'Hail to the Chief.'" A deep, resonating cheer spread quickly along
the lines. Young Alabama private Joab Goodson felt that he "never
saw the men cheer General Lee so much before." Occasionally the
neat ranks would break as Lee was surrounded by mobs of reverently
happy soldiers. Private Frank Mixson of South Carolina was among
them: "The men hung around him and seemed satisfied to lay their
hands on his gray horse or to touch the bridle, or the stirrup, or the
general's leg — anything that Lee had was sacred to us fellows who
had just come back."

One officer who was more objective than most took a hard look
at Lee and gauged the effects of the worrisome winter just past.
"When I saw him the year before, his skin was healthy pink," noted
Asbury Coward, a South Carolina colonel. "Now it was decidedly
faded. . . . But he sat on Traveller as firmly as ever."

There was a devotion beyond simple affection that bound together Robert E. Lee and his soldiers. "The effect was as of a military
sacrament," one artillerist felt. A First Corps chaplain turned to one
of Lee's aides and asked, "Does it not make the general proud to see
how the men love him?" The lieutenant colonel shook his head. "Not
proud," he answered. "It awes him."

Army of the Potomac Headquarters, Brandy Station, Virginia

Andrew Atkinson Humphreys felt no sense of triumph as he finished
work on the plan. Humphreys, George Meade's chief of staff, was
described this way by Morris Schaff, an ordnance officer: "A small,
bow-legged man, with chopped-off, iron gray moustache; and when

he lifted his army hat you saw a rather low forehead, and a shock of iron-gray hair. His blue-gray dauntless eyes threw into his stern face the coldness of hammered steel. I never saw it lit up with joy. . . ." Humphreys had cause to look dour. It had fallen on his shoulders to draw up the logistical plan for Grant's advance into Virginia.

The dimensions of that advance were staggering. First there was the very size of the Army of the Potomac. There would be — if one included Burnside's independent Ninth Corps in the count — nearly 120,000 men poised above the Rapidan for the spring campaign. Put into a line two ranks deep, the army would stretch more than thirty miles. Add to this the supplies needed by men and animals, enough to fill 4,300 supply wagons. Everything — men, horses, wagons, guns — had to be moved as compactly, swiftly, and effectively as possible. An army on the move in enemy country must be able to concentrate promptly to meet any threat that might arise. These matters all bore down on Andrew Atkinson Humphreys as he scratched out the orders to guide the great military aggregation.

The path of the Union advance took it directly into a seventy-mile-square region of Virginia that fringed the south banks of the Rapidan River about ten miles west of Fredericksburg and was known as the Wilderness. Humphreys began his planning with the assumption that the last thing anyone wanted was to fight there. That area, with its tangled underbrush and gully-ridden ground, would make the handling of large bodies of troops "exceedingly difficult," Humphreys thought, and would nullify any Federal numerical superiority. Also, the best roads in the region ran west to east (the direction the Confederate army would likely take) rather than north to south (the direction in which the Union army would be proceeding), so the plan called for the Federal force to move quickly through the Wilderness.

Humphreys split the Union advance into two parallel columns. The westernmost would be led by James Wilson's 3rd Cavalry Division. Behind it would come Gouverneur Warren's Fifth Corps and John Sedgwick's Sixth. This column would cross the Rapidan at Germanna Ford and tramp to Wilderness Tavern on the first day. To the east, and moving simultaneously, there would be a force with David Gregg's 2nd Cavalry Division. Behind it would be Winfield Hancock's Second Corps and the Union Artillery Reserve. These would cross the Rapidan at Ely's Ford and head to Chancellorsville. Ambrose Burnside's Ninth Corps would cover the rear of the strung-out army, screening the huge supply train, which would also cross at Ely's Ford. To steal a march on the sharp-eyed Confederate observers posted on Clark's Mountain, Humphreys planned the Federal advance to begin early on the target day. By the end of day two — well before Lee was anticipated to be able to mount any significant countermove — the Union army would be through the Wilderness. Crucial to the success of this rapid movement was the speed of the supply wagons. "The question," Humphreys realized, "was as to the practicability of moving the great trains of the army that distance simultaneously with the troops, so as to keep them under cover of the army."

Myriad small details weighed on Humphreys's mind. Routes had to be laid out to avoid congestion and tie-ups; start times needed to be calculated for the various units that were beginning the march at differing distances from the river; bridging materials needed to be ready so they could span the Rapidan; and allowances had to be made for possible enemy countermeasures. All this planning was a thankless task, and it rankled Humphreys that any credit for the success of this grand maneuver would be going elsewhere. "It is impossible not to perceive," he wrote this day, "that without in the least lessening my labors and responsibility or those of General Meade, the reputation justly due to those labors, responsibility and deeds will go to General Grant." Humphreys closed his letter on a bitter note: "I made a mistake in accepting this position of Chief of Staff and I am vexed at myself for doing it. . . . It has been almost unendurable to me at times."

Confederate Army Camps, Army of Northern Virginia

As the Army of the Potomac steadily increased in size, Confederates across the Rapidan watched it grow with a mix of emotions. George Clark, a member of A. P. Hill's Third Corps, spoke for many when he stated, "The men knew that the coming campaign was to be a severe one." Artilleryman Cary Eggleston viewed the disparate sizes of the two armies with grim fatalism: "I think we must have known from the beginning of the campaign of 1864 that the end was approaching and that it could not be other than a disastrous one." Others were firmly optimistic: "The thought of being whipped never crossed my mind," Captain Samuel Buck of Virginia declared, "and I felt positive that we would get the best of Grant."

SATURDAY, APRIL 30

Union Army Headquarters, Culpeper, Virginia

Horace Porter, a witness to the first meeting of Lincoln and Grant, now rode proudly alongside his new boss, Lieutenant General U. S.

Grant. More than one string had needed to be pulled to get Porter out of his desk job in the Ordnance Bureau and onto Grant's staff, but, to Porter's pleased amazement, the general had been willing to pull them. Porter had reported for duty at army headquarters on Friday. Today Grant asked his new aide to come along on a visit to General Meade's headquarters, six miles away at Brandy Station. Grant was riding his favorite horse, a long-legged bay thoroughbred named after the Ohio city of Cincinnati. The usually taciturn lieutenant general reminisced to Porter about their experiences together when Porter was an aide to George Thomas, and then he changed the topic to President Lincoln. Grant recalled their first interview, during which the commander in chief had admitted "that he did not pretend to know anything about the handling of troops, and it was with the greatest reluctance that he ever interfered with the movements of army commanders." Further, Grant continued, Lincoln had said "that he did not want to know my plans, that it was, perhaps, better that he should not know them, for everybody he met was trying to find out from him something . . . and there was always a temptation 'to leak.'"

Meade came out quickly to greet the lieutenant general with a warm handshake. "General Meade," Porter noted, "was then forty-nine years of age, of rather a spare build, and graceful in his movements. He had a full beard, which, like his hair, was brown, slightly tinged with gray. He wore a slouched felt hat with a conical crown and a turned down rim, which gave him a sort of Tyrolese appearance."

Listening to the pair talk, Porter learned one important piece of information: "Two days before, the time had been definitely named at which the opening campaign was to begin, and that on the next Wednesday, May 4, the armies were to move."

Richmond

The day began well for Jefferson Davis, the President of the Confederate States of America. Sitting in his office adjoining Capitol Square, he reviewed the good news from all fronts. Everywhere, it seemed, the Union forces were in check or in retreat. Davis's wife, Varina, arrived at midday with a tray of food; the pressures and tensions of the war were wasting the once-vital Davis into a gaunt, almost emaciated figure, and today Varina hoped to tempt him into eating a little extra.

The two had just begun to spread out the meal when a servant broke in breathlessly with the news that there had been an accident, a terrible accident. The Presidential Mansion was under repair, its rear face covered with scaffolding. Joe Davis, the President's five-year-old son, had climbed out onto the scaffolding while the workmen were eating lunch and had fallen thirty feet onto the brick-paved courtyard.

Varina, seven months pregnant, was on the verge of hysteria and Jefferson's face was a stone mask as the two hurried home. They found Joe with his skull fractured and both legs broken. While both parents stood by helpless, Joe died.

Jefferson Davis turned away, struggling with his emotions. Joe was his favorite; he had "set his hopes" on him. Davis tried to overcome his despair by returning to work immediately. A dispatch arrived from Robert E. Lee, and Davis stared bleakly at it for a long time. "Did you tell me what was in it?" he asked his wife plaintively. Finally, grief triumphed over self-control. "I must have this day with my little son," Davis cried. He went up to the room where the child was laid out in a casket. For the rest of the day and long into the night, he paced beside the broken body, saying over and over again, "Not mine, O Lord, but thine."

SUNDAY, MAY 1

Union Army Headquarters, Culpeper, Virginia

Among the communications U. S. Grant received this day was one from Abraham Lincoln:

> LIEUTENANT-GENERAL GRANT: NOT EXPECTING TO SEE YOU AGAIN BEFORE THE SPRING CAMPAIGN, I WISH TO EXPRESS IN THIS WAY MY ENTIRE SATISFACTION WITH WHAT YOU HAVE DONE UP TO THIS TIME, SO FAR AS I UNDERSTAND IT. . . . WHILE I AM VERY ANXIOUS THAT ANY GREAT DISASTER, OR THE CAPTURE OF OUR MEN IN GREAT NUMBERS, SHALL BE AVOIDED, I KNOW THESE POINTS ARE LESS LIKELY TO ESCAPE YOUR ATTENTION THAN THEY WOULD MINE. IF THERE IS ANYTHING WANTING WHICH IS WITHIN MY POWER TO GIVE, DO NOT FAIL TO LET ME KNOW. AND NOW WITH A BRAVE ARMY, AND A JUST CAUSE, MAY GOD SUSTAIN YOU.

Richmond

Jefferson Davis's young son Joe was buried in Richmond's Hollywood Cemetery this afternoon. More than a thousand children walked behind the hearse as the funeral procession moved slowly up Oregon Hill. As the young people filed solemnly past the tiny grave, they left on it sprays of flowers and sprigs of evergreen.

Union Army Headquarters, Culpeper, Virginia

Sometime this day Ulysses Grant sent a reply to Abraham Lincoln, which read, in part,

> SINCE THE PROMOTION WHICH PLACED ME IN COMMAND OF ALL THE ARMIES, AND IN VIEW OF THE GREAT RESPONSIBILITY AND THE IMPORTANCE OF SUCCESS, I HAVE BEEN ASTON-ISHED AT THE READINESS WITH WHICH EVERYTHING ASKED FOR HAS BEEN YIELDED, WITHOUT EVEN AN EXPLANATION BEING ASKED. SHOULD MY SUCCESS BE LESS THAN I DESIRE AND EXPECT, THE LEAST I CAN SAY IS, THE FAULT IS NOT WITH YOU.

MONDAY, MAY 2

Richmond

The newly elected Second Congress of the Confederate States of America convened for its first day of business on Capitol Hill. As was customary, President Jefferson Davis's welcome was read to the legislators by the congressional clerk. "It is enough for us to know," the proclamation declared, "that every avenue of negotiation is closed against us, that our enemy is making renewed and strenuous efforts for our destruction, and that the sole resource for us, as a people secure in the justice of our cause and holding our liberties to be more precious than all other earthly possessions, is to combine and apply every available element of power for their defense and preservation."

Clark's Mountain, Virginia

Confederate brigadier John Gordon long remembered the view from atop Clark's Mountain. Located along the southern side of the Rapidan River, its eleven-hundred-foot peak commanded an area encompassing twenty Virginia counties. Most important, from Gordon's perspective, was the sight it provided of the enemy's Army of the Potomac: "A more peaceful scene could scarcely be conceived than that which broke upon our view day after day as the rays of the morning sun fell upon the quiet, wide-spreading Union camp, with its

thousands of smoke columns rising like miniature geysers, its flutter-
ing flags marking, at regular intervals, the different divisions. . . ."

This day Robert E. Lee was paying one of his frequent visits to
the mountaintop. What made the occasion special was the company
he had brought along: three corps and eight division commanders,
comprising virtually the entire high command of the Army of Northern Virginia.

Lee took his officers to Clark's Mountain to familiarize them with
the terrain. His military success owed a great deal to his uncanny
ability to size up an opponent and then act accordingly. Thus far Lee
had faced five different Union commanders — George B. McClellan,
John Pope, Ambrose Burnside, Joseph Hooker, and George Gordon
Meade — and beaten or cowed them all. Now there was a new officer
to contend with: Ulysses S. Grant. Lee's First Corps commander,
James Longstreet, believed that this Federal would be different.
"That man," Longstreet told a staff officer who asked his opinion,
"will fight us every day and every hour till the end of this war."

Lee had spent the past few weeks pondering what Grant's first
move would be with the Army of the Potomac. Now he was certain
enough of his conclusions to share them with his subordinates. "I
think those people over there are going to make a move soon," he
thought aloud. Lee's hand pointed east to where the Rapidan brushed
against a hellishly tangled mass of trees, undergrowth, and furrowed
ground known as the Wilderness. With no preamble and no explanation, Lee said, "Grant will cross by one of those fords."

With a few more comments and warnings about being prepared,
the conference broke up. As he turned to go, Lee stopped to talk
with young B. L. Wynn, who was in charge of the signal station atop
Clark's Mountain. A few days earlier the two had had another conversation. "Sergeant," Lee had asked, "do you keep a guard on watch
at night?" "No sir," Wynn had replied. Lee had taken a look back at
the unstirring Union camps and said, "Well, you must put one on."

TUESDAY, MAY 3

Union Camps, Army of the Potomac

"On the morning of May 3d, 1864," noted New Jersey private J. Newton Terrill, "orderlies were seen riding in all directions. That something unusual was going on was apparent to all."

HEADQUARTERS ARMY OF THE POTOMAC
SOLDIERS: AGAIN YOU ARE CALLED UPON TO ADVANCE ON
THE ENEMIES OF YOUR COUNTRY. . . . YOU HAVE BEEN REOR-
GANIZED, STRENGTHENED, AND FULLY EQUIPPED IN EVERY
RESPECT. YOU FORM A PART OF THE SEVERAL ARMIES OF YOUR
COUNTRY, THE WHOLE UNDER THE DIRECTION OF AN ABLE
AND DISTINGUISHED GENERAL, WHO ENJOYS THE CONFI-
DENCE OF THE GOVERNMENT, THE PEOPLE, AND THE ARMY.
YOUR MOVEMENT BEING IN CO-OPERATION WITH OTHERS, IT
IS OF THE UTMOST IMPORTANCE THAT NO EFFORT SHOULD BE
LEFT UNSPARED TO MAKE IT SUCCESSFUL. SOLDIERS! THE
EYES OF THE WHOLE COUNTRY ARE LOOKING WITH ANXIOUS
HOPE TO THE BLOW YOU ARE ABOUT TO STRIKE IN THE MOST
SACRED CAUSE THAT EVER CALLED MEN TO ARMS.

A *New York Herald* correspondent, Sylvanus Cadwallader, had
the presence of mind to stake out Grant's headquarters. He got an
eyeful and earful: "Officers and clerks . . . worked without intermis-
sion. Quartermaster and Commissary departments were taxed to the
utmost. . . . Cartridge boxes, haversacks and caissons were all filled,
fires were burning . . . for many miles in all directions, troops and
trains were taking assigned positions, staff officers and orderlies were
galloping in hot haste, carrying orders, whilst the rumble of artillery
wheels, the rattling and clanking of mule teams and the shouting,
song, and laughter of thousands of men, were 'faint from farther distance borne.'"

REMEMBER YOUR HOMES, YOUR WIVES AND CHILDREN, AND
BEAR IN MIND THAT THE SOONER YOUR ENEMIES ARE OVER-
COME THE SOONER YOU WILL BE RETURNED TO ENJOY THE
BENEFITS AND BLESSINGS OF PEACE. BEAR WITH PATIENCE
THE HARDSHIPS AND SACRIFICES YOU WILL BE CALLED UPON
TO ENDURE.

David Craft, chaplain to the 141st Pennsylvania, observed that
"All day the frequent coming and going of swift-riding orderlies [and]
a noticeable excitement about Headquarters convinced the soldiers
that an important movement of the army was near at hand."

HAVE CONFIDENCE IN YOUR OFFICERS AND IN EACH OTHER.
KEEP YOUR RANKS ON THE MARCH AND ON THE BATTLE-
FIELD, AND LET EACH MAN EARNESTLY IMPLORE GOD'S

BLESSING, AND ENDEAVOR BY HIS THOUGHTS AND ACTIONS
TO RENDER HIMSELF WORTHY OF THE FAVOR HE SEEKS. WITH
CLEAR CONSCIENCES AND STRONG ARMS, ACTUATED BY A
HIGH SENSE OF DUTY, FIGHTING TO PRESERVE THE GOVERN-
MENT AND THE INSTITUTIONS HANDED DOWN TO US BY OUR
FOREFATHERS — IF TRUE TO OURSELVES — VICTORY, UNDER
GOD'S BLESSING, MUST AND WILL ATTEND OUR EFFORTS.

GEO. G. MEADE,

Major-General, Commanding

Confederate Camps, Army of Northern Virginia

G. W. Nichols, a Georgia private in Ewell's Second Corps, remembered that "On May 3rd we noticed that couriers were riding around,
sometimes in quite a hurry. We felt sure that something was on the
verge of happening." In A. P. Hill's Third Corps, Cadmus Wilcox, a
divisional commander, related that "an order was issued to have, in
the language of the camp 'three days' cooked rations, thus putting an
end to all suspense."

Confederate Camps near Verdiersville, Virginia: Night

Tom Barclay, a Virginia boy who belonged to the famous Stonewall
Brigade, wrote a long letter home. Among other things, he said, "Our
army is certainly in fine condition and we have a leader in which all
have confidence. But more than this our cause we believe to be a just
one and our God is certainly a just God, then why should we
doubt. . . . [You] may confidently expect a glorious issue in the impending campaign, a campaign between right and wrong, we are
backed by an army of good and true men, the other by a bunch of
lawless outcasts and mercenaries. True the struggle will be a bloody
one but it is noble to die in so just a cause."

Union Camps, Army of the Potomac: Night

Artilleryman Levi Baker and his fellow cannoneers in the 9th Massachusetts Battery felt the tension. "Although many of us are anxious
for more active service, yet there is a minor strain running through
our conversation, as we sit around our fireplaces on our boxes, three-
legged stools and blocks, eat our last loaf of soft bread and drink our
coffee, sort over our letters, burn all but the last."

Brigadier General James Wadsworth was an old man in a young man's
war. A wealthy planter, philanthropist, and politician from upstate

New York, he had sacrificed more than most to defend the Union cause. Nominated by the Republicans as their candidate for governor of New York in 1862, Wadsworth declined to leave the army to campaign and so lost the election. Although not a professional military man, Wadsworth was an able one. He had led a brigade with distinction at Gettysburg and now commanded a division in Warren's corps. At fifty-six, James Wadsworth was one of the oldest of Meade's generals. He wrote this night:

> My Dear Wife:
>   . . . We have just received marching orders . . . and all is bustle and confusion. . . . [I] feel sure of a victory. — I wish I could tell you how much I love you, and our dear children, how anxious I am that all should go well with you, that you will all live in affection and kindness, and that none of our dear children will ever do anything to tarnish the good name which we who are here hope to maintain on the battlefield. . . . [With] all the love and affection I can express . . . believe me, my dear wife, fondly and truly yours,
>
> JAS. S. WADSWORTH

The mood around Grant's headquarters was tense with anticipation. His aide-de-camp Horace Porter marveled at the very immensity of the Grand Strategy. The essence of the plan was simplicity itself: hit 'em everywhere at once. From Chattanooga, William T. Sherman was to take on Joseph E. Johnston's Confederate army in northwest Georgia, with Atlanta as his goal. Supporting him from New Orleans, Major General Nathaniel P. Banks would march on Mobile, Alabama. In the rich Shenandoah Valley west of Washington, Franz Sigel had orders to push a Union force down through the Rebel breadbasket. Most importantly from Grant's standpoint, Benjamin Butler "was directed to move up the James River, and endeavor to secure Petersburg. . . ."

Grant finished a last set of messages. He then "turned his back to the table, crossed one leg over the other, lighted a fresh cigar, and began to talk." Porter leaned forward as Grant discussed the advantages of moving against Lee's right flank. Such a move, he explained, would simplify the Union resupply process, help support Butler's expedition, and also screen Washington, D.C. Grant emphasized that the object of the coming campaign was *not* the capture of Richmond; the target was Lee's army. "Wherever Lee goes," Grant's orders made clear to Meade, "there you will go also." Then the unpretentious lieutenant general made a sudden, dramatic gesture. He "rose from his seat, stepped up to a map hanging upon the wall, and with a sweep of his forefinger indicated a line around Richmond and Petersburg." Grant looked at his aides and said plainly, "When my troops are there, Richmond is mine. Lee must retreat or surrender."

Clark's Mountain: Night

It was near midnight. Confederate signalman B. L. Wynn heard someone calling his name softly in the darkness. The young sergeant rose quickly when the night guard told him that something was afoot in the Yankee camps. Wynn took his perch and looked through the observation glass. "Occasionally I could catch glimpses of troops as they passed between me and their campfires, but could not make out in which direction they were moving."

Wynn promptly signaled this intelligence back to Lee's headquarters near Orange Court House. Lee's reply came quickly. The General wanted to know if the Federal troops were heading west, toward Liberty Mills, or east, toward Germanna Ford. Wynn had to admit that it was too dark for him to be certain. Lee's next order, Wynn remembered, "was that I make a report to him as early in the morning as possible."

Union Camps: Night

In the late hours of May 3 and the early hours of May 4, the Army of the Potomac launched its spring campaign. "The march began silently, without call of bugle or beat of drum," recollected Private Warren Goss of Hancock's Second Corps. "The veterans, as a rule, silently following the file leaders, marched forward, reserving their strength, while the recruits laughed and noisily joked." John Haley, a Maine veteran, was one of those silent old-timers. "We moved on through the interminable forest and endless night," he later recalled. "The winds tossed the leafless branches of the trees, seeming to moan and shudder."

Cavalryman Alphonso Rockwell of Ohio was feeling anything but chipper. "The air was chilly and damp; the blood was circulating at lowest ebb in our veins, and I recall the feeling of inertness and inefficiency that well-nigh overwhelmed me as I imagined all sorts of unknown terrors ahead."

★

Decision

WEDNESDAY, MAY 4

Germanna Ford: 3:00 A.M.

Colonel George Chapman, leading the advance guard of James Wilson's 3rd Cavalry Division, made his dispositions quietly. When the signal was given, dismounted squads from the 3rd Indiana splashed across the Rapidan and clambered up the south bank of the river. Confederate pickets from the 1st North Carolina Cavalry scattered into the darkness. A young Pennsylvania cavalryman felt that the Rebels "gave evidence of great fright, running off and leaving blankets and overcoats and a half cooked breakfast on the ground." The rest of Chapman's men came over in force, taking up a position two or three miles inland.

The first Rapidan crossing was secure. Behind Chapman, Federal engineers led by Captain William Folwell cracked whips and moved their little wagon train of bridging material toward the ford. Poised to follow in Folwell's wake were the heavy columns of Warren's Fifth Corps. In his official report, Colonel Chapman described the Confederate resistance as nonexistent.

A few miles to the east, Union riders under Brigadier General Alfred T. A. Torbert cleared Ely's Ford for Hancock's infantry.

Once more the Army of the Potomac was across the Rapidan.

Clark's Mountain: 5:00 A.M.

The sun was up now, and the Confederate signalman, B. L. Wynn, got a clear view of the activity below. "I signaled General Lee that the enemy was moving down the river. Clouds of dust were rising from all the roads leading southeast and toward Fredericksburg and that Germanna Ford seemed to be their objective point."

Union Army Headquarters, Culpeper, Virginia: 8:00 A.M.

Ulysses Grant, according to his military secretary, Adam Badeau, "started from Culpeper . . . at about eight o'clock and rode along the column amid the cheers of the troops whenever they recognized their new commander."

Roads Leading South to Germanna Ford and Ely's Ford: Morning

The massive Army of the Potomac uncoiled from its camps and filled the roads south. Grant's aide Horace Porter marveled, "As far as the eye could reach the troops were wending their way to the front. Their war banners, bullet-riddled and battle-stained, floated proudly in the morning breeze." The *New York Herald* correspondent, Sylvanus Cadwallader, always remembered "the shimmer of . . . bright bayonets resembling the glitter of frost on hedgerows in winter." "The roads were hard and excellent, full of wagons and black with troops," added Meade's perspicuous aide Theodore Lyman; "there were the little green leaves just opening, and purple violets in great plenty by the wayside. . . ." The image of so many men was itself a morale booster. "It was," declared one Connecticut soldier, "a sight of grandeur and power, the view of acres of soldiers with the bristling steel of their arms gave the idea of great strength and majesty, and one might conclude that they could overcome the world."

"The day had not been oppressively warm," observed Abner Small, a Maine officer, "but in the narrow defile among the trees no air was stirring, and the heat of long marching under a heavy load provoked some of our men to throw away overcoats and blankets." The trail of castoffs amazed New York artilleryman Warren Works: "I believe it would be no exaggeration to say that one could have marched . . . to the Rapidan on overcoats and blankets that were thrown away by the tired soldiers." Sergeant Austin Stearns of Massachusetts declared, "Some boys threw away everything but their rations." An irate Connecticut chaplain estimated the government's loss at between twenty and thirty thousand dollars. Its magnitude surprised even U. S. Grant, who declared it "an improvidence I had never witnessed before."

Few of the soldiers thought of the matter in any terms other than personal ones. In this Augustus Brown, a captain in the 4th New York Heavy Artillery, was typical: "I myself debated for some time which I would part with — my overcoat or my blanket — and finally actually threw the blanket away."

Chancellorsville: 9:30 A.M.–3:05 P.M.

One by one, the various units of Winfield Hancock's Second Corps reached the old Chancellorsville battleground and settled into camp. A year earlier the Army of the Potomac, then commanded by Joseph Hooker, had grappled here with Robert E. Lee and the Army of Northern Virginia. Union soldiers killed, wounded, or missing had totaled more than seventeen thousand. Many of the Yankee dead had been hastily buried by the Confederates who were left in possession of the battlefield.

Ordnance Lieutenant Morris Schaff now declared, "The ground . . . everywhere was strewn more or less with human bones and the skeletons of horses. In a spot less than ten rods square, fifty skulls with their cavernous eyes were counted, their foreheads doming in silence above the brown leaves that were gathering about them." Ohio cavalryman Alphonso Rockwell picked up a piece of bone and held it for a moment. "Just as on the street, we meet a passing stranger and wonder what his name is, — what of his history, — what his past or his future, so I wondered of what personality this dry bone had been a part."

"It made my heart sick to look over the ground," a New York captain wrote this afternoon. "The omen," added a Vermont rifleman, "was not a happy one." Lieutenant Colonel Richard C. Dale of the 116th Pennsylvania was also deeply affected. "He stood gazing upon the ground, wrapped in thought, and spoke in a strangely poetic strain of the goodness of the Creator in covering with beauty and perfume the last resting places of these brave men. He . . . talked of the matter for a long time. . . ." Private John Haley of Maine found little to encourage him as he crisscrossed the old fighting ground. The water he drank from one well had "a most horrible flavor. I desired no second taste." Trying to shrug off the gloomy thoughts these sights of past defeat gave him, Haley reflected, "True, there might be nothing ominous in such coincidences, but they do have their effect on morale. Hooker has been strongly censured for allowing himself to be shut up here in the Wilderness. Is Grant to repeat this stupendous piece of folly?"

On the Road to Germanna Ford: Late Morning

As Grant and his staff rode past the marching columns, the soldiers stared with open-mouthed curiosity at one member of the party. An officer in the 5th Maine stated the question many had asked themselves: "Who was the elderly gentleman in a plain black suit and stove pipe hat?" Riding with Grant's group, Horace Porter overheard other comments from the foot soldiers who wanted "to know whether the general had brought his private undertaker with him, or whether it was a parson who had joined headquarters so as to be on hand to read the funeral service over the Southern Confederacy. . . ." Porter allowed himself a smile. He knew the answer to these questions. "The person was Mr. E. B. Washburne, member of Congress from General Grant's district, who had arrived at headquarters a few days before, and had expressed a desire to accompany the army upon the opening campaign, to which the general had readily agreed."

Confederate Camps near Gordonsville, Virginia: Morning

Colonel Asbury Coward of South Carolina looked for his friend, Brigadier General Micah Jenkins, and asked him for news.

"From all I can learn," Jenkins answered, "the enemy is crossing Ely's Ford. A. P. Hill has already gone to meet him but his Corps is too small to hold back eighty thousand or more of Meade's men."

Coward nodded grimly and turned to prepare his command for its marching orders. Jenkins stopped him and continued to talk. "He told me of a singular dream he had had in Petersburg which seemed to bother him. In his dream he had lived all his life until he came to a blank after the coming battle."

"Why have I not forgotten this dream, as I have all the dreams I've had before?" Jenkins asked Coward. "It's as clear and the details as sharp as though I had actually lived it."

Germanna Ford: Midday

Meade's aide Theodore Lyman sat on the high bank overlooking the Rapidan and allowed himself a curious reverie. Below, the last units of Warren's Fifth Corps were carefully breaking cadence and marching over the temporary river bridges. Forming up behind them were the divisions of John Sedgwick's Sixth Corps. Watching the blue columns tramp across the pontoons, Lyman thought "how strange it would be if each man who was destined to fall in the campaign had some large badge on!"

It may be that passing before Lyman's gaze were the 296 men and twenty officers of the 18th Massachusetts Regiment, with Colonel Joseph Hayes in command. Among the otherwise anonymous foot soldiers was Private Charles Wilson of Company I. One thing alone separated Wilson from his fellow troopers this day. In less than twelve hours Charles Wilson would be dead, the first man to be killed in Grant's spring campaign of 1864.

Wilderness Tavern: Noon–3:05 P.M.

The road south from Germanna Ford was a roughly finished, packed-earth affair that climbed up slowly from the Rapidan and, after a wobbly run of four and a half miles, came out into an open space by an intersection. There it crossed a thoroughfare coming in from the west, known as the Orange Turnpike, an impressive name for what was little more than a common dirt road. The Turnpike continued in an easterly direction on its way to Fredericksburg, passing the Brock Road less than a mile further on. The path of the Union march led south along the Germanna Ford Road, jogged east on the Orange Turnpike, then turned south again on the Brock Road. Just east of where the Orange Turnpike met the Germanna Ford Road, there was a tumble of wood and ruin that had once been a busy stage station called Wilderness Tavern. West of the tavern site, dominating one of the few hillsides in the area with a clear, sweeping view of the surrounding ground, was a large house that belonged to J. Horace Lacy. Crossing the Turnpike at a right angle, just about a quarter-mile east of where the Germanna Ford Road and the Orange Turnpike crossed, was Wilderness Run.

Charles Griffin's division, leading the Fifth Corps this day, arrived near the crossroads at about noon. "All was quiet," reminisced New York captain Porter Farley. "An ominous silence was our only welcome." This was fine, for few of the Federals had much energy left. Some regiments had been on the go since midnight. A bone-weary member of the 22nd Massachusetts recalled the march as being "long, tedious and severe." Still, several Pennsylvanians from the Corn Exchange Regiment (the 118th) managed to do a little scouting. They came back to camp subdued by what they had seen of the Wilderness. "It was a wild, weird region. Everywhere was dense and trackless forest. . . . No other idea of the country can be given save that it was a forest apparently without limit, with clearings so few and their space so contracted as scarcely to be considered as breaking the solemn monotony of tree, chaparral and undergrowth."

The commander of the Fifth Corps, Gouverneur Warren, was a slight-figured, sallow-faced man with an engineer's love of well-coordinated parts and a pedant's distaste for impulsive, reckless actions. The thirty-four-year-old major general could be moody and was usually obsessed with details to the point of distraction. Warren's mood this afternoon was upbeat. Morris Schaff passed by Warren's headquarters around suppertime and found the corps commander to be "in fine spirits." Just about everyone around Wilderness Tavern was feeling good about this day. A captain in the 24th Michigan voiced the thoughts of many: "All were in high spirits, being sanguine of success."

Germanna Ford: 1:30 P.M.

Ulysses Grant established temporary headquarters in an old farm-house on a bluff overlooking the river. Horace Porter was standing nearby when Grant said, "Well, the movement so far has been as satisfactory as could be desired."

A newspaperman in Grant's entourage stepped forward and asked, "How long will it take you to get to Richmond?" "I will agree to be there in about four days," Grant returned quickly. Catching the look of disbelief on the reporter's face, he continued, "That is, if General Lee becomes a party to the agreement, but if he objects, the trip will undoubtedly be prolonged."

Confederate Camps near Verdiersville: Early Afternoon

The word came to the men of Richard Ewell's Second Corps late in the morning: pack up and march at once. A Georgia soldier named George Washington Hall was overwhelmed by the sounds that followed: "The drums resounded and echoed from the various brigades and regiments from every direction, their hoarse monotonous sound . . . warned us to prepare for battle." From that moment, remembered Lieutenant Robert Funkhouser of Virginia, "All was hurry and confusion."

By the time Ewell's column set out, the sun was well up and the day hot. Alabama private James Roberts readily admitted that "not a few of the 'Hardy Veterans' of Lee were compelled to stop and seek rest beneath the tempting shades of the forest trees along the line of march." Nothing, however, could dampen the enthusiasm of a young Virginian, James McCown: "All nature seems smiling on this spring morning. What a grand sight is the [Army of Northern Virginia] in motion. The . . . [Stonewall] brigade is all life — seems as though they are never to be conquered."

The gray files headed eastward, passing through Mine Run. There John Casler, the pragmatic Virginia private, took a brief leave from the Stonewall Brigade and ran to Mollie Kube's house. "I called in and gave her farewell," Casler remembered fondly forty-nine years after the war, "and have never seen or heard of her since."

Union Cavalry Headquarters, near Wilderness Tavern: Afternoon

Phil Sheridan, the cavalry chief of the Army of the Potomac, was angry. The hard-driving officer believed that his riders should be given an offensive role in the current campaign, but that was not the thinking of the infantry-minded Federal high command. Instead, most of Sheridan's cavalry was tied down watching over the huge Union supply train. Of his three divisions, only James Wilson's — numerically Sheridan's weakest — was out scouting in the enemy's direction.

For all intents and purposes, the Federal army was marching past an alert and aggressive enemy with its eyes closed.

Gordonsville: 4:00 P.M.

There was something in the makeup of James Longstreet that cast him forever as the outsider. In the Army of Northern Virginia, dominated by Virginians, the North Carolina–born Longstreet was a geographic outsider, one who also spoke openly of his profound doubts about the offensive strategy practiced by Robert E. Lee. The cause of the Confederacy would be best served, Longstreet believed, by husbanding its meager resources and forcing the enemy to attack it. Yet James Longstreet was one of the few senior officers whom Lee trusted to run a corps, so — profound doubts and all — he commanded one third of Lee's army.

Lee's marching orders to Longstreet came at around 1:00 P.M., and as usual, James Longstreet had an improvement to suggest. The order designated a route that would send the First Corps in *behind* A. P. Hill's Third Corps. Longstreet proposed taking roads that would bring his corps up to a point *alongside* Hill's men, on their right flank. Lee approved the change, and the ten-thousand-man First Corps set out from Gordonsville — about forty miles southwest of Parker's Store — at around 4:00 P.M.

Verdiersville: Late Afternoon–Early Evening

Marching orders for A. P. Hill's Third Corps came at about 11:00 A.M. "A universal stir ensued," one South Carolina officer noted wryly. By early afternoon the corps was advancing along the Orange Plank Road toward Fredericksburg. (The Plank Road got its name from the wooden paving that had been laid down years before the war in a plan to make the passage a toll route.) Hill's goal was Verdiersville, a crossroads hamlet eleven miles beyond Orange Court House and nine from Parker's Store. For the rearmost units in Hill's column it meant covering twenty-eight miles. His long, spiky files moved on a parallel course with Ewell's corps, which was marching on the Orange Turnpike to the north.

Robert E. Lee rode quietly at the head of Hill's column. A cavalry courier who saw him this afternoon noted that Lee "is looking remarkably well and as calm, as courteous and as considerate today as on the most ordinary occasions."

The reports that were coming in were sketchy, so Lee had an imperfect picture of Union movements. Grant might be gathering his force across the river for a lunge at the Mine Run entrenchments, planning an advance on Fredericksburg, or intending to push rapidly south down to the open country around Spotsylvania Court House. Lee's only option at the moment was to pull his units together and seek any opportunity that might arise.

Even as he pondered Grant's movements, Lee was also dealing with the politics of command. The Confederate President, Jefferson Davis, tended to view matters from a national perspective and was fond of moving military units about the Confederacy as if they were pieces on a chessboard. Lee was firmly committed to the defense of Virginia and the integrity of his army. His exchanges with Davis often consisted of patient explanations of why a particular plan to detach portions of the army was not a good idea, and why it would be best to return those units that had previously been borrowed. From his field headquarters near Verdiersville, Lee now dictated another such letter. "It is apparent," he began, "that the long threatened effort to take Richmond has begun." Lee then brushed aside Davis's idea of diverting Yankee designs by launching small-scale offensives in North Carolina. "Success in resisting the chief armies of the enemy will enable us more easily to recover the country now occupied by him," Lee lectured. Quickly he moved to the point he had made time and time again: "We are inferior in numbers, and as I have before stated to Your Excellency the absence of the troops belonging to this army weakens it more than by the mere numbers of men."

Robert E. Lee signed the letter, "With great respect, your obt servt."

Locust Grove: Late Afternoon

The Union cavalry patrol edged warily into the crossroads settlement of Locust Grove. The officer in command stood in his stirrups and squinted westward into the setting sun. His orders from James Wilson were to scout to Locust Grove and then, if no Confederate troops were spotted, to continue southward to Parker's Store. The officer saw nothing and waved his troop onto the forest path south.

Minutes later the sunset glare settled into clouds of dust thrown up by the lead elements of Richard Ewell's Second Confederate Corps. Ewell's men would make camp this night in Locust Grove, miles closer to the Federal columns than anyone in the Union high command would have thought possible.

Germanna Ford: 6:00 P.M.

Couriers departed from Grant's temporary headquarters with orders for the next day's movement. Hancock's Second Corps was to march from Chancellorsville southwest to Shady Grove Church. Warren's Fifth would move from Wilderness Tavern southwest to Parker's Store. John Sedgwick's Sixth Corps would turn over the defense of Germanna Ford to Burnside's Ninth Corps and then move down to Wilderness Tavern.

Sometime after sunset George Meade ambled over and joined Grant before a large campfire made of fence rails. Ordnance officer Morris Schaff watched as "Grant's staff withdrew to a fire of their own, and left them alone." Schaff nosed around and learned that "from all accounts they were both cheery over having the army across the Rapidan. Anxiety over their first move was all gone." All the reports on hand readily lent themselves to the interpretation that Lee was reacting as he had when Meade had crossed the Rapidan in November, and was taking up a defensive line along the old Mine Run position. Even fretful Andrew Humphreys, the master planner of Grant's advance, felt gratified. "It was a good day's work," he insisted, "in such a country for so large an army with its artillery and fighting trains to march twenty miles, crossing a river on five bridges of its own building, without a single mishap, interruption, or delay." However, the bulky, plodding wagon train would not clear the river crossings until the middle of the next day, the fifth. That meant that the Union army would not be able to march clear of the Wilderness until then. It was a risk, but as long as Lee kept the Confederate army digging in near Mine Run, it should all work out as planned.

In the Fifth Corps camps, spread about Wilderness Tavern, the men for the most part slept easily. Slumber in the 155th Pennsylvania was "serene and undisturbed," and in the 20th Maine the night was "quiet and restful." Lieutenant John Dusseault of the 39th Massachusetts never forgot the image formed by the flickering campfires of the twenty-five-thousand-man corps at rest. It was, Dusseault felt, "a most impressive sight."

Ordnance officer Morris Schaff sat alone on an old rail fence, watching thoughtfully as "evening deepened into a twilight of great peace." In the distance Schaff heard a brigade singing hymns and songs. Then, "slowly out of the sky bending kindly over us all, — woods, the Lacy fields, the old tavern, and murmuring runs, — the light faded softly away and on came night."

Orange Turnpike, near Locust Grove: Night

In an army full of distinctive characters, Richard Stoddert Ewell was in a class by himself. So nervous and fidgety that he could not sleep regularly, the Confederate Ewell had "bright, prominent eyes, a bomb-shaped, bald head, and a nose like that of Francis of Valois." He spoke in a high, piping voice and tended to lisp when he was excited. In the early months of the war, Ewell had gained a reputation as a hard-fighting, aggressive officer. He had lost a leg at Second Bull Run in 1862 and returned to the army a more subdued man. The Army of Northern Virginia was then sorely in need of senior officers, and "Baldy" Ewell became a corps commander.

Then came Gettysburg, where, some said, Ewell's indecisiveness on July 1 had robbed the Confederacy of its golden opportunity for victory. Others muttered that Ewell was being disproportionately influenced by his subordinate Jubal Early, and that he was apt to act erratically when given no firm directives. Now, in the spring of 1864, Ewell's Second Corps lay closest to the invading Yankee columns.

At 8:00 P.M. Robert E. Lee dictated orders for Ewell to his aide Walter Taylor. "General Lee," Taylor wrote, ". . . wishes you to be ready to move on early in the morning. If the enemy moves down the river [toward Fredericksburg], he wishes you to push on after him. . . . The general's desire is to bring him to battle as soon now as possible."

Quirky Dick Ewell read the dispatch and nodded absently in the flickering firelight. These were the kind of orders he understood.

A few miles farther east, near the western edge of an open field, advance pickets from the 44th Virginia settled in for the night. Less than a mile away, unseen through the cordons of brush and trees, lay the forward outposts of the Union Fifth Corps, and behind them the main camps of the Federal army. Private Charles Wilson of Massachusetts now had only a few hours of life left.

★

The Wilderness

THURSDAY, MAY 5

Early Morning

A Virginia artilleryman, Robert Stiles, riding ahead of his command, came upon Richard Ewell's headquarters near Locust Grove. The air was heavy with the smell of woodsmoke and alive with the clank-clatter-murmur of men coming awake. Portions of the Confederate Second Corps were already in motion on the Orange Turnpike, marching east. Ewell, Stiles noticed, was unusually "thin and pale . . . but bright-eyed and alert." The corps commander gave a friendly wave, inviting the cannoneer to dismount for some coffee. As they chatted, Major Stiles diplomatically asked Lieutenant General Ewell "if he had any objections to telling me his orders." Ewell's response was brisk. "Just the orders I like," he piped, "to go right down the . . . road and strike the enemy wherever I find him."

Morris Schaff joined in an early breakfast at Gouverneur Warren's headquarters near the Lacy House. The Fifth Corps commander had made some changes in the plan for the day's march. Each corps was advancing with its own collection of supply wagons, and Warren's orders were to send the slow-moving train by way of the Brock Road while his troops advanced on a more direct route to Parker's Store. Warren decided that it would be just as efficient for his men to bring their wagons along. It was a routine operational decision that would have dramatic consequences.

Robert E. Lee's aide Charles Venable found his chief cheerful and talkative this morning at the army's headquarters near Verdiersville. During the night Lee had received more scouting reports, which indicated that Grant was moving neither east toward Fredericksburg nor west toward Mine Run, but was instead pushing south into the Wilderness. To Venable, Lee "expressed his pleasure that the Federal general had not profited by General Hooker's Wilderness experiences, and that he seemed inclined to throw away to some extent the immense advantage which his great superiority in numbers . . . gave him."

Horace Porter, along with the other officers at Grant's temporary headquarters near Germanna Ford, had gotten little sleep during the night. Everyone wondered what daylight would bring. The staff consensus was that it would be either a footrace to secure good positions or a fight.

Grant waited for most of his aides to finish eating before he sat down to breakfast. The lieutenant general was maintaining his headquarters at the Rapidan crossing pending the arrival of Burnside's Ninth Corps. While Grant sipped coffee and stared thoughtfully into the distance, a young reporter slipped up to the far end of the well-stocked table and began helping himself. "The general," Porter noted with amusement, "paid no more attention to this occurrence than he would have paid to the flight of a bird across his path."

A. P. Hill's Third Corps was on the road early, marching east along the Orange Plank Road. A short distance outside Verdiersville, the head of the column came upon the great Mine Run entrenchments, built to block Meade's winter assault. The troops swung past them without hesitation. Now there could be no doubt that Lee's plan was an offensive one. William Palmer, an aide on Hill's staff, overheard the soldiers chatter as they loped through the Mine Run lines: "Mars Bob is going for them this time."

As dawn brightened the sky, Colonel David Jenkins saw it with his own eyes. Jenkins, commanding the advance picket line of Charles Griffin's division, was posted along the Orange Turnpike; he was the farthest west from the main Union camps around Wilderness Tavern. Only moments before, a courier had ridden in with orders for the picket line to be held in place until the main body of the Fifth Corps cleared the Tavern area on its way to Parker's Store. Jenkins barely glanced at the note before turning it over to scribble on its back, "The Rebel Infantry have appeared on the Orange . . . Turnpike and are forming a line of battle, three-quarters of a mile in front of General

Griffin's line of battle. I have my skirmishers out, and preparations are being made to meet them. There is a large cloud of dust in that direction."

Dawn–1 P.M.

Some of the men in Winfield Hancock's Second Corps "turned out stiff and sore this morning, . . . drenched to the skin with dew, which falls so heavily here that . . . the appearance of the . . . fields, is very much like that after a severe storm."

William Corby, a chaplain in the Irish Brigade, awoke to an unpleasant surprise. Corby and a fellow cleric had spent the night about ten feet from a country road, comfortably sandwiched between two army blankets. Before the chaplain fell asleep, he had propped a soft military hat over his face to keep out the damp air. Now, as Corby came awake, he discovered that during the night some dexterous Union soldier had swapped headgear with him. Gone was his new felt hat. In its place Corby found one that "must have been in use for two or three years. . . . The lining had been torn out . . . and the bell of the hat had assumed the form of a . . . pineapple!"

He could wear this caricature of a hat or go bareheaded. Grumbled Chaplain Corby, "The thought of it spoiled my morning meditation."

The Second Corps fell into line at around 5:00 A.M. to begin its southwest movement from Chancellorsville toward Shady Grove Church. The pace of the march, recalled one New Yorker, was "a moderate gait . . . with occasional short halts."

Lieutenant Colonel John Hammond was not expecting any serious trouble as his mounted command ambled west along the Orange Plank Road. Hammond led the 5th New York Cavalry, a force of five hundred riders assigned to patrol the Plank Road and "keep an active lookout for the enemy." Some four miles south James Harrison Wilson was leading the bulk of the 3rd Cavalry Division on a sweep west toward Craig's Meeting House. Hammond and his men were to secure the area around Parker's Store and hold it until they were relieved by Warren's Fifth Corps.

It was shortly after dawn when carbine fire crackled around the head of Hammond's column. Confederate skirmishers from the 47th North Carolina, pushing ahead of A. P. Hill's corps, brought the prowling New Yorkers to a halt and began to drive them back. Hammond was not about to be shoved out of the way, and he fed most of his men into the fighting. The Federals were armed with rapid-firing, breech-loading Spencer carbines, and their gunfire stalled the Tarheel infantrymen, who were carrying standard single-shot, muzzle-loading rifles. The sharp bark of the Spencers "made the dense woods ring," according to one New Yorker, while a Confederate made the grudging admission that the Yankees "were picked men and hard to move."

The Confederate line thickened with reinforcements and then lengthened to overlap the Federal flanks. Again and again Hammond gave ground, only to re-form his lines a short distance back and once more check the enemy advance. The blue-coated riders, one Mississippi soldier remarked ruefully, "fought us on every hill for several miles."

Hammond's five hundred men were slowing, but not stopping, the advance of A. P. Hill's corps. As the minutes passed, the cavalry officer repeatedly looked back over his shoulder, wondering when he would see the leading elements of Warren's Fifth Corps, due to arrive from Wilderness Tavern.

Morris Schaff was riding near Gouverneur Warren when a staff officer brought word of the picket sighting from Charles Griffin. "I do not believe," Schaff declared, "that Warren ever had a greater surprise in his life. . . ." The Fifth Corps commander at once dictated a message to Meade, passing along the report of Confederate troops and indicating that for the moment he was halting his command to await further developments. Warren then sent an order back to Griffin: "Push a force out at once against the enemy, and see what force he has."

Despite the weight of evidence before him, Robert E. Lee still had to check the other Rapidan crossings to be certain that the movement of the Union army across Germanna Ford and Ely's Ford was not some massive feint.

Private George Peyton, part of Company A of the 13th Virginia Infantry, was among those who were roused early this morning and hustled off to investigate the other crossing points. Peyton's unit drew Summerville Ford, perhaps ten miles west (as the crow flies) from Germanna Ford. Peyton was battling a cold. "I felt very bad," he confessed to his diary, "and my knapsack hurt my shoulders so I almost cried. We marched very fast and got to the ford about sunrise and not a Yankee in sight. You can imagine what we thought. We were deployed up and down the river and laid down and went to sleep."

Warren's order to Charles Griffin to "push a force out at once against the enemy" moved down the chain of command. Griffin took the note and endorsed it: "General Bartlett will please execute the within order." It was 7:00 A.M.

The marching men of Richard Ewell's corps were spread out along the Orange Turnpike, feeling their way east. For all his bluster over his morning coffee, Ewell was not rushing forward. A young Alabamian in Rodes's division insisted, "We advanced carefully — cautiously, and quite slowly."

George Meade found Warren's headquarters and listened to the Fifth Corps commander's report. Morris Schaff heard Meade exclaim emphatically, "If there is to be any fighting this side of Mine Run, let us do it right off."

Warren's reconnaissance order to Griffin was now in the hands of Joseph Bartlett, the commander of the 3rd Brigade, who decided that two regiments could do the job. He called in Colonel Joseph Hayes, ordering him to ready the 83rd Pennsylvania and the 18th Massachusetts for an advance. In the camps of the two regiments, men kicked dirt over fires, pulled apart neat pyramids of stacked rifles, and formed up to the growling accompaniment of noncommissioned officers. Private Charles Wilson of Company I grumbled with the rest and shambled into formation.

At 7:30 A.M. U. S. Grant, still waiting near Germanna Ford for Burnside's column to appear, received George Meade's report that a Confederate force of unknown size had appeared on the Orange Turnpike, smack on the Union right flank. Meade seconded Warren's halting of the Fifth Corps' advance and, further, indicated that he was sending word to Hancock to stop the Second Corps at Todd's Tavern, about four miles short of Shady Grove Church. Grant scribbled a quick reply, stating his own situation and adding, "If any opportunity presents itself for pitching into a part of Lee's army, do so. . . ."

Major Campbell Brown served as a staff officer to his father-in-law, Richard S. Ewell. The fact that camp rumor suggested that he owed his appointment to his mother's influence did little to endear the young officer to the other aides.

Brown was in the saddle early this day, picking his way along barely discernible forest paths, looking for Robert E. Lee. He found the army commander at around 8:00 A.M. and passed along Ewell's request for further orders.

Lee first told Major Brown that he wanted Ewell to regulate the pace of his march to that of A. P. Hill's. The two Confederate corps were separated by perhaps two and three-quarter miles of often impenetrable wilderness, but Lee was anxious that the advance toward the enemy be as closely synchronized as possible. Lee's second point puzzled Brown. As the young aide remembered it, "Above all General Ewell was not to get his troops entangled so as to be unable to disengage them, in case the enemy was in force." This seemed to contradict Lee's dispatch of the night before, with its orders to "bring [the enemy] to battle as soon as possible."

Campbell Brown nudged his horse back onto the trail, hoping to get the restraining order to Richard Ewell before things got out of hand on the Orange Turnpike.

The two regiments that had been picked to reconnoiter the Confederate force in Griffin's front on the Orange Turnpike pushed through heavy brush on the right side of the road. When the pair — the 18th Massachusetts and the 83rd Pennsylvania — came up to the line held by the most forward of the Union pickets, Colonel Joseph Hayes stopped their advance. Two companies from each regiment were now detailed to probe forward. In the 18th, Company I was one of those chosen. Private Charles Wilson dropped his knapsack, readied his combat gear, and stepped out along with the rest.

Brigadier General Samuel W. Crawford's division, leading the way for the Fifth Corps this morning, emerged from the confining underbrush of the Wilderness onto the open fields of a farm owned by William V. Chewning. It was a good position, providing well-cleared ground situated on one of the higher plateaus in the area. In the near distance Crawford could hear the sharp crack of carbines. He guessed that Union and Confederate cavalry were fighting. It never occurred to him that the enemy on the Orange Plank Road might be Rebel infantry instead.

Crawford already had scouting parties moving in the direction of Parker's Store when an orderly arrived from Warren's headquarters with a startling message:

THE MOVEMENT TOWARD PARKER'S STORE IS SUSPENDED.
YOU WILL HALT, FACE TOWARD MINE RUN [i.e., to the west], AND
CONNECT WITH GENERAL WADSWORTH ON YOUR RIGHT.

The Federal division commander at once acknowledged his receipt of the dispatch, noted that he could hear firing near Parker's
Store, and closed with the comment, "I am halted in a good position."

Even as the first files of the Ninth Corps column hauled into sight,
U. S. Grant decided not to wait any longer for Burnside himself to
show up. The Federal chief commander hurriedly dictated a note
urging the corps commander to speed the crossing and to join his
force as quickly as possible to John Sedgwick's Sixth Corps, which
was already spreading along the feeble Wilderness paths toward a
junction with Warren's right flank. Then, recalled Grant's aide Horace Porter, "the general immediately . . . directed the staff to mount
and move forward with him along the Germanna Road." An officer in
one of the Sixth Corps regiments posted along the way watched Grant
pass: "He was on a fine, though small, black horse, which he set well;
was plainly dressed, looked the picture of health, and bore no evidence of anxiety about him. His plain hat and clothes were in marked
contrast with a somewhat gaily dressed and equipped staff. He saluted and spoke pleasantly, but did not check his horse from a rather
rapid gait."

It was not quite 9:00 A.M.

By this time the reconnaissance that Gouverneur Warren had
ordered at 6:20 A.M. was complete. The official report put the results
this way: "It was quickly ascertained that the enemy was present with
strong infantry force, and that he was busily engaged throwing up
breastworks, and upon making this report to the brigade commander
[Bartlett] the skirmishers were ordered to retire." The Confederates,
added a member of the 83rd Pennsylvania, "came up on the Orange
[Turnpike] and were seen about half a mile ahead filing off to the right
and left for the purpose of forming a line of battle. Nothing could be
seen of their movements except what was seen upon the road. The
moment they plunged into the woods they were lost to the sight."

Couriers hurried back up the command chain with the informa-
tion. Only one Union soldier had been killed in the operation: Private
Charles Wilson, Company I, 18th Massachusetts. No one who left an
account saw him die. Morris Schaff asked around and found out that
Wilson "was only eighteen years old, and the son of a farmer." A *New
York Tribune* reporter, Charles Page, also made note of Wilson's

death, writing, "Let Charles Wilson . . . be remembered as the first man to give his life in this (God willing) the last grand campaign of the war."

The head of Winfield Hancock's Second Corps column was already past Todd's Tavern and on its way to Shady Grove Church when things began to change. A member of the 124th New York watched as a "mounted officer whose horse was almost covered with foam went dashing past us toward the front. A few moments later a halt was ordered. . . . As soon as the pickets were posted we stacked arms; and while the majority threw themselves down by the gun-stacks, not a few old soldiers scouted the idea of lying down to rest until they had first fortified themselves against the scorching rays of the sun by 'getting outside of a pint cup of piping hot *Old Java.'*"

It was 9:00 A.M.

Virginia lieutenant Robert Funkhouser could hear gunfire to the east when his brigade, part of Ewell's corps, paused and the men were allowed to rest. "Whilst we were halted," Funkhouser relates, "I wrote sort of a will and gave it to our preacher with directions to send it home in case I was killed, which seemed very likely. . . ."

Gouverneur Warren kept hurrying more units forward to build up the line spreading across the Orange Turnpike, but it was hard going on the troops. James Wadsworth was told to slide his division through the woods and into position on Griffin's left flank. This was easier said than done. One of Wadsworth's men recalled, "The troops were compelled to cut alley-ways through the thickets with axes and hatchets, in order to proceed, and finally brought up on the bank of a swamp with short, briery undergrowth, which it seemed impossible to penetrate."

The plan also called for elements of John Sedgwick's Sixth Corps to take up a position on Griffin's right. Sedgwick's advance down an old lumbering trail from the Germanna Ford Road was also bedeviled. "We advanced for two miles through the awfullest brush, briers, grapevines, etc. I was ever in," a member of the 96th Pennsylvania declared.

Warren himself remained uncertain as to the strength of the Confederate force before him. "About ten o'clock," according to a member of Ayres's brigade, "a staff officer came out and said that

General Warren and others believed that there was nothing in our front but dismounted cavalry, that had been left there to delay our advance."

U. S. Grant and his staff rode "at an accelerated pace" down the Germanna Ford Road, arriving at the Orange Turnpike intersection at around 10:00 A.M. There, remembered Horace Porter, "General Meade was seen standing, near the roadside. He came forward on foot to give General Grant the latest information."

The news confirmed Grant's worst fears about the Army of the Potomac. Nearly two and a half hours had passed since his telling Meade to pitch into the Confederate force that was confronting Griffin on the Orange Turnpike. The Union army was no closer to launching an attack now than it had been when Grant sent his message. Griffin was reporting that the Confederate force in front of him was larger than previously assumed, and both Wadsworth and Sedgwick had yet to extend Griffin's flanks. Crawford was sending word that a Confederate force of unknown size was pushing down the Orange Plank Road.

Grant's patience came to an abrupt end, and he dictated orders to Meade. Charles Griffin was to attack at once — the flanks be damned. Sedgwick was to push his lead brigades into position on Griffin's right immediately. A glance at the field maps made clear the importance of the intersection of the Brock and Orange Plank roads. If the Confederates managed to seize that crossroads, the Federal army would be cut in two; Hancock's corps to the south would be isolated from the rest of the army, which was fighting west of Wilderness Tavern. One division of Sedgwick's corps was awaiting orders near the Tavern. That division (George Getty's — minus Thomas Neill's brigade, which was already moving to help Griffin) was to hustle to the Brock–Orange Plank Road intersection to stop the enemy force reported by Crawford. And finally, Hancock's Second Corps was to come up from Todd's Tavern to help Getty. Grant's purpose was clear. Any thought he might have had of continuing the planned movement of the Army of the Potomac was discarded; his only plan now was to strike the enemy wherever he found him.

Couriers clambered onto horses and galloped off in various directions. A Sixth Corps soldier watching them go was reminded "of the lively manner the hornets flitted around when their nest was disturbed." "General Grant," Horace Porter observed, "lighted a cigar, sat down on the stump of a tree, took out his penknife, and began to whittle a stick."

It was about 11:00 A.M. when the Confederate corps commander Richard Ewell noted that he could see "a column of the enemy crossing the pike from [Germanna] Ford towards the plank-road." The one-legged officer sent word of his observations back to Lee, entrusting it this time to his young chief of staff, Lieutenant Colonel Alexander "Sandie" Pendleton. The tall, plain-faced aide soon returned with "substantially the same instructions as before." Ewell told his brigadiers that they were "not to allow themselves to become involved, but to fall back slowly if pressed."

Throughout the morning Ewell built up his line across the Orange Turnpike. It was spread thin in places to cover a broad front. Marcus Toney, a Virginia private in Jones's Brigade, reported that "on my part of the line we did not have a rear rank, and that the front ranks were so far apart that they could not touch elbows."

It was around 11:00 A.M. when Winfield Hancock received Grant's orders — via Meade — to move his command north from Todd's Tavern and march to the Brock–Orange Plank Road intersection. The Union Second Corps commander issued the necessary instructions, then rode ahead to find out what was happening. Behind him, his corps struggled to cover the distance. "Our march," recalled Ohio private William Kepler, "was most of the time hurried, at times on the double-quick, with horsemen, guns and caissons obstructing the way."

A deceptive calm settled over the two sides as they readied their respective positions across the Orange Turnpike. The main Union line lay midway between the Wilderness Tavern crossroads and Saunders Field. According to a member of the 20th Maine, "The trees were all cut down for a distance of some 10 rods in front of the line, and their trunks trimmed of all their branches, and piled up for breastworks. . . ."

North of the roadway, on the Confederate side, the soldiers commanded by Leroy Stafford "seized the opportunity to take their dinner, smoke, sleep and take such ease as the circumstance admitted."

The officers of the 6th Wisconsin, part of James Wadsworth's division, also enjoyed the moment. "It was a bright and pleasant morning, and the woods were filled with the twitter of birds. . . . All of our officers gathered under a great oak tree and were chattering and chaffering in the highest spirits."

U. S. Grant fixed his headquarters at a point "about half-way between the Germanna Ford and Todd's Tavern, and immediately in rear of Warren's corps." Soon the headquarters wagons arrived, and tents began to go up around a little knoll. Adam Badeau, Grant's military secretary, described the view: "Here and there is a ravine or a brook, and one or two houses are visible, with a bit of open land around them; all the rest is one tangled mass of stunted evergreen, dwarf chestnut, oak and hazel, with an undergrowth of low-limbed bristling shrubs, making the forest almost impenetrable." Added Horace Porter, "It was a wilderness in the most forbidding sense of the word."

From the moment they received the order to move to the Brock–Orange Plank Road intersection, George Getty's men advanced to that point "flanked by heavy undergrowth, without skirmishers or flankers." Gouverneur Warren's earlier decision to keep his bulky wagon trains off the cramped Brock Road allowed Getty's men to make good time.

Captain Hazard Stevens, Getty's chief of staff, told what happened next: "Just as [Getty and his staff] reached the crossroads, a detachment of cavalry came flying down the Plank Road strung out like a flock of wild geese." This was John Hammond's 5th New York Cavalry, finally giving way after holding up the advance of A. P. Hill's Confederate corps since dawn. A few of the cavalrymen paused long enough "to cry out that the rebel infantry were coming down the road in force. . . . Getty instantly hurried back an aide to bring his troops up at the double-quick. Surrounded by his staff and orderlies, with his headquarters flag flying overhead, he took position directly at the intersection of the roads. Soon a few gray forms were discerned far up the narrow Plank Road moving cautiously forward, then a bullet went whistling overhead, and another and another. . . . Getty would not budge. 'We must hold this point at any risk,' he exclaimed. . . . In a few minutes, which seemed an age to the little squad, the leading regiments of [Brigadier General Frank] Wheaton's brigade . . . came running . . . along the Brock Road . . . and then at the commands 'Halt!' 'Front!' 'Fire!' poured a volley into the woods and threw out skirmishers in almost less time than it takes to tell it."

For the moment the vital crossroads that protected the fragile link with Hancock's Second Corps at Todd's Tavern was in Union hands. Getty's men made it with seconds to spare.

Tension was building like a storm cloud over the Union headquarters, spread near the Lacy House hill. Grant's impatience was transmitted to Meade, who passed it along to Warren. According to one staff officer, Morris Schaff, "Again and again inquiries were made of Warren when Griffin would move and each time with more edge, for no one at headquarters shared his conviction that the situation called for a thoroughly organized and formidable attack. . . ."

Caught in the middle was young William Swan, an aide to Griffin's brigade commander Romeyn Ayres. "I remember that Ayres sent me back to Griffin to say that in his judgment we ought to wait, for the enemy was about to attack . . . and I remember that Griffin went . . . to the front, and then sent me back to say to General Warren that he was averse to making an attack. I think I went twice to General Warren with that message. The last time I met him on the road, and I remember that he answered me as if fear was at the bottom of my errand. I remember my indignation."

After failing for hours to convince anyone at Fifth Corps headquarters that the Chewning Farm position was worth holding, Samuel Crawford reluctantly ordered his men off the open ground and back onto the forest paths to link up with James Wadsworth's division farther north. Crawford's message announcing this closed with the terse observation, "The enemy hold the [Orange] plank road and are passing up."

Robert E. Lee spent the morning riding with Henry Heth's division at the head of A. P. Hill's column. Soon after the pesky Union cavalry was pushed out of Parker's Store, Lee's party, "consisting of Generals Lee, Hill and Stuart and their staff-officers," rode up to a large field, "dismounted and sat under the shade of the trees." Hill's aide William Palmer was with the group when "suddenly a force of the enemy, in skirmishing order, came out of the woods on the left. General Lee walked rapidly off toward Heth's troops, calling for Colonel Taylor, his adjutant-general. General Stuart stood up and looked the danger squarely in the face; General Hill remained as he was. We were within pistol shot, when to our surprise the Federal officer gave the command 'right about' and disappeared in the timber, as much alarmed at finding himself in the presence of Confederate troops as we were at this unexpected appearance."

1:00–3:00 P.M.

It was, remembered one of the 529 men of the 140th New York, "a lovely morning." The soldiers sat around their bivouac fires and discussed the rumors that "were afloat that the enemy had been found in force in our immediate front."

The 140th was an upstate outfit, recruited largely from Monroe County, clad in colorful red and blue uniforms patterned on the garb worn by the elite French North African troops. "Our distinctive zouave uniform had made us well known throughout the army," Captain Porter Farley bragged, ". . . and . . . we had the vanity to think there was no organization in the army superior to us."

Colonel George Ryan commanded the 140th. A man "of an active temperament," the West Point graduate was also a strict disciplinarian. Anticipating that there might be a fight, Ryan had called into the ranks every able-bodied man in the commissary and quartermaster departments of the regiment. His orders were that "if all were not armed . . . they should follow the regiment and take the arms and accouterments of the first men who were hurt."

Sometime before 11:00 A.M., orders came to form up. Each company piled together its knapsacks "in charge of a guard of two men." Then the men stood in formation for more than an hour. Mounted staff officers and orderlies hurried past on unexplained errands. In the distance the New Yorkers could hear the *pop-pop-pop* of skirmishers at work. The day got hotter, the air stuffier.

It was a little after noon when word came: "Forward!" The men marched, with guns unloaded, "through the woods where one thinks that not even a hare can get through." The lines of battle, so neat and orderly on the parade ground, were thoroughly shuffled by the passage through the woods. Soon the men could smell the pungent residue of burnt gunpowder. The uneven line moved past scattered pockets of friendly skirmishers, who watched with detached curiosity as the combat formation pushed on; unfriendly skirmishers fired a few shots before sizing up the weight of the advancing force and scrambling back.

"In about five minutes," remembered Captain Farley, "we reached an opening in the woods some acres in extent and forming a sort of valley or hollow two or three hundred yards in width, directly across our line of march." This was Saunders Field. Another New Yorker guessed it to be "about forty acres in size." As if attracted by the light that was splashed across the clearing, the double battle lines of the regiment stumbled out of the woods. "The very moment we appeared," said Porter Farley, Confederates posted on the west side of the field "gave us a volley at long range, but evidently with very deliberate aim, and with serious effect." Colonel Ryan's horse was grazed, causing it to kick and plunge so badly that the regimental commander had to dismount and have the mare led to the rear. "Right-about! March!" Ryan called out, and the regiment pulled back to the eastern folds of the woods. Once they were safely under cover, Ryan shouted, "Right-about! Halt! Order Arms! Load at will! Load!" Then the men were told to lie down and fix bayonets.

Virginia private James McCown still held the image of the "grand sight" of the Army of Northern Virginia in his mind as the Stonewall Brigade turned off the Orange Turnpike to file into the woods north of the road. The lean, sunburned Confederate veterans pushed through the underbrush and went into line of battle on the left of George Steuart's brigade, along the western edge of Saunders Field.

"After forming in line there is an awful silence," remembered McCown. "He that a short time ago jested is now grave. . . . How awful is this inaction. Home flashes up the dear ones and thousands of thoughts crowd in on me. . . . Our skirmish line is advanced. Now we are ordered to lie down. . . . All nature seems to expect some awful shock."

It was nearly 1:00 P.M. before Charles Griffin had his division in position to attack. To the north of the Orange Turnpike, on the eastern edge of Saunders Field, was Romeyn Ayres's brigade. The ground in front of Ayres's men sloped downward for about a third of the distance across to the west side, and then it leveled off into the woods. Brigade and staff officers rode past the prone ranks of the 140th New York, checking that the regiment was ready to advance. Colonel George Ryan sent word along that the regiment was to "charge the enemy in the opposite woods, without firing a shot until we reached them." The men braced themselves.

Then, remembered Porter Farley, "the order was passed along the line by the staff officers, to charge. Colonel Ryan gave us the word of command, and the regiment started at full speed, with a shout which drowned all other sounds."

Waiting on the other side of the brambly field, in position on the western fringes of the clearing, were three Confederate brigades belonging to Edward Johnson's division. McHenry Howard served on the staff of one of Johnson's brigadiers, George Steuart. Howard was standing near his chief when Johnson rode by, calling out for both to hear "that it was not intended to bring on a general engagement [this] day."

Porter Farley said that he and Colonel Ryan were "running so near together that we exchanged words as we went across the field. Of course the moment we sprang to our feet the enemy opened fire on us. . . ." "The bullets fly like hail," another New Yorker recalled, "men fall by the dozen. . . ."

When Colonel Ryan had sent his wounded horse back earlier, he had inadvertently left his sword in the saddle-girth. Doing his best with what he had, Ryan advanced on foot ahead of the color guard, "waving his soft hat over his head to encourage his men as they charged."

The Confederate aide McHenry Howard was listening to the rising tempo of gunfire when his division commander, Edward Johnson, rode past for the second time. "Remember, Captain Howard," Johnson called out again, "it is not meant to have a general engagement."

Howard motioned toward the firing. "The two lines will come together in a few moments," he shouted over the increasing din. "Will it not be better for our men to have the impetus of a forward movement in the collision?"

"Very well," Johnson replied. "Let them go ahead a little."

Just as Johnson finished, Howard later recollected, "the bullets were flying thicker . . . the men were getting restive and the moment seemed critical." He raised his sword and cried "Forward!" and "the men responded with alacrity and almost immediately a tremendous fire rolled along the line."

"We expected to close upon the enemy with the bayonet," insisted New York captain Porter Farley, "but they fell back just as we were about to reach them. . . . The moment we reached the woods . . .

we opened fire, but still kept advancing slowly." Added Captain Henry Cribben of the 140th, "Often the burning powder from the discharged rifles in the hands of the enemy would drop at the foot of our men who would instantly thrust their rifle bayonets through the brush and vines and kill or wound those in their front."

For Virginia private James McCown, the awful waiting came to an abrupt end. "Just then," he remembered, "there jumps from my front a rabbit. . . . [At] that moment our brave Captain was yelling, 'Give it to them Company K.' Amid this storm of lead . . . we stood until we were reported to be flanked. . . . We then fell back."

Seven battalions of U.S. Regulars were supposed to be advancing on the right flank of the 140th; instead, they veered northward and stalled at the edge of the woods. So, as the New York Zouaves pushed ahead, they were no longer screened on their right flank. Captain Cribben was one of the first to discover this: "Without notice we received a destructive fire of musketry from our rear and right which killed and wounded more of our men than the firing from our front." According to Porter Farley, "Men disappeared as if the earth had swallowed them. . . . It seemed as if the regiment had been annihilated." Farley ran back to look for the supporting line and arrived at the western edge of the clearing in time to see the 146th New York advance. This was another Zouave regiment, clad in a similar manner. "Just then there were two terrific explosions in the hollow behind us, accompanied by the crash of shot through the trees and followed by a dense cloud of smoke which completely enveloped us."

At Charles Griffin's hard-eyed insistence, two guns of a New York battery pushed to within rifle range and went into action to support the Federal attack. Amid the yelling and smoky confusion, cannon shots plowed into both blue and gray.

Rifle fire continued to chew into the backs of the 140th. Colonel Ryan, fearing that it was the supporting line doing the damage, yelled to Henry Cribben to investigate. He quickly found Colonel David Jenkins of the 146th, who complained that his men were also getting hit. Cribben continued to scout for the source of the shooting until a rifle burst shredded some nearby branches, throwing particles of twigs and bark into his face. The Federal officer lurched to the ground, scrubbing at his burning eyes. As his vision slowly cleared, Cribben found himself looking across Saunders Field, where he "beheld a sight that made my blood run cold for there in plain view was a Confederate line of battle which was deliberately loading and firing into the backs of our men, apparently without any opposition."

In the Stonewall Brigade, Brigadier General James Walker rallied his men. "Remember your name!" he shouted to the sweaty, powder-smeared faces of the soldiers who could hear him. Private James McCown was one of these. "The colors advance in the face of a deadly fire from the Yankees. . . . We advance and sweep everything before us. . . . Dead and dying lie around us."

Captain Henry Cribben, his eyes red and watering, scrambled back into the woods and found Colonel Ryan. His words coming in frantic gulps, Cribben told the commander of the 140th New York that Confederate troops were in behind the Zouave regiment. Ryan cursed. The supports he had been promised had not come up; what had begun as a glorious charge had become a deadly trap. Ryan sent Cribben with Major Milo Stark to tell Colonel Jenkins of the 146th New York what was going on. The two had walked only a short distance when Cribben went down. His fingers frantically probed the bloody hole in his leg. "Flesh wound," he gasped. "Bone's not broken." Stark nodded. "You get off the field," he said. "I'll see that Colonel Jenkins is notified."

Using his sword and scabbard as a crutch, Henry Cribben hobbled painfully back toward the main Union lines, east of Saunders Field. Stumbling out onto the open ground, he made a clear target for the Rebel riflemen. The earth spouted in little geysers all around. "I made a short race for life," Cribben remembered, "every jump carrying me farther from the fire of the enemy."

Recalled the Confederate aide McHenry Howard, "We [drove] the enemy through the jungle to an open field extending on both sides of the [Orange Turnpike] and as they were pressed across it a destructive fire was poured into them, so that it appeared to me the ground was more thickly strewn with their dead and wounded than I had ever seen." John Worsham, a Virginian, added, "We captured many prisoners; behind every tree and stump were several who seemed to remain there in preference to running the gauntlet of our fire."

The shattered remains of the two colorfully uniformed New York regiments scrambled back across Saunders Field. One New Yorker from the 146th described the moment: "The bright red of our zouave uniform mingled with the sober gray and butternut of the Southerners, creating a fantastic spectacle as the wearers ran to and fro over the field, firing and shouting. . . ." In the melee the two cannon ordered up to point-blank range by Charles Griffin were overrun, and their crews killed, captured, or driven off.

Colonel David Jenkins, whose early-morning picket report had changed the Union plans this day, was down somewhere in the brush across the field, mortally wounded. Adjutant Porter Farley of the 140th made it back to the eastern side of the field and eventually found Colonel Ryan, along with perhaps a dozen men and officers from the regiment. "It was a wild meeting," Farley admitted. "Overcome by our conflicting emotions of wrath, excitement and mortification, we all talked at once." "My God," anguished Ryan, "I'm the first colonel I ever knew who couldn't tell where his regiment was."

McHenry Howard remembered mopping up the two New York regiments: "Large bodies were taken prisoners, one regiment . . . in new uniforms with heavy yellow trimmings, being captured almost as an organization — many of them, however, lay dead or wounded. For some time the woods road . . . on which we had diverged from the [Orange Turnpike] and across which our line extended, was blocked by a mass of prisoners. None but our slightly wounded were allowed to guard them to the rear and they were simply directed, for the most part, to keep that road back until they would meet troops having more leisure to take charge of them. Probably many escaped."

Even as the initially ragged line of the 140th New York emerged from the woods north of the Orange Turnpike, the regiments of Joseph Bartlett's brigade belatedly joined in the attack from along the southern side of the road. Bartlett's men struck John M. Jones's thinned line and broke it. Jones made a desperate attempt to rally his men but was killed in a flurry of bullets. His aide-de-camp, Captain Robert D. Early, the nephew of General Jubal Early, fell nearby.

"What a medley of sounds," said Maine private Theodore Garrish: "the incessant roar of the rifle; the screaming bullets, the forest on fire; men cheering, groaning, yelling, swearing and praying!" "We kept on yelling and firing into the woods at every jump," added Amos Judson of the 83rd Pennsylvania. "On we went, o'er briar, o'er brake, o'er logs and o'er bogs, through the underbrush and overhanging limbs, for about three quarters of a mile, yelling all the while like so many demons, until we came to another small opening and there halted. We had by this time got into such a snarl that no man could find his own company or regiment."

Jones's troops were scattered everywhere. "The woods were filled with demoralized men and we ascertained that the lines of Jones' Brigade had been broken, and that the regiments comprising the brigade were quitting the field in the utmost confusion," noted a North Carolina sergeant in Daniel's Brigade, which was positioned well behind and south of the line ruptured by Bartlett's assault. Directly to the rear of Jones's line was Brigadier General Cullen A. Battle's supporting brigade. The signs of panic in front unsettled some of Battle's men. "[Our line] became unsteady," admitted Alabama private James Roberts, "each man appearing as if halting between two opinions." Nearby, Captain W. H. May was hit in the foot and leg. "After being wounded I called my men who had been thrown into some confusion by the troops on our front giving way and closely followed by the Yankees, but only one came back to me and knowing he could not do anything by himself, [I] told him to get away. I then tried my leg and foot to see if I could locomote, found I could, and I locomoted."

Ewell's son-in-law and aide, Major Campbell Brown, later declared, "I don't believe these brigades would have been so easily broken had it not been for the general understanding that we were to retire to Mine Run if attacked in force."

Bartlett's men now began to have problems of their own. Their steady advance through the dense thickets shuffled the units until their organization was effectively lost. The lead elements were outpacing the supporting units on either flank. Ayres's brigade was supposed to be on the right, but already the New York Zouaves were being ambushed by Confederates who were coming down the Union right flank. On Bartlett's left, Wadsworth's men were stalled by a swamp and were lagging behind. With angry pockets of Confederates sniping at their exposed flanks, the men felt their nerves chill and their resolution slip away in the spooky smoke and ghostly shadows of the Wilderness. A Pennsylvanian in the 118th told what happened next: "The command was given to 'about face' and for some distance a good line was preserved. But the impression soon gained ground that they were hopelessly flanked and liable to be surrounded and captured, and then the line broke into little knots which, falling back some distance, would turn and face the enemy, and then fall back."

──── ★ ────

The Confederate brigadier general John B. Gordon had the kind of fiercely dominating gaze that provoked both fear and respect. He was a thin ramrod of a man, with jet-black hair, a deeply scarred cheek, and eyes that blazed with unremitting intensity. He also had a penchant for the dramatic gesture.

Gordon's brigade of Georgia troops moved at the head of Jubal Early's division this day. The men marched in tightly closed columns, listening to the rattle of gunfire ahead.

Suddenly a rider came galloping furiously toward Gordon. It was the Second Corps commander himself, one-legged Richard Ewell. "With a quick jerk of his bridle rein just as his wooden leg was about to come into an unwelcome collision with my knee," Gordon recalled, "he checked his horse and rapped out his few words with characteristic impetuosity."

"General Gordon," Ewell piped excitedly, "the fate of the day depends on you, sir!"

Gordon, with one eye cocked toward posterity and the other toward the soldiers who were crowding near to hear what the brass was saying, replied melodramatically, "These men will save it, sir!" He turned and snapped out his orders: "Forward into line on the right!" "Right oblique!" "Load as you march!"

As each regiment filed past, Gordon called out, "Boys, there are Yankees in front and lots of them . . . *we* must move them. Now all who are faint-hearted, fall out . . . we do not want any to go but *heroes — we want brave Georgians.*"

Gordon skillfully led his men through the woods and into position to the right of where the Union attack had breached the line. Adrenaline pumping, Gordon rode to the center of his line and shouted "Forward!" He recalled: "With a deafening yell which must have been heard miles away, that glorious brigade rushed upon the hitherto advancing enemy, and by the shock of their furious onset shattered into fragments all that portion of the compact Union line confronting my troops." Private G. W. Nichols always remembered the moment of Gordon's attack: "I never heard such a yell as we raised. We could scarcely hear a gun fire, and could hardly tell when our own gun fired, only by the jar it gave us."

Gordon's counterattack came crashing down on James Wadsworth's three brigades: Lysander Cutler's, Roy Stone's, and James Rice's.

The 6th Wisconsin, on the left of Cutler's line, was among the first to be hit. "There came the enemy stretching as far as I could see through the woods and rapidly advancing and firing on us," said the regimental commander Rufus Dawes. Added Philip Cheek of Company A, "A murderous volley from the left and front was poured into our ranks, followed by another from the right, both at short range, which caused surprise, confusion and some disorder."

Portions of Roy Stone's brigade were floundering in an uncharted swamp when Gordon's advance found them. According to a Pennsylvanian in the 121st, "When the order to retire was given, the scrambling to get out of that mud hole was amusing as well as ridiculous. . . . During this stampede it very naturally followed that the men became somewhat confused and more or less scattered, many not being sure which way to run."

James Rice's men, the last in line to be hit, fared no better. "The line on the right fell back in disorder," reported a New Yorker in the 76th, "and was followed by this Brigade. The underbrush was very dense, and the men found great difficulty in making their way through it. The enemy, still unseen, continued to pour in a very destructive fire."

Ignited by powder sparks, fed by the dry underbrush, and stoked by the wind, flash fires flared up across the battle lines. The flames exploded many of the cartridge boxes strapped to the bellies of the fallen, blowing bloody holes in the helpless, screaming victims. A New York Zouave viewed the horror: "The almost cheerful 'Pop! Pop!' of cartridges gave no hint of the almost dreadful horror their noise bespoke. . . . The bodies of the dead were blackened and burned beyond all possibility of recognition."

Campbell Brown rode back to Robert E. Lee to confirm that Ewell's orders were to "fall back to Mine Run if pushed." Once again Lee surprised the young aide. "He told me that Colonel P[endleton] and myself had misinterpreted him, that he only meant us to fall back in case we could not hold our position."

After the war, reflecting on this confusion of orders, Brown said, "General Lee's instructions to his Corps commanders are of a very comprehensive and general description and frequently admit of several interpretations."

It was a little after 1:00 P.M. when Winfield Hancock appeared from the south on the Brock Road, accompanied by his chief of staff, Lieutenant Colonel Charles H. Morgan, along with a gaggle of aides and orderlies. Since establishing his division to protect the vital cross-roads, George Getty had received no news of events west of Wilderness Tavern and could offer the Second Corps commander no enlightenment. Getty was sure he would soon be hit by at least two divisions of A. P. Hill's Confederate corps, and he felt that the best thing he could do at the moment was prepare a strong defensive position.

It was about 2:00 P.M. when a heavy dust cloud to the south marked the arrival of David Birney's Second Corps division. The pale, ascetic-looking, Alabama-born Union officer was riding ahead of his men, seeking orders. The first of Birney's regiments to arrive, the 93rd New York, was immediately sent out along the north side of the Orange Plank Road. In a matter of minutes shooting could be heard as the New Yorkers pushed against the Confederate skirmish line. Other units coming from Todd's Tavern began to build light breastworks along the Brock Road.

From his field headquarters near the Widow Tapp's house, Robert E. Lee listened to the distant firing and tried to make sense of it. The sound was indistinct and, coupled with the lack of any new communication from Richard Ewell, left Lee in the dark as to developments on the Orange Turnpike. Worrying about the gap between Ewell's and Hill's men, Lee ordered Major General Cadmus Wilcox to turn his division off the Plank Road and stretch Hill's battle line north to connect with Ewell's position. It was about 2:30 when the first of Wilcox's four brigades disappeared into the folds of the Wilderness, heading north. Brigadier General Edward L. Thomas's men were second in order today. A young Georgian in the brigade described the movement: "Our division files out to the left of the plank road, forms line of battle, and marches through an old field and through a dense thicket of undergrowth." J. F. J. Caldwell, a South Carolinian in McGowan's Brigade, the last in Wilcox's column, recalled crossing an open space near the house owned by the Widow Tapp. "There were several pieces of artillery here, and near them General Lee and General Stuart, on foot."

Lee, suddenly hesitant to force the issue on the Orange Plank Road with so much unknown about the Orange Turnpike, let the advance of A. P. Hill's corps ease to a stop. Henry Heth's division was closest to the enemy. Heth later recalled, "My skirmish line was unable to drive the enemy's skirmishers any further; they halted, and the division came up, line of battle was formed. All was quiet for an hour or more."

——— ★ ———

New York Tribune correspondent Charles Page sketched the moment at Union headquarters near the Lacy House: "At this hour the enemy has ceased to make demonstrations, and we are waiting for Hancock to join on our left. General Grant is smoking a wooden pipe, his face as peaceful as a summer evening, his general demeanor indescribably imperturbable. I know, however, that there is great anxiety that Hancock should fall into position, for it is believed that the entire Rebel force is massing upon us."

Near 2:30 P.M., the Union Second Corps commander, Winfield Hancock, received a message that Meade's headquarters had sent an hour earlier. The army officer had scarcely digested its contents when another orderly appeared, this time with a headquarters message that had been sent at noon. The gist of each was that Hancock was to attack down the Orange Plank Road immediately. The tenor of the messages suggested that Meade believed the Second Corps to be present in greater strength at the Brock–Orange Plank Road intersection than it in fact was. In his reply, sent at 2:40 P.M., Hancock gently tried to disabuse the army brass of its notions: "I am forming my corps on Getty's left, and will order an advance as soon as prepared. The ground over which I must pass is very bad — a perfect thicket."

George Meade's observant aide Theodore Lyman reckoned the time to be 2:45 P.M. when Charles Griffin, accompanied by a single staff officer, rode angrily up to army headquarters. Griffin, Lyman said, "called out loudly that he drove Ewell three quarters of a mile, but got no support on his flanks and had to retreat. He implied censure on General Wright [the Sixth Corps divisional commander who was supposed to support Griffin's right], and apparently on his corps commander, General Warren. [Grant's chief of staff] General Rawlins was very angry, considering his language mutinous. Grant was of the same mind, and asked Meade: 'Who is this General *Gregg*? You ought to arrest him!' Grant's coat was unbuttoned, and Meade began to button it up, as if he were a little boy, saying in a good-natured voice, 'It's Griffin, not Gregg, and it's only his way of talking.'"

On both sides, wounded men stumbled back while fresh troops hurried forward.

"[Never] did it look so much like marching right into the jaws of death . . . ," said Lieutenant Robert Funkhouser of the 49th Virginia, "for now we began to meet officers wounded on horseback & men walking, the ambulances loaded with the desperately wounded & dieing, & the ambulance corpsmen walking & carrying the wounded." Added Captain Samuel Buck of the 13th Virginia, "This is the most trying time of a soldier's life, to see wounded men with blood and powder all over their faces. It does not speak well for safety in front." From the Confederate artillery reserve, Private Henry Berkeley observed surgeons operating on the wounded. "It is a beautiful spring day on which all this bloody work is being done," he remembered thinking.

A Federal field hospital was put up directly behind the position taken by a Union battery. Artilleryman Frank Wilkeson watched. "Soon men, singly and in pairs or in groups of four or five, came limping slowly or walking briskly, with arms across their breasts and their hands clutched into their blouses, out of the woods. Some carried their rifles. Others had thrown them away. All of them were bloody." According to William Swan, an aide, "Every soldier . . . seemed to know the way to the Lacy house." A young drummer boy in Roy Stone's brigade also watched some surgeons at work. "[There] was a man whose leg was being taken off at the thigh, and who, chloroformed into unconsciousness, interested everybody by singing at the top of his voice, and with a clear articulation, five verses of a hymn to an old-fashioned Methodist tune, never once losing the melody or stopping for a word." Still limping badly from his leg wound, Captain Henry Cribben found the Fifth Corps field hospital "located in the woods on the north side of the turnpike." The regimental surgeon in charge asked Cribben where he was wounded. "Before I could reply," Cribben later recalled, "the rebel bullets came flying through the woods. . . . The doctor requested me to get all the men together who were able to walk and take them to the rear."

With admirable promptness, Richard Ewell reestablished his battle line along the western fringes of Saunders Field. Orders were issued to all commands to entrench.

Around this time the first regiments of John Sedgwick's Sixth Corps finally arrived on Griffin's right flank. New Jersey chaplain Alanson Haines described what he saw: "The dead and wounded of both sides lay around. . . . It was impossible to see the enemy. . . . We soon began intrenching. Our men scraped the stones and earth before them as best they could, until spades were brought. All the time the enemy were sending a shower of bullets over and past us. It would at times lessen, then start again afresh." G. Norton Galloway of the 95th Pennsylvania cursed the Wilderness as "one of the waste places of nature." Years afterward there was still distaste in his memories of a region "so wild and forbidden that we were compelled to crawl like snakes whilst worming our bodies through some devilish entanglement."

Griffin gradually yielded the area north of the Orange Turnpike to Wright's Sixth Corps division and reorganized his men south of the road. Wadsworth's shaken command assembled on open ground near the Lacy House to re-form. Samuel Crawford's men, up from their morning on the Chewning Farm, took the extreme left of the Fifth Corps line. On Crawford's right was Jacob Sweitzer's brigade, and on Sweitzer's right were the battered units of Romeyn Ayres. John Robinson's three hitherto unused brigades connected with Wright's men north of the road.

Also on the roads leading from Saunders Field were squads of prisoners. Edwin Forbes, a combat artist for *Frank Leslie's Illustrated Newspaper*, turned his trained eyes on one group of Rebels: "[They] had in the lead a stalwart red-whiskered fellow, who carried a patchwork quilt . . . under his arm. Behind him came a youth with light-gray jacket and trousers, and a gray infantry cap trimmed with light blue. The next one to him wore a striped worsted sailor cap. And the last in order was an old man with long white hair, who was evidently a recruit, for he still wore . . . an old-fashioned stove-pipe [hat]."

Walking with pain, Captain Henry Cribben led his party of thirty Union wounded toward the Lacy House. Along the way he saw "General Grant with three or four staff-officers looking up the road in the direction of the firing. He asked me to what regiment the wounded men belonged. I gave him the desired information, and told him they had been driven out of the temporary field hospital by rebel musketry." If Grant had anything further to say, Henry Cribben took no notice of it.

Among the decisions made by Grant during this bloody day was one that called for "all the bridges over the Rapidan to be taken up except one at [Germanna] Ford." There would be no turning back.

3:00–5:00 P.M.

At 3:00 P.M., three brigades of John Sedgwick's Sixth Corps attacked the Confederate lines north of the Orange Turnpike. The gunsmoke and thick underbrush combined effectively to blind the combatants to each other. "Failing to see the enemy," said one Wisconsin soldier, Evan Jones, "[we] soon began to fire by *ear-sight*." The Federals managed a gain of perhaps two hundred yards before being stopped by violent Confederate counterattacks.

"At one point," remembered Oliver Wendell Holmes, Jr., a young Sixth Corps aide, "General Sedgwick's . . . headquarters were very accurately shelled from the left — one struck within a yard of quite a number of us who were sitting on horseback & bounced under the horses." Another staff aide, Thomas Hyde, was standing near the corps commander when a stray cannonball decapitated a New Jersey private a few yards away. The bloody head struck Hyde full in the face, momentarily blinding him and filling his mouth with brains and gore. Friends moved to help the shaken aide to his feet, finding to their astonishment that he was otherwise untouched. "I was not much use as a staff officer for fully fifteen minutes," Hyde recalled with a shudder.

Meade's aide Theodore Lyman found his way to George Getty's command near the Brock–Orange Plank Road intersection at about 3:25 P.M. Lyman carried dispatches that revealed something of the frustrated impatience now gripping the army's high command. They ordered Getty to attack down the Orange Plank Road at once, with or without Hancock's help. Lyman could tell that the spare-faced, hazel-eyed Getty was less than pleased with the peremptory instructions. "Plainly he thought it poor strategy to attack before more of the 2d Corps was up, but he ordered an immediate advance."

Confederate major general Henry Heth remembered that it was between three and four o'clock when a staff officer arrived from General Lee with this message: "The General is desirous that you occupy the Brock Road if you could do so without bringing on a general engagement." Heth shrugged. "The enemy are holding the Brock Road with a strong force," he told Lee's emissary. "Whether I can drive them from the Brock Road or not can only be determined by my attacking with my entire division, but I cannot tell if my attack will bring on a general engagement or not. I am ready to try if he says attack."

The staff officer rode back to Lee with the reply.

The Union Second Corps commander, Winfield Hancock, read the latest orders from Meade's headquarters with a mixture of disbelief and frustration. The message informed him that Getty's division would attack at once along the Orange Plank Road, and further, it specified that Hancock must support Getty's advance by putting one

Second Corps division on Getty's right flank and another on his left, while holding two more in reserve. Up to this moment Hancock had been methodically planning to attack with all his strength along the south side of the Plank Road, while Getty took the north. Hancock shook his head. Certainly the staff officers back at Wilderness Tavern had not the slightest idea of the true situation on the Orange Plank Road. Two of the four divisions that headquarters wanted Hancock to use were still in column, marching up from Todd's Tavern. It would be at least another hour before they could be successfully deployed.

Couriers raced from Hancock's position with new instructions. David Birney was to pull his two-brigade division out of the line it held on Getty's left; it was to march in behind Getty and come up into position on his right. Meanwhile, Brigadier General Gershom Mott was to move his own two-brigade division to fill in the gap left by Birney. Putting these units in motion through Wilderness thickets just at the beginning of the attack was courting disaster, but Winfield Hancock felt he had no choice.

All of the action was taking place near the roads, north of the Orange Turnpike, where Sedgwick was attacking, and along the Orange Plank Road, where Getty and Hancock were stepping off. Since leaving the Orange Plank Road and pushing north, the four Confederate brigades of Cadmus Wilcox's division of A. P. Hill's corps had found themselves listening to the sounds of distant gunfire. Eventually they connected with troops belonging to Gordon's brigade of Ewell's corps, so for the moment, at least, Lee had linked his two corps on the field.

Taking advantage of the lull, Chaplain Mullally of McGowan's Brigade held a brief prayer service. Lieutenant J. F. J. Caldwell remembered it as "one of the most impressive scenes I have ever witnessed. On the left thundered the dull battle; on the right the sharp crack of rifles, gradually swelled to equal importance, above was the blue, placid heavens; around us a varied landscape of forest and fields, green with the earliest foliage of spring, and here knelt hirsute and browned veterans shriving for another struggle with death.

"In the midst of the prayer, a harsh, rapid fire broke out right on the plank road we had left; the order was issued to face about . . . and then we went [quickly] . . . towards the constantly increasing battle."

George Getty's men pushed forward with Colonel Lewis A. Grant's all-Vermont brigade south of the Orange Plank Road; Frank Wheaton's and Brigadier General Henry L. Eustis's brigades were advancing along its north side. The Federals literally blundered into battle. "Nothing was visible for ten paces ahead," a Pennsylvanian in Wheaton's brigade recalled. Chaplain A. M. Stewart was pacing his comrades in the 102nd Pennsylvania just north of the Plank Road when all hell broke loose. "Suddenly these hitherto quiet woods seemed to be lifted up, shook, rent, and torn asunder. Thousands and thousands of Minnie balls united in their sharp crack and ear-piercing sound, rendering the tumult one of terrible grandeur." A North Carolinian on the shooting end of the equation described the combat this way: "A butchery pure and simple it was, unrelieved by any of the arts of war in which the exercise of military skill and tact robs the hour of some of its horrors."

With David Birney's division not yet in position to shield Getty's right, it was that flank that first unraveled. The 2nd Rhode Island took quick, brutal punishment. "The woods and brush were so thick and dark that the enemy could not be seen," said Elisha Rhodes of that regiment. "They flanked our right, driving it back in confusion." This, in turn, uncovered the right flank of the next regiment in line, the 10th Massachusetts.

South of the Plank Road, Lewis Grant's Vermonters became confused and disoriented in the wooded thicket. Grant's men came up against the Confederate defenses in uncoordinated, piecemeal packets, with all formation lost. In a move of pure desperation, Grant pulled his regiments back into a semicircular defensive position and called for help. A Vermonter in the midst of the fighting described the moment: "The men's faces grew powder-grimed, and their mouths black from biting cartridges. The musketry silenced all other sounds; and the air in the woods was hot and heavy with sulphurous vapor."

Lewis Grant's call for help caught the two brigades of David Birney's division in the process of shifting over to Getty's right flank. Acting quickly, Birney let Alexander Hays's brigade complete its movement to Getty's right, but he turned J. H. H. Ward's brigade around and sent it in on the south side of the Plank Road after Grant's Vermonters. "We rushed forward to the attack with the utmost vigor," recalled Sergeant Fred Floyd of the 40th New York.

Ward's brigade surged over Lewis Grant's semicircular position and smashed into the Virginians of Henry Walker's brigade. Confederate counterattacks drove Ward's men back, but not before the colors of the 55th Virginia were captured and carried triumphantly back to the main Union lines. North Carolinians from William Kirkland's reserve brigade helped stop Ward's men. In one attack W. J. Martin led his men in a yelling charge that passed over a prone portion of Brigadier General John Cooke's brigade. As they ran by, Colonel William MacRae of Cooke's brigade sneered sardonically, "Go ahead, you'll soon come back." Remembered Martin, "And sure enough, we did. We struck, as he had done, the Federal line behind entrenchments, from which in vain we tried to dislodge it, and recoiled, lying down behind MacRae's men. I fancy he *smiled* sardonically then."

By now Alexander Hays had placed his brigade in the woods on George Getty's punished right flank. With all sense of direction gone, all formation lost in the twisted ground and brush, Hays waved his brigade forward in bits and pieces. Brigadier General Joseph R. Davis's entrenched Mississippi troops found the range, and for a few terrible minutes carnage reigned. As one Michigan color sergeant, Daniel Crotty, recalled, "The slaughter is fearful, men fall on every side, and my flag is receiving its share of bullets. Charge after charge is made on both sides. Sometimes we drive the enemy, and then they rally and drive us. . . ."

Charles Page of the *New York Tribune* steadied his horse and tried to make sense of the images before him on the Brock Road. "The wounded stream out, and fresh troops pour in. Stretchers pass with ghastly burdens, and go back reeking with blood for more. Word is brought that the ammunition is failing. 60 rounds fired in one steady, stand-up fight, and that fight not fought out. Boxes of cartridges are placed on the returning stretchers, and the struggle shall not cease for want of ball and powder."

Now Gershom Mott's division completed its move into the line vacated by Birney's men and advanced along the south side of the Plank Road, into the fray. The result was disastrous. Stumbling blindly toward the fighting, Colonel Robert McAllister's brigade bumped into Lewis Grant's grimly held pocket. This threw McAllister's men into a fatal confusion, which was compounded by the relentless hammering of Confederate gunfire. "Along the whole division the movement became at once and rapidly retrograde," recalled Chaplain Warren Cudworth of the 1st Massachusetts. "Branches of trees tore off knapsacks and haversacks, knocked guns out of men's hands, and, in two or three cases, completely stripped them of their accouterments."

Meade's aide Theodore Lyman found Winfield Hancock at the point where the Brock and Orange Plank roads intersected. "The musketry was crashing in the woods in our front," Lyman recalled vividly, "and stray balls — too many to be pleasant — were coming about. It's all very well for novels, but *I* don't like such places. . . ."

"Report to General Meade," Hancock shouted, "that it is very hard to bring up troops in this wood, and that only a part of my Corps is up, but I will do as well as I can." He had hardly finished speaking when an officer rode in.

"Sir! General Getty is hard pressed and nearly out of ammunition!"

"Tell him to hold on and General Gibbon will be up to help him," Hancock answered, turning to face yet another officer.

"General Mott's division has broken, sir, and is coming back."

"Tell him to stop them, sir!" Hancock roared.

As Lyman watched, the first squads of disorganized Union soldiers, like the scud clouds before a storm, broke from the woods onto the Brock Road. Instantly Hancock rode in among them.

"Halt here! Halt here! Form behind this rifle-pit!"

Lyman observed all this with open-mouthed astonishment and admiration. It was no wonder to him that Hancock was nicknamed the Superb.

Then, almost as if all of this had been rehearsed, the first brigade of John Gibbon's division came marching up from Todd's Tavern. "Left face — Prime — Forward" came the commands. Then, according to Lyman, "the line disappeared in the woods to waken the musketry with double violence."

Another sight caught Lyman's eye. Out of the woods north of the Plank Road came a small, sorrowful procession carrying the body of Brigadier General Alexander Hays. "He was a strong-built, rough sort of man, with red hair, and a tawny, full beard," Lyman observed. "He had been shot in the head while leading his troops on horseback."

It was approximately 5:00 P.M.

Like most of the artillerymen accompanying A. P. Hill's corps, William Dame of the Richmond Howitzers sat in reserve near Parker's Store. Ordered to halt here because the thicketed Wilderness ground made it impossible to employ many cannon, the artillerymen could at first only hear the battle. As time went on, they began to see its results. Remembered Dame, "Numbers of wounded men streamed past us, asking the way to the hospitals, some limping painfully along, some, with arms in a sling, some, with blood streaming down over neck or face, some, helped along by a comrade, some, borne on stretchers. . . . Eagerly we stopped these wounded men to ask how the fight was going. . . . One fellow . . . expressed it, 'Dead Yankees were *knee deep* all over about four acres of ground.' The blood was running down and dropping, very freely, off this man's arm; while he stood in the road and told us of this."

Horace Porter was busy this day carrying messages and passing news along. Just back from the Orange Plank Road, he told U. S. Grant of Hancock's fight and Hays's death. Grant was sitting on the ground with his back against a tree, still whittling pine sticks. Porter remembered, "He sat for a time without uttering a word, and then, speaking in a low voice, and pausing between the sentences, said: 'Hays and I were cadets together for three years. . . . I am not surprised that he met his death at the head of his troops; it was just like the man.'"

Porter learned something else. Despite the terrible battering that the Army of the Potomac had taken so far, Grant was not ready to call it a day. Already a force made up of James Wadsworth's Fifth Corps division and one brigade from John Robinson's division was feeling its way southward to help Hancock. Grant's intentions were clear: they would continue the attack.

5:00 P.M.–Sunset

James Longstreet's corps was coming. Captain D. Augustus Dickert, part of Kershaw's Brigade, remembered May 5: "All day we marched along unused roads — through fields and thickets, taking every cut possible. Scarcely stopping for a moment to rest, we found ourselves, at five o'clock in the evening, twenty-eight miles from our starting point. Men were too tired and worn out to pitch tents, and troops stretched themselves on the ground to get such comfort and rest as possible."

The head of Longstreet's column was at Richard's Shop, perhaps ten miles from the Orange Plank Road and A. P. Hill's men.

Pushing grimly over the debris of two hours' fighting, two fresh Union brigades attacked along either side of the Orange Plank Road. Samuel Carroll's men were north of it. A Delaware soldier recalled, "Our line had not moved more than 50 yards down a gentle slope towards a swamp, and through a dense thicket of scrub-oak and dwarf-pine, when the enemy . . . opened upon us a terrific fire of musketry by volleys." Carroll's well-disciplined troops pressed on and were soon at close quarters with Confederates from John Cooke's and

Joe Davis's brigades. "It wasn't like a battle at all — it was more like Indian warfare," remembered John McClure, a young private in the 14th Indiana. "I hid behind a tree and looked out. Across the way . . . was a rebel aiming at me. I put my hat on a stick . . . and stuck it out from behind the tree — as bait. Then I saw him peep out of the thicket and I shot him. It was the first time I'd ever seen the man I'd killed, and it was an awful feeling."

Brigadier General Joshua T. Owen's brigade was less successful south of the Plank Road. His men had to contend with the confused pockets of Lewis Grant's brigade and Gershom Mott's division. "We entered the woods, passing over the bodies of those who had fallen before," said a New Yorker in the 152nd. "We forced a passage through the thick undergrowth, becoming separated and considerably mixed up."

It was at this time that troops from Cadmus Wilcox's division, urgently recalled from their brief connection with Ewell's right flank, came up to reinforce the sagging Confederate line. Lieutenant J. F. J. Caldwell was in McGowan's Brigade, the first to arrive. "The [Orange Plank] road was crowded with non-combatants, artillery and ordnance wagons . . . ," he said. "The order to advance was given. Balls fired at Heth's division, in front of us, fell among us at the beginning of our advance. We pressed on . . . through the thick undergrowth, until we reached Heth's line, now much thinned and exhausted. . . . We passed over this line cheering. . . . We drew upon ourselves a terrific volley." The two battle lines — McGowan's and Carroll's — lunged back and forth in a deadly grapple. Confusion reigned everywhere. Admitted Caldwell, "It began to look like every man would have to be his own general." During one of the forward surges of the Southern line, portions of the 11th North Carolina took cover behind "a line of dead Federals so thick as to form a partial breastwork." Years later an officer in the regiment still had a vivid memory of that moment: "It was a novel experience and seems ghastly enough in the retrospect."

South of the Plank Road, the four North Carolina regiments belonging to Brigadier General Alfred Scales's brigade pushed into the woods against Joshua Owen's Yankees. "It was like fighting a forest fire," said Captain R. S. Williams of the 13th North Carolina.

For perhaps an hour the two sides surged against each other like competing tides driven by rival moons. William Haines, a New Jerseyman, never forgot the sounds of "that long swelling roll of musketry, which would die down to a few spattering shots, then break out again with all the terrible power and grandeur of a mighty church organ." At Grant's headquarters, the sound of Hancock's attack could be heard, but no sense could be made of it. Grant's military secretary, Adam Badeau, noted that it was "like one incessant peal of thunder, and most remarkable to those familiar with battle, because so seldom interrupted by artillery."

Each side had managed to place a few cannon along the narrow Plank Road. In both cases the cannoneers made clear targets for opposing infantrymen sheltered in the woods, and they sustained terrible losses. At various times during the back-and-forth fighting one side overran the other's guns. Neither, however, kept possession long enough to haul them away. When night fell, all the cannon were reclaimed.

More men pushed into the fighting. On the Union side, Alexander Webb's brigade tried to bring order to the chaotic situation south of the Plank Road. "The roll of musketry reverberating in the front was like the roar of a mighty cataract," noted Lieutenant T. J. Hastings of the 15th Massachusetts. Captain John G. B. Adams, leading the tiny Company A of the 19th Massachusetts, testified to the ebb and flow of the combat: "Sometimes the rebels drove us, sometimes we drove them." On the Confederate side, Wilcox committed the last two brigades of his division. The Georgians of Edward Thomas's brigade turned off the Plank Road to the north and relieved Joe Davis's Mississippians. Behind Thomas came the five North Carolina regiments of Brigadier General James H. Lane's brigade. These filed off to the south of the road. As the last troops available to Lee entered the battle, a North Carolinian in the 37th Regiment recalled, "the whole Wilderness roared like a fire in a canebrake."

Lane's men were in turn hit by portions of Francis Barlow's division of Hancock's corps. Dusk seemed more like night in the thick embrace of the Wilderness forest as Barlow's men groped forward. "Only by the flash of the volleys of the firing lines can we know where is posted the enemy with which we are engaged," said a New York officer. "The woods light up with the flashes of musketry, as if with lightning . . . Death holds high carnival in our ranks."

Only by heroic efforts did Lane's exhausted troops hold back the Union attacks. Squads of men who had been separated from their outfits in the confused fighting reorganized themselves and headed back to the battle, sharpshooter Barry Benson among them. Benson ran past General Lane, "who sat on horseback a little in rear of his Brigade. Seeing us and supposing we were of the detail who kept the line supplied with cartridges from the wagons at the rear, he called to us, 'Are you bringing in cartridges?'

"'Yes, in our cartridge boxes,' we answered, holding them up and shaking them at him.

"'That's right,' he said."

General A. P. Hill's aide William Palmer was busy throughout the afternoon carrying orders and urging troops into line. The rattling fire from Lane's fighting could be heard clearly as Palmer rode past two officers on horseback, whom he recognized as the cavalry chief, "Jeb" Stuart, and Lee's aide Charles Venable. Palmer distinctly recalled hearing one of them exclaim helplessly, "If night would only come!"

Following the Union troops into battle, Chaplain William Corby, grimly wearing his pineapple-shaped hat, came across a badly wounded soldier named Daniel Lynch. Corby had disapproved of the way Lynch, a good-natured but simple-minded boy, had squandered his advancement opportunities "for want of system and education." Corby now counted eight bloody holes in Lynch's body. "His mind was clear," the chaplain later wrote. "I prepared him for death, and, dropping a parting tear, was obliged to leave him to his fate in the Wilderness of Virginia."

Sometime between five and six o'clock, James Longstreet received a change of orders that puzzled him. Instead of proceeding as planned, on a route that would bring his corps to the Brock Road around Todd's Tavern, Longstreet was now told to veer northward and to "unite with the troops of the Third Corps on the Plank Road." Longstreet continued, "The accounts we had of the day's work were favorable to the Confederates; but the change of direction of our march was not reassuring."

Shortly after 7:00 P.M. the smoldering embers of combat around Saunders Field flared violently to bright flame again. Another Sixth Corps assault struggled across the difficult ground toward the Confederate lines. It was not successful. According to Virginia lieutenant Robert Funkhouser, "the Yankees made a tremendous onslaught upon us, but we held our ground & after about half an hour the Yanks gave it up. . . ."

The Federal attack caught John Casler and his fellow pioneers working in the front lines, building up the entrenchments for the Stonewall Brigade. Casler ducked behind a tree and watched as

"Doggie" Bradley of Company F stood out in the open and fired again and again at the Yankees. Bradley believed that if he was fated to be hit, then hiding behind a tree would not save him. "In a few moments he was shot dead," Casler noted, adding, "I never believed in such a theory, and would shield myself all I could."

After leaving Army headquarters near the Lacy House at around 6:00 P.M., James Wadsworth's division inched slowly and fearfully southward through dense and darkening thickets. These brigades had already been pushed around by Gordon's counterattack; their confidence was sorely shaken. Yet through some odd flash of fortune, Wadsworth's men moved exactly toward the critical point of the battle. Their route, if completed, would put them squarely on the left flank and rear of A. P. Hill's troops, fighting north of the Orange Plank Road.

Word of Wadsworth's approach found Hill with his manpower accounts all overdrawn; every available brigade had been committed to the fighting. Somehow this new threat had to be parried. Hill's aide William Palmer recalled that at that moment "There was nothing out of the line except the Fifth Alabama Battalion (125 strong) under Major Vandegraff, who had charge of the prisoners." Hill ordered the captives to be turned over to noncombatants and told Vandegraff to take his provost unit forward against the Yankees, yelling as though they were skirmishing for a fresh brigade. The Alabamians formed a loosely open line, waited for the nervous Federals to get close, and then fired fast and whooped loud.

Roy Stone's Federals, who had already run once this day, broke and scattered a second time. By the time Wadsworth's officers could get matters back in hand, darkness had put an end to any further action. James Wadsworth halted his men in the thickets about a half mile north of the Orange Plank Road.

Sometime near eight o'clock the fighting ended.

Noted Morris Schaff, "When the firing ceased on Hancock's front, to those of us around the Lacy House and at Grant's headquarters, the silence was heavy and awesome."

Confederate: Night

Virginia private James McCown fell asleep with reflection and brief prayer: "So closed this awful day, the first fighting I have ever done and the Lord delivered me. All thanks to him."

On some parts of the Confederate line, sleep was a long time coming. McHenry Howard of Edward Johnson's division, in Ewell's corps, recalled wearily, "It was half a dozen times reported that the enemy were advancing . . . but no serious attack was made, . . . and after rushing to arms more than once under the impression that a charge was imminent, we presently grew accustomed to the situation and received such claims more stolidly."

Samuel Buck, a Virginian, was part of Pegram's Brigade, posted north of the Orange Turnpike. After the firing died down, Buck sagged in place, grateful for the chance to get some sleep. Hardly had he closed his eyes, however, when he was shaken awake by the brigade adjutant, with orders to set up the picket line for the night. Buck suggested testily that someone else be volunteered, but the officer repeated the order, promising to send relief as soon as possible. Under grumbling protest, Buck gathered together enough men for a picket line and moved forward, "stumbling over the dead and dying [who] lay thicker than I ever saw them. . . . It was hard to keep off of them in the darkness." Buck never forgot "the terrible groans of the wounded, the mournful sound of the owl and the awful shrill shrieks of the whippoorwill. . . . These birds seemed to mock at our grief and laugh at the groans of the dying."

Henry Heth, whose division had begun the fighting along the Orange Plank Road this day, rode wearily to Third Corps headquarters and sought out A. P. Hill. Heth found the Confederate corps commander huddled near a campfire, looking ill. Hill began to praise the fight Heth's men had waged, but the divisional officer cut him short. Hill's aide William Palmer listened intently as Heth described the jumbled position the Southern troops now occupied. This confirmed the information they had already been provided by Cadmus Wilcox. According to Palmer, the two officers "said their lines in the woods were like a worm fence, at every angle, and when they had undertaken to straighten them the enemy had captured our men and we captured theirs."

Heth never forgot Hill's reply: "Longstreet will be up in a few hours. . . . I don't propose that your division shall do any fighting tomorrow, the men have been marching and fighting all day and are tired. I do not wish them disturbed."

It was about 10:00 P.M. when young Major Henry McClellan of "Jeb" Stuart's staff rode into Lee's headquarters, angry and upset. Three hours earlier McClellan had been sent to Longstreet's corps with verbal orders that they were to press on without delay to assure an early arrival in Hill's rear on May 6. McClellan had come across Longstreet's lead division, which was under the command of Charles Field, a West Pointer and a stickler for procedure. Major General Field had politely heard out the young major (McClellan later termed his reception "somewhat cold and formal") and then flatly refused to wake his men on the word of an officer unknown to him. Field had clear orders from Longstreet: the men would march at 1:00 A.M. (Years afterward McClellan wrote, "General Field's reply has never escaped my memory. It was, 'I prefer to obey General Longstreet's orders.'") Embarrassed and angry, McClellan picked his way over the dark roads back to Parker's Store and told his story to Robert E. Lee. McClellan offered to ride back at once with written orders, which even the punctilious Field would not be able to ignore. Lee shook his head. "No, Major," he said quietly. "It is now past 10 o'clock, and by the time you could return to General Field and he could put his division in motion, it would be 1 o'clock. At that hour he will move."

Twice more Henry Heth returned to A. P. Hill to ask for permission to pull back some of the troops that were scattered across the Orange Plank Road, in order to regroup them. Once more Cadmus Wilcox added his voice to the request. The third time Heth asked, Hill exploded. "Damn it, Heth," he said sharply, "I don't want to hear any more about it; the men shall not be disturbed."

At 11:00 P.M. Robert E. Lee dispatched a battle report to the Confederate war secretary, James Seddon. It read, in part:

> THE ENEMY CROSSED THE RAPIDAN YESTERDAY. . . . TWO CORPS OF THIS ARMY MOVED TO OPPOSE HIM. . . . A STRONG ATTACK WAS MADE UPON EWELL, WHO REPULSED IT. . . . THE ENEMY SUBSEQUENTLY CONCENTRATED UPON GENERAL HILL, WHO . . . RESISTED REPEATED & DESPERATE ASSAULTS. . . . BY THE BLESSING OF GOD WE MAINTAINED OUR POSITION . . . UNTIL NIGHT, WHEN THE CONTEST ENDED.

The unhappy picket officer Samuel Buck spent a weary night walking up and down the outpost line. The promised relief had not appeared, and Buck was betting he would not be seeing any help until dawn. "The only thing to break the monotony," he recalled, "was the constant tramp of the men removing the wounded and preparing for the coming struggle."

It was midnight when A. P. Hill, suddenly anxious about the arrival of Longstreet's corps, rode west on the Orange Plank Road to Parker's Store and Robert E. Lee's headquarters. According to Hill's aide William Palmer, "General Lee repeated his orders . . . to let the men rest as they were; that General Longstreet would be up . . . and would form in the rear of the line before daylight."

Seemingly satisfied, Hill and his staff rode back to their Tapp Farm headquarters. Palmer remembered that despite Lee's assurances, "the anxious night wore slowly away. . . . We could not sleep, but waited for news of Longstreet."

"About midnight," noted William Perry, an officer of Field's Division, in Longstreet's corps, "the men were aroused by marching orders." It was closer to 1:00 A.M., according to Longstreet himself, before the lead elements in his long column actually began to march. William Perry's men were farther down the line. They did not step off until almost 2:00.

James Longstreet later wrote, "The road was overgrown by the bushes . . . and . . . difficult to follow." William Perry added, "The progress made before light was slow."

Union: Night

Morris Schaff painted this image of Grant's headquarters this night: ". . . soldiers, in groups of two or three, were sitting around their little dying fires, smoking; some with overcoat and hat for a pillow, already asleep. The black cooks, coatless and bareheaded, were puttering around their pot and kettle fires. . . . And around them all . . . are the baggage and supply wagons, their bowed white canvas tops, although mildewed and dirty, dimly looming, outlined by being the resting place for stray beams winding through the night."

Nearby, Grant and Meade talked over the day's battle. Horace Porter heard Grant remark, "I feel pretty well satisfied with the results of the engagement; for it is evident that Lee attempted by a bold movement to strike this army in flank . . . but in this he has failed." As Grant later added, "I was anxious that the rebels should not take the initiative in the morning." Porter continued, "The plan agreed upon that night for the coming struggle was as follows: Han-

cock and Wadsworth were to make an attack on Hill at 4:30 A.M. . . .
Burnside . . . was to send one division . . . to Hancock, and to put
. . . two divisions between Wadsworth and Warren's other divisions,
and attack Hill in flank . . . while Warren and Sedgwick were to attack along their fronts."

Throughout the afternoon and evening the battered survivors of the
140th New York had stumbled back through the brush to the site of
that morning's bivouac to find the neat rows of knapsacks they had
left behind before the advance. Adjutant Porter Farley always remembered the sad scene: "Of the knapsacks which had been piled
together only half had been reclaimed by their owners. . . . [The]
unclaimed knapsacks were opened, and the friends of the missing
men tried to save such trifling momentos of their lost comrades as
would be most precious to their families."

By Henry Cribben's count, of the 529 men of the 140th New
York who dropped their packs and attacked across Saunders Field,
238 failed to return.

Not everyone who had been killed or captured was mourned this
night. Private John Haley of the 17th Maine learned that Major Mat-
tox of his regiment had been taken prisoner. Haley grinned in the
darkness as he thought, "I can't think of any officer I'd sooner part
with for he was very pompous and had yards and yards of superfluous
red tape about him."

Members of the 118th Pennsylvania, entrenched along the eastern
fringes of Saunders Field, recalled this as "a woeful night. . . . [The]
moans and wailings of the Wilderness battle-field stirred the stoutest
hearts, and yet they could not be relieved. . . . War's hard rules
would not permit it. . . . There was no helping hand to succor, no
yielding of the stern necessities of war."

Bored with the inactivity of the artillery reserve, cannoneer
Frank Wilkeson had spent the day watching the fighting up close.
Still driven by curiosity, Wilkeson prowled the ground where the
wounded lay in careless profusion. "I saw one man," he remembered,
"both of whose legs were broken, lying on the ground with his cocked
rifle by his side and his ramrod in his hand, and his eyes set on the
front. I know he meant to kill himself in case of fire — knew it as
surely as though I could read his thoughts."

Wilkeson saw something else that disturbed him. "The dead men lay where they fell. . . . The battlefield ghouls had rifled their pockets. I saw no dead men that night whose pockets had not been turned inside out."

A few officers in Gershom Mott's division were incensed over its poor showing today. Captain Henry Blake of the 11th Massachusetts recalled that the regimental colonel gathered up the soldiers who he was convinced had run and assigned one apiece to the steadfast veterans. His speech went this way: "Private, you are responsible for this cowardly skulker. If he tries to run away, blow his brains out; but if we are fighting, crack his skull with the butt of your gun, and he will never trouble you again."

George Meade called his corps commanders together to discuss Grant's attack plans. During the meeting, the bushy-whiskered Ambrose Burnside showed up, in receipt of orders directly from Grant to close the gap in the Union lines between Warren near the Orange Turnpike and Hancock and Wadsworth along the Orange Plank Road.

Burnside, as Morris Schaff noted this night, "had a very grand and oracular air." Confidently assuring everyone in sight that his troops would be marching by 2:30 A.M., the onetime commander of the Army of the Potomac disappeared into the darkness.

"After he was out of hearing," Schaff continued, "Duane, Meade's Chief of Engineers, who had been with the Army of the Potomac since its formation, said: '*He* won't be up — I know him well!'" Years later Schaff could still muse, "I can see Duane's face, hear his quiet voice, see his hands slowly stroking his full, long, rusty beard, as he says, '*He* won't be up — I know him well!'"

As Captain John G. B. Adams tallied up the casualties for Company A of the 19th Massachusetts, he thought about Ben Falls, whose decision to reenlist had helped convince the other members of the company to do the same. Falls had been hit in the leg today, and Adams had ordered him to the rear. Adams was privately glad to see the veteran get off with such a light wound. Falls was the color-sergeant and was always apt to be at the point of worst fighting. For the moment, at least, Ben Falls was safely out of danger.

The Northern newspapermen who were accompanying the army on this campaign gathered around a campfire to count their losses and make plans. One of their number had been mortally wounded in the fighting, while another nursed an arm wound.

All knew they were sitting on a great story; the problem was, how to get it back to Washington and New York? All telegraph lines had been pulled up when the army had moved, and the roads north swarmed with murderous Confederate guerrillas.

Homer Byington, the senior of the *New York Tribune* men present, decided that one of his cub reporters would have to go. All eyes turned to the youngest and least experienced. Henry Wing swallowed and nodded. A grateful Byington promised him a hundred dollars if he made it, telling him to leave at dawn.

Wing showed his resourcefulness immediately. He wandered over to Grant's campfire, found the Union commander, told him of his trip, and blithely asked if he had any message for the country. Grant glanced over at the reporter and said levelly, "You may tell the people that things are going swimmingly down here." Wing jotted down some notes, smiled, and turned to go; he had hardly left the campfire glow behind when he felt a firm hand on his shoulder. Wing turned and saw that Grant had followed him out of the hearing of the others. "You expect to get through to Washington?" Grant asked. Wing nodded. Grant paused, then leaned close and spoke to the young reporter in a low voice.

From his field headquarters near Chancellorsville, Phil Sheridan put the best face he could on the dismal performance of the Union cavalry this day.

MAJOR-GENERAL HUMPHREYS:
GENERAL: I HAVE THE HONOR TO REPORT THAT GENERAL WIL-
SON WAS ATTACKED TO-DAY AT CRAIG'S MEETING HOUSE.

Ambitious, outspoken, quick to find fault in others, James Harrison Wilson was a newcomer to cavalry command, yet his division — the smallest in Sheridan's corps — had been given the toughest assignment. While Sheridan had sat with two of his divisions near Chancellorsville, Wilson's men had been scattered to the west to protect the Union line of march. When the cavalry officer had ridden out of Parker's Store at five o'clock that morning, it was with the understanding that he would provide patrols for the Orange Turnpike and the Orange Plank Road, as well as for other avenues leading from the west and southwest toward the places that were to be occupied by Hancock's Second Corps. In point of fact, Wilson had failed to screen the Turnpike in front of Charles Griffin's infantry, left John Hammond's small force to battle alone along the Plank Road, and nearly gotten himself chewed up by Confederate riders in a clattering, clanky firefight that had lasted most of the day.

> AT FIRST HE DROVE THE ENEMY ON THE CATHARPIN ROAD FOR SOME DISTANCE THEN THEY DROVE HIM BACK TO TODD'S TAVERN. GENERAL GREGG ATTACKED THE ENEMY AND DROVE THEM BACK TO BEACH GROVE, DISTANCE ABOUT 4 MILES.

Prodded by a message from George Meade at Wilderness Tavern, complaining that no reports were coming in from Wilson, Phil Sheridan had dispatched David McM. Gregg's division to investigate. At 2:45 that afternoon Gregg had ridden into Wilson's fighting retreat. Reacting quickly, Gregg had ordered an attack that rocked the Confederate riders back. And there the fighting had ended for the day.

Sheridan's frustration at his own inability to take an aggressive role while he was tied to the lumbering army supply train strained his patience.

> I CANNOT DO ANYTHING WITH THE CAVALRY, EXCEPT TO ACT ON THE DEFENSIVE, ON ACCOUNT OF THE IMMENSE AMOUNT OF MATERIAL AND TRAINS HERE. . . . WHY CANNOT INFANTRY BE SENT TO GUARD THE TRAINS AND LET ME TAKE THE OFFENSIVE . . . ?

Horace Porter put the time at before 11:00 P.M. when Grant told his staff, "We shall have a busy day tomorrow, and I think we had better get all the sleep we can to-night. I am a confirmed believer in the restorative qualities of sleep, and always like to get at least seven hours of it, though I have often been compelled to put up with much less."

The staff separated, each man heading to his own little corner. Before he drifted off, Porter noted, "The marked stillness which now reigned in camp formed a striking contrast to the shock and din of battle which had just ceased, and which was so soon to be renewed."

Amid the groaning and screaming wounded at the division hospital for David Birney's men, a life-and-death vigil was taking place. Only a few hours earlier, at sunset, Colonel Calvin A. Craig had been shot in the jaw. After being patched up at an aide station, he had insisted on returning to the fighting line. Craig had gone only a short distance forward when his facial wound reopened, this time with the blood spouting out in great jets. Frantic work by Dr. Stevens at the divisional hospital determined that the facial artery was severed, and Stevens finally stopped the terrible bleeding by pressing his thumb on the artery. Since there were constant demands on Dr. Stevens, Colonel Craig's friends were drafted to join in an urgent relay, each in turn holding his finger on the artery to keep the officer from bleeding to death. The friends were required to stand this watch for thirty-six hours before the wounded Federal passed out of danger.

After conversing with his corps commanders, George Meade sent a message to U. S. Grant to request that the attack that was planned for May 6 be postponed from 4:30 A.M. to 6:00. Grant, already asleep when the messenger came, was awakened and given the note, in which Meade indicated that the difficult terrain and fatigue of the men would make it necessary to delay things for ninety minutes. As Grant later wrote, "Deferring to his wishes as far as I was willing, the order was modified and five was fixed as the hour to move."

The *New York Tribune* correspondent Charles Page closed his notes on this day with a truculent, if slightly inaccurate, observation: "Today we have fought because the enemy chose that we should. Tomorrow, because we choose that he shall."

FRIDAY, MAY 6

Early Morning

Captain D. Augustus Dickert described the morning march of Longstreet's corps: "Along blind roads, overgrown by underbrush, through fields that had lain fallow for years, now studded with bushes and briars . . . the men floundered and fell as they marched. . . . Sometimes the head of the column would lose its way, and during the time it was hunting its way back to the lost bridle path, was about the only rest we got."

During the night, as Richard Ewell reordered his lines, John Gordon's brigade was shifted from its position on the extreme right to a new one on the extreme left — north of the Orange Turnpike — where it rejoined Jubal Early's division. The aggressive and meticulous Gordon moved quickly to size up his new position. "Scouts were at once sent to the front to feel their way through the thickets and ascertain, if possible, where the extreme right of Grant's line rested."

It was 4:00 A.M. as Henry Wing, the young *New York Tribune* reporter entrusted with the stories of the May 5 fighting, rode out from the Union camps around Wilderness Tavern and headed for Ely's Ford. Wing was dressed for the adventure in Irish corduroy pants, a buckskin jacket, calfskin boots, Alexandria kid gloves, and a dark, soft felt hat.

John Gordon later recalled it as being "early dawn" when his scouts returned with a story he thought hard to believe. They reported their probe of the Union right flank: they had found it to be "wholly unprotected" and, further, had discovered that "the Confederate lines stretched a considerable distance beyond the Union right, overlapping it." Gordon immediately ordered a second scouting party to verify the report of the first and "to proceed to the rear of Grant's right and ascertain if the exposed flank were supported by troops held in reserve behind it."

Even as Gordon was assessing this intelligence, his division commander, Jubal Early, heard a conflicting report from cavalry scouts who told him that "a column of the enemy's infantry was moving between our left and the [Rapidan] river, with the apparent purpose of turning our left flank; and information was also received that Burnside's corps had crossed the river, and was in rear of the enemy's right. I received directions to watch this column, and take steps to prevent its getting to our rear."

As the first units of Burnside's Ninth Corps came in sight of army headquarters, Grant's military secretary, Adam Badeau, checked his watch. It was 4:00 A.M.

The noise of the corps' passing woke up Grant's staff. Wolfing down a "hasty breakfast," his aide Horace Porter wondered at the skimpy meal Grant ate. The general, Porter noted carefully, "took a cucumber, sliced it, poured some vinegar over it, and partook of nothing else except a cup of strong coffee."

The coming of dawn was remembered in different ways by different men. Virginia captain Samuel Buck greeted it dourly. Barely a half hour earlier he had been relieved from what had turned out to be all-night picket duty. Having missed supper the evening before, Buck "decided to run the two meals into one and take supper and breakfast together." Thomas Galwey of the 8th Ohio (Carroll's brigade, Hancock's corps) noted that the sky was clear and the "screaming of the birds . . . was terrifyingly shrill." Henry Berkeley, a young gunner in reserve behind Ewell's main line, had fallen asleep the night before as field surgeons were beginning to work nearby on the wounded. This morning Berkeley awoke to find "a big pile of amputated arms, hands, legs and fingers within a foot or two of me. A horrid sight."

Even as he labored to set up the morning attack down the Orange Plank Road — now involving units from three different corps — Winfield Hancock worried about James Longstreet. Along with orders to begin the assault at 5:00 A.M., Hancock received this disturbing intelligence assessment from Meade's chief of staff, Andrew Humphreys: "An examination of prisoners during the night . . . drew from them the statement that Longstreet was expected to be up in the morning to attack our left." Hancock anticipated a Confederate thrust from around Todd's Tavern northward along the Brock Road. To counter this, the Second Corps commander ordered Barlow's division and most of the corps artillery into blocking positions on the left flank.

Despite all the assurances he had been given, Henry Heth had gotten no sleep this night. "When I imagined I saw the first streak of daylight," he said, "I . . . rode down the Plank Road to see if Longstreet was coming. I rode two or three miles in the direction of Mine Run. No Longstreet. I hurried back."

During the fighting yesterday, a Confederate cannon positioned along the Plank Road had been briefly overrun. Night found the gun between lines, and during the late hours a few enterprising North Carolina soldiers ran it in by hand. The sky was beginning to lighten as gunner William Poague set out from his battalion near the Widow Tapp's farm to reclaim the field piece. "As I went along the Plank Road to get the gun," the twenty-eight-year-old Poague later wrote, "I was surprised to see the unusual condition of things. Nearly all the men were still asleep. One long row of muskets was stacked in the road. Another row made an acute angle with the road and still another was almost at right angles, and here and there could be seen bunches of stacked guns." Poague asked an officer what it all meant and was told that reinforcements were expected at any moment. "He struck me as being very indifferent and not at all concerned about the situation. I could not help feeling troubled," Poague said.

It was, noted George Meade's aide Theodore Lyman, "in the gray of morning" when the Union general rode out to the Germanna Ford Road to find out why Burnside's march was proceeding so slowly. Another aide reported that only a single division of the Ninth Corps had passed and that the rest had been held up by the corps artillery, which was blocking the road. The aide offered to order the guns to move. "No, sir," Meade said. "I have no command over General Burnside."

Lyman shook his head fretfully. Grant's face-saving decision to put the Ninth Corps directly under his orders instead of subordinating it to Meade's was already having ominous consequences. Lyman thought, "Here was a mishap, at once, from a divided leadership."

It was 4:30 A.M.

In the gloom of early dawn, firing broke out once more north of the Orange Turnpike. Keyed-up Confederate pickets scrapped fiercely with their Union counterparts over meaningless pieces of turf. Federal Sixth Corps troops were moving forward, but more than one Union observer believed that the Confederates attacked first this day.

The gunfire was fierce. A Sixth Corps surgeon, George Stevens, remembered, "The volleys of musketry echoed and re-echoed through the forests like peals of thunder." Virginia captain Samuel Buck was hit while trying to get a skulker to fire his gun. "I grabbed hold of my right hand with the left and pulled it up to see if it was broken and when I let go the blood ran out as if all the blood in my body was in that sleeve. . . . I stayed until the last charge was . . . repulsed and then went back to the hospital."

Barry Benson, a sharpshooter, stood a weary watch in A. P. Hill's picket lines, perhaps two hundred yards advanced from the main body of the corps. It was shortly after dawn, he later recalled, when another picket nearby waved frantically at him. Benson scuttled over. "As I stooped beside him, he pointed toward the front, saying 'Look there!'

"When I could see nothing in particular, he said, 'Don't you see? It's the Yankee line-of-battle!'"

Fourteen thousand Confederates were about to be hit by twenty-five thousand Federals.

5:00–11:45 A.M.

As the double-ranked battle line of the 141st Pennsylvania prepared to advance along the south side of the Orange Plank Road, the men could see ahead of them a mound marking the Confederate position. It was topped by an enemy regimental flag "hanging lazily from the staff which was conspicuously placed upon the crest of the works."

"Fix bayonets," came the order. The Pennsylvanians slithered their long knives out of their scabbards and snapped them into place. Sergeant Stephen Rought found that he had lost his bayonet, "so clubbing his musket, he remarked . . . 'I'll have that flag.'" "Soon," added Rought's fellow sergeant J. D. Bloodgood, "the order to charge was given and with a ringing cheer our boys rushed for the enemy's works."

Captain R. S. Williams stretched slowly, trying to shake off the morning dampness. Most of the 13th North Carolina was scattered behind a rough breastwork of old logs and dirt. According to Williams, his brigade commander, Alfred Scales, and regimental colonel, J. H. Hyman, were talking nearby when one of the sergeants called, "Look in front!" Williams craned his neck around to peer over the rude earthwork. "The woods," he remembered, "were blue with the enemy."

Cheering, yelling Pennsylvanians burst into a small clearing in front of the North Carolina position. The Federals "were greeted with a shower of bullets, but on they sped through the stifling smoke, and, reaching the enemy's works, they scaled them without a moment's hesitation."

Captain Williams was momentarily paralyzed by the suddenness of the Yankee attack. He glanced over to where General Scales and Colonel Hyman were standing. "I told them to look — we were almost surrounded. General Scales waved his sword about his head and called on the men to follow him. He dashed off at right angles to his brigade and took . . . [it] out by the right flank."

Not all of the North Carolinians scattered. More than fifty rallied to the regimental flag and fought a short, vicious battle for it. Rought, the Yankee sergeant, came face-to-face with the Rebel color-bearer and clubbed him down. Then, said Sergeant Bloodgood, "A rebel soldier leveled his musket at Rought, but before he could fire Captain Warner, of Company D, shot the assailant with his revolver. A large number of the enemy threw down their arms and surrendered, while those who could get away precipitately fled."

From his position south of the Plank Road, Confederate Major General Cadmus Wilcox clutched the faint hope that the Federals would delay their assault until Longstreet arrived. Now the spreading crackle of gunfire made it clear that the Yankees were attacking in force: "A few shots were heard on [the] right, and the firing extended rapidly along to the left, to the road and across this, and around to [the] extreme left, which was considerably in the rear of [my] line on the right of the road."

The Union soldiers were everywhere.

It was about daylight, remembered Lieutenant Richard Lewis, a South Carolinian in James Longstreet's corps, when the men were allowed to rest from the double-quick time they had kept up for hours. Lewis painted this foreground scene against a backdrop of distant gunfire: "Our noble and beloved Chaplain, McDowell, called on us to rally around him, and we knelt down and had prayers for a few minutes; but before we got through the troops were already moving ahead of us."

Not all of the Federals along the Plank Road were as immediately successful as those in the 141st Pennsylvania. The soldiers in Hays's brigade seemed to have an especially difficult time. According to Daniel Crotty, a Michigan color sergeant, "The order comes to forward, and we go in, thinking to surprise the Johnnies, but they are up and waiting for us in the thick chaparral." Even at this early stage it was difficult for the Federal units to keep together. "The density of the woods," said a captain in the 57th Pennsylvania, "rendered it impossible to maintain a regular line of battle, so we commenced bushwhacking with the enemy on a grand scale."

The quick success enjoyed by the Federals against Scales's Brigade punched a hole in the Confederate front line, throwing Union firepower into the flanks of the Southern units on either side. Troops from Edward Thomas's brigade, battling on the extreme right of

A. P. Hill's forward line, now caught it. A young Georgia diarist, George Washington Hall, noted bitterly, "The enemy advanced in three columns cross-firing on our Brigade from three directions from the front, right flank and rear. . . . We were ordered to fall back which was reluctantly done. . . ."

McGowan's South Carolina brigade, posted north of the Plank Road, on Scales's left flank, also gave way. According to Lieutenant J. F. J. Caldwell, "There was no panic and no great haste; the men seemed to fall back from a deliberate conviction that it was impossible to hold the ground."

Still with the Confederate artillery reserve near Parker's Store, cannoneer William Dame stopped orderlies and wounded men to ask the news. He recalled, "Reports began to float back that the Federals were heavily overlapping A. P. Hill's right, and things looked dangerous. . . . This immediately threw our crowd into a fever of excitement; the idea of lying there, doing nothing, when our men were falling back was intolerable. . . . One fellow near me, voiced the feelings of us all — 'If we can't get in there, or Longstreet doesn't get here pretty quick, the devil will be to pay.'"

The second party of scouts, sent by John Gordon to verify the remarkable report of the first, returned with even more astounding news. Not only was the Union right flank hanging in the air — not anchored to any blocking piece of terrain and vulnerable to being turned — but "there was not a supporting force within several miles of it." Gordon related, "My brain was throbbing with the tremendous possibilities." The Confederate brigade commander now decided to check this intelligence himself.

In the wake of their frustrating experiences on May 5, the men under James Wadsworth's command began this day auspiciously. Attacking from the north on an angle toward the Plank Road, they crashed into William Kirkland's brigade. "Our left flank," said Colonel W. J. Martin of the 11th North Carolina, "rolled up as a sheet of paper would be rolled without power of resistance."

Theodore Lyman came pounding down the Brock Road in search of a progress report. He found Winfield Hancock on the Plank Road, looking, as Lyman put it, "radiant." "Tell General Meade," Hancock

yelled over the steady roar of gunfire, "we are driving them beautifully."

After getting the good news from Hancock, Theodore Lyman
passed along the bad news. "I am ordered to tell you, sir, that only
one division of General Burnside is up, but that he will go in as soon
as he can be put in position." Recorded Lyman, "Hancock's face
changed. 'I knew it!' he said vehemently. 'Just what I expected. If he
could attack *now* we would smash A. P. Hill all to pieces!'"

Robert E. Lee listened to the rising sound of gunfire, watched the
slowly growing trickle of wounded and routed men stumbling past,
and made preparations to retreat. According to his staff officer
Charles Venable, "Lee sent his trusted Adjutant, Colonel W. H. Taylor, back to Parker's store, to get the trains ready for a movement to
the rear." This did not mean that Lee was ready to give up the fight.
Continued Venable, "He sent an aid[e] also to hasten the march of
Longstreet's divisions."

Exultant Federals from Wadsworth's division pushed down to and
across the Plank Road. This threw them into the advance of Birney's
assault column. Precious time was lost as officers struggled frantically
to separate the tangled units.

Hancock's adjutant Francis Walker saw the problem clearly.
"The Union columns had become terribly mixed and disordered in
their forward movement, under the excitement and bewilderment of
battle, through woods so dense that no body of troops could possibly
preserve their alignment. In some cases they were heaped up in
unnecessary strength; elsewhere great gaps existed unknown to
the staff; men and even officers had lost their regiments in the
jungle. . . ."

In fits and starts, the milling soldiers were reoriented, and the
offensive resumed. The Union battle line across the Orange Plank
Road stretched for nearly a mile.

A current of excitement rippled among the reserve artillerymen waiting near Parker's Store. "Look out down the road," someone shouted.
"Here they come!"

William Dame ran down to the Plank Road with the rest of the
idle cannoneers. Already the head of Longstreet's column was swinging past at a double quick. Recalled Dame, "Crowding up to the road,
on both sides, we yelled ourselves nearly dumb to cheer them as they
swept by. . . . Our feeling of relief was complete as the Brigades dis-

appeared into the woods in the direction of Hill's breaking right. . . .
We all felt, 'Thank God! it's all right now! Longstreet is up!'"

A feeling of impending disaster hung in the air around the Tapp Farm
clearing. All along A. P. Hill's line, the Confederate resistance was
collapsing. Cadmus Wilcox rode up to report that the Confederate
position south of the Plank Road was in shambles. "Longstreet must
be here," Robert E. Lee replied. "Go bring him up." Wilcox spurred
down the Plank Road in search of the officer known as Lee's War
Horse.

Large groups of men appeared on the eastern folds of the Tapp
Farm clearing and drifted across the field to the protective cordon of
artillery that Hill had ordered drawn up along the western edge of
the opening. Lee recognized the dispirited form of Brigadier General
Samuel McGowan and rode over to him.

"My God!" Lee said — at this time he was speaking "rather
roughly," according to one of McGowan's aides — "General Mc-
Gowan, is this splendid brigade of yours running like a flock of
geese?" The weary brigadier general replied pridefully, "General, the
men are not whipped, they only want a place to form, and they will
fight as well as ever they did."

Behind them the twelve guns of William Poague's battalion began to bark out shots into the woods across the road. In his frantic
effort to hold this last line, A. P. Hill himself helped man the pieces.
Shells burst in the forest, sending squads of Federals ducking. Lee
felt the bitter taste of miscalculation rise in his throat like bile. As a
member of McGowan's Brigade put it, "We had reckoned too confidently on the coming of the War Horse!" Turning to an aide, Lee
asked plaintively, "Why does not Longstreet come?"

It was 6:30 A.M., perhaps an hour and a half since Hancock's men
had begun the attack.

Longstreet's aide G. Moxley Sorrel, riding near the head of the First
Corps column, was appalled by what he saw up close to the fighting.
"Fugitives from the broken lines of the Third Corps were pushing
back in disorder and it looked as if things were past mending."

By now the hard-riding Cadmus Wilcox had met Joseph Kershaw, of Longstreet's leading division, and apprised him of the situation before galloping farther along the column in search of the War
Horse. Kershaw scouted ahead to the Tapp Farm field, sized things
up, and deployed his men for the most part south of the road. Kershaw rode along the forming ranks. "I expect you to do your duty,"

he shouted. A soldier who was watching noted, "It seemed an inspiration to every man. . . . The columns were not yet in proper order, but the needs so pressing to check the advance of the enemy, that a forward movement was ordered, and the lines formed up as the troops marched."

The Confederate and Union lines came together. Said D. Augustus Dickert of the 3rd South Carolina, "Men rolled and writhed in their last death struggle; wounded men groped their way to the rear, being blinded by the stifling smoke. All commands were drowned in this terrible din of battle — the earth and elements shook and trembled with the deadly shock of combat."

Even in the midst of such terribly impersonal carnage, brief moments of individual struggle stood out. Dickert remembered, "A soldier from Company C, 3rd South Carolina . . . had been shot in the first advance, the bullet severing the great artery of the thigh. The young man . . . struggled behind a small sapling. Bracing himself against it, he undertook deliberative measures for saving his life. Tying a handkerchief about the wound, and placing a small stone underneath and just over the artery, and putting a stick between the handkerchief and his leg, he began to tighten by twisting the stick around. But too late; life had fled, leaving both hands clasping the stick, his eyes glassy and fixed."

Even as Joseph Kershaw rushed his division into the fighting south of the Plank Road, Charles Field swung his men into a battle line north of it. All around were retreating Confederate soldiers. "The numbers, manner, and words of the troops all told too plainly that [Hill's] divisions were being driven back in confusion," Field later stated. "Such [confusion] . . . ," added a Texas soldier named Joseph Polley, "we had never witnessed before in Lee's army."

John Gregg's Texas brigade was the first of Field's command to move from column into combat formation. According to one Texan, A. C. Jones, "We had to push our way through a dense thicket of underbrush, coming up finally into line of battle upon the margin of a small clearing." As the spiky files of Texas and Arkansas troops took shape behind William Poague's busy cannon, Hill's aide William Palmer observed Longstreet steadying the soldiers: "Keep cool, men, we will straighten this out in a short time — keep cool." It was, admired Palmer, "inspiring."

Robert E. Lee peered into the obscuring swirls of cannon smoke clinging to the branches behind Poague's belching guns and caught sight of the slowly building force of men. The long, dressing ranks were like a seawall against a storm. He rode over to them. In the years after the war, the next few moments were to become an indelible part of the Lee legend.

"Who are you, my boys?" Lee cried.

"Texas boys," they yelled back.

Lee felt the sudden, warm rush of a gamble won. These were Longstreet's men! "Hurrah for Texas," he shouted, waving his hat. "Hurrah for Texas!"

As the snaky file of Gregg's battle line wriggled past Poague's guns, the cannon fell silent. Lee stopped his horse on the flank of the advance and pulled the reins to follow the attacking infantrymen. William Palmer watched what happened next: "The tall Texan on the left [of the line] lifted his hat and called to General Lee to go back, and it was taken up by the others. General Lee lifted his hat to them, and moved slowly to the rear. It did not strike me as remarkable at the time."

Gregg's violent attack stunned the poorly ordered pockets of Federals in the woods. "The Union line began to waver, break up and fall back in confusion," admitted O. B. Curtis of the 24th Michigan. Just as quickly, Federal supports came up. Gregg's men took heavy losses and rolled back to a position about two hundred yards in front of Poague's cannon. Soon after the Texans disappeared into the obscuring woods, Georgians from Henry Benning's brigade followed. Benning's men also took many casualties before falling back.

After bringing word that Burnside's corps would be delayed getting into position on Hancock's right, Theodore Lyman stayed to watch the action. Prudently holding a position near the Brock Road, he listened approvingly as the sounds of fighting receded to the west. Shortly after Lyman made a note that "the firing seemed to wake again with renewed fury," a soldier came up with a captured Confederate in tow.

"I was ordered to report that this prisoner here belongs to Longstreet's Corps," the Federal infantryman said. Lyman looked the man over. "Do you belong to Longstreet?" he asked. "Ya-as, sir," the Rebel replied, and he was motioned to the rear.

Theodore Lyman felt a chill despite the warm day. "It was too true!" he thought. "Longstreet, coming in all haste from Orange Court House, had fallen desperately on our advance."

There was confusion around the Tapp Farm as Law's Brigade, under the temporary command of Colonel William F. Perry, came into line of battle on the north side of the Plank Road. A young Alabamian in the 4th remembered that things were "squally" as the men came up to the row of Poague's guns. Colonel William Oates, commanding the 15th Alabama, watched grim-faced as Henry Benning of Georgia was carried to the rear on a litter, seriously wounded. Perry's men moved toward the woods where the battle lay, and the 15th passed near General Lee as he sat on his horse, Traveller. The face of the commander of the Army of Northern Virginia was "flushed and full of animation," Oates recalled. As Lee became aware of the new battle line, he called out, "What troops are these?" "Law's Alabama brigade," came the reply. According to Oates, Lee "exclaimed in a strong voice, 'God bless the Alabamians!'" The image of Lee watching the line of armed men sweep past remained fixed in Oates's memory. "I thought him at that moment the grandest specimen of manhood I ever beheld. He looked as though he ought to have been and was the monarch of the world."

From a concealed position, the Confederate brigadier general John Gordon viewed the extreme right flank of the Army of the Potomac. "As far as my eye could reach," Gordon recalled, "the Union soldiers were seated on the margin of the rifle-pits, taking their breakfast." Gordon sucked in his breath slowly. The scouting reports were true; the right flank of the Union army lay unprotected and unsupported. A sharp, strong attack on it would make the entire Federal position collapse like a row of dominoes. Gordon could barely contain his excitement. "The revelation had amazed me and filled me with confident anticipation of unprecedented victory."

John Gordon hurried back to inform his superiors of his discovery.

Opposite Kershaw, south of the Orange Plank Road, a mixture of Federal units from Hays's, Ward's, McAllister's, and Brewster's brigades fought in confusion. In the tangle of underbrush and smoke north of the Plank Road, James Wadsworth struggled to hold his command together. He rode frantically from point to threatened point as Perry's Alabama regiments began killing his men. A member of the 150th Pennsylvania recalled that time and again the gray-haired Union general appeared alongside their battling line to steady it, calling out, "Come on, Bucktails!"

It was about 8:00 A.M. when John Gordon's aide Thomas Jones rode to report the news to the Second Corps commander, Richard Ewell.

The wispy-haired, one-legged general listened without expression to the aide's story. Even as Jones was completing his report, Gordon's immediate superior, Jubal Early, rode up. Jones dutifully repeated the results of Gordon's personal reconnaissance: the extreme right of the Union army was wide open to a flanking attack. Early was unmoved by the intelligence. He believed that a Federal "column was threatening our left flank and Burnside's corps was in rear of the enemy's flank, on which the attack was suggested." Even as they talked, a courier arrived with a message from Major W. H. H. Cowles confirming Early's assessment. The dispatch rider had been stopped by Gordon, however, and the latter had scratched his own message on the report: "This must be a feint — I don't think it can be intended for a serious movement." At last Ewell spoke up, telling Jones to return to Gordon with instructions to do nothing. At some later point the corps commander would confer directly with his brigadier. Frustrated and not a little surprised, Jones rode back to Gordon.

At around 8:00 A.M., blue-coated skirmishers from Burnside's corps emerged from the woods onto an open field north of the Chewning Farm. Whatever possibilities there might have been of flanking the forces battling against Hancock quickly disappeared as Confederates from Ewell's corps plugged the line. Led by their fiery brigadier, Stephen D. Ramseur, four North Carolina regiments checked the Union advance at this point.

Before the Ninth Corps soldiers could re-form and counterattack, they received orders directing them to move to their left "and attack on the right of General Hancock, near the Plank Road."

Thomas Jones reported his unsuccessful interview with generals Ewell and Early to John Gordon. Not willing to accept "Wait" as an answer, Gordon turned Jones around and rode back with him. According to Jones, Gordon argued his case before Ewell and Early for fifteen or twenty minutes before retiring in defeat. He told Jones with some bitterness, "General Early evidently didn't believe a word of what I told him of what I had seen myself."

Ewell's aide Campbell Brown remembered the discussion with this variation: "I know of my own personal knowledge that General Ewell was in favor of . . . [Gordon's plan] but begged out of it by Early's strong personal appeals *until* he could go to examine the ground himself." Early, Brown added, was delayed for several hours in making his own reconnaissance of the Confederate left because

General Ewell was summoned to a conference with Lee, and Early had to mind the Second Corps.

Ordnance officer and aide Morris Schaff was carrying a message from Meade's headquarters to James Wadsworth when he saw the unmistakable signs of a beaten army. First there were groups of stragglers, then units falling back under some discipline. Schaff located the officer in charge, who turned out to be Wadsworth's brigade commander Lysander Cutler. Schaff noted, "He was rather an oldish, thin, earnest-looking Roundhead sort of a man, his light stubby beard and hair turning gray. He was bleeding from a wound across his upper lip, and looked ghastly. . . . On my asking him where Wadsworth was, he said, 'I think he is dead.'" Schaff continued, "I started back for Meade's headquarters. When I reached there and reported the serious break in Wadsworth's lines no one could believe it; but just then Cutler's men began to pour out of the woods in full view on the ridge east of the Lacy house, and the seriousness of the situation at once appeared to all."

It was not yet 9:00 A.M.

From his position near the intersection of the Brock and Plank roads, Winfield Hancock turned from crisis to crisis. Even as he struggled to clarify the confused fighting across the Plank Road, Hancock decided that the time had come to gamble. At 7:05 A.M. he ordered John Gibbon to move his division out of its blocking position on the extreme left, facing south, and attack westerly, toward Longstreet's right on the Plank Road. Gibbon, a dependable, imaginative, and generally aggressive officer, ignored Hancock's dispatch and, when he was later pressed, released only a single brigade to demonstrate on Longstreet's right. Hancock meanwhile shuffled the other units on hand in an attempt to restart his stalled assault.

Even as the crackling gunfire melded into the steady roar of close-in combat, a breathless rider came in with word of a Confederate force moving along the Brock Road from Todd's Tavern. Nightmare recollections of the chaos caused by a similar Confederate flank attack a year earlier at Chancellorsville chilled Hancock's will. George Meade's chief of staff, Andrew Humphreys, later voiced the fear on everyone's mind: "It must be remembered that according to our information Pickett's Division was with Longstreet, and only Field's and Kershaw's divisions had as yet been encountered; and that Anderson's division of Hill's corps had not then been felt by our troops, nor its presence become known to them." George Pickett's men were, in fact, near Richmond, but no one in the Union high command knew that. So the Federal units that were waiting to support the renewed drive now shifted to back up Gibbon.

Hardly had those orders been sent when a new directive came in from army headquarters, revealing its fear that the Confederates were penetrating the gap between Warren's left and Hancock's right. The harassed Hancock was told to "make immediate disposition to check this movement of the enemy." He ordered more troops diverted from the fresh attack along the Plank Road to deal with this new threat.

Horace Porter returned from a futile exercise in trying to hurry along Burnside's Ninth Corps column, only to find Grant's headquarters knoll dotted with Fifth Corps stragglers and under fire by long-range Confederate cannon. Grant stood "watching the scene, and mingling the smoke of his cigar with the smoke of the battle, without making any comments." An officer nearby ventured his opinion: "General, wouldn't it be prudent to move headquarters . . . till the result of the present attack is known?" As Porter later recorded, "The general replied very quietly, between the puffs of his cigar, 'It strikes me it would be better to order up some artillery and defend the present location.'"

According to Lee's aide Charles Venable the Southern commander never faltered in "his profound confidence in the steady valor of his troops, and in their ability to maintain themselves successfully against very heavy odds." Lee's confidence was not misplaced this day. Within a few hours of being thoroughly overwhelmed by Hancock's dawn attack, the men of Heth's and Wilcox's divisions had been reorganized and moved northward to permanently close the yawning gap that separated Ewell, along the Turnpike, from Hill and Longstreet, near the Plank Road.

A weary A. P. Hill led his men in their march toward the open fields around the Chewning Farm. Riding several hundred yards ahead of the column's vanguard, Hill and his staff reined up alongside a deserted farmhouse "in the lower end of the field and dismounted." Continued Hill's aide William Palmer, "We had been there only a short while when we were startled by the breaking down of a fence just below, and in plain view was a long line of Federal infantry clearing the fence to move forward. General Hill commanded, 'Mount, walk your horses, and don't look back.'" With agonizing slowness, the command group regained the woods and safety. At Hill's request, Palmer rode to Lee, asking for and obtaining reinforcements from Richard Anderson's division. By the time the fresh troops arrived, Hill had things well in hand.

For the first time since the fighting began, the Confederate line from the Orange Turnpike to the Orange Plank Road was complete. Now Lee and Longstreet could pursue their designs on the Confederate right, no longer fearful of being turned from the north.

For perhaps an hour and a half, from 8:30 to 10:00 A.M., Unionist battled Confederate in a succession of small-unit actions along the Orange Plank Road.

A member of the Philadelphia Brigade remembered the fighting this way: "At no time during the morning . . . could there be seen a body of the enemy numbering fifty men, and yet the heavy volleys of musketry sent the balls flying into and about our ranks. The line of fire in response to these attacks was indicated by the direction from which the shots were received."

Although the fighting along the lines north of the Orange Turnpike would continue sporadically throughout the day, the net result was inconclusive. Union attacks carried out by soldiers from the Fifth and Sixth corps met with no lasting success.

As one of the last Federal waves ebbed out of sight, Virginia private Marcus Toney turned to his cousin, who was lying alongside him, and said, "That was an impetuous charge." Getting no answer, Toney shook his companion. "I . . . saw that a bullet had pierced his forehead, killing him instantly. I wrapped him in his oilcloth blanket, and . . . buried him with a black-jack tree for his headstone."

Sometime after 10:00 A.M. a lull settled along the Orange Plank Road. The men on the firing line, whose heads throbbed with the deafening ring of constant gunfire, noticed the reduction in volume less quickly than did the artillerymen who were posted farther back.

Private Frank Mixson of South Carolina took quick advantage of the calm to do a little pillaging of the Yankee bodies that were lying nearby. Mixson checked with Colonel James Hagood, who felt "it was mighty risky, but if I chose to take chances . . . to go ahead. I lay flat [on] my belly and crawled up to the first one, then to the second, until I had visited eight of those fellows. I was always careful to keep

them between me and the Yankees. . . . When I got back Jim Hagood said, 'What have you got?' . . . I unloaded my pockets . . . I
had six watches, three or four knives, some rations and a few other
trinkets. Col. Hagood took his choice of the watches and I gave Capt.
Wood another. The other I sold to Sid Key . . . who had some Confederate money."

It was about 10:00 A.M. as James Longstreet listened thoughtfully to
a report that appealed to him greatly. Martin Smith, chief engineer
for the Army of Northern Virginia, was back from a scout of the Confederate right and said he had found an unfinished railroad bed not
shown on any Confederate field map. The cleared right-of-way, which
was virtually invisible unless one was right on top of it, led around
the left flank of the forward Union line, posted south of the Plank
Road. Longstreet thought quickly. He much preferred flanking ma-
neuvers, and this seemed to be a golden opportunity to swing a portion of his force around the enemy. The more Longstreet thought
about it, the better he liked it. Smith had not scouted as far as the
Brock Road, so it was not clear whether the Union flank he had seen
represented the actual left of the main Union line or just the end of
its most advanced position in the Wilderness.

"General Smith," Longstreet later wrote, "was . . . asked to take
a small party and pass beyond the Brock Road and find a way for
turning the extreme Union left on that road." Lee's War Horse then
turned to his aide C. Moxley Sorrel. "Colonel," Longstreet said,
"there is a fine chance of a great attack by our right. If you will quickly
get into those woods, some brigades will be found much scattered
from the fight. Collect them and take charge. Form a good line and
then move, your right pushed forward and turning as much as possible to the left. Hit hard when you start, but don't start until you
have everything ready."

Sorrel, a twenty-six-year-old former bank clerk who had never
before commanded troops in battle, hurried away to carry out his
mission.

Even as Longstreet planned his surprise blow, Winfield Hancock
learned that the enemy infantry force that was reported to be pushing
north along the Brock Road toward his left flank was in fact, as he
later stated, "a body of several hundred [Union] convalescents who
had marched from Chancellorsville and were now following the route
of the Second Corps around by Todd's Tavern." The lack of proper

intelligence concerning this force, Hancock afterward complained, "paralyzed a large number of my best troops, who would otherwise have gone into action at a decisive point . . . [in] the morning."

The morning's fighting had greatly fatigued James Wadsworth. His aide Robert Monteith later recalled that the senior general took him aside and "told me that he felt completely exhausted and worn out; that he was unfit to command, and felt that he ought, in justice to himself and his men, to turn the command of the division over to Gen. Cutler. He asked me to get him a cracker, which I did."

It was around 11:00 A.M. when G. Moxley Sorrel guided the assault force into the woods on its way to the unfinished railroad bed that led beyond the Union left flank. Sorrel managed to gather together three brigades: William Wofford's Georgians from Kershaw's Division, G. T. "Tige" Anderson's Georgia brigade of Field's Division, and William "Billy" Mahone's Virginians, from Richard Anderson's division of A. P. Hill's corps. Even as the movement began, a fourth brigade was volunteered by Colonel John M. Stone, who was temporarily in command of Joe Davis's Mississippi troops, in Henry Heth's division. As the senior brigadier, Mahone was actually in charge of the operation.

In anticipation of the flank attack, James Longstreet readied a force to advance straight ahead the moment gunfire erupted on the right. On hand were Brigadier General Micah Jenkins's brigade, three brigades from Kershaw's Division, and three more from Richard Anderson's.

Longstreet and his subordinates clustered near their command post on the Plank Road, waiting for the sound of gunfire to the south.

It was still not yet noon.

11:45 A.M.–7:00 P.M.

Brigadier General William Mahone later reported the start of Longstreet's flank attack this way: "Wofford and Anderson were already in motion, and in a few moments the line of attack had been formed, and the . . . brigades, in imposing order and with a step that meant to conquer, were now rapidly descending upon the enemy's left." A soldier in the 12th Virginia remembered, "After going some distance through a thicket, we encountered the enemy apparently bivouacking, and little expecting any attack from that direction."

The first Union brigade hit was Colonel Robert McAllister's, in Mott's division. The colonel reported, "I heard firing on my left and rear. I

soon discovered we were flanked. I immediately ordered a change of
front to meet it. . . . Held the enemy in front and delivered volley
after volley into their ranks, but I soon discovered that they had
flanked my left and were receiving a fire in my front, on my left flank,
and rear. . . . At this time my line broke. . . ." Added Chaplain
Warren Cudworth of the 1st Massachusetts, "Confusion reigned
supreme."

According to Lieutenant Colonel Sorrel, "The lines in front of us
made some sharp resistance, but they were quickly overcome. . . ."
A member of the 12th Virginia described Sorrel's participation more
vividly: "We had not proceeded very far . . . when Col. Sorrel . . .
appeared on the scene, and placing himself in front . . . with his hat
in one hand and grasping the reins of his horse with the other . . .
exclaimed 'Follow me, Virginians! Let me lead you!'"

Joshua Owen's Second Corps brigade came next after McAllister's in
the Union line. Its undoing was curiously deliberate. According to
the adjutant, Charles Banes, "Without any apparent cause that could
be seen from the position of the brigade, the troops on our left began
to give way. . . . Those pressing past . . . [our] left flank . . . did not
seem to be demoralized in manner, nor did they present the appearance of soldiers moving under orders, but rather of a throng of armed
men who were returning dissatisfied from a muster. . . . [Our] men
soon caught the infection and joined in the retreat."

Years afterward a member of the 12th Virginia named George
Bernard wrote down the images he remembered from this moment:
". . . the men loading and firing as they moved forward, all yelling
and cheering as they saw the enemy hastily retiring, the woods echo-
ing with the rapid discharge of musketry and the 'rebel yell' sounding
from more than a thousand Confederate throats, the men in the finest
spirits as they pressed on. . . ."

Carroll's brigade was the closest in Hancock's forward line to the
south side of the Orange Plank Road. Lieutenant Colonel Franklin
Sawyer of the 8th Ohio looked to his left: "The woods were literally
black with ranks of men as far as we could see. Now a terrific volley
of musketry struck us, and our officers and men went down all along
the line." Continued another Ohioan, Thomas Galwey, "[Many] of
the recruits . . . began to give way one by one, then in twos and
threes, until at last they went in such numbers as to give the appear-

ance of a general skedaddle. The Confederates shouted exultantly, for they could see the tops of the heads, here and there, of men running through the brush. Our Veterans halloed to the faint-hearted to come back, showering bitter curses on them, but all to no purpose. . . . All that remained for us to do was to get back to our lines, running if possible. . . . A sharp prong projecting from a clump of bushes caught against the hind portion of my pantaloons, exposing me unmercifully to the enemy! . . . I picked up a shirt which I found . . . on the ground and stuffed it into the woeful rent. Then I continued my retreat in a more dignified manner."

Close by, two Confederates, George Bernard and Leroy Edwards, fired simultaneously at a huddled Yankee who flopped to the ground. Bernard and Edwards rushed to the body, both claiming the kill. Continued Bernard, "In a few seconds we were at his side and to our surprise he did not appear to be badly hurt." Edwards solicitously helped the wounded bluecoat to his feet and "said in the most sympathetic way, 'I hope you are not hurt!'"

What remained of the advanced Federal position in the woods along the Plank Road now came apart. Charles Weygant served in the 124th New York. "The terrible tempest of disaster swept on down the Union line," he recalled, "beating back brigade after brigade . . . until upwards of twenty thousand veterans were fleeing, every man for himself, through the disorganizing and already blood-stained woods toward the Union rear. . . . Hancock's officers . . . planted their colors on nearly every rising piece of ground they came to; and, waving their swords and gnashing their teeth shrieked the order, 'Rally men, rally' . . . but to no purpose."

South Carolina private Frank Mixson had just disposed of the last of the watches he had pilfered from the Yankee dead when his brigade commander, Micah Jenkins, rode near.

"Men of the First," Jenkins said, "we are going to charge. Now I want each and every one of you to remember that you are South Carolinians. Remember your wives, your sweethearts, your sisters at home. Remember your duty."

Jenkins also rode up to Colonel Asbury Coward of the 4th South Carolina, who was told, "Old man, we are in for it today. We are to break the enemy's line where the Brock Road cuts across the pike. The point lies just over there, I think." (Coward recalled that Jenkins indicated the direction "with his extended arm.")

Jenkins smiled what Coward called "his charming smile" and continued, "Tell your men that South Carolina is looking for every man to do his duty to her this day." Then, said Coward, "[Jenkins] reached down and seized my hand for a moment then rode off. . . ."

A few minutes later came the command to "Charge!" and Jenkins's men moved forward in support of Longstreet's flank attack.

North of the Plank Road, James Wadsworth's men were assailed in the front and on the left. Wadsworth had two horses shot out from under him, but the elderly division commander clambered onto a third to hold his brigades together. After the battle Colonel Rufus Dawes of the 6th Wisconsin asked the brigadier's aide Earl M. Rogers why Wadsworth had insisted on exposing himself so recklessly. Rogers replied, "My God, Colonel, nobody could stop him!"

In a desperate ploy to halt the Confederate wave that was breaking across the Plank Road, Wadsworth ordered the 20th Massachusetts, of Webb's brigade, to charge straight up it. The Yankees took heavy losses and reeled back. Even as the Bay State regiment came apart, Wadsworth was nearby, his old Revolutionary War saber flashing in the mottled sunlight. Then his horse bolted toward the Confederate lines. Afterward Morris Schaff pieced together what happened next: "The heroic Wadsworth did not or could not check his horse till within twenty odd feet of the Confederate line. Then, turning, a shot struck him in the back of the head, his brain spattering the coat of Earl M. Rogers, his aide at his side. The rein of Wadsworth's horse, after the general fell, caught in a snag, and, Rogers's horse having been killed by the volley, he vaulted into the saddle, and escaped through the flying balls." "At that very instant," continued an officer in the 149th Pennsylvania, "the whole line of our army, so far as I could see, gave way, and we were compelled to leave the brave old General, in a senseless and dying condition, to the mercy of his foes."

The Union forces along the Orange Plank Road faced utter disaster.

James Longstreet was exultant. He felt certain, he later declared, that he had pulled off "another Bull Run" on the Union army. His subordinates shared the moment. Micah Jenkins rode up and said, "I am happy; I have felt despair of the cause for some months, but am relieved, and feel assured that we will put the enemy back across the Rapidan before night."

Longstreet then turned to a one-armed artilleryman named John

Cheeves Haskell, ordering him to bring up a pair of guns to support the infantry that was fighting along the Plank Road. Haskell rode with his cannoneers. "While we were advancing I noticed a large, fine-looking man in the uniform of a general, who was lying on the side of the road in the dust and heat. Noticing that he was still alive, I had two of my orderlies to move him out of the dust. . . . He was General Wadsworth. . . ." A few moments earlier, Longstreet's aide Sorrel had stopped by the mortally wounded Union officer. "Some of his valuables — watch, sword, glasses, etc. — had disappeared among the troops," Sorrel recalled. "One of the men came up with, 'Here, Colonel, here's his map.' It was a good general map of Virginia, and of use afterwards."

Theodore Lyman, on the Brock Road, tried helplessly to stem the Union retreat. "The musketry now drew nearer. . . . Stragglers began to come back, and, in a little while, a crowd of men emerged from the thicket in full retreat. They were not running, nor pale, nor scared, nor had they thrown away their guns. . . . They had fought all they meant to fight for the present, and there was an end of it! . . . I drew my sword and rode in among them, trying to stop them. . . . I would get one squad to stop, but, as I turned to another, the first would quietly walk off. . . ."

Flushed with success, G. Moxley Sorrel rode down the Plank Road, signaling the First Corps commander to send up fresh troops. "There was no need with him," Sorrel said. "He had heard our guns, knew what was up, and was already marching . . . to finish it with the eager men at his heels.

"There was quite a party of mounted officers and men riding with him — Generals Kers[h]aw and Jenkins, the staff, and orderlies. Jenkins, always enthusiastic, had thrown his arm about my shoulder, with, 'Sorrel, it was splendid; we shall smash them now.'"

Gruff, imperious, and gray-whiskered, Marsena Patrick represented the law within the Army of the Potomac. As provost marshal, Patrick commanded a small force of cavalry and infantry charged with keeping order. His diary for this day recorded the following actions: ". . . Hancock was then fighting furiously on the left and hundreds and thousands of stragglers were pouring out of the woods in rear of his Corps — I put in my cavalry & rode down & drove back & sent to Corps multitudes of these fellows, handling them very roughly."

— ★ —

The victorious Confederates along the Plank Road new fell prey to the same confusion that had bedeviled the Union advance a few hours earlier. In the hazy gunsmoke and confusing thickets, no one could be quite sure who was who.

Riding eastward on that Plank Road, James Longstreet considered his next move. As J. B. Kershaw recalled, "[Longstreet] rapidly planned and directed an attack to be made by Brigadier Jenkins and myself upon the position of the enemy upon the Brock Road, before he could recover from his disaster. The order to me was to break their line and push all to the right of the road towards Fredericksburg."

Suddenly, remembered Lieutenant Colonel Sorrel, "firing broke out from our own men on the roadside in the dense tangle. . . . [Longstreet] was struck. He was a heavy man, with a very firm seat in the saddle, but he was actually lifted straight up and came down hard." Even as staff officers helped the wounded lieutenant general to the ground, General Kershaw spurred ahead to halt the firing. "They are friends," he shouted. The firing stopped.

Four men lay on the ground, among them Longstreet and Micah Jenkins. Colonel Asbury Coward ran from the nearby battle line of the 4th South Carolina and bent down next to his friend. "Jenkins," he said, "Mike, do you know me?" Coward continued sadly, "I felt a convulsive pressure of my hand. Then I noticed that his features, in fact his whole body, was convulsed."

Longstreet was in a bad way. The bullet had struck him in the throat and crashed into his right shoulder. Even as the corps medical director worked to stop the bleeding, Longstreet blew bloody foam from his mouth and whispered instructions: "Tell General Field to take command and move forward with the whole force and gain the Brock Road."

Lieutenant Colonel Sorrel carried word of the tragedy to Robert E. Lee. "I found him greatly concerned by the wounding of Longstreet and his loss to the army," Sorrel later wrote. "He was most minute in his inquiries and was pleased to praise the handling of the flank attack. Longstreet's message was given, but the General was not in sufficient touch with the actual position of the troops to proceed with it as our fallen chief would have been able to do; at least, I received that impression because activity came to a stop for the moment."

Horace Porter recalled that during the late afternoon lull, Ulysses Grant, "in company with two staff officers, strolled over toward the

Germanna road. While we stood on the bank of a small rivulet, a drove of beef cattle was driven past. One of the animals strayed . . . [and one] of the drovers yelled to the general . . . 'I say, stranger, head off that beef-critter for me, will you?' The general, having always prided himself upon being a practical farmer . . . threw up his hands, and shouted to the animal. It stopped, took a look at him, and then, as if sufficiently impressed with this show of authority, turned back into the road."

Despite the wounded Longstreet's urging him to continue the attack toward the Brock Road immediately, Major General Charles Field found ample reasons for not doing so. His own troops, he quickly discovered, "and some others, probably, were perpendicular to the road . . . whilst all those which had acted as the turning force were in line parallel to the road, and the two were somewhat mixed up. No advance could be possibly made till the troops parallel to the road were placed perpendicular to it. . . . To rectify this alignment consumed some precious time. . . ."

General Alexander Shaler's brigade, one of the smallest in the Army of the Potomac, consisted of just three regiments. At around midday it had been ordered from a reserve position to the extreme right flank of the Union army in support of General Truman Seymour's brigade. Shaler unhappily found his men taking responsibility for the very end of the Federal line; he also learned that there were no supports and no reserves to call upon in an emergency. Complained a historian in the brigade, "Our regiments had to be placed in the first line, thus presenting to the enemy a single attenuated line where a strong, well-supported one should have been." Shaler himself remarked on "the most extraordinary fact . . . that an army of 100,000 men had its right flank in the air with a single line of battle without entrenchments. . . . I lost no time in informing General Seymour that I would not be held responsible for any disaster that might befall the troops at this point, calling on him for at least 4,000 or 5,000 more men to properly defend that point."

Seymour's own line was stretched thin, and he had no troops to spare. Shaler's plea for reinforcements fell on deaf ears.

James Longstreet never forgot his painful trip to the field hospital. "As my litter was borne to the rear my hat was placed over my face, and soldiers by the roadside said, 'He is dead, and they are telling us he is only wounded.' Hearing this repeated from time to time, I raised my hat with my left hand, when the burst of voices and the flying of hats in the air eased my pains somewhat." Longstreet would survive; Micah Jenkins would not.

Sometime after 1:00 P.M., John Gordon once more sought out Richard Ewell to press for permission to swing around and attack the Union right flank north of the Orange Turnpike. In the hours since he had first proposed the action, the picture had changed considerably. The column of Federal soldiers that Jubal Early had feared might be moving to attack the Confederate left had not materialized. Any questions as to the whereabouts of Burnside's Ninth Corps were answered when a large portion of that force appeared in the fields north of the Chewning Farm, well out of supporting distance of the Union right flank. Additionally, reinforcements from R. D. Johnston's brigade now provided enough strength on the Confederate left to complete a strike force for the assault.

This time Gordon was accompanied by William Seymour, a member of Louisianan Harry T. Hays's staff. Gordon, according to Seymour, "begged permission to make the attempt, but Gen. Ewell expressed the opinion that a movement of that kind so early in the day would be inadvisable, insomuch as Gordon would have to cross some open fields, and thereby the smallness of his force would become apparent to the enemy who would be able to make preparations for his reception. He ordered Gordon to wait until late in the afternoon."

According to Hancock's adjutant Francis Walker, "The next hour or two was, it must be confessed, an anxious time along the Brock Road." A Sixth Corps officer, Hazard Stevens, described the scene: "Hundreds of fugitives were crossing the road and plunging out of sight into the woods in the rear, and others were going down the road and to the right, and hundreds of others were breaking out of the woods into the open ground near [Wilderness] tavern." Nevertheless, order slowly emerged out of this chaos. Charles Weygant of the 124th New York felt that the three-foot-high barrier of dirt and logs that Hancock's men had been building since the day before along more than two miles of the Brock Road represented "one of the strongest lines of temporary works it had ever been my fortune to stand behind. . . . Staff officers from the various brigades and divisions were there directing those who came in to the particular portions of the works where their respective commands had been ordered to rally; . . . [In] an incredibly short space of time Hancock's command was substantially re-formed, re-supplied with ammunition, and ready for action."

At around 2:00 P.M., blue-coated battle lines from Ambrose Burnside's untested Ninth Corps moved to the attack. The raw troops enjoyed a quick initial success but were then shoved back by Confederate counterattacks.

Meade's aide Theodore Lyman rode with Winfield Hancock, whom the young officer described as "very tired indeed." Hancock, according to Lyman, "said that his troops were rallied but very tired and mixed up, and not in a condition to advance. . . . At 2 P.M. Burnside . . . made a short attack with loud musketry. . . . [I ventured] to urge Hancock . . . to try and attack too; but he said with much regret that it would be to hazard too much."

One Rhode Island artilleryman, Ezra Parker, passed the afternoon watching Grant and Meade through a field glass. "Grant smoked imperturbably as the Sphinx, while General Meade seemed to show nervousness and anxiety. A stream of staff officers and orderlies were continually reporting to General Meade. Occasionally General Grant would appear to take part in the conversation."

Here was the situation around 4:00 P.M., as summarized by Horace Porter: "Sedgwick and Warren had been ordered to intrench their fronts and do everything possible to strengthen their positions. . . . Every one on the right was on the alert, and eager to hear particulars about the fighting on the left. . . . Generals Grant and Meade, after discussing the situation, now decided to have Hancock and Burnside make a simultaneous attack at 6 P.M. . . . I started for Hancock's front to confer with him regarding this movement."

Massachusetts captain Henry Blake commanded a portion of the Union skirmish line that was posted a short distance west of the Brock Road breastworks. As he remembered it, the pickets had just been established "when the tramp of a heavy force resounded through the woods. Orders were excitedly repeated, 'Forward!' 'Guide right!' 'Close up those intervals!' and finally a voice shouted, 'Now, men, for the love of God and your country, forward!'"

It was 4:15 P.M. Robert E. Lee was throwing everything he

had — perhaps as many as thirteen brigades — at the Brock Road line.

Success this day in the Wilderness could be measured in minutes. Hancock's success had given way to Longstreet's success, which now in turn gave way. "[The] change of commanders after the fall of Longstreet and the resumption of the thread of operations, occasioned a delay of several hours," said the Confederate brigadier general Evander Law, "and then the tide had turned. . . . When at 4 o'clock an attack was made upon the Federals along the Brock road, it was found strongly fortified and stubbornly defended."

Morris Schaff reckoned that the two sides exchanged volleys for the better part of thirty minutes. "The incessant roar of these crashing volleys, and the thunder of the guns as they played rapidly, struck war's last full diapason on the Plank Road in the Wilderness."

According to Robert E. Lee's mapmaker Jed Hotchkiss, "The dried leaves of the preceding autumn took fire from blazing cartridges, and their smoke, joining that of battle, clouded the day and concealed the combatants from each other."

Carrying orders for Hancock to attack at 6:00 P.M., Horace Porter arrived in time to witness the climax of the battle. "The woods in front of Hancock had now taken fire, and the flames were communicated to his log breastworks. . . . The wind was . . . blowing in our direction, and the blinding smoke was driven in the faces of our men, while the fire itself swept down upon them. . . . At last . . . the breastworks became untenable, and some of the troops . . . now fell back in confusion."

In an action report prepared after the war, Charles Field wrote, "The almost impenetrable growth of wood and brush prevented some of the troops from reaching the enemy at all, but one of my brigades, the gallant South Carolina — now led by Colonel Bratton, since Jenkins's death — rushed up to the enemy's works under a withering fire and got into them. . . ."

A Pennsylvanian in the 106th remembered the Confederates "advancing like so many devils through the flames." A New Yorker from the 152nd added, "On they came, like maddened demons, charging directly into the flames."

Colonel Asbury Coward took the flag of the 4th South Carolina from a wounded color-bearer, lunged up to the Federal works, and planted it on the crest. "My men followed cheering and jumped on the parapet with loud huzzas. The enemy was just disappearing in the shrubbery and trees on the opposite side of the road. As I was pushing the flagstaff firmly into the wattlework, I saw James Hagood and Adjutant Clourey doing the same thing with their flags."

New Yorker Josiah Favill, a young aide to Colonel John Brooke, noted, "The horses plunged and reared; the balls whistled around our ears, and the noise was simply too terrible to describe. . . . I saw a rebel officer mount the parapet with a flag in his hand, waving it over the heads of his men. . . ." Union officers moved to pinch shut the breach from both sides. John Gibbon, who commanded an area south of where the Rebels broke the Brock Road line, recalled, "Having a part of Brooke's brigade disposable, I directed him to form it in line, perpendicular to the Brock Road and move up to the right to the sound of the guns." North of the rupture, David Birney found his ace shock-force commander, Samuel Carroll. According to a member of the 10th New York, Birney said, "Carroll, you must put your brigade in and drive the enemy back." Union batteries on either flank of the breach opened fire with canister, and the artillerymen in Dow's 6th Maine, Battery A, added buckets of musket balls to the blasts.

Charles Cowtan of the 10th New York described the dramatic end of the Confederate attack: "[With] a ringing cheer, . . . [Carroll's men] are over both breastworks, driving the Rebels furiously through the abatis far into the woods beyond, and pouring a hot fire into their fleeing lines."

The Confederate Charles Field concluded his report of the action: "[My men] having no support were driven back again, save those who were killed or captured in the works."

WINFIELD HANCOCK TO GEORGE MEADE — 5:30 P.M.
   GENERAL: OWING TO THE FACT THAT I CANNOT SUPPLY MY COMMAND WITH AMMUNITION, MY WAGONS BEING SO FAR TO THE REAR, HAVING BEEN SENT FURTHER BACK ON ACCOUNT OF THE ENEMY'S ASSAULT THIS MORNING, I DO NOT THINK IT ADVISABLE TO ATTACK THIS EVENING. . . .

Sometime around 5:30 P.M., nearly twelve hours after he had first discovered the opportunity, John Gordon was given permission to attack the right flank of the Army of the Potomac. Jubal Early, finally persuaded by the weight of evidence that Gordon's proposal had merit, now backed the idea of an assault. The punctilious Richard Ewell gave the overall command to Early, who later wrote, "I determined to make [the attack] with Gordon's brigade, supported by

[R. D.] Johnston's and to follow it up, if successful, with the rest of my division."

ANDREW HUMPHREYS TO WINFIELD HANCOCK — 5:45 P.M.
   YOUR DISPATCH IS RECEIVED. THE MAJOR-GENERAL COM-
MANDING DIRECTS THAT YOU DO NOT ATTACK TO-DAY. RE-
MAIN AS YOU ARE FOR THE PRESENT.

According to Horace Porter, Grant twice left his headquarters knoll during the day to inspect portions of the Union line. "It was noted," Porter continued, "that he was visibly affected by his proximity to the wounded, and especially by the sight of blood. He would turn his face away from such scenes, and show by the expression of his countenance, and sometimes by a pause in his conversation, that he felt most keenly the painful spectacle presented by the field of battle."

Soon after the Brock Road line had been reestablished, an impromptu prayer meeting took place along the portion of it that was held by the 86th New York. "All we did to get ready," reported Stephen Chase, "was to call out that there would be a meeting ten feet in rear of Company H and in two minutes there were from 20 to 40 formed in a circle. Someone was named as a leader and every man would say: 'So say we all.' The next thing would be a familiar hymn in which everyone took part and always there would be three parts carried and sometimes four and you would think of almost anything else before you thought of fighting."

7:00 P.M.–Night

One Georgia soldier, G. W. Nichols, never forgot his part in Gordon's evening attack on the right flank of the Union army. "Our brigade was marched around on a circuit-flank movement on the extreme right of the Yankees. We found them . . . all resting, cooking and eating; with their guns stacked, their blankets spread down and some of their little tents stretched. We came up in thick woods in the wilderness and were in about 100 yards of them before their guards saw us. . . . We fired one volley at them, raised a yell and charged them."

   Alexander Shaler's brigade was the first to be unhinged by the attack. Theodore Poole, a major in the 122nd New York, wrote in his diary, "Our regiment and the entire brigade were driven back in great confusion and with heavy loss . . . many of our regiment being killed and wounded and others falling and being taken prisoner." Truman Seymour's brigade, the next in line, was also shattered.

F. L. Hudgins, a Georgian in the 38th Regiment, recalled, "My company struck the Federal breastworks squarely on the end[,] I advanced up in rear of their works . . . and at each step their confused mass become more dense. On bark fires in rear of these works were well filled coffee pots with steaming coffee, and frying pans with pickled pork."

The ripples of panic that radiated out from the disorganized Federals dissipated at the next Union brigade in line, Thomas Neill's. This unit was also being assaulted in front by Pegram's Virginia brigade. "On came the enemy," read a report of the 7th Maine, "and opened fire on us from front, flank and rear, and ordered us to surrender. Major Jones replied, 'All others may go back, but the Seventh Maine, never!'" Another of Neill's units moved to halt the fleeing Union troops. Colonel George F. Smith of the 61st Pennsylvania ordered his regiment, "Shoot them, bayonet them, stop them any way you can."

Despite its initial success, Gordon's flank attack began to come up short. R. D. Johnston's North Carolina brigade should have swept along the Federal line on Gordon's left. But in the deepening shadows of the Wilderness, Johnston's men veered eastward and floundered toward the Germanna Ford Road, proving to be more a nuisance than a threat. The squeezing pressure that might have helped Gordon, from John Pegram's brigade on his right, failed to materialize. "Our Brigade," complained a soldier in the 49th Virginia, ". . . was badly managed." Virginia captain James Bumgardner described his experience in Pegram's advance: "Conflicting orders, were [repeatedly] given, one . . . was to dress and close to the right, the other . . . was to close and dress to the left. I heard both orders several times. . . . On reaching the immediate front of the Federal works the men were in scattered groups . . . and no company under effective control of its captain."

Even as other Union troops moved to form a new defensive line, rumor and panic spread magnified tales of Confederate success. The reporter for the *Philadelphia Inquirer* jotted down, "At Grant's headquarters it looked like disaster." Horace Porter was with Grant when the first stories came in. "It was soon reported that General Shaler and part of his brigade had been captured; then that General Seymour and several hundred of his men had fallen into the hands of the enemy; afterward that our right had been turned, and Ferrero's division cut off and forced back upon the Rapidan." Baggy-eyed George Meade, however, was not buying the reports that all was lost. "Nonsense," he shouted to one shaken orderly. "If they have broken our lines they can do nothing more tonight." Grant heard out a staff officer who insisted that Lee was now blocking the army's retreat to the Rapidan. Grant, for the first time since the campaign had begun, became angry. "Oh, I am heartily tired of hearing about what Lee is going to do," he snapped. "Some of you always seem to think he is suddenly going to turn a double somersault, and land in our rear and on both of our flanks at the same time. Go back to your command, and try to think what we are going to do ourselves, instead of what Lee is going to do."

Flashes of gunfire continued well into darkness, but it soon became apparent that John Sedgwick had not only checked the Confederate attack but also drawn in the Sixth Corps line somewhat and tightened up the defensive perimeter. On the Confederate side, Jubal Early remained anxious about the number of Federal troops opposing him. Grateful that the fading light had hidden the small numbers of Gordon's force from Union view, Early now resolved not to be caught in the open when morning came. As he later wrote, "All of the brigades engaged in the attack were drawn back and formed on a new line in front of the old one, and obliquely to it."

The Battle of the Wilderness was over.

The Federal cavalrymen bivouacked near Chancellorsville were feeling upbeat this evening. "We drove the enemy all day long," bugler Carlos McDonald noted cheerfully in his diary. "Went into camp at night with everybody in good spirits and ready for more fighting on the morrow."

While the Union horsemen chattered in nervous release, their chief, Phil Sheridan, fumed. His fighting today had been loud, fluid, and indecisive. The daylong scrap had taken place across the rolling fields around Todd's Tavern as Sheridan's riders had fanned out in an attempt to intercept Longstreet's column. What they had found instead was Confederate cavalry spoiling for a fight. Charge had been followed by countercharge, and then the combat had continued dismounted as the cavalrymen battled on foot.

The racket of gunfire had been audible to John Gibbon's men, guarding Hancock's left flank only a few miles to the north. Given the lack of any clear intelligence from Sheridan until late in the day that he was fighting Confederate cavalry and not infantry, it had remained easy for Gibbon to believe that a portion of Longstreet's corps was threatening from the south.

The Army of the Potomac's headquarters had grown increasingly apprehensive about the security of its left flank. In the early afternoon Sheridan had received a dispatch from Andrew Humphreys, reporting that "General Hancock has been heavily pressed, and his left turned." Then had come the bitter orders: "The major-general commanding thinks that you had better draw in your cavalry so as to secure the protection of the trains."

As Sheridan later noted in his official report, "I obeyed this order, and the enemy took possession of the Furnaces, Todd's Tavern and Piney Branch Church." With this withdrawal, the Federal army had relinquished its hold on the crossroads at Todd's Tavern, cutting off its main route of advance to the south. Sheridan, who knew Grant well, believed that the lieutenant general would never retreat, and he realized that in order for the army to resume its advance, the Union cavalry would have to fight all over again for the ground it had been told to give up.

Gone were the buckskin jacket, corduroy trousers, calfskin boots, and natty kid gloves. The cub reporter Henry Wing now wore a butternut suit, a pair of coarse brogans, and a dilapidated, quilted cotton hat. Gone also were the dispatches and letters from the *New York Tribune* staff. Outside the door, a Union sentry stared sleepily at his curious prisoner. It was about 10:00 P.M.; Federal authorities had stopped Henry Wing cold in his attempt to report the story of the Wilderness.

Henry Wing's confident plan for carrying the *Tribune* dispatches north through guerrilla-infested territory had quickly gone awry. After riding the short distance from Wilderness Tavern to Ely's Ford, Wing had stopped to talk with a civilian of Union sympathies, who had convinced him that his best disguise would be to pose as a pro-Southerner carrying word of Lee's victory to Confederate agents in Washington. The masquerade had appealed to the young newspaperman, and he had promptly changed his clothes and chucked out all the incriminating *Tribune* documents before setting out again. Near Richardsville, he had run into a band of Mosby's riders, who had warned him against the "nigger" soldiers of Ferrero. They had believed his story and escorted him to Kelly's Ford, farther north. There things had fallen apart. A bitter, one-armed secessionist who lived near the Ford had seen through Wing's disguise, but while the Rebels were arguing his case, the young correspondent had splashed across the river to safety. In the breathless hide-and-seek that followed, Wing had abandoned his horse and set off on foot to distant Manassas Junction. Near the Bull Run trestle, he had been scooped up by Federal pickets, who had found his story difficult to accept.

Wing finally wrangled permission to telegraph an influential Washington acquaintance, and the minutes passed slowly until the telegraph key chattered a reply. The answer came from Lincoln's war secretary, Edwin Stanton, who demanded that the reporter tell *him* of Grant's progress. The government controlled the telegraph lines in and out of the capital, and since Wing's request for help had come in on the army line, it had been received at the War Department and promptly forwarded to the secretary. Wing stubbornly stood his ground and insisted that he first be allowed to send a hundred words to the *Tribune*. Back came Stanton's reply: put the obstinate reporter under arrest. "That settled it," Wing later wrote. "I would not have told him one little word to save my life."

Resigned to his fate, Henry Wing sat wearily under guard, awaiting dawn. Then the staccato clicking began again. The field telegrapher grinned. "Mr. Lincoln wants to know if you will tell *him* where Grant is." Wing was respectful but unbudging. Back came Lincoln's acceptance of Wing's terms, on the condition that the reporter also release a summary to the Associated Press. Wing agreed and dictated a half-column dispatch that brought the first word of the Battle of the Wilderness to the North.

After he had finished, Wing sagged gratefully, his mission accomplished. Again the telegraph clattered. A special locomotive would be stopping by on another mission. Would Wing ride it back to Washington and meet with Lincoln? Henry Wing agreed.

Remembered Private Frank Mixson of South Carolina, somewhere along the Orange Plank Road, "We did not sleep much this night, for we were right in among the dead and dying, and many a poor fellow, especially from the Yankee army, would beg for water. . . . Our men got some canteens from the dead, some with a little water and some with brandy. All this was given to the poor fellows without any regard to which side he belonged. All we cared for was that he was a human being and a brother, though we had fought him hard all day."

Exhausted, weary beyond measure, Horace Porter fell into a fitful sleep. Vivid images pursued him into his dreams. "Forest fires raged; ammunition-trains exploded; the dead were roasted in the conflagration; the wounded, roused by its hot breath, dragged themselves along, with their torn and mangled limbs, in the mad energy of despair, to escape the ravages of the flames; and every bush seemed hung with shreds of blood-stained clothing. It was as though Christian men had turned to fiends, and hell itself had usurped the place of earth."

Virginia cannoneer William Dame, who had only heard about the fighting for the past two days, remembered the end of this one. "We drew off some distance to the right, and lay down, supperless, on the ground around our guns; it was very dark and cloudy and soon began to rain. . . . Lying out exposed on the untented ground, with only one blanket to cover with, we got soaking wet, and stayed so."

Grant's aide Cyrus Comstock, an engineer, noted in his diary, "Orders issued to stand on defensive tomorrow. . . ."

★

Roads South: 1

SATURDAY, MAY 7

Washington

It was 2:00 A.M. when Henry Wing met with Abraham Lincoln. Under steady questioning from the President and several cabinet members, Wing told what he knew. When the gathering at last broke up, he lingered so he could be alone with Lincoln.

"Mr. President," the young reporter said hesitantly, "I have a message for you — a message from General Grant."

"Something from Grant for me?" Lincoln said.

Wing swallowed and spoke quickly. "He told me I was to tell you, Mr. President, that there would be no turning back."

Lincoln smiled the first smile he had enjoyed since Grant had gone into the Wilderness "and pulled in the hole after him." Wing explained what happened next in the title of his memoirs, *When Lincoln Kissed Me*.

The Wilderness

Recorded George Meade's perceptive aide Theodore Lyman, "At daybreak it would be hard to say what opinion was held in regard to the enemy, whether they would attack, or stand still; whether they were on our flanks, or trying to get in our rear, or simply in our front."

At Ulysses Grant's headquarters, Horace Porter reported that "General Grant was almost the first one up. He seated himself at the campfire at dawn, and looked thoroughly refreshed after the sound sleep he had enjoyed. . . . A fog, combined with the smoke from the smoldering forest fires, rendered it difficult for those of us who were sent to make reconnaissances to see any great distance, even where there were openings in the forest."

——— ★ ———

Dawn found the Union right flank pulled back tight toward the intersection of the Turnpike and the Germanna Ford Road.

According to George Peyton, a Virginian in Pegram's Brigade, "[I] got up at daybreak expecting either to make or expel an attack. Pickets soon came in and said all the Yankees were gone." Thomas Doyle, a member of the Stonewall Brigade, was among those who now crowded forward into the abandoned entrenchments. "The ground was strewn with plunder of all kinds in great abundance, and such of the Confederates as needed them supplied themselves with tent-flies, oil clothes, blankets, canteens, guns, etc."

Remembered Theodore Lyman, "About five this morning a novel sight was presented to the Potomac Army. A division of black troops, under General Ferrero, and belonging to the 9th Corps, marched up and massed in a hollow near by."

Marching with the white officers in command of the troops was Lieutenant Freeman S. Bowley, who recalled, "Our men, aware that they were objects of criticism, closed up their ranks, brought their guns to the right shoulder, and presented a credible military appearance."

"As I looked at them," Lyman continued, "my soul was troubled and I would gladly have seen them marched back to Washington. . . . We do not dare trust them in the line of battle. Ah, you may make speeches at home, but here, where it is life or death, we dare not risk it."

Said Lieutenant Bowley, "The white soldiers were not disposed to let them pass without some 'chaffing,' to which the black men were quite equal. One colored soldier, with a clear, mellow voice, raised the song 'Will you, will you, Fight for de Union?' Instantly the whole line took up the chorus: 'Ah-ha! ah-ha! We'll fight for Uncle Sam!'"

The few Confederates who expressed any clear opinion on the matter believed that their side had won the Battle of the Wilderness. Bryan Grimes, an aggressive colonel in Ewell's corps, wrote home today that everything "looks bright for [the] Confederacy." There was no uncertainty in the mind of A. P. Hill's division commander Cadmus Wilcox, who, years after the war, declared unequivocally, "The battle of the Wilderness was a Confederate victory."

But the fight had extracted its toll, especially among the senior officers. Robert E. Lee spent a portion of this day reorganizing the Army of Northern Virginia to cover the loss of James Longstreet and others.

(Lee's losses in the Wilderness fighting were substantial. Recent examinations of Confederate casualty data suggest these figures as *minimums:* killed and wounded, 8,949; captured, 1,881; total, 10,830. Federal losses for the same period are: killed and wounded, 14,283; captured, 3,383; total, 17,666.)

ULYSSES GRANT TO GEORGE MEADE — 6:30 A.M.
 GENERAL: MAKE ALL PREPARATIONS DURING THE DAY FOR A NIGHT MARCH TO TAKE POSITION AT SPOTSYLVANIA COURT HOUSE.

Captain Z. Boylston Adams lay among the wounded Union soldiers who were now prisoners of the Confederates. Lying next to him was a "rather tall, an eminently handsome man of commanding presence, but showing gentle breeding." On a small piece of paper attached to the unconscious man's coat, someone had scrawled, "General James S. Wadsworth."

A steady stream of Southerners came to view the wounded general. A few were impressed. "Do you mean to say that this is James S. Wadsworth, of New York, the proprietor of vast estates in the Genessee Valley, the candidate for governor in 1862?" someone asked. Another swore at Adams and the insensible Wadsworth, "declaring that he knew that our officers were crazy abolitionists, mercenaries, low politicians, hirelings from foreign armies, etc. . . ."

Throughout the day, Adams watched the dying officer carefully. "Occasionally," Adams later wrote, "he heaved a deep sigh, but otherwise lay in calm slumber."

At around 7:30 A.M., skirmishers inched forward from Burnside's and Hancock's corps and determined that during the night, Robert E. Lee had pulled back his lines across the Plank Road, to a point about a mile from the Union position along the Brock Road.

Meade's aide Theodore Lyman later penned this succinct summary of the situation on May 7: "There lay both armies, each behind its breastworks, panting and exhausted, and scowling at each other."

According to young Walter Taylor of Robert E. Lee's staff, "The 7th passed without any serious encounter between the two armies. General Lee spent the time in visiting all parts of his line of battle, seeking to ascertain the probable designs of his adversary."

Today Brigadier General James H. Wilson of the Union cavalry paid a visit to Grant's headquarters and met with two old friends, Chief of Staff John Rawlins and Theodore S. Bowers, an aide. The pair took the cavalryman aside with the air of those who have important secrets to share. "[They] made haste to say that the night before had tested Grant's . . . self-control more seriously than any event of his past career." As panic-laden reports had poured in following the late-evening attack on the Union right, it had quickly become "apparent that the General was confronted by the greatest crisis of his life." All the western officers' suppressed fears about the lack of fighting quality in the Army of the Potomac had begun to seem only too true. Rawlins and Bowers believed that Grant's will alone had kept the army from retreating at dawn, but only at a terrible personal cost. Wilson related, "When all proper measures had been taken and there was nothing further to do but to wait, both Rawlins and Bowers concurred . . . that Grant went into his tent, and, throwing himself face downward on his cot, gave way to the greatest emotion. . . ." The two staff officers agreed that "they had never before seen . . . [Grant] so deeply moved as upon that occasion."

Private John Haley of Maine might have survived yet another battle, but he was none too cheerful about his current situation. Colonel George West, the able commander of the 17th Maine, was wounded and out of action. Captain John Perry, in temporary charge of the regiment, scored almost no points in Haley's book. "A very earnest man," Haley noted, "and as ignorant as he is earnest. His lack of knowledge is apparently bottomless."

Haley's regiment was part of a small force that pushed out along the Plank Road at around noon, looking for trouble. When the probing Federals found the Confederate main line, they were greeted by blasts of canister that sent them running. Admitted Haley, "Such agility as we displayed hunting for the rear has few parallels in this war. Captain John Perry . . . kept yelling, 'Halt!' but failed to set an example, except in the way of speed. We could hear the voice of our gallant officer, but nothing was visible but two coat-tails and loose heels enveloped in a cloud of dust."

——— ★ ———

At 10:00 A.M., the Union cavalry commander, Phil Sheridan, was finally freed from his orders to protect the great army supply trains
parked around Chancellorsville. His riders were replaced by Burnside's black division, and the pugnacious cavalry general was given
permission "to detach any portion of your command for offensive
operations."

By noon, mounted Federals had cleared most of the Brock
Road down to Todd's Tavern, retaken the Tavern area itself, and
were pressing Confederate cavalry westward along the Catharpin
Road.

Captain C. A. Stevens of the U.S. Sharpshooters passed over ground
where dead of both sides lay. Stevens stared at the lifeless lumps
clothed in blue and gray, trying to discover a pattern to it all. He at
last concluded that there was none. "They fall every way — forward,
backward, sideways, gently sinking down, hurriedly pitching ahead,
and all regardless of the way they are going, quick or slow, forward
or backward."

Near the northernmost end of the opposing battle lines, where
the Confederate left faced the Union right, the Southerners held
fields filled with dead. Private Marcus Toney of Virginia was working
the body squad this day. "There is very little ceremony in burying
the dead of the enemy. With a shovel the dirt is removed the length
of the soldier and to the depth of eight or ten inches, and then with
the shovel the body is turned into the little trench, sometimes falling
on side or back and sometimes on the face; the dirt removed from the
little trench is then shoveled onto the body. . . ."

Never far from Grant's mind were the other moving parts in his grand
military design to squeeze the Confederacy. Noted his aide Horace
Porter, "At 3 P.M. dispatches were received by way of Washington,
saying that General Butler had reached the junction of the James and
Appomattox rivers the night of the 5th, had surprised the enemy, and
successfully disembarked his troops, and that Sherman was moving
out against Johnston in Georgia, and expected that a battle would be
fought on the 7th."

At 3:00 P.M. new orders were received by all Army of the Potomac
commands:

THE FOLLOWING MOVEMENTS ARE ORDERED FOR TO-DAY
AND TONIGHT:

... AT 8:30 P.M. MAJOR-GENERAL WARREN, COMMANDING THE FIFTH CORPS, WILL MOVE TO SPOTSYLVANIA COURT-HOUSE BY WAY OF THE BROCK ROAD AND TODD'S TAVERN.

... AT 8:30 P.M. MAJOR-GENERAL SEDGWICK, COMMANDING SIXTH CORPS, WILL MOVE BY THE PIKE AND PLANK ROADS TO CHANCELLORSVILLE, ... THENCE BY WAY OF ALRICH'S AND PINEY BRANCH CHURCH ... TO SPOTSYLVANIA COURT-HOUSE.

... MAJOR-GENERAL HANCOCK, COMMANDING SECOND CORPS, WILL MOVE TO TODD'S TAVERN BY THE BROCK ROAD, FOLLOWING THE FIFTH CORPS CLOSELY.

... CORPS COMMANDERS WILL SEE THAT THE MOVEMENTS ARE MADE WITH PUNCTUALITY AND PROMPTITUDE.

... IT IS UNDERSTOOD THAT GENERAL BURNSIDE'S COMMAND WILL FOLLOW THE SIXTH CORPS.

BY COMMAND OF MAJOR-GENERAL MEADE.

In the precise and unemotional language of command, Andrew Humphreys explained a source of agony for many of the Union wounded: "Early in the morning of the 7th, the bridge at Germanna Ford was taken up, and relaid at Ely's Ford, for the passage of the ambulance train carrying the wounded, who were to be sent to Washington by the Orange and Alexandria Railroad. In the course of the day their destination was changed and they were subsequently sent to Washington by way of Fredericksburg."

Pennsylvanian William Roberts, one of the walking wounded, remembered it differently: "After proceeding on our way quite a distance we were ordered in another direction, as it was reported that Mosby's guerrillas were lying in wait to capture us. Then we marched back and forth in the hot sun, with no attention paid to our wounds. . . . Many of the poor boys died in the ambulances while going over the rough corduroy roads. It was heartrending to hear their groans and cries for water without being able to relieve them."

It was late in the morning when Lee decided to turn Longstreet's corps over to Richard H. Anderson. Anderson himself recalled receiving the word "a little after mid-day, if I remember correctly." Responsibility for one third of Lee's army now rested on the shoulders of a West Point graduate from South Carolina, whose career in the Confederate military had been one of occasional brilliance interspersed with equally occasional stretches of indolence.

——— ★ ———

Threading its way to Orange Court House was a column of Federals taken in the two days' fighting. A young Confederate scout named John Jackson rode with the escort. He remembered being so impressed by the proud courage of Colonel Walter Harriman of New Hampshire that for a few dusty miles he let the Federal ride in his stead. As they trudged along, the Southerner boasted "that we had at least foiled Grant, if not beaten him." At this Harriman rose tall in the saddle and cried out, "Never! Your success is only ephemeral. God Almighty is back of our army!"

For Federal officers in the prisoners' ranks, the road out of the war led to Richmond and then to various points farther south. For the enlisted men, the destination was generally a new prison camp established in February, located well out of the way, some sixty miles south of Atlanta. Officially designated Camp Sumter, it would soon become better known from the name of a nearby village — Andersonville.

Wrote Charles Coffin, a *Boston Journal* correspondent, "Grant was thoughtful through the day. He said but little. He had a cigar in his mouth from morning till night. I saw him many times during the day, deeply absorbed in thought."

A. P. Hill's aide William Palmer noted that it was late "on the 7th" when Robert E. Lee rode up to consult with his Third Corps commander at the latter's headquarters, located in an abandoned farmhouse between the Plank Road and the Turnpike. Palmer continued, "From the roof some shingles had been broken out, and we had a fine marine glass, and could see clearly the open ground around the Wilderness tavern over the tops of the trees. . . . In a field near the headquarters was a large park of heavy guns, and as I looked these guns moved into the road and took the road to our right, their left. I went down and reported the movement and direction taken by these heavy guns."

The weary Yankee boys got what rest they could today, wondering what the next move would be. In the 19th Massachusetts, "most of us thought it was another Chancellorsville, and that the next day we should recross the river." Comparisons to that battle, which had occurred almost exactly one year earlier, had an eerie exactitude. All this suggested to cynical Union veterans that another retreat was in the works. In the 57th Pennsylvania they were saying, "We have had the usual three days' fighting on this side of the river, and by about tomorrow night we will be back in our old camp."

Washington

Edwin M. Stanton was feeling the tension. Earlier this day the Federal war secretary's friend and adviser Major General Ethan Allen Hitchcock had noted in his diary, "I saw the Secretary about 11 . . . [in the] morning, and I noticed that, in reaching for a piece of paper his fingers showed a nervous tremor which I never observed before."

On the street corners of Washington, newsboys hawked the story brought in late the previous night by Henry Wing: "News from the army! Grant found!"

In a statement released to the public at 7:10 P.M., Stanton summarized what the government knew: "We have no official reports from the Army of the Potomac since Wednesday's dispatch from General Grant announcing his crossing of the Rapidan. . . . The report of the *Tribune* correspondent, published this morning and forwarded from here last night, is the substance of all that is known here at this hour. . . ."

The *Tribune* story was good enough for President Lincoln. This afternoon, for the first time since 1861, the Marine Band had played on the south lawn of the White House. The crowd had been large and enthusiastic. The President had appeared on the portico and, according to a *Washington Star* reporter whose notes confused Grant's rank, said to the crowd, "In lieu of a speech, I propose that we give three cheers for Major-General Grant and all the armies under his command."

The Wilderness

"Throughout the entire day succeeding this first great contest," reported John Esten Cooke, a Southern staff officer, "General Lee remained quiet, watching for some movement of his adversary."

Even as he struggled to patch up his battered command structure and resupply his exhausted army, Robert E. Lee pondered Grant's next move. Lee's thinking was dominated by a desire to hold "those people" outside the natural barrier provided by the Rapidan and Rappahannock rivers. Back in April Lee had confessed to Jefferson Davis, "If I am obliged to retire from this line . . . great injury would befall us."

Each fresh report brought a new piece of the puzzle. The enemy had taken up its pontoon bridges across the Germanna Ford, so clearly no retreat was planned in that direction. Cavalry reports came in indicating that large numbers of Union wagons were moving to the east, toward Chancellorsville. That might mean a general fallback to Fredericksburg, or it could indicate a repositioning in preparation for a southward movement to Spotsylvania. More of "Jeb" Stuart's riders reined up, telling of a big cavalry fight going on around Todd's Tavern. Lots of Federal horsemen were piling into the melee, but no enemy infantry had been seen. Sheridan's assaults could be merely spoiling attacks to cover a Yankee retreat to Fredericksburg, or they could be a move to pry the Brock Road open to allow for a general Federal advance toward Spotsylvania.

Lee made preparations for covering both possibilities. An order was sent to Stuart requesting that he scout the roads leading south, "should the enemy continue his movement toward Spotsylvania Court House, or should we desire to move on his [retreating] flank in that direction." Early in the morning Lee's artillery chief, William Pendleton, was ordered to cut a rough military road "through the pines in rear of the artillery position, crossing the Plank Road to White Hall Mill." The route Pendleton selected had been plotted that spring by the Confederate engineering chief, M. L. Smith, as part of Lee's anticipating various contingencies.

It was late in the day before Lee finally believed he had put the puzzle together. He would report early on May 8 to his war secretary, James Seddon, "The enemy has abandoned his position and is moving towards Fredericksburg."

Once again Lee had won against impossible odds, and once again Virginia was safe.

Pursuit of the retreating Union army meant that a strong force would have to be sent down to Spotsylvania to block any sudden southward turn that might put the Federals between Lee and Richmond. At 7:00 P.M., orders were cut for the new First Corps commander, Richard Anderson, to march his men to Spotsylvania. There was no urgency in the dispatch, which allowed Anderson (who was known throughout the army for deliberation rather than quickness) to start the march anytime before 3:00 A.M. on May 8.

Shortly before sunset the Fifth Corps commander, Gouverneur Warren, and his staff left their headquarters at the Lacy House and headed for the Brock Road. Morris Schaff rode with the group and recalled, "just as we gained the brow of the hill at the old Wilderness

Tavern there was borne from the enemy's lines on the still evening air the sound of distant cheering. I halted and turned my horse's head in the direction whence it came. . . . The sun was now lodged half-way in the treetops, and looked like a great, red copper ball. I think I can hear that Confederate line cheering yet. . . . [Like] a wave on the beach, it broke continuously along their entire line. And after dying away, from their right beyond the unfinished railway to their extreme left resting on Flat Run, it was followed by two more like surges."

It was, as the Confederate artillery chief, William Pendleton, later noted, "about dark" when he briefed Richard Anderson about the military road that had been cut that day. Pendleton carefully "described the route, and left an officer as guide." The artilleryman continued, "Here a circumstance occurred which should be specially noticed. General Anderson stated that his orders were to march by 3 next morning. He was preparing to start at 11 that night."

At about 8:30 P.M., "Generals Grant and Meade, with their staffs and escort, . . . started out by the Brock Road, along which Hancock's men were lying behind the works in which they had been fighting so hard."

Recalled one of those Second Corps soldiers, "Shortly after dark a loud cheer suddenly uprose on the right, and was taken up by regiment after regiment, as Generals Grant and Meade, with their staffs, moved toward the left in the direction of Spottsylvania Court House."

It was shortly after 9:00 P.M. when Warren's Fifth Corps began its march to Spotsylvania.

"[We] moved as silently as possible from our breastworks in the Wilderness," said John Parker of the 22nd Massachusetts. A Pennsylvanian in the 83rd recorded this last impression: "The rebels seemed to understand what was going on, and began at the same time to leave our front and march to their right. They yelled as they went, and as their voices kept going further and further away, this was the first evidence we had that they were also on the move."

Remembered a soldier in the 19th Maine, "About nine or ten o'clock . . . while the Regiment was resting by the roadside and awaiting developments, Generals Grant and Meade, accompanied by their staffs, rode along and halted at General Hancock's headquarters. . . .

The burning woods lighted up the scene, and when the faces of the Commanders were recognized, wild cheers echoed through the forest."

Charles Coffin, a *Boston Journal* reporter, put the time at 11:00 P.M. "when Generals Grant and Meade, accompanied by their cavalry escorts, left the Wilderness headquarters of General Hancock, for a ride to Todd's Tavern, a place of two or three houses, exhibiting the usual degree of thriftlessness which characterizes the Old Dominion."

Grant hoped that Lee would not immediately catch on to what was happening and that he would hold on to his position in the Wilderness. His aide Cyrus Comstock noted the feeling in his diary: "Uncertain whether enemy has fallen back a little or to Mine Run."

According to Lee's new First Corps commander, Richard Anderson, "General Lee . . . directed me to retire the troops quietly and as soon after nightfall as practicable, and when I should have reached a suitable place in rear of the line they had been occupying, to let them rest. . . . Upon withdrawing the Corps . . . I found the woods, in every direction on fire and burning furiously and there was no suitable place for rest. The road by which I was conducted was narrow and frequently obstructed . . . and the guide . . . informed me that it preserved the same character until near Spotsylvania [so] I decided to continue the march until I should be within easy reach of that place."

U. S. Grant, his military secretary, Adam Badeau, and his aide Horace Porter related an incident from this night's ride down the Brock Road:

> PORTER: "At 11 o'clock word came to Grant and Meade that their headquarters escorts and wagons were delaying the advance of Warren's corps, and they decided to move on to Todd's Tavern in order to clear the way."
>
> GRANT: "Meade and I rode in advance. We had passed but a little way beyond our left when the road forked."
>
> BADEAU: "The party soon struck off from the main road into a dark and tangled wood-path; and whether the guide was false, or only ignorant, he professed to have lost his way."
>
> GRANT: "We had not gone far, however, when Colonel C. B.

Comstock, of my staff, with the instinct of the engineer, suspecting that we were on a road that would lead us into the line of the enemy . . . dashed by at a rapid gallop and all alone."

PORTER: "Colonel Comstock rode on in advance, and hearing the sound of marching columns not far off on our right, came back with this news. . . ."

BADEAU: "It was then discovered that Grant and Meade, with their staffs and escort, hardly a hundred men in all, were moving on a road directly between the two armies. . . ."

PORTER: "It was decided to return to the Brock Road. General Grant . . . urged the guide to try and find some cross-road leading to the Brock Road, to avoid retracing our steps. This was an instance of his marked aversion to turning back, which amounted almost to a superstition."

None of Warren's Fifth Corps soldiers remembered this night march to Spotsylvania with pleasure. Abner Small of the 16th Maine was typical in his remarks: "We marched, that night, through a forest of black pines; the road was narrow, and the trees made it very dark; it was a desolate and dismal track." "All night we marched and halted," complained Francis Parker of the 32nd Massachusetts, "but halted more than we marched." The Brock Road, added the Fifth Corps artillery chief, Charles Wainwright, "was literally jammed with troops moving one step at a time. . . . It was so dark that you could not see at all where your horse was stepping."

Part of the delay grew out of pure spite. The tough, veteran 3rd Pennsylvania Cavalry decided to "swap" horses with a newly arrived, green regiment. Fists flew; by the time the mess was sorted out, the Pennsylvanians had their remounts, and the marching columns had stood stock-still for an hour and a half.

The marching was little better for the Sixth Corps, which began its withdrawal at around 9:30 P.M., moving on a longer route that swung east to Chancellorsville, then south on the Catharpin Road. Captain Mason Tyler of Massachusetts remembered it as "a night of sweltering heat." "The march . . . proved one of intolerable severity," added James Bowen of the 37th Massachusetts. "[The] roads were dry as tinder, and the dust rose in stifling clouds which hung with tortuous persistency close to the earth, choking the lungs, the throat, the eyes, and settling in disgusting quantity upon the sweaty flesh wherever it could penetrate." A soldier in the 10th Vermont recalled a macabre scene: "[The Regiment] crossed on its way the field of Chancellors-ville, still covered by the debris of the battle a year before, and the men kicked human skulls from their path as they marched on to new scenes of carnage."

Throughout the night, Federal unit after Federal unit came to the point of decision — the point where a turn one way meant retreat, and a turn the other, advance. For two years the Army of the Potomac had turned back; no more. The feeling of many was summed up by a Ninth Corps artilleryman: "The rank and file of the army wanted no more retreating, and from the moment when we . . . continued straight on towards Spotsylvania, I never had a doubt that General Grant would lead us on to final victory."

SUNDAY, MAY 8

Alabama colonel William Oates had this to say about Anderson's march south to Spotsylvania: "Our progress was slow on account of the crowded condition of the inferior road which was being opened through the woods by the pioneer corps."

At 1:00 A.M., Meade and his staff, riding in advance of Warren's Fifth Corps column, broke out of the Wilderness near Todd's Tavern to find two divisions of Union cavalry camped there with nothing to do. Dashing off a prickly note to Sheridan — "I find Generals Gregg and Torbert without orders. They are in the way of the infantry and there is no time to refer to you" — Meade ordered Gregg to move out to the west along the Catharpin Road toward Corbin's Bridge, while Torbert's men (Torbert was sick, so Wesley Merritt was in command) were to push south along the Brock Road to Spotsylvania.

Richard Lewis, a South Carolinian, marched with Richard Anderson's First Corps: "The men were so completely worn out that when the column halted they would lie down and go fast asleep, and it was very difficult to wake them up and get them started again."

According to Meade's chief of staff, Andrew Humphreys, Merritt's men finally got moving at about 3:30 A.M., with Warren's column massed right behind them. Said Humphreys, "General Fitzhugh Lee's [Confederate] cavalry division was on the road, which they had barricaded by felling trees across it, and disputed every foot of ground, and in the darkness of night General Merritt found it exceedingly difficult to make any progress."

Shortly after sunrise, Robert E. Lee realized he had guessed wrong. At about that time he received a report from Wade Hampton, one of "Jeb" Stuart's cavalry commanders, containing intelligence gathered by a scout named Channing Smith. Smith had ridden boldly along the Federal lines and felt certain that the Yankee Fifth Corps was on the road to Todd's Tavern, not Fredericksburg.

Lee now recognized that he was in a race to Spotsylvania. Richard Ewell's Second Corps, spread across the Orange Turnpike farthest from that point, would have to move first. Couriers raced off to Ewell with new orders:

> I DESIRE YOU TO MOVE ON WITH YOUR CORPS AS RAPIDLY AS YOU CAN, WITHOUT INJURING THE MEN, TO SHADY GROVE CHURCH. ANDERSON BY THIS TIME IS AT SPOTSYLVANIA COURT HOUSE AND MAY NEED YOUR SUPPORT. . . .

Although Winfield Hancock's orders specified that he should move out his Second Corps before midnight, the slow passage of Warren's Fifth Corps delayed his start until "some time after daylight."

"The day was hot and the roads very dusty," a New York officer recalled, "and we were obliged to tie handkerchiefs over our mouths and noses in order to breathe." Groups of Fifth Corps stragglers could be seen everywhere. A Massachusetts infantryman in the Second Corps admitted to having "considerable fun at . . . [their] expense. . . . One of . . . [our] men cried out 'Close up and serve your country.' Another 'advance in line' and many more funny jokes were cracked at their expense."

Early in the morning, a battalion of Confederate sharpshooters eased into the empty trenches left by Sedgwick's Sixth Corps north of Saunders Field. The Southerners discovered something else as well: "the richest field of spoils we had ever seen. . . . [The] battalion [was] ordered to stack arms, break ranks and help themselves. Instantly the command, from a compact body of daring men, was converted into a wild and reckless mob, rushing hither and thither in search of plunder."

—— ★ ——

During the morning, James S. Wadsworth died.

Attending him were the wounded Captain Adams of Massachusetts and a local farmer, Patrick McCracken. Earlier in the war Wadsworth had helped McCracken in a dispute with authorities, and though the Confederates strongly discouraged him, McCracken promised Adams that he would provide anything Wadsworth might need. The elderly Union general, however, had slipped beyond helping.

Burnside's Ninth Corps was the last sizable Federal force to leave the Wilderness. Throughout the night of May 7, Burnside's men moved to a rendezvous point near Wilderness Tavern, where they massed and waited for the tail of the Sixth Corps column to clear the area. Early on the morning of the eighth, the Ninth Corps began its movement toward Chancellorsville; the rear guard would not get out until well after daylight. According to the detail's commander, Byron Cutcheon, "The enemy followed at a short distance, but did not press us at all."

The crisis in Robert E. Lee's command structure continued. As he rode south toward Spotsylvania, Lee learned that the Third Corps commander, A. P. Hill, was sick. Hill's physical condition had always been a matter of concern. Although he was capable of sustained bursts of high-strung energy, the frail, fever-eyed Hill had never fully recovered from a youthful case of venereal disease that had left him vulnerable to prostate infection and generally weakened his immune system. Incapacitating onsets of illness, often during periods of great stress, had marred Hill's record with the Army of Northern Virginia, and now he had been put out of action once again. Lee responded quickly to the news. A follow-up order went to Ewell, detailing him to detach Jubal Early for temporary command of the Third Corps. Lee designated John Gordon to take over Early's division.

Throughout the morning, the men of Richard Ewell's Second Corps pulled out of their trenches north and south of the Orange Turnpike and headed for Spotsylvania.

Their route took them along the whole course of the battle — past Saunders Field, where the New York Zouaves had been ambushed; past the open fields around the Chewning Farm, where Crawford had briefly held the advantage and A. P. Hill had almost been captured; past the lines across the Plank Road, where Union and Confederate victories had each seemed possible for fleeting minutes. But there was no time for reflection, only a sense of dogged urgency to push on. The foot soldiers paid the price:

> Lieutenant James Thompson (6th Alabama): "On the 8th of May we had the hardest march of the war."
>
> Sergeant Joseph McMurran (4th Virginia): "The weather was very hot, water scarce and the road thro' the Wilderness thick set with undergrowth which had been set on fire and was so warm that the troops almost suffocated."
>
> Private George Peyton (13th Virginia): "Moved very slowly at first, but as soon as we got strung out, we went like race horses. . . . The woods were on fire on each side of the road and it was suffocating marching through the smoke and fire. Men fainted, broke down and fell out all the way."

It was late afternoon or early evening before A. P. Hill's corps, now commanded by Jubal Early, pulled out of its trenches across the Plank Road and joined the movement to Spotsylvania.

Grant's headquarters were fixed near Piney Branch Church, and Meade's close by. Grant was doggedly optimistic, already thinking past Spotsylvania and on to Richmond. "My efforts will be to form a junction with General Butler as early as possible," he informed Henry Halleck. "My exact route to the James river I have not yet definitely marked out."

Horace Porter remembered an incident at this time: "A drum corps in passing caught sight of the general, and at once struck up a then popular negro camp-meeting air. Every one began to laugh, and [John] Rawlins cried, 'Good for the drummers!' 'What's the fun?' inquired [Grant, who was tone deaf]. 'Why,' was the reply, 'they are playing *Ain't I glad to get out ob de wilderness!*'"

"Meanwhile," noted Meade's aide Lyman, "there was firing towards Spotsylvania, an ill omen for us."

★

Spotsylvania

SUNDAY, MAY 8

Laurel Hill: Dawn–Midday

The day began with laughter. As the first rays of the sun caught their faces, the men of the 13th Massachusetts looked at one another and howled "at the comical appearance we presented." The Federals had spent most of this humid night marching slowly along the Brock Road through clouds of dust and sooty ash, which had left them looking "more like drivers of charcoal wagons than soldiers."

The men, part of John Robinson's division of Warren's Fifth Corps, were leading a stop-and-go procession south along the Brock Road. Just ahead, the infantrymen could hear a thin crackle of carbine fire where Federal cavalrymen were pushing ineffectively against dismounted Confederate horsemen from Major General Fitzhugh Lee's division. The sun had been up for only a few minutes when some other Massachusetts men at the very head of the column saw a solitary rider appear from the direction of the skirmishing. When the horseman began ordering deployment of the lead regiments, a harassed infantry colonel demanded that he identify himself. "The figure raised the flapping brim of his felt hat and answered with the single word: 'Sheridan!'"

The Yankee soldiers spread out into lines of battle and began a slow advance along the Brock Road, finally breaking the early-morning stalemate despite some hard going. Just ahead, perhaps three miles distant, was the strategic crossroads village of Spotsylvania Court House; Ulysses Grant's bold flank march to cut off the Army of Northern Virginia from its shortest route to Richmond was that close to succeeding. It was now almost 8:00 A.M.

——— ★ ———

Richard Heron Anderson was a forty-two-year-old regular-army man from South Carolina. In a Confederate military only too well stocked with colorful and eccentric personalities, the courteous, capable Anderson had served with quiet competence rather than dramatic distinction, rising to lead a division in A. P. Hill's corps. He now commanded James Longstreet's corps in its march from the Wilderness to Spotsylvania. Walking for fifty minutes of each hour, the Southern column struggled along a narrow, hastily cut military road, stumbling over partially cleared tree trunks and choking on the smoke from forest fires along the way. What the Confederate officer did not know — and what Robert E. Lee had just realized — was that the Union Army of the Potomac was moving on a parallel track a few miles to the east. The race to Spotsylvania was on.

It was, Anderson remembered, "a little after daylight" when he found "some open fields and halted there to let the troops close up and rest a little." The First Corps commander put the distance to Spotsylvania at about three miles. He continued, "The orders . . . [for rest] had scarcely been given, when a courier from Fitz-Hugh Lee arrived with an urgent call . . . to . . . come to his support with all speed, for his cavalry was hard pressed and could not hold . . . [near Spotsylvania] much longer."

The dispatch rider had already passed his message along to Major John Cheeves Haskell, in command of an artillery battalion that was marching ahead of Anderson's infantry. Haskell immediately moved his men toward the sound of the gunfire, prompting one of the cannoneers to observe wryly that "a great many people were bound for Spotsylvania that morning besides ourselves."

At Alsop's Farm the Brock Road to Spotsylvania split, with a small path running alongside to the right for about a mile. "When the fork was reached General Robinson with Lyle's brigade* in the lead, followed by Coulter's[,]† kept on the main road, while Denison's brigade took the narrow road to the right." When the strung-out Federal columns came back together, it required some time to get them in order again. While the officers worked to straighten things out, the division commander, John Robinson, scouted ahead. At forty-seven,

---

*Colonel Peter Lyle took command of Colonel Samuel H. Leonard's brigade on May 6.
†Colonel Richard Coulter replaced Brigadier General Henry Baxter, who was wounded on May 6.

Robinson was Wadsworth's successor as the oldest division commander in the army. His gaze rested on a gently sloping rise known
locally as Laurel Hill, which effectively dominated the Brock Road,
the route the Federals would have to take if they were going to roll
into Spotsylvania. "I could plainly see the enemy's line in the edge of
the timber beyond," Robinson later wrote. A Massachusetts officer
recalled what happened next: "General Warren here rode up and,
saying to General Robinson that his orders were to go to Spotsylvania
Court House, ordered him forward. Robinson asked for time to get
up his other brigades, but after a few moments of waiting Warren
became impatient, and General Robinson ordered an immediate
charge upon the enemy's line."

Adjutant Y. J. Pope of Kershaw's Division, which was leading Anderson's march this day, remembered that the last few miles to Spotsylvania were filled with ominous portents. First a frantic civilian rode
up, warning that the Confederate cavalrymen ahead on Laurel Hill
could not hold out much longer. Then, as the leading brigade was
turning toward the threatened hill, a rider galloped close and yelled,
"Run for our rail piles; the Federal infantry will reach them first, if
you don't run." Despite their weariness, Kershaw's men made a dash
for the fence-rail breastworks that had been piled up by Fitzhugh
Lee's dismounted riders. Adjutant Pope continued, "We occupy the
rail piles in time to see a column, a gallant column, moving towards
us, about sixty yards away. Fire, deadening fire, is poured into that
column by our men. . . . The column staggers and then falls back."

That Yankee column, from Richard Coulter's brigade, "was struck
with such a tremendous fire of artillery and infantry that the Federals
recoiled and fell back in some confusion." John Robinson re-formed
his division, more completely now, for another assault.

"Once more they come to time," said Adjutant Pope of South Carolina. "We are better prepared for them."

"Knowing that my brave men would follow wherever I led the way,"
said Robinson, the Union general, "I placed myself at their head and
led them forward to the attack." Robinson was putting everything he
had into the assault, with Peter Lyle's brigade in the center, the all-
Maryland brigade, commanded by Andrew Denison, on the right,
and Richard Coulter's shaken brigade supporting on the left.

The Federals were tired. "There wasn't any double-quick in us," a weary member of the 13th Massachusetts admitted. Added Lieutenant Colonel Charles Peirson of the 39th Massachusetts, "The enemy's line . . . was protected by an incomplete breastwork, with small pine-trees felled for abatis and a rail fence parallel with the line to the front. Lyle's brigade . . . charged over 500 yards of open, badly gullied ground under a rapid fire. The troops went over the rail fence into the abatis, and up to within 30 feet of the works. . . . Here they lay to recover their wind . . . and while waiting saw the . . . [Maryland brigade] advancing . . . to their support." As the Marylanders moved ahead, they filed past the Fifth Corps commander, Gouverneur Warren, who yelled to them, "Never mind cannon! Never mind bullets! Press on and clear this road."

A member of the 7th Regiment remembered the Maryland brigade's assault on Laurel Hill: "The enemy opened with shell, followed by canister and then double-canister, from the cross-fire guns on the right. . . . [The] front rank was goaded into a return fire, individual progress was . . . retarded by the act of aiming and loading. . . . In this way, ranks and regiments soon became intermingled . . . [and] the time of exposure was fatally prolonged. . . . What remained of the movement was no longer a column, but a bunched and ragged line."

Then John Robinson was down with a bullet-shattered knee, followed by Denison, the Maryland brigade's commander, punched from his horse with a serious wound in his right arm. The historian of the 1st Maryland finished the story: "The 1st, 7th and 8th regiments pushed on to within 15 yards of the rebel entrenchments, but the terrific fire poured into their ranks forced them to give way."

Even as Robinson's men came hobbling back, the leading brigade of Charles Griffin's division moved forward. Brigadier General Joseph Bartlett pushed his men ahead quickly. "Hurry up or you won't get a shot at them," he called out to one New York regiment. "The troops were very weary," a Pennsylvanian in the 83rd later wrote, "and little enthusiasm in the charge could be excited." Said Captain Amos Judson of that regiment, "We started . . . and endeavored to get up a yell and a double quick, but the men were too much exhausted either to run or to yell." Portions of Bartlett's ragged battle line lurched close enough to the Confederate works to use their bayonets. Other sections found themselves flanked and without support. "There appeared to have been miscalculation somewhere," New York captain Eugene Nash noted bitterly. After what Captain Judson remembered as thirty minutes of close-in killing — "so close that the discharges of our muskets almost flashed in their faces" — the 83rd Pennsylvania fell back "without much regard to order." The nearby battle line of the 44th New York "quickly dissolved, some to escape, some to fall and some to be captured."

Other bits and pieces of Griffin's division got into the fighting, most of them seemingly by accident. No one was quite sure if there was a battle plan or, if there was one, what it might be. "The affair was certainly very poorly managed," a member of Ayres's brigade complained. In the confused combat, Colonel George Ryan, who just three days before had led the 140th New York in its attack across Saunders Field to open the Battle of the Wilderness, was shot from his horse and mortally wounded. In an attempt to inspire his men, General Ayres' "ordered his magnificent brigade brass band . . . to render most cheerful and inspiring music as his Brigade advanced against the enemy."

More and more troops were arriving to bolster the Confederate line that was now spreading across Laurel Hill. The first Federal attacks were thrown back by Benjamin Humphreys's Mississippi brigade and by Kershaw's brigade of South Carolinians, with artillery support from Haskell's Battalion. Even before Bartlett's men began their ill-coordinated assault, Alabamians from William Perry's brigade began coming onto the field. Two Alabama regiments led by Colonel William Oates swung around the left of the Confederate position to hit yet another line of Federal support, this one from Lysander Cutler's Fifth Corps division.* Oates's men scrapped fiercely with Yankees from Wisconsin in the woods on the Confederate left, or the Union right. Cutler later reported, "My right, being uncovered and unsupported, was attacked in flank from the woods and we were obliged to retire a slight distance."

By 12:30 P.M. Gouverneur Warren had had enough. He sent this message to Meade's chief of staff, Andrew Humphreys:

> . . . I HAVE DONE MY BEST, BUT WITH THE FORCE I NOW HAVE I CANNOT ATTACK AGAIN. . . . [ASSISTANT ADJUTANT FRED] LOCKE IS BADLY WOUNDED IN THE FACE. I HAVE LOST THE OLD WHITE HORSE. . . . MY STAFF IS ALL TIRED OUT. . . . I IN-

---

*Cutler had succeeded James Wadsworth.

CLINE TO THINK . . . THAT IF I LET THE ENEMY ALONE HE
WILL ME. . . . I AM OUT OF AMMUNITION.

Army of the Potomac Headquarters, near Piney Branch Church

The explosion came, Horace Porter later figured, "between eleven
and twelve o'clock that morning." George Meade called Phil Sheridan to headquarters, and the sparks flew. Meade, Porter said, "had
worked himself into a towering passion regarding delays encountered
[on the Brock Road] . . . and when Sheridan appeared went at him
hammer and tongs, accusing him of blunders, and charging him with
not making a proper disposition of his troops, and letting the cavalry
block the advance of the infantry. Sheridan was equally fiery, and . . .
all the hotspur in his nature was aroused."

Phil Sheridan felt he had cause. In his view, Meade's meddling
with his riders along the Brock Road had thoroughly disrupted the
cavalry chief's control of events and scattered his horsemen all over
the countryside. Only James Wilson's division had operated this
morning under Sheridan's orders, and it had managed to take Spotsylvania Court House. But it had done so without support, and as
Confederate infantry had begun showing up at the crossroads, Sheridan had ordered Wilson to withdraw lest his division be trapped.
In his *Personal Memoirs*, Sheridan recalled lashing into Meade
about the "disjointed operations . . . he had been requiring of the
cavalry . . . [which] would render the corps inefficient and useless. . . . One word brought on another until, finally, I told him I
could whip ["Jeb"] Stuart if he (Meade) would only let me." Sheridan's language, Horace Porter took care to note, "was highly spiced
and conspicuously italicized with expletives." After Sheridan stormed
out, Meade went over to Grant's tent and related the gist of the argument. According to Porter, "When Meade repeated the remarks
made by Sheridan, that he could move out with his cavalry and whip
Stuart, General Grant quietly observed, 'Did Sheridan say that?
Well, he generally knows what he is talking about. Let him start right
out and do it.'" "By one o'clock," Porter continued, "Sheridan had
received his orders in writing from Meade for the movement."

Todd's Tavern

Throughout the morning and afternoon, Winfield Hancock concentrated his Second Corps around a crossroads halfway between the
Wilderness and Spotsylvania. Should Lee want to move men behind
the rest of the Federal army at Spotsylvania or strike at the Union

supply train that was lumbering southward on roads to the east, he would have to make his move through this crossroads next to Todd's Tavern.

Hancock sent a large scouting force to the west along the Catharpin Road at about midday. The Federals made it to high ground overlooking Corbin's Bridge, where, in the distance, they could observe the dusty smudges of Richard Ewell's Confederate Second Corps heading toward Spotsylvania. Late in the day fighting broke out as this scouting force was attacked by Confederate troops moving south from the Wilderness. These troops, part of A. P. Hill's Third Corps, were under the temporary command of Jubal Early. Combat flared brightly, briefly. It ended when Hancock withdrew his men to the entrenchments that had been built around Todd's Tavern and Early's men pulled back to continue their march.

As Hancock's adjutant later closed his account of this forgotten affair, "[The] sun went down, and darkness came on, and the great battle of Todd's Tavern was never fought."

Laurel Hill: Afternoon–Night

The Confederate commander, Robert E. Lee, arrived near Spotsylvania at around 2:30 P.M. Sorting through the reports coming to him, Lee realized that the Army of Northern Virginia was holding its advantage, thanks to the superb tactical skill of "Jeb" Stuart and Richard Anderson. Stuart had begun the morning under heavy attack from two directions — on one side from Federal infantry pressing resolutely down the Brock Road, and on the other from a division of Yankee cavalry that had come boiling into Spotsylvania Court House from the northeast. Stuart had detailed Fitzhugh Lee's division to stall the foot soldiers, sent everything else he had against the Yankee riders in Spotsylvania, and rushed couriers to Anderson's approaching infantry columns with urgent requests for assistance. Once on the scene, Richard Anderson had acted without hesitation. His leading pair of brigades went to Laurel Hill to help Fitzhugh Lee. The next two in line marched off to the Court House to assist Stuart in levering out the Federals, now identified as belonging to James Wilson's cavalry division. By the time Lee showed up, matters were sorting themselves out favorably. Field's Division had joined Kershaw's to extend the Laurel Hill position to the left, or westward. ("We formed a line, advanced near the enemy's and threw up breast works of rails and logs," one Georgian soldier noted in his diary.) Several Federal infantry attacks on Laurel Hill in the morning had been beaten back, and the Yankee horsemen in Spotsylvania had withdrawn without giving serious challenge to Anderson's two brigades. The day was not yet won, but as more and more Confederate troops arrived, Lee felt the satisfaction of knowing that the odds were shortening in his favor all the time.

Throughout the early afternoon Ulysses Grant fretted over the lack of progress on Laurel Hill. "I was anxious to crush Anderson before Lee could get a force to his support," Grant later said. At Grant's urging, Meade sent messages to his corps commanders exhorting them to take Laurel Hill and gain the crossroads beyond, at Spotsylvania. By 1:00 P.M., when it was clear that Warren could not do the job, Meade sent word to John Sedgwick to bring the Sixth Corps. "Use every exertion to move with the utmost dispatch," Meade implored. Then he sent his aide Theodore Lyman to check things out. Lyman did not like what he saw. "It was plain that many of the men were jaded," he noted, "and I thought some of the generals were in a like case." The usually dependable Sedgwick was far from confidence-inspiring. "Where's the Vermont Brigade?" he asked. When told that it was not yet up, the grizzly-bearded Sixth Corps commander muttered, "Just when I wanted it. Everything unlucky." Warren, the Fifth Corps commander, was also showing the signs of stress. When Meade informed him that he would have to cooperate with Sedgwick, Warren exploded. "You . . . can give your orders and I will obey them," he snapped, "or you can put Sedgwick in command and he can give the orders and I will obey them; or you can put me in command and I will give the orders . . . but I'll be God d——d if I'll *cooperate* with General Sedgwick or anybody else."

It was a little after 6:00 P.M. when the "combined" Fifth and Sixth corps attack on Laurel Hill got under way. One reporter, Charles Coffin, watched the advance: "[A] long line of men in blue, picking their way, now through dense underbrush, in a forest of moaning pines, now stepping over a sluggish stream, with briers, hazel thorn-bushes and alders impeding every step, and now emerging into an old field where the thriftless farmers had turned the shallow soil for spring planting." Actually, only one of Sedgwick's brigades advanced — William Penrose's, which had been temporarily attached to Samuel Crawford's Fifth Corps division. Penrose's all–New Jersey outfit made a costly dash to the Rebel entrenchments but then had to fall back for lack of support.

A Pennsylvanian in Samuel Crawford's division remembered it

as being "half-past six o'clock in the evening" when "a great shout
rolled along the line and the columns of attack moved forward." "The
men fought forward and upward desperately," added another. This
attack too failed for reasons that had a familiar ring: "[The advance of
Crawford's men] was not supported, and there was no adequate result
from their brilliant charge."

South Carolina private Frank Mixson remembered stopping
Crawford's men, adding, "We did not follow them, I suppose because
we were too tired and broken down to run when we met them."

To add to the confusion of the moment, Union supports arrived
at the firing line in time to see Crawford's men scuttle rearward.
Close behind the retreating Federals, their silent battle lines seeming
especially eerie in the gloomy twilight, were the dimly seen shapes
of a Southern counterattack.

Brigadier General Stephen Dodson Ramseur arrived at Spotsylvania at about 5:00 P.M., leading the first units from Richard Ewell's
Confederate Second Corps to reach the battlefield. His men, having
endured "a very warm and fatiguing march," "were so tired and worn
out they could hardly halloo," but Ramseur pushed them toward the
sounds of gunfire on Laurel Hill. Handsome, black-eyed, and with
an open, friendly manner that endeared him to his troops, Dodson
Ramseur led his men into combat with a fierce joy. "His whole being
seemed to kindle and glow amid the excitements of danger," one ad-
mirer later wrote. A North Carolinian standing in the ranks this day
recalled, "After maneuvering for some time with the enemy, General
Ramseur rode to the front and ordered a charge. The men moved off
in a double-quick. . . . We encountered a line of battle on the top of
the ridge."

The Yankee line of battle stood its ground and fought. A Maine
private who later became a minister confessed that these Federals
forgot "all the noble and refined elements of manhood, and for that
hour on Laurel Hill they were brutes, made wild with passion and
blood, engaged in a conflict as deadly and fierce as ever raged upon
the continent. . . ."

Ramseur's counterattack was joined by elements from Cullen
Battle's brigade, but the men from North Carolina and Alabama were
just plain fought out. "I took the colors of the Third Alabama in my
hand, went forward, and asked the men to follow," Battle later reported. "I regret to say that the result did not correspond with my
high hopes. . . . General Ramseur came up and we united our efforts, but with results scarcely better than before." Battle continued,

"My left was originally nearest the enemy and as a consequence the Twelfth Alabama, Sixth Alabama and Sixty-First Alabama Regiments first encountered the [Federal] works and the colors and some officers of the Sixth and Sixty-First were captured." The stubborn Federal line of battle held its place until 3:00 A.M., when it withdrew to the main position "well to . . . [the] rear."

The first battle of Laurel Hill was over. Federal casualties numbered about 1,740, while the Confederates lost fewer than that. John Robinson's division had been dealt a death blow; as a Massachusetts soldier noted in his diary the next day, "Owing to scarcity of officers and men, the division was broken up."

Years later, when he tried to reconstruct the events surrounding the Federal repulse at Laurel Hill, Thomas Hyde, a Sixth Corps staff aide, could only remember, "The dim impression of that afternoon is of things going wrong and of . . . much bloodshed and futility." "Time wasted till dark," Grant's aide Cyrus Comstock noted dourly, "when it was too late to produce any result." In the end, it all came down to minutes. Again and again Confederate reinforcements arrived where they were needed, when they were needed. It was a day when the chaplain of the 11th Pennsylvania Reserves could observe that "time was now more precious than life."

"The race [to secure the strategic crossroads at Spotsylvania Court House] had been finished," Fitzhugh Lee later wrote, "and [Robert E.] Lee, between Grant and Richmond, cried Check!"

Night

Darkness had fallen by the time Edward Johnson's division of Richard Ewell's corps completed its march from the Wilderness to Spotsylvania. Johnson was told to extend the Confederate line to the right by taking a position on that flank of Robert Rodes's division, something that was easier said than done. William Whitehurst Old, Johnson's aide-de-camp, recalled, "Rodes' right rested on the edge of the woods, and to extend his line, we had to go through the woods. We had no guides and no lights. . . . We came upon a thicket, mostly pine, so thick that the darkness was almost impenetrable.

"I remember well that I kept my hands before my eyes . . . to protect them, and . . . more than once I was nearly dragged off my horse by the trees. . . . We knew nothing of the topography of the country, but soon . . . saw camp fires before us, almost directly in the line of our march.

"The ground was examined and General Johnson found we were on the brow of a ridge, which turned somewhat shortly to the right. The camp fires in our front seemed to us to be considerably below the plane of our position, as they were in fact. It was now quite late in the night and General Johnson deflected his line and followed the ridge. . . . It was under these circumstances that Johnson's division was placed in line, and fortified it." This decision would have serious consequences.

MONDAY, MAY 9

According to his aide Horace Porter, "Every one at [Grant's] head-quarters was up at daylight . . . prepared for another active day's work." A glance at the map showed that the Army of the Potomac was slowly bringing its strength to bear on the Confederate lines before Spotsylvania. Already on hand were Warren's and Sedgwick's corps. During the morning Hancock's men would leave their positions around Todd's Tavern and march down the Brock Road to form on Warren's right. Also moving was Burnside's Ninth Corps, which was pushing toward Spotsylvania from the northeast, along the Fredericksburg Road.

According to his aide Charles Venable, "It was General Lee's habit in those days of physical and mental trial to retire about 10 or 11 at night, to rise at 3 A.M., breakfast by candle-light, and return to the front, spending the entire day on the lines." Sometime early this day Lee wrote to President Davis of the Confederacy, "We have succeeded so far in keeping on the front flank of [Grant's] army, and impeding its progress, without a general engagement, which I will not bring on unless a favorable opportunity offers, or as a last resort. . . . With the blessing of God I trust we shall be able to prevent Gen. Grant from reaching Richmond."

Three divisions of Yankee cavalry — perhaps ten thousand men — rode out of their camps near Alrich's Farm this morning. Phil Sheridan was getting his chance. Under orders "to engage the enemy's cavalry, and after cutting the Fredericksburg and Central Railroads to threaten Richmond, and eventually communicate with and draw supplies from [Butler's army] . . . on the James River," Sheridan was expecting to defeat the vaunted "Jeb" Stuart in open-field fighting. "I know we can beat them," Sheridan told his division commanders.

Dawn arrived, and Confederate engineers found that Edward Johnson's late-night decision had created a neat little problem. The ridge Johnson was fortifying did not follow the curve of the entrenchments to his left. Instead, it jutted forward, creating a huge bulge, or salient, in the Confederate position. The engineers preferred the lines to fit more closely into a smooth curve, so that any attack could come only from the front. A salient could be assaulted from both front and sides. Ewell, the Second Corps commander, felt that the line should nevertheless be held. If they were to pull back and straighten things out, he argued, the Yankees would have high ground in front of them. Said Johnson's aide William Old, "My recollection is that on the 9th of May the engineer officers, with General M. L. Smith at their head, went over the line and considered it safe with artillery." So cannon were pushed into the salient to strengthen it against attack. This compromise pleased some officers and worried others. Brigadier General James Walker, whose Stonewall Brigade held a position in the heart of the salient, pronounced it "one of the best lines of temporary field works I ever saw. It was apparently impregnable." But one artillery-man, Thomas Carter, who commanded some of the guns that were being rolled along the twisty forest paths to the apex of the salient, thought it "was a wretchedly defective line."

By now, A. P. Hill's Third Corps had come onto the field and gone into position on Ewell's right. Hill's men — Jubal Early was still in temporary command of the corps — had to cover Spotsylvania itself, so their line bent back sharply and followed a more conventional layout toward the south. Seen on a map, the salient now took on a familiar shape. The Southern farm boys began to call it the "Horse Shoe" or the "Mule Shoe."

"A little before eight o'clock," said Grant's aide Porter, "the general mounted his horse, and directed me and two other staff-officers to accompany him to make an examination of the lines in our immediate front." Grant stopped for a brief discussion with the Sixth Corps commander, John Sedgwick, and then rode on. Another thought came to Grant, so he sent Horace Porter back to Sedgwick with a message. On the way, Porter came across a sorrowful procession of officers who told him that John Sedgwick was dead, killed by a Confederate sharpshooter as he prowled the exposed forward lines. The aide returned to Grant, who was stunned by the news. Porter remembered, "For a few moments he could scarcely realize it, and twice asked, 'Is he really dead?'" The pace of war allowed no time for sentiment, however, and Porter noted that "General [Horatio] Wright was at once placed in command of the Sixth Corps."

George Meade's aide Theodore Lyman later wrote down the story of Sedgwick's death: "General Sedgwick, with a carelessness of consequences for which he was well known, had put his Headquarters close on the line of battle and in range of the sharpshooters. As he sat there, he noticed a soldier dodging the bullets as they came over. Rising from the grass, he went up to the man, and, laying his hand on his shoulder, said, 'Why, what are you dodging for? They could not hit an elephant at that distance.' As he spoke the last word, he fell, shot through the brain by a ball from a telescopic rifle."

At 8:00 A.M., Robert E. Lee got his first inkling that there was something doing with Grant's cavalry. A message came from "Jeb" Stuart, reporting, "There is a demonstration of the enemy's cavalry on the Fredericksburg road about one mile and a half from Spotsylvania Courthouse. If it amounts to anything serious I will be sure to inform you."

Then Stuart was gone, taking as many men as he could gather in pursuit of what turned out to be most of the Army of the Potomac's cavalry corps.

"The 9th of May passed without any serious encounter with the enemy," said Lee's aide Walter Taylor. "Each army was engaged in strengthening its own line and in endeavoring to discover the position of the other."

At around noon Ulysses Grant received communications from Washington that brought him up to date on the other forces involved in the grand campaign of 1864. As Horace Porter later recalled the news contained in the dispatches, "Sherman's columns were moving successfully in northwestern Georgia. . . . A report from Butler, dated the 5th, stated that he had landed at City Point, and reports of the 6th and 7th announced that he had sent out reconnoitering parties on the Petersburg Railroad . . . that he had had some hard fighting, and was then intrenching, and wanted reinforcements. . . . Sigel [in the Shenandoah Valley] reported that he had not yet met the enemy."

Earlier this morning Grant had penned a quick note to Major General Henry Halleck in Washington, which began, "The enemy hold our front in very strong force, and evince a strong determination to interpose between us and Richmond to the last. I shall take no backward steps."

Po River: Afternoon–Night

It was just about noon when the men of the 148th Pennsylvania shouldered their gear and began a three-mile march from Todd's Tavern to Spotsylvania. The Pennsylvanians were a veteran outfit; mustered into service in 1862, they had fought at Chancellorsville and Gettysburg. Since March 1864 they had been assigned to Brooke's brigade of Barlow's division in Hancock's Second Corps. Major R. H. Forster later recalled the march to Spotsylvania, a march that took the men through dense woods: "There were ominous and gloomy recesses in that dark forest, but all was quiet as the weary column silently pursued its march, save such sounds as were occasioned by the rapidly repeated orders sent along the line by the commanding officers, the steady tramp, tramp of the soldiers, and the monotonous rumble of the artillery teams."

By now Ulysses Grant had a rough picture of the Rebel defenses opposing him. "It was found," reported Horace Porter, "that the Confederate army occupied an almost continuous line in front of Spotsylvania, in the form of a semi-circle, with the convex side facing north." A miscommunication with Burnside, who was approaching Spotsylvania from the northeast, led Grant to believe that Lee had moved a strong force in that direction. Without Sheridan's riders to confirm it, Burnside's report had to be accepted at face value. Grant concluded that "Lee was about to make the attempt to get to, or towards, Fredericksburg to cut off my supplies." Grant's combative response was to look for a place to hit back, and at that moment Lee's left flank, where Hancock's Second Corps was coming into line, seemed to be it.

It was early afternoon when the 148th Pennsylvania completed its march to Spotsylvania, along with the rest of Francis Barlow's division. The Pennsylvanians, recalled Major Forster, "filed into place upon high, cleared ground overlooking the valley of the Po River." They immediately began to throw up breastworks.

Grant's suspicion that Lee was weakening his western flank for a push to Fredericksburg brought him to inspect Hancock's lines at a propitious moment. According to Francis Walker, a Second Corps adjutant, Grant and Meade rode to a hillside overlooking the Po River valley to discuss matters with Hancock. "While the conversation was in progress," Walker said, "a Confederate wagon train was seen passing along a road on the opposite side of the river . . . [and] a battery was ordered up to open fire upon it." The shelling had an instant effect. An Ohio soldier who was watching nearby remembered that the first explosion caused the train to move "in a lively and amusing manner . . . spilling out large quantities of corn and black beans." There was, however, a somber side effect, as Walker explained: "Hancock was directed to throw a division over the river and try to capture the train."

It was around 6:00 P.M. when the order came down to John Brooke's brigade to fall into line and cross the Po River. Pushing out ahead of it were skirmishers from the 148th Pennsylvania. H. C. Campbell of Company D recalled crossing the Po, "jumping down in the water which was about four feet deep, holding up our cartridge box." Behind the Pennsylvanians, the rest of Brooke's brigade came across, followed by most of Barlow's division. Then the stakes got higher, as Hancock committed two other divisions: John Gibbon's, east of Barlow, and David Birney's, crossing to the west. The pretense of grabbing the Confederate wagon train was gone now, and Francis Walker believed that Grant "thought he saw an opportunity of getting . . . upon the flank of the Confederates at Spotsylvania." Hancock had hoped to quickly seize the Shady Grove Road, which led to Lee's left flank, but, related Walker, "it was nearly dark when the last two divisions succeeded in getting over . . . and Hancock found it impossible to push the troops forward as he desired."

In the 148th Pennsylvania they counted their losses: "The movement cost the regiment one officer and eleven men wounded." One of the eleven was Private George W. Walker, hit "in the fleshy part of the right arm, severing an artery, from which the blood, on certain movements of the arm, gushed out higher than his head." When told to get himself to an aid station, Walker defiantly fired one more shot at the enemy before obeying.

Part of the regiment "slept in the fields," while another portion "bivouacked in woods near Waite's Shop." Behind them, Federal engineers labored in the darkness to put up temporary bridges over the Po River so that artillery could be brought up in the morning.

Washington

Newspaper headlines proclaimed victory: "MORE GLORIOUS NEWS FROM THE FRONT . . . LEE RETREATED 12 MILES, LEAVING HIS DEAD AND WOUNDED IN OUR HANDS." In a telegram to governors in Ohio, Illinois, Indiana, Iowa, and Kentucky, War Secretary Stanton expressed his belief that "General Grant has driven the enemy on all points and is achieving a complete victory." Crowds once again came to the White House for an evening serenade, this time by the band of the 27th Ohio. Lincoln made a brief appearance and said, "Grant was moving on the line he had marked out. It was a great victory for the army to be where it was, yet there was a great deal of work yet to do before the rebellion could be suppressed and the Union restored."

TUESDAY, MAY 10

Spotsylvania
Po River: Morning–Afternoon

The 148th Pennsylvania spent the first hours of the morning of May 10 digging in along "a ridge which ran south of the Po." On all sides of the regiment, the men could see the battle flags of three Federal divisions. Winfield Hancock now controlled the Shady Grove Road south and west of the Po River. The road obligingly led eastward and in behind Lee's left flank, anchored on Laurel Hill, but to get there Hancock had to cross the twisty Po once more at Block House Bridge. He found it being defended by William Mahone's division and promptly began preparations to flank the position. But as Hancock readied his men to carry out this plan, he was handed a dispatch from army headquarters:

> YOU WILL IMMEDIATELY TRANSFER TWO DIVISIONS OF YOUR CORPS TO GENERAL WARREN'S POSITION, AND MAKE ARRANGEMENTS, IN CONJUNCTION WITH THE FIFTH CORPS, TO MAKE A VIGOROUS ATTACK ON THE ENEMY'S LINE PUNCTUALLY AT 5 P.M.

In the light of a new day, Ulysses Grant had thought better of yesterday's impulsively ordered turning movement. He now realized that Hancock's advance effectively isolated that corps from the rest of the Union army, so the idea of flanking Lee on his left, Grant later wrote, "was therefore abandoned. Lee had weakened the other parts of his line to meet this movement of Hancock's, and I decided to take advantage of it."

"Early on the morning of the 10th," wrote Jubal Early in his *Memoirs,* "I was ordered to move one of my divisions [Mahone's] . . . to cover the crossing of the Po on the Shady Grove Road; and to move with another division [Heth's] to the rear and left, by the way of Spottsylvania Old Court House, and drive back a column of the enemy which had crossed the Po and taken possession of the Shady Grove Road, thus threatening our rear and endangering our trains."

No one in the 148th Pennsylvania had the slightest idea of what the larger scheme of things was. All that the men knew, related their adjutant, J. W. Muffly, was that the regiment "occupied a dozen or more different positions during the day." As a member of the Second Corps staff, Francis Walker could see the larger plan: "Gibbon at once recrossed to the north bank of the [Po] river . . . while Birney followed. . . . The withdrawal of two divisions had left Barlow alone to hold the position south of the Po. . . . It also placed Barlow in a singularly exposed and isolated position." The time was about 2:00 P.M.

Even as Birney's division was crossing back to the north side of the Po, a crackle of gunfire sputtered into an ominous roar south of Shady Grove Road. Jubal Early, completing his circuitous march, was striking at the suddenly exposed Federals, and Henry Heth's division was spearheading the attack. "I found the troops opposed to me to be Hancock's Corps," Heth recalled. "My division . . . steadily drove the enemy."

The sudden Confederate attack so worried George Meade that he told Hancock to supervise the withdrawal of the last Federal division south of the Po. While Heth's men aggressively probed the Union position, Hancock and his officers worked out a plan using three successive fallback lines. The first (closest to the enemy) consisted of Nelson Miles's and Thomas Smyth's brigades, holding earthworks just south of the Shady Grove Road. About halfway between the Road and the Po was a second line of works, held by Hiram Brown's* and John Brooke's brigades. The third line stretched along the south side

---

*Colonel Hiram L. Brown took command from Colonel Paul Frank on May 10.

of the Po itself, covering the three military bridges that had been constructed during the night. As soon as Brown's and Brooke's brigades fell back to the middle line of works, Hancock ordered Miles and Smyth to leave their position in the first line and to retire to the third before crossing on the bridges. Hancock's report continued, "Encouraged doubtless by the withdrawal . . . from our front line, which it is supposed . . . [the Confederates] mistook for a forced retreat, they reformed their troops and . . . assaulted Brooke's and Brown's brigades. The combat now became close and bloody." Chaos spread as timber to the right and rear of the defending units was ignited. "The woods were on fire and the flames crackling and roaring. The surroundings were appalling," a Pennsylvanian remembered. Maine private John Haley later wrote, "There was a continual roar, like the voice of many waters: the crash of artillery, the yells and cheers of the combatants, the groans and cries of the wounded, and the general confusion of charging and counter-charging. . . . I regard this as one of the hardest days of fighting this army has ever seen."

The 148th Pennsylvania was in a small stand of trees, holding the extreme right of Brooke's position in the second Union fallback line. "All the afternoon the regiment lay at its post," wrote one reporter, Frank Burr, "its commander aware that hour by hour its comrades were crossing in safety." The tempo of gunfire increased, and smoky little fires sprang up in the woods, obscuring any visual connection with the rest of Brooke's brigade to the left. "It looked as if our Regiment was fighting the whole Rebel Army," observed H. C. Campbell.

Confederate soldiers now occupied the first Union fallback line. According to Colonel James Beaver, commanding the 148th Pennsylvania, the Rebels "poured a murderous fire into our exposed line." Beaver was beginning to suspect that his men were all alone. He had received no communication from John Brooke for the better part of an hour, and it was no longer clear whether Brown's brigade was still protecting his right flank. Beaver sent Sergeant Robert Kissinger to scout that way. Kissinger, Beaver later recalled, "returned on a full run, with eyes blazing, and, in emphatic language said: 'Colonel, the rebels are in there!'" Adjutant Muffly remembered the moment: "Our men were falling like game before hunters. . . . Beaver, . . . calling me to his side, . . . said: 'Adjutant, we can not stand this. You go swing the right back while I hold the left and we will retire. . . . I will take the responsibility of withdrawing my Regiment without orders.' So we made good our retreat, gathering up our dead and wounded as we went toward the river, and as we were about to cross, Beaver looked back at the procession of stretcher bearers with their burdens and said with tears in his eyes, 'Oh, my brave boys! What a pity.'"

Behind the retreating Federals, Confederates from Heth's Division took over the abandoned second-line position and were sickened by what they saw. Burton Conerly of Mississippi remembered, "The ground in front of us was covered by the dead and wounded Yankees, and the pine straw and leaves caught fire from the exploding shells, and long lines of fire lighted the woods and burned over the dead and wounded. The flashes of the exploding cartridge boxes on the dead and wounded could be seen as the long sweep of flame went over them, and the cries of the wounded for help, which could not come, was something heart rending."

Beaver recalled, "The bank of the river was very marshy and in urging the passage of the men . . . I became mired. . . . I finally crossed and fell exhausted upon the opposite bank of the river. . . . As soon as I had revived myself, I found, to my surprise, that our Brigade had withdrawn and that we had been left alone to confront an entire division of the enemy. . . ."

The end of the Po River affair was described by A. L. Long, an artilleryman: "With a fierce foe in front and a burning forest in rear Hancock's men found themselves in a critical situation, and were very severely handled in the effort to extricate themselves. On crossing the stream they destroyed the bridges, and thus checked the Confederate pursuit."

Events elsewhere on the battlefield quickly overshadowed the fighting south of the Po. In Barlow's division the officers believed that a choice opportunity to tackle a Confederate division — Heth's — on equal terms had been passed up. Also, in the confusion a single gun from Captain William Arnold's 1st Rhode Island Light Artillery had been caught between two trees and left behind. *"This was,"* Winfield Hancock reported with emphasis, *"the first gun ever lost by the Second Corps."* At General Lee's request, Henry Heth published a congratulatory order to his troops, praising them for their valor in driving the Yankees from their entrenched lines. One of the Southern regiments that had been heavily engaged, the 11th Mississippi, noted in its history, "In this fight the Confederates lost many good and true soldiers." Among them was Brigadier General Henry H. Walker, down with a serious foot wound that would eventually require amputation.

The final summation in a history of the 148th Pennsylvania was not without irony: "This battle, though unimportant in results, was fiercely contested, the regiment losing two hundred officers and men, of whom twenty-one were killed and two died of the wounds."

Laurel Hill: All Day

Of the five corps commanders marching with Grant in this army, Gouverneur Kemble Warren was the least proven. Since the opening guns of May 5, he had struggled to achieve the kind of success that would show his peers once and for all that he was worthy of the rank. "Let me have a fair chance," he wrote his wife on May 4, "and I do not fear the result." That chance had eluded Warren, however, in the confused tangles of the Wilderness and on the open fields of Laurel Hill. Today would be different. A Pennsylvania soldier who saw him this morning declared, "General Warren never appeared to better advantage. . . . Wearing his full uniform, he was conspicuously prominent."

Warren's corps held much the same line it had held at the end of the day on May 8. At 10:00 A.M., Warren received a dispatch from George Meade that promised the action he had been waiting for: a combined Fifth and Second corps force was to launch "an attack on the enemy in your front . . . at 5 P.M. this day." But this tonic came with a bitter taste: "Major-General Hancock will by virtue of seniority have the command of the combined operation."

Warren had already set about his end of it. The first order of business was to get a clear picture of the main Confederate position, and so reconnaissance was ordered.

Charles Griffin sent out about eight hundred men from two regiments at 11:30 A.M. to secure the rifle-pits covering the Confederate position. "Our line swept forward at a run," remembered one Massachusetts soldier, "and with a wild hurrah, drove them out pellmell." "At this point," said a Federal soldier who was watching from back along the Fifth Corps line, "a heavy artillery and infantry fire opened on them from the enemy in the woods as they took refuge in the rifle-pits and earthworks now in their possession." Blue-coated soldiers scattered frantically for cover. "Nothing could be done," recalled one of them, "but to lie down, hug close and wait our doom and coming events."

South Carolina private Frank Mixson was among the Confederate skirmishers ejected from the rifle-pits. Safely back in his main line, he got his revenge: "We were well protected behind the good breastworks of logs, and the way we did give it to those Yankees would have done your heart good to see. . . ."

At 12:30 P.M., two regiments from Cutler's division moved to uncover the Rebel lines in their front. Rufus Dawes was in charge of the 6th Wisconsin, which had been given the mission along with the 12th Massachusetts. The probing force got within two hundred feet of the main enemy line before it was pinned down by "a continual storm of bullets." As Dawes later wrote, "Major General Warren soon came running up the hill to have a look at the rebel works, when I seized his yellow sash and pulled him violently back. . . . To have exposed himself above the hill was certain death. I accompanied General Warren to another point where we secured a good view of the rebel works."

Under orders to join the Fifth Corps in the 5:00 P.M. attack, Brigadier General John Gibbon of the Second Corps personally scouted the ground ahead. "It was a dense piece of woods where dead cedar trees were scattered about, their stiff ragged arms standing out like so many bayonets, in such a way that a movement by a line of battle . . . was entirely out of the question. . . . I told Gen. Warren no line of battle could move through such obstacles . . . and we rode together to Gen. Meade's Headquarters where I [again] stated . . . the objections. . . . [Meade], however, seemed to rely wholly upon Warren's judgment in the matter, and the latter seemed bent upon the attack with some idea that the occasion was a crisis in the battle of which advantage must be taken."

By now Hancock was caught up in organizing the withdrawal of Barlow's division across the Po River. Gouverneur Warren would direct the attack on Laurel Hill.

The First Assault: 4:00 P.M.

Thomas Chamberlain (150th Pennsylvania): "Warren's troops, in advancing, were obliged to traverse a ravine thickly covered with heavy timber on the sides, and with a tangle of underbrush at the bottom which proved well-nigh impenetrable. Necessarily the ranks were much disordered in forcing their way through."

Franklin Sawyer (8th Ohio): "The lines struggled stubbornly through the woods, cheering and undaunted, but only to meet a terrible repulse."

John G. B. Adams (19th Massachusetts): "Grape and canister ploughed through our ranks. Both color-bearers were shot down. . . . Among the first to go down was Color-Sergeant Ben Falls. . . . As he fell he said, 'John, your old uncle has got his quietus this time.'. . . [He] died the next day. . . . No army on earth could capture the works with such odds against it, but we charged once more. . . ."

The Second Assault: 5:00 P.M.

Confederate First Corps diary: "The enemy began a series of attacks on [Major General Charles] Field's position. . . . Some of the enemy succeeded in gaining the works, but are killed in them."

D. H. Hamilton (1st Texas): "[We] fight at the battle of Spotsylvania Court House where the Federals charged over the works of our regiment and we had a hand to hand fight with them. We killed nine of the Federals in front of our company, inside of the works. They killed one man and frightened a good many very badly, myself among the number."

William Oates (15th Alabama): "The charge on the Texas brigade was for a time partially successful. They did not have any bayonets . . . but the Texans, by desperate fighting and clubbing their guns, hand-to-hand, drove out the assaults and recaptured the line."

Anonymous Confederate reminiscence: "Captain James Hunter . . . commanding Company E of 7th Georgia, was frying his meat at the time, . . . seeing the lines broken, snatched his frying pan from the fire . . . rushed in among the Texans calling loudly to stand their ground, which they did. . . . Captain Hunter was remembered as the man who rallied the Texans with his frying pan."

Winfield Hancock, who had spent the afternoon supervising Barlow's withdrawal across the Po River, rode over to Warren's front at 5:30 P.M. He was in time to see the second assault fail. Hancock's orders left no room for argument: "I was . . . to assault the enemy again at the same point at 6:30 P.M." Farther to the left of the Union line, an attack by Horatio Wright's Sixth Corps was taking place, and Hancock's assault was to support it. This time David Birney's division would join with Gibbon's along with troops from Warren's Fifth Corps.

The Third Assault: 7:00 P.M.

Charles Weygant moved up into position along with the rest of the 124th New York. "Just as we had completed our formation," he remembered, "General Crawford, of Warren's corps, came walking along the front, accompanied by several of his staff. He was gesticulating in an excited manner . . . and exclaimed in a tone of intense anguish, . . . 'I tell you this is sheer madness, and can only end in wanton slaughter and certain repulse.'"

According to Sergeant J. D. Bloodgood of the 141st Pennsylvania, "The troops had witnessed the failure of Warren's men to take the ridge and the terrible slaughter which resulted, and moved forward with a great deal of reluctance, for they all felt it to be a hopeless undertaking and that they were like sheep being led to the slaughter."

Reported Winfield Hancock, "The troops encountered the same obstacles which had forced them to retire when they had assaulted this point at 5 P.M. They were again repulsed with considerable loss."

Just before sunset yet another assault was set up, only to be called off, to the great relief of the troops that were lined up to attack. In his after-action report, Gouverneur Warren wrote, "Toward evening two assaults were made with a part of my corps and Gibbon's division and a part of Birney's, but failed to carry the enemy's works, which were defended by musketry and flanked by canister. Loss heavy."

The second battle of Laurel Hill was over. "In the . . . attacks of this day," said Charles Banes of the Philadelphia Brigade, "the Second and Fifth Corps lost over five thousand men, while it is probable that the enemy did not lose one thousand." "The only results of . . . [these] assaults," wrote a Massachusetts soldier, "was to kill and wound a large number of men." Michigan color-sergeant Daniel Crotty expressed the frustration that many Union soldiers were feeling: "Now what is the reason that we cannot walk straight through them with our far superior numbers? We fight as good as they. They must understand the country better, or else there is a screw loose somewhere in the machinery of our army."

Upton's Charge: 6:10 P.M.–Dark

Do not weep, maiden, for war is kind.
Because your lover threw wild hands toward the sky
And the affrighted steed ran on alone,
Do not weep.
War is kind.*

"On the 10th orders were received to inspect the fronts of the line with reference to making an assault," wrote Major Henry R. Dalton of Horatio Wright's Sixth Corps. "[The First Division commander,] General [David A.] Russell, after a thorough personal examination, reported a favorable point in the vicinity of the Scott house."

May 10 was shaping up as a fairly quiet day for the regiments of the Sixth Corps. A corporal in the 121st New York noted that the day was "bright and it was warm, but the air felt damp, indicating rain." At around noon, men were dozing near the regiment's headquarters when, according to F. W. Morse, an aide, "a staff officer rode up, saying that 'General Wright would like to see Colonel Upton.' There was no use in sleeping now," Morse added ruefully, "for we knew we would have fighting soon if Upton had any thing to say about it."

There was something hard and menacing about Colonel Emory Upton. The thin, wiry Union officer was a driven man, driven by an unsatiated ambition and an outspoken disdain for the way this war was being waged. Despite his having received five promotions since the beginning of the war, Upton still hungered after a general's star. "I ought to have had it a year ago," he had grumbled back in April. Upton believed in personal leadership — "I have never heard our generals utter a word of encouragement, either before or after entering a battle," he wrote — and he believed that modern warfare required new solutions. The problem, as Upton saw it, was time. Men charging an entrenched position across an open space took too much time to reach their destination. The long, thin battle lines that were always used would inevitably stop and exchange fire with the dug-in foe (taking heavy losses in the process); if they managed to move forward again at all, they would do so with most of their punch gone. Upton felt that the key to taking an entrenched strong point was to

*This and the following excerpts are taken from Stephen Crane, "War Is Kind," from *The Complete Poems of Stephen Crane*, ed. Joseph Katz (New York: Cornell University Press, 1972).

attack it with a swiftly moving, compact column that did not pause once it began its charge, but instead rushed right over the enemy works. Emory Upton was coldly confident that with this formation and some intelligent, inspiring leadership, any fortified position could be taken. He had made his feelings perfectly clear to his superiors. Now, as Upton reported to the Sixth Corps headquarters, he learned that he was going to get an opportunity to test his method.

> Hoarse, booming drums of the regiment,
> Little souls who thirst for fight,
> These men were born to drill and die.
> The unexplained glory flies above them,
> Great is the Battle-God, great, and his Kingdom —
> A field where a thousand corpses lie.

The position picked for Upton's attack was not promising — located perhaps half a mile southeast of a house owned by a local family named Scott, it represented part of the western face of an immense, northward-jutting salient in the Confederate line. The line itself was a solid piece of trench work, well buttressed with logs and dirt, shielded in front by an abatis of felled trees whose sharpened branches pointed toward the Federals. Before the defenders lay a cleared area perhaps two hundred yards wide, providing an ample killing ground. Seen from above, the trenches looked like a series of three-sided bunkers with heavy traverses — running back at right angles from the main embankment — built to prevent enfilade fire should an enemy somehow get into the main trench system. And some hundred yards to the rear was a second defensive line, not yet wholly finished but strong nonetheless. "The point of attack," Upton wrote afterward, "was shown me by Captain Mackenzie, of the U.S. Engineers. . . . [The enemy's works] were of a formidable character. . . ."

Back at divisional headquarters, General Russell selected the twelve regiments that would take part in the desperate attack. His aide Thomas Hyde looked at the first draft of the list and saw that his old regiment — the 7th Maine — was on it. Hyde knew Upton and his ambition and decided that the 7th was not going to be a part of it. At his coaxing, the staff officers substituted another regiment. The final list was handed to Upton, who pronounced it "a splendid command."

Now Upton laid his plans. There would be four battle lines, with three regiments in each. Only the first line would attack with rifles capped — that is, ready to fire. That line would rush over the enemy works and then fan out to the left and right. The guns carried in the remaining three lines would be loaded but not capped. These weapons could be fired in the few seconds it would take the soldier to put a copper percussion cap on the nipple, but their not being capped insured that no one would stop to fire while on the run to the works. The second line would advance to hold the center of the captured line after the first line had spread right and left. "The third line," according to Upton, "was to lie down behind the second, and await orders. The fourth line was to advance to the edge of the wood, lie down, and await the issue of the charge."

At 4:00 P.M., Federal skirmishers filtered forward, driving their Rebel counterparts back into the main trenches. This allowed Upton to bring his twelve regimental commanders up close to see the ground and be assigned their individual roles in the upcoming assault. To each Upton stressed that the command "Forward!" was to be repeated constantly "from the commencement of the charge till the works were carried."

At around 5:00 P.M., the twelve regiments began moving to their jump-off positions. "The men," said a member of the 5th Maine, "were ordered to unsling knapsacks, and to divest themselves of every incumbrance, preparatory to a charge." A Pennsylvanian in the 96th Regiment recalled, "We were marched a short distance from camp. . . . We then had orders to lie down." In the 121st New York, Dorr Danvenport turned to his tentmate Clinton Beckwith and said, "I dread the first volley, they have so good a shot at us."

The time was just about 5:50 P.M.

> Do not weep, babe, for war is kind.
> Because your father tumbled in the yellow trenches,
> Raged at his breast, gulped and died,
> Do not weep.
> War is kind.

The Confederates in the trenches opposite were Georgians belonging to George Doles's brigade, in Ewell's Second Corps. Supporting Doles were the cannon of the 3rd Company of the Richmond Howitzer Battalion.

When his skirmishers came scurrying back to the main line at 4:00 P.M., Doles sent word of the fact to his corps commander, Ewell. As soon as the one-legged Confederate general learned of the matter, he ordered Doles "to regain his skirmish line at any cost." It was just about 5:50 P.M.

"At 5:51 P.M.," reported the Sixth Corps artillery chief, Colonel Charles H. Tompkins, "Cowan's, McCartney's, and Rhodes' batteries fired with all rapidity for nine minutes." The preassault barrage was supposed to stop promptly at 6:00 P.M., but it went on a bit longer than planned. "Owing to some delay," said Captain Andrew Cowan of the 1st New York Battery, "I was obliged to continue firing until 6:10 P.M." In the waiting ranks of the 5th Maine, the men recalled "the shells howling and shrieking over the heads of the charging column, and plunging into the works of the enemy."

Then it was time. A member of the 5th Maine remembered the moment: "Colonel Upton's clear voice rang out, 'Attention, battalions! Forward, double-quick! CHARGE!'"

> Swift blazing flag of the regiment,
> Eagle with crest of red and gold,
> These men were born to drill and die.
> Point for them the virtue of slaughter,
> Make plain to them the excellence of killing
> And a field where a thousand corpses lie.

"I felt my gorge rise, and my stomach and intestines shrink together in a knot, and a thousand things rushed through my mind," remembered Beckwith, the New Yorker. "As soon as we began to run the men . . . commenced to yell, and in a few steps farther the rifle pits were dotted with puffs of smoke, and men began to fall rapidly. . . ." For what seemed like hours, the leading Federals tore frantically at the jagged abatis. Men spun around and died; others cursed and ripped open pathways. A "leaden hail swept the ground," said a Maine soldier in the first line, "while the canister of the artillery came crashing through our ranks at every step." Then, incredibly, they were through the abatis, over a ditch, and onto the breastworks. As Upton later reported, "The first of our men who tried to surmount the works fell pierced through the head by musket-balls. Others, seeing the fate of their comrades, held their pieces at arms length and fired downward, while others, poising their pieces vertically, hurled them down upon their enemy, piercing them to the ground."

A stunned Georgian recalled, "They came at us with a yell and never made any halt. . . . We were simply overwhelmed and forced to retire, *every man for himself.*"

Now the second line was in with the first, pushing the breach wider open. "Our boys are using bayonets, butts of guns and fists — anything to get the rebels back out of our way," a Pennsylvanian in the 49th said. A young farm boy in the 44th Georgia, Thomas Dingler, fought in lonely desperation to save the regimental flag. "When his body was found after the fight," an eyewitness claimed, "he had received fourteen bayonet wounds and he held tightly clutched in each hand fragments of the flag." Colonel Upton himself remembered, "A private of the 5th Maine, having bayoneted a rebel, was fired at by the captain, who, missing his aim, in turn shared the same fate. The brave man fell by a shot from the rebel lieutenant."

While squads of screaming Federals rushed ahead and took the second line of works, large bunches of Confederate prisoners were sent running wildly to the Union rear, through curtains of fire laid down by Southern troops on either side of the breach. Other groups of Union men jabbed into flanking trenches held by North Carolinians from Junius Daniel's brigade.

Upton's desperate plan had succeeded; it had broken the Confederate line. Now was the time for a fresh body of troops to widen the hole and roll up the Confederate defenses. This had been anticipated; a full division of troops from Hancock's Second Corps had been held ready all day for just this reason. Led by Gershom Mott, it was assigned to punch in on Upton's left to finish the job. But Gershom Mott was not Emory Upton. Earlier this day, young Oliver Wendell Holmes, Jr., had brought Mott some orders and noted that the Second Corps officer "seemed somewhat stupid and flurried." Mott's division now swung out of the woods on cue, onto an open field a half mile from the Confederate lines and in clear view of the rows of cannon that were posted there. The Southern artillerymen opened a devastating fire. One of Mott's men later recalled the advance of the division this way: "It went forward through the woods, pressing the enemy's pickets back until near the breastworks, when it was met by an enfilading fire from their batteries, which caused it to fall back in some confusion." Ulysses Grant was less charitable in his assessment. "Mott," Grant wrote in his *Memoirs*, ". . . failed utterly." Diversionary actions were also ordered on Upton's right, but these troops — from Hancock's Second and Warren's Fifth corps — had already failed in several bloody attacks this day, and their commanders had had enough.

By this time, fully aroused Confederate defenders were counterattacking on all sides of Upton's pocket. Richard Ewell himself helped rally portions of Daniel's Brigade, posted to Doles's right. "Don't run boys," the Rebel commander shouted excitedly. "I will have enough men here in five minutes to eat up every damned one of them." Battle's Alabama brigade moved to block any further forward movement by the Federals, while troops led by John Gordon and R. D. Johnston pushed on the flanks. "The Yankees fought with unusual desperation," remembered one Alabama soldier, James Roberts. "The sun was just setting and the immense volumes of smoke which rose from the musketry so darkened its rays as to give it the appearance of a bright moon-shining night." Robert E. Lee's young aide Walter Taylor later recorded, "General Lee started for the breach, with the purpose of leading the troops in the effort to regain the lost ground, when his staff and other officers surrounded him and urged him . . . not . . . to expose himself to an almost certain death. To their expostulations he replied that he would relinquish his purpose if they would see to it that the lines were reestablished — that that 'must be done.' And it was done!"

"Our position," Emory Upton later reported, "was three quarters of a mile in advance of the army, and, without prospect of support, was untenable. Meeting General Russell at the edge of the woods, he gave me the order to withdraw." Corporal Clinton Beckwith of the 121st New York remembered, "Getting back into the open field, it was covered with dark forms, lying on the ground, and many more moving back." (According to Asbury Jackson of Georgia, the Confederate general George Doles was captured in the first rush, "but when the enemy was driven back he fell & when our line came up he arose & resumed command.") A squad of retreating Pennsylvanians from the 49th Regiment stopped by some Confederate cannon. The captain in charge of the squad looked for something to jam into the vents of the artillery pieces to put them out of action. "Who has a rat-tail file or nail to spike these pieces?" he yelled. "This is a hell of a place to ask for a file," someone in the squad muttered back. The absurdity of the moment broke over the men, and a member of the squad recalled looking up into the captain's face and laughing.

One of the Confederate counterattackers noted that it was "an hour after dark" before the last of Upton's men were driven out. As Upton later related, "Our loss in this assault was about 1,000 in killed, wounded, and missing. The enemy lost at least 100 in killed at the first intrenchments, while a much heavier loss was sustained in his effort to regain them. We captured between 1,000 and 1,200 prisoners and several stand of colors." (The Confederate estimates were, not surprisingly, different from Upton's. The historian of Doles's Brigade said, "Our loss was about six hundred and fifty, three hundred and fifty of the number being prisoners." A soldier in Junius Daniel's

North Carolina brigade, which was posted close on Doles's flank and was partially overrun, put the total at about "225 enlisted men of our Rgt. captured and six officers.") The Yankee wounded were scattered everywhere. According to F. W. Morse of the 121st New York, "The woods were full of these unfortunate creatures, and sounded all night with their cries and groans." A Pennsylvanian in the 96th made a bitter entry in his diary: "The many killed and wounded had done their duty for nothing." Clinton Beckwith spent part of the night looking for his tentmate Dorr Davenport, who had become separated from him during the worst of the fighting. Beckwith searched everywhere and finally realized that his friend was not coming back. "I sat down in the woods, and as I thought of the desolation and misery about me, my feelings overcame me and I cried like a little child."

> Mother whose heart hung humble as a button
> On the bright splendid shroud of your son,
> Do not weep.
> War is kind.

Emory Upton got his general's star. "I conferred the rank of brigadier general upon Upton on the spot," Ulysses Grant said. Upton's feat gave Grant an idea. The theory worked; what it had lacked today was enough weight to complete the job. Luman Tenney, an Ohio cavalryman who was serving as an orderly at army headquarters, saw Grant talking with George Meade about it, and he heard the lieutenant general say, "A brigade today — we'll try a corps tomorrow."

Richmond: Night

For days now the alarm bells had been sounding throughout the Confederate capital, summoning civilians to arms. War Clerk John Jones sat down to his diary and recalled this day as one of "excitement . . . but it is sullen rather than despairing." The news from Robert E. Lee was generally good. Carefully cataloguing the numerous repulses of the enemy that had been reported by Lee, Jones tittered, "Grant's tactics seem to be to receive his stripes by installments." There had been no definite news today from Bermuda Hundred, where "Beast" Butler's Army of the James had landed. But there was a bit of disturbing information from north of the city: a Yankee force of unknown size had "cut the railroad at Beaver Dam Station, and destroyed some of our stores." This worried Jones, who was something of an armchair strategist. With so much of Richmond's defense force tied up south of the city, it seemed to him eminently possible "that a cavalry raid from the north may dash into the city and burn the bridges on the James; then our army [to the south] would be in a 'fix.'"

Spotsylvania: Night

Virginian John Casler had so far enjoyed a spectator's seat for the great battles of Spotsylvania. Earlier this evening some of his brigade had helped beat back Upton's attack. Now it was dark. Casler's friend Sam Nunnelly crawled close and suggested that the two wriggle out in front of the works to pick over the dead Yankees. Casler shook his head. The odds of getting shot by one side or the other were pretty great, he thought. Nunnelly shrugged and went over the works alone. Remembered Casler, "He got three watches, some money, knives and other things. He would risk his life any time for plunder."

Since witnessing the "chaffing" of his black soldiers by white troops near Wilderness Tavern on May 7, Lieutenant Freeman S. Bowley had marched his men east toward Fredericksburg, where they guarded roads and watched over supply wagons. Bowley wandered around the brigade camps this night and was drawn to a prayer meeting at a nearby regiment. "Grouped under the quiet pine-trees, the scene lighted up by the fires of pine-knots, the men, all wearing their accouterments, gathered. Every black face was sober and reverent.

"The leader 'lined off' the words of the hymn, and all sang the line together. The voices rose sweet and mellow. . . . One powerful black soldier prayed. 'O Lord Jesus, you know we'se ready an' willin' to die for de flag, but O Lord! if we falls, comfort de lubbed ones at home.'

". . . I turned away with tears in my eyes, for I too was thinking of my home, and the black soldier had spoken my unuttered prayer."

Sometime after midnight it was completed — the dreary task of removing the wounded who were lying inside the lines pierced by Upton's charge. According to the historian of Doles's Brigade, "[To] vary the monotony a little, a Confederate band moved up to an elevated position on the line and played 'Nearer my God to thee.' The sound of this beautiful piece of music had scarcely died away when a Yankee band over the line gave us the 'Dead March' [from Handel's *Saul*]. This was followed by the Confederate band playing 'Bonnie Blue Flag.' As the last notes were wafted out on the crisp night-air a grand old-style rebel yell went up. The Yankee band then played 'The Star-Spangled Banner,' and . . . it seemed by the response yell, that every man in the Army of the Potomac was awake and listening to the music. The Confederate band then rendered 'Home, Sweet Home,' when a united yell went up in concert from the men on both sides."

WEDNESDAY, MAY 11

Morning

Remembered Grant's aide Horace Porter, "The 11th of May gave promise of a little rest for everybody, as the commander expressed his intention to spend the day simply in reconnoitering for the purpose of learning more about the character and strength of the enemy's intrenchments, and discovering the weakest points in his line, with a view to breaking through. . . ." By three o'clock Grant had found the weak point — the "Mule Shoe" salient.

The Confederate brigadier George Steuart's staff officer McHenry Howard was returning from a visit to the brigade's field hospital when he "saw General Lee examining the rear of that part of Rodes' line which had been broken the day before." Recalled Edward Johnson's aide William Old, "General Lee, with General Smith[,] visited our lines, and [they] were of the opinion, as I was later informed[,] that they could be held with our artillery."

Confederate confidence was high. Bryan Grimes, who led a regiment in Ramseur's Brigade, wrote home today, "We now have good breastworks and will slay them worse than ever."

Washington

Today the *Washington Star* printed a telegram from Brigadier General Rufus Ingalls, the chief quartermaster for the Army of the Potomac, to Senator J. W. Nesmith of Oregon. Ingalls's communication (for which he would later be reprimanded by George Meade) said in part, "We are fighting now and have been all the time. We are 'busting them up.' Our losses heavy. . . . The world never heard of war before."

Spotsylvania

The dark, somber man whom the Union troops had jokingly tagged Grant's personal undertaker prepared to depart for Washington. Before he left, Senator Elihu Washburne asked Grant for a personal message to deliver to the President and the secretary of war. Grant sat down and began to write. "We have now ended the sixth day of very heavy fighting," he scribbled. In the middle of the two-hundred-word dispatch, and with no special emphasis whatsoever, Grant said, "I . . . propose to fight it out on this line if it takes all summer."

Washburne thanked Grant, pocketed the message, and rode off.

Mixed in with the ambulances and walking wounded winding their way from Spotsylvania to Fredericksburg and Belle Plain were columns of Confederates who had been captured in the fighting. The first stop for these men would be a natural enclosure created by a series of ravines near Belle Plain, which came to be known as the Punch Bowl. Some seventy-five hundred prisoners would pass through this place on their way to Federal camps in the north. One young Union soldier assigned to guard the POW's remembered them as being sulky and unwilling to answer questions. "I don't blame them for that," he wrote home. "They don't look like soldiers any more than a gang of Irishmen that work on the canal in New York State."

Some of the captured Confederates would end up at Point Lookout, Maryland, situated on a barren, swampy bit of land near the mouth of the Potomac River. Here some twenty thousand men were crammed into a facility designed to hold half that number. More than three thousand inmates would die before the war's end. Other prisoners would be packed off to Fort Delaware, on an island in the Delaware River, south of Philadelphia. One Alabama officer imprisoned there declared that "a respectable hog would have turned up his nose in disgust at it."

Today some of the Confederates on their way to Belle Plain met a detail of black guards, and a Massachusetts man was there to watch. "A regiment of Rebel prisoners passed us during the day. Seeing some negro soldiers guarding one of the [supply] trains, they were quite free in use of strong language towards them, to which the negroes answered as sharp."

All along the entrenched battle lines, Confederates watched the Union wounded who were caught in the no-man's land suffer and die. George Peyton of Virginia was manning some of the trenches that had formerly been held by George Doles's men. "In front were a great many wounded Yanks whose cries were awful," he wrote in his diary. "Our ambulance went out to bring them in but the Yankee Sharpshooters ordered it back. So the poor fellows were left to die in agony."

——— ★ ———

The mood at Meade's headquarters this day was foul. The Army of the Potomac's provost marshal, Marsena Patrick, wrote in his diary, "Miserable camp! Wet, stinking, disgusting Rain, too, much of the time. . . . [Meade] is cross as a Bear, at which I do not wonder, with such a man as Grant over him."

Robert E. Lee met with some of his officers this evening at Henry Heth's headquarters, to discuss various reports about Union movements. Scouts told of some activity on the Confederate left and even more on its right. Lee listened as several officers made light of Grant's generalship. Lee commented, "Gentlemen, I think that General Grant has managed his affairs remarkably well up to the present time." The gray-haired army commander turned to Heth: "My opinion is the enemy are preparing to retreat tonight to Fredericksburg. I wish you to have everything in readiness to pull out at a moment's notice, but do not disturb your artillery, until you commence moving. We must attack these people if they retreat."

Though he was still too ill to command, A. P. Hill was not too sick to have an opinion. "General Lee, let them continue to attack our breastworks; we can stand that very well." Lee, still thinking in terms of offense, not defense, disagreed. "This army cannot stand a siege," he said, rising wearily to continue his rounds. "We must end this business on the battlefield, not in a fortified position."

It was his eyes that marked Francis Barlow as a soldier to be reckoned with; they were cold, hard, emotionless shutters hiding the fiercely burning inner fires that had propelled this New York lawyer from his first post as a private in the ranks to his present status as a general in charge of a division. Everything else about Barlow seemed almost too casual. George Meade's aide Theodore Lyman saw Barlow in a typical state of presentation around this time: "He looked like a highly independent mounted newsboy; he was attired in a flannel checked shirt; a threadbare pair of trousers, and an old blue *képi*; from his waist hung a big cavalry sabre; his features wore a familiar sarcastic smile."

It was now about 7:00 P.M. Barlow, along with his fellow Second Corps division commanders David Birney and John Gibbon, had been summoned to Hancock's headquarters. "We were told," Barlow later recalled, "that an attack upon the enemy's right flank by the 2d corps was intended to be made at daylight on the next day. We were told that it was a movement of more than usual importance, and were reminded of the gratitude which the country would feel for those officers who should contribute to the success of the enterprise."

What happened next, or rather, what did *not* happen next, shook the normally phlegmatic Barlow: "No information whatever . . . was given to us as to the position or strength of the enemy, or as to the troops to be engaged in the movements . . . or as to the plan of the attack, or why any attack was to be made at that time or place. The sole information and the only orders given were that the leading division was to report at corps headquarters at an hour named of that night . . . and that the others were to follow closely. At the headquarters we were to meet staff and engineering officers who would conduct us on the ground, and give us all the information needed."

As the three division commanders left for their various headquarters, it came to Barlow that with his division spearheading the attack, all the responsibility for its success rested on his slim shoulders.

Soon after his meeting with A. P. Hill, Henry Heth, and others, Robert E. Lee rode up toward the "Mule Shoe" and at the Harrison House took part in yet another unplanned conference, this one with generals Ewell, Long, and Rodes, and their staffs. Ewell's chief of staff, Campbell Brown, was present and later recalled, "Scouts and skirmishers kept coming in to report that the enemy appeared to be moving artillery and trains away from the front. Gradually, the conviction spread that they were retreating towards Fredericksburg. General Lee was himself of this opinion and, as no enemy had yet appeared in front of Johnson, he directed General Ewell to withdraw the troops from the trenches and General Long to do the same with the artillery. . . . The evening had been very wet and General Ewell suggested that the men would be more comfortable in the trenches than if moved, as they already had shelters there. Accordingly, they were allowed to remain."

Incredibly, no one bothered to tell Edward Johnson, whose troops manned the "Mule Shoe," of the decision to withdraw the cannon. The Confederate officer later related his amazement: "On the night of the 11th, in riding around my lines, I found the artillery which had occupied a position at the salient — a point which with artillery was strong, but without it was weak — leaving the trenches and moving to the rear. I inquired the cause of the moving, and was informed that it was in obedience to orders, and that a general movement of troops was contemplated." James Wood of Virginia, a regimental officer with George Steuart's brigade, remembered, "It was a matter of comment at the time as to what . . . [the removal of the cannon] meant, men wondered if it was the beginning of a withdrawal."

Between 8:00 P.M. and 1:00 A.M., the various regiments making up Barlow's, Birney's, and Gibbon's divisions left their camps overlooking the Po River valley and slowly headed eastward, behind the Fifth and Sixth corps.

Gibbon's men brought up the rear of the long column. "This march was fearful," a New Yorker in the 108th Regiment recalled. "The mud and water was anywhere from ankle to knee deep." "The men were in dense ignorance as to their destination," said George Bruce of the 20th Massachusetts, "and, as they pulled their feet from out [of] the thick and sticky mud for mile after mile, indulged themselves to the limit in the soldiers' privilege to grumble." David Birney's men marched in the middle of Hancock's column. David Craft, a Pennsylvanian in the 141st, recorded it as being "so dark that often one could not see the man in front of him, nor even his hand held before his face."

Francis Barlow's men plodded at the head of the line. According to the historian of the 140th Pennsylvania, "After an hour or more had passed the heavy rain fall was succeeded by a dense, chilling, searching mist amid which the men moved like phantoms of the night." At the very front of the column, Francis Barlow fought hard to keep from shouting angrily in the darkness. The attack plans, haphazard at best, had gone from bad to worse. The staff officers who were to have scouted the ground and provided Barlow with all the information he needed had botched the job. No one knew the layout of the Confederate defenses. It did not help a whit that one of the two officers who had been supplied by Hancock to guide the corps persisted in filling Barlow's ear with "his criticisms on the 'conduct of the war.'" Barlow also suffered visits from two of his brigadiers, Miles and Brooke, both of whom "were loud in their complaints of the madness of the whole undertaking." Brooke carried on so much that Barlow finally had to tell him to shut up. It all got to be too much when his Second Corps "guides" confessed that they were not sure which way the Confederate positions lay. "For Heaven's sake," Barlow snapped, "at least, face us in the right direction, so that we shall not march away from the enemy, and have to go round the world and come up in their rear."

★

The night was cold and wet; the Confederates on picket duty shivered miserably in their advanced positions. But there was something else: there were strange sounds in the air on this drizzly, sodden night. For some reason the Yankee bands were out in force. And that was not all. Thomas Doyle of the Stonewall Brigade recalled hearing "the jingling of the canteens and even the heavy tramp of the enemy's infantry." George Steuart's staff officer McHenry Howard finally sloshed out to the main line to hear the noises for himself. "I . . . stood for an hour on the breastwork, listening to the subdued roar or noise, plainly audible in the still heavy night air, like distant falling water or machinery." Convinced that a Yankee attack was in the making, Howard woke his brigade commander, who immediately sent an urgent request to the division commander, Edward Johnson, that the missing cannon be returned to the front at once.

THURSDAY, MAY 12

George Steuart's report of unusual noises in his front was enough for Edward Johnson, who sent his aide Robert W. Hunter off at once to find General Ewell, "to tell him he was sure that the enemy would attack his division next morning." Major Hunter continued, "I rode to General Ewell and gave him the message. General Ewell said that 'General Lee had positive information that the enemy was moving to turn his right flank . . . and that it was necessary for the artillery to move accordingly.' I rode back to General Johnson. . . . I told him I could not impress General Ewell with his views, and that he had better go and see him in person. General Johnson arose and said: 'I will go at once.'"

Between midnight and 3:00 A.M., the various Second Corps units reached the assembly point for the dawn attack. The ground chosen was an open hillside near the Brown House, close enough to the Confederate lines that Rebel campfires could be seen flickering in the distance. A few thoroughly confused Federals believed that the lights represented the bivouacs of the Union Sixth Corps.

Francis Barlow now learned that the fourth Second Corps division — Mott's — was nearby and would be joining the attack. In fact, Mott's men had held this ground since May 10, and presumably there were officers present who might know the lay of the land. Splashing over to Mott's headquarters, Barlow found just the man he was looking for, Lieutenant Colonel Waldo Merriam of the 16th Massachusetts. Merriam, as Barlow later remembered, "drew upon the [headquarters] wall a sketch of the position, and this was the sole basis on which the disposition of my division was made."

When Major General Edward Johnson and his aide Major Robert Hunter found Richard Ewell, the Confederate Second Corps commander was, according to Hunter's recollections, "apparently very uneasy. He got up and told General Johnson . . . [what] he had told me as to General Lee's information, but was soon convinced . . . that the assault would be made. . . . General Ewell then sent orders for the artillery to be returned to our front, close up, and General Johnson, on his return, instructed me to issue a circular of warning and direction."

As each of the Union Second Corps divisions came up, its commander picked a formation that made sense to him. Barlow chose a compact column, while the other division generals settled on more traditional, spread-out lines of battle. By the time all the shuffling and pushing was done, it was nearly 2:00 A.M. The men were allowed to get what rest they could in the open with no cover. Francis Barlow used some of the time to give all of his personal possessions to a friend for safekeeping. Deep in his heart, the young Union brigadier knew he would not survive this attack.

On hand to support the action directly were two divisions from Wright's Sixth Corps. In all, almost nineteen thousand Union troops were poised to attack, three quarters of a mile from the tip of the "Mule Shoe."

A. L. Long, the Confederate Second Corps artillery chief, logged it as being "half-past three o'clock A.M." when he "read a note from General Johnson, endorsed by General Ewell . . . to replace immediately the artillery that had been withdrawn the evening before. . . . I immediately ordered Page's battalion to proceed with all haste to the assistance of General Johnson."

General Long's note went to Thomas H. Carter, then in command of Major Richard Page's artillery battalion. "Striking a light," Carter recalled, "I endorsed on the order that it was then twenty minutes to daybreak, and the men all asleep, but the artillery would be in place as soon as possible."

Along the Confederate lines that made up the "Mule Shoe," soldiers stood ready and anxious. "Nothing was said by our officers," remembered Virginian M. S. Stringfellow, "but there was a nameless something in the air which told each man that a crisis was at hand." Farther down the line to the right, Steuart's staff officer McHenry Howard recalled, "Owing to the fog the day was late in breaking and even then there was no sign for a while of an attack, which I began to believe would not be made."

The air was damp and a fog hung low as officers and noncoms moved along the sleeping ranks of the Federal Second Corps to wake up the men. Winfield Hancock peered into the dank gloom and decided to delay the assault until things cleared up. The scheduled jump-off time came and went, and Hancock watched the slowly lightening sky. "A funeral silence pervades the assembly, and like spectres the men in blue await the order to attack," wrote the historian of the 152nd New York. "Objects can only be seen at four or five rods. An occasional musket shot can be heard in the distance."

At last it was light enough, and Hancock gave the order to advance. Staff officers checked their pocket watches. It was 4:35 A.M.

As the great mass of men moved past him, Hancock was heard to say, "I know they will not come back! They will not come back!" No one was exactly sure what he meant.

One young Confederate aide, Henry Kyd Douglas, spent this night in the saddle, running messages to and from various Second Corps headquarters and, toward dawn, "helping as I could to speed the guns to their places. . . . The artillery began to arrive [back in the salient]. . . . Light streaks which heralded the coming dawn were appearing in the sky. I had just spoken to General Johnson who was in the trench and was starting with a message for General Ewell when the storm burst." Farther along to the right of the bending Confederate line, a Tennessee picket noticed something odd to his left: "flocks of small birds and owls" were fleeing the woods as if running before a fire. Cannoneer William Dame, posted with his battery along the portion of the Confederate line that was held by Richard Anderson's corps, peered toward the right and caught "a vague glimpse of movement among the trees." Dame called his battery mate Dan McCarthy over to look. "I don't like this," McCarthy said. "Who can they be?"

The stage was set for the longest sustained hand-to-hand combat of the Civil War.

The Bloody Angle

John D. Black was a lieutenant with the 145th Pennsylvania: "Advancing perhaps half a mile, we passed the [Landrum] house on our left, when a shot from the enemy's picket reserve mortally wounded [the officer] . . . in command of the skirmishers protecting the left flank. A short distance beyond . . . our advance was obstructed by dense second-growth timber or thickets, passing through which we came to a cleared space showing a rise of ground . . . running parallel with our line of battle. The men, taking it for granted that this was the enemy's works, contrary to orders opened the yell that always accompanies a charge and sprang forward, but on mounting the crest, the red earth of a well defined line of works loomed up through the mists on the crest of another ridge, distant about 200 yards with a shallow ravine between. . . . We moved quickly forward and just as the command reached the bottom of the . . . ravine, there belched forth from the works a volley of shot and shell that . . . fortunately . . . had been trained on the ridge we had just crossed. . . . At once came the order from General Barlow repeated by every officer in the command, 'Forward!!' 'Double-quick!' 'Charge!'" The Federals would strike the Confederate salient almost at the very tip of its apex.

Virginian John Worsham was moving out to the skirmish line in front of William Witcher's brigade,* which was manning trenches near the apex, "when the stillness was broken by a cannon shot and the screaming of a shell! I put my hands instantly to my head to see if it was on my shoulders; the shell seemed to come so near me that it certainly took off my head! . . . Before I reached our line I could hear the sound of the marching of [what sounded like] 40,000 men. . . . I saw the line approaching to my left, ran back to the colonel and reported to him; and he immediately called the regiment to attention."

In William Monaghan's consolidated Louisiana brigade,† the men were startled by "a sound like the roaring of a tempestuous sea." One soldier caught sight of the great mass of Barlow's men about to crash into the lines to the right, and he shouted, "Look out, boys! We will have blood for supper!"

---

*formerly John M. Jones's brigade
†made up of regiments from Brigadier General Harry T. Hays's and Leroy Stafford's brigades

"Tearing away the abatis with their hands," said Lieutenant Black, "Miles' and Brooke's Brigades dashed over the entrenchments and with bayonet and clubbed musket beat down everything before them." Afterward, Major Nathan Church of the 26th Michigan claimed that his regiment "was the first to reach the works (striking them immediately at the Angle), which we gained after a fierce hand-to-hand fight with the bayonet." "For a time every soldier was a *fiend,*" Maine private John Haley remembered. An officer in the 148th Pennsylvania paused long enough atop the captured breastworks to yell back to his men, "Come on boys, the last day of the Rebellion is here!"

Barlow's men broke over the trenches near the apex held by William Witcher's soldiers. Private Marcus Toney of Virginia remembered turning around in his rifle-pit and seeing that "some of our men were being shot and clubbed to death with guns after they had thrown down their arms." Even as the Union tide crested over the position, the cannon that had been withdrawn during the night on Lee's orders returned. The artillery battalion's commander, Thomas Carter, described their fate: "Most . . . reached the salient . . . just in time to be captured." Nearby, Major Robert Hunter of Edward Johnson's staff watched the major general try to stem the blue flood single-handedly. The forty-eight-year-old division commander had been wounded while fighting under Jackson, and he walked with the help of a heavy hickory stick. "I could see General Johnson with his cane striking at the enemy as they leaped over the works, and a sputtering fire swept up and down our line, many guns being damp. I found myself . . . in the midst of . . . a general melee in full blast. . . . I came upon an artillery horse of Carter's battery, jumped on him, and sinking in my spurs, galloped to the rear, with bullets buzzing around me."

Having obliterated Witcher's command, Barlow's troops surged to their left and hit George Steuart's brigade in the flank and rear. Steuart's aide McHenry Howard tried desperately to organize a defense but was caught in one of the bunkers with a handful of his men. Union soldiers ringed the pit's rim, with their rifles pointed down. For a moment Howard thought that he and his men were all going to be killed, but the Federals merely knocked aside the Confederate muskets and ordered the group out. "I retained my sword in hand," Howard remembered, "after some hesitation whether or not to throw

it away or stick it in the ground." Two passing Yankees quickly relieved the Confederate officer of his sword and scabbard. Howard
continued, "We were ordered to their rear and in going I passed up
the breastwork and out the angle." As he scrambled back, Howard
looked at the mobs of Union troops and thought bitterly that "if our
artillery had been in position at the angle it would have inflicted a
terrible loss and perhaps have checked the assault." Also taken prisoner was Howard's brigade commander, George H. Steuart.

Pennsylvania adjutant John Black rode back to Hancock's headquarters with a request from Francis Barlow for reinforcements on the
left. By now, Confederate cannon positioned outside the salient were
throwing shells into the Federal lines. On his return, Black was
stopped by an officer who had a question to ask. "But before he could
speak," Black recalled with a shudder, "a shell took off that part of
the head above the lower jaw, as smooth as if it had been cut with a
knife, and as I passed he fell backward and in looking down at him
the tongue was moving in its socket as if in the act of speaking —
a horrible sight I can never forget." Another image of horror remembered by a Union survivor was of the Federal officer who had
"both eyes shot out, the ball passing just back of the eyeballs. He
stood blind and helpless, never uttering a word of complaint, but
opening and closing the sightless sockets, the blood leaping out in
spouts."

Even as Barlow's men swept down the eastern portion of the salient,
Birney's and Mott's divisions crashed into the western lines held by
Monaghan's Louisiana troops and James Walker's all-Virginia Stonewall Brigade. Private James McCown, who eight days earlier had
marveled at the grand sight of the Army of Northern Virginia, spoke
for his comrades when he stated, "We . . . [fought] desperately not
dreaming of [capture] until we were completely surrounded by their
overwhelming numbers." Two Southern brigades virtually ceased to
exist.

Success was everywhere, but Francis Barlow was worried. "We had
carried the enemy's line at its extreme right, and, practically destroyed its defenders. The occasion for 'charging,' for rush and confusion, was past and troops ought to have been soberly and deliberately put in position, and ordered to sweep down the rebel line
towards his left." Barlow tried to get his officers to restore order, but

their work was undone from an unexpected quarter. Fresh Union troops appeared on the scene and piled into the milling throng of disorganized Federals in the captured trenches.

Clinging to the harness of the artillery horse he had mounted, the Confederate aide Robert Hunter broke out through the rear of the fighting and almost immediately found himself facing Robert E. Lee. "He was mounted on Traveller," Hunter recalled, "and with his hat off was endeavoring to halt the retreating men. I saw in a moment that General Lee did not know the extent of the trouble in front, and hailed him with the exclamation: 'General, the line is broken at the angle in General Johnson's front.' His countenance instantly changed, and he said: 'Ride with me to General Gordon.'"

It was a critical moment. As the Southern soldier, writer, and Lee biographer John Esten Cooke later stated, "Unless General Lee could reform his line at the point, it seemed that nothing was left him but an abandonment of his whole position. . . . It is probable that at no time during the war was the Southern army in greater danger of a bloody and decisive disaster."

It was never Ulysses Grant's intention that Hancock's movement against the salient be the only Federal attack this day. The whole Confederate line was to be hit, and an important part of the action was entrusted to Burnside's Ninth Corps. A division under Brigadier General Robert Potter drove into the lower eastern side of the salient and enjoyed a momentary success. But Confederate defenders, under the cool leadership of Virginian James Lane, struck back and pushed Potter's men out of the trenches they had taken. A follow-up attack organized by Orlando Willcox's division failed to make a dent. Burnside did manage to sidle one division northward, linking up with Hancock's men at around 9:00 A.M. to form a continuous battle line that hugged the whole "Mule Shoe" and extended southward toward the eastern approaches to Spotsylvania. The best Burnside could claim afterward was that his men had kept Lee from drawing troops from his right to support his beleaguered center.

After today's fighting was over, staff officers had little good to say about Burnside's lackluster performance. Young Oliver Wendell Holmes, Jr., termed the bushy-whiskered general "a d'd humbug," while one diarist, Cyrus Comstock, considered him "Rather weak & not fit for a corps commander."

—— ★ ——

John Gordon of Georgia, now commanding a three-brigade division,* was awakened at around 5:00 A.M. by a soldier who told him, "General, I think there's something wrong down in the woods where General Edward Johnson's men are." Gordon roused his staff and got them in their saddles, all the while receiving reports that confirmed that a serious break had occurred in the salient's defenses. By 5:30 or so, Gordon had a portion of his reserve force heading toward the fighting. Robert D. Johnston's North Carolina brigade moved out first from its camps around the Harrison House. Hoping to buy enough time to let the rest of his division form up for a counterattack, Gordon told Johnston to advance his men into the fighting. The North Carolina soldiers swung past the McCoull House and had reached the lower edge of the woods below the salient's works when they were hit by a tremendous volley. Johnston's brigade "was thrown inevitably into great confusion," Gordon later wrote, "but did not break to the rear." Even though Johnston was down with a serious head wound, his soldiers held on as best they could and managed to slow the uncoordinated advance of the lead Federal elements.

Francis Barlow was becoming frantic. There were too many Federal soldiers crammed into the captured "Mule Shoe" salient. All combat formation had been lost in the milling mass, and more troops kept coming up to join the mob. Barlow rode back to Hancock's headquarters and threw military etiquette out the window as he shouted, "For God's sake, Hancock, do not send any more troops in here." Behind him, the cheering of yet another Union reserve regiment as it plunged over the works told its own story.

John Gordon moved his remaining two brigades — John Pegram's Virginians and Clement Evans's Georgians — into attack position. Then Robert E. Lee rode up, trailed by Edward Johnson's aide Robert Hunter. "Lee looked a very god of war," Gordon recalled. "Calmly and grandly, he rode to a point near the centre of my line and turned his horse's head to the front, evidently resolved to lead in person the desperate charge and drive Hancock back or perish in the effort." Gordon would have no sacrificial heroics from his army chief. "Instantly I spurred my horse across old Traveller's front, and grasping his bridle in my hand, I checked him." Young Robert Hunter recalled

---

*Two — Pegram's Brigade and Gordon's old brigade — came from Jubal Early's division; the third was R. D. Johnston's, from Rodes's Division.

the next few moments as "Gordon exhorting and the men clamoring for General Lee to go back. As Lee retired through Gordon's line (Pegram's Virginia brigade) . . . both that brigade and Evans' . . . moved forward."

Grant's military secretary, Adam Badeau, remembered the army commander's camp as "a strange sight in that early morning — the general-in-chief, with a few officers, standing beside a fire that was almost quenched by the driving rain; within sound of the musketry, receiving reports, issuing orders, directing the battle, but unable to perceive any of its movements — shut in entirely by the trees. . . . [At] 5:30 an officer rode up hurriedly . . . with Hancock's first report. . . . Instantly after, a second aide brought news of many prisoners. . . . At 5:45, Hancock reported the capture of three generals. . . . At 5:50 2000 prisoners were reported. . . . At half-past six, the rebel General Johnson was brought in a prisoner, to Grant's headquarters. He had been an old army friend of Grant and Meade in other days, and the three shook hands." Meade's aide Theodore Lyman was nearby. He recalled Johnson as "a strongly built man of a stern and rather bad face. . . . He was most horribly mortified at being taken, and kept coughing to hide his emotion." With Johnson was Brigadier General George H. Steuart, who, Lyman remembered, "insulted everybody who came near him." One of the first of these was Hancock, who had met Steuart soon after he had been taken prisoner. Hancock recognized a fellow West Pointer and offered the captured officer a friendly handshake. "Under the circumstances I must decline to give my hand," Steuart said sourly. "Under any other circumstances, General Steuart," Hancock snapped back, "I should not have offered mine."

With a shout, John Gordon led his men in a violent counterattack against the Federals in the salient. Virginian George Peyton took part in the charge: "We had gone only a few steps into the pines when we were saluted by a heavy volley of musketry. We did not stop for this, but rushed forward driving a mob of Yankees in front of us. We did not know that the Yankees had broken our front line and had penetrated nearly a mile behind our front. . . . We drove out of the pines, then through a body of big oak trees, down a hill, through a mud-puddle over our knees, up a long naked hill at [the] top of which was our breastworks which they had captured." It was a savage fight. "Pistols, guns, bayonets, swords, all came into play," recalled another

Virginian, M. S. Stringfellow. "A lieutenant of the Fifty-second Virginia was just to my right, almost touching me. I saw him put his hand upon a Yankee's shoulder, ordering him to surrender. The Yankee jerked away, and making a half turn, drove his bayonet through the lieutenant's body, killing him instantly." In a portion of the trenches that had been retaken from the 14th Connecticut, it was remembered, "One Fourteenth man had thrust his bayonet through the breast of a Confederate, the Confederate also having thrust his bayonet through the neck of the Fourteenth man, the two stood dead against the breastworks, the guns of each serving to brace them and hold them in this standing position." "Gordon's troops fought like demons," added a member of the 152nd New York.

Gordon's men cleared the east side of the salient and pushed near the apex. Francis Barlow's fears were coming true; the numerically superior but disorganized Union host was no match for the smaller body of disciplined Confederate soldiers. Gordon's men were spent, though. Help in regaining the rest of the lost position would have to come from another quarter.

From his headquarters near the Landrum House, Winfield Hancock tried to keep the faltering Union momentum going. When Confederate counterattacks began to stem the Federal tide, he ordered up artillery to the Landrum House to shell the enemy lines. Couriers raced in with requests for help, and the military telegraph clicked away as the various corps commanders sent terse messages back and forth. Inwardly Hancock fumed at the poor command setup. The three corps — Hancock's Second, Wright's Sixth, and Burnside's Ninth — were cooperating with one another, but they were not acting with a single purpose. The problem, Hancock later explained, was that "there was no Corps commander there who was invested with the General Command. Had General Meade come up, or had there been another Commander-in-Chief on the spot, . . . a great deal more might have been done."

Another Confederate battle line now appeared out of the gunsmoke fog, moving across the muddy ground, sliced by gullies, toward the western side of the salient. This counterattack was led by Stephen Ramseur, whose North Carolina troops stormed forward and recaptured a section of the trenches. Hancock's grip on the "Mule Shoe" was slowly being pried loose, though only at great cost to the counterattacking forces. The officers at Union army headquarters, how-

Hancock's corps crossing the Rapidan River at Ely's Ford (Waud)

The Wilderness: Barlow's division in action (Waud)

THE WILDERNESS: Carrying the wounded from the flames (Waud)

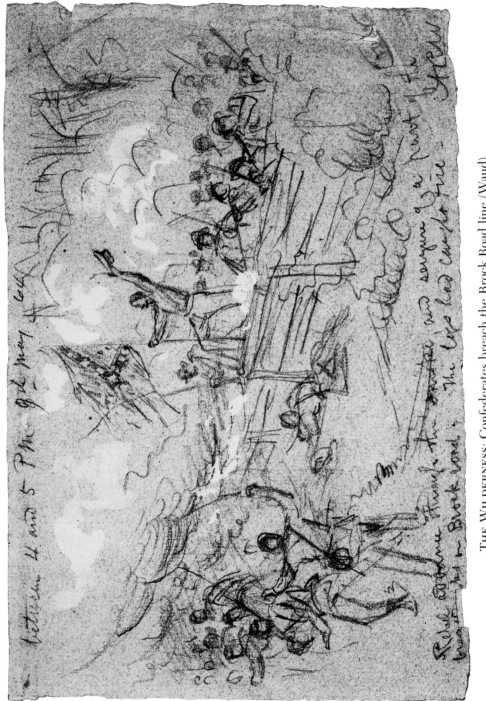

THE WILDERNESS: Confederates breach the Brock Road line (Waud)

ROADS SOUTH: The Army turns south — Grant cheered by troops (Forbes)

SPOTSYLVANIA: The spot where John Sedgwick was killed (Waud)

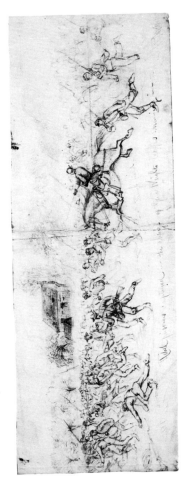

SPOTSYLVANIA: Confederate prisoners being herded to the Union lines after Upton's charge (Waud)

SPOTSYLVANIA: "The toughest fight yet" — the Bloody Angle (Waud)

Finished

SPOTSYLVANIA: A Union field hospital (Forbes)

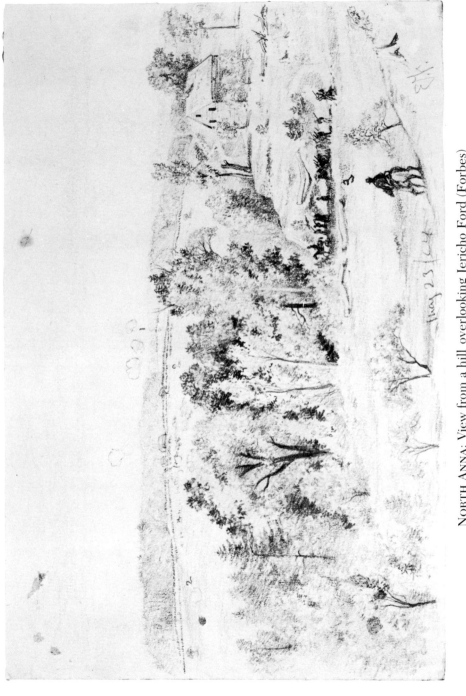

NORTH ANNA: View from a hill overlooking Jericho Ford (Forbes)

NORTH ANNA: Warren's troops crossing at Jericho Ford (Forbes)

NORTH ANNA: Union engineers building a pontoon bridge (Waud)

ROADS SOUTH: Union Army crossing the Pamunkey at Hanovertown (Waud)

BETHESDA CHURCH: Last fight of the Pennsylvania Reserves (Waud)

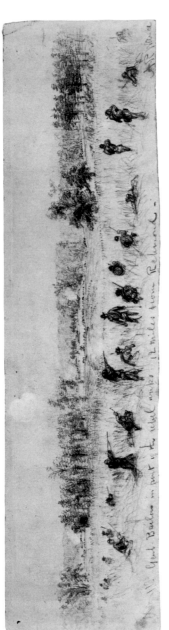

TOROPOTOMOY: General Barlow and his skirmish line scout the Confederate lines (Waud)

COLD HARBOR: General Smith's corps disembarks at White House (Forbes)

COLD HARBOR: June 3 — the 7th New York Heavy Artillery breaks the enemy line (Waud)

COLD HARBOR: June 3 — death of
Colonel James P. McMahon (Waud)

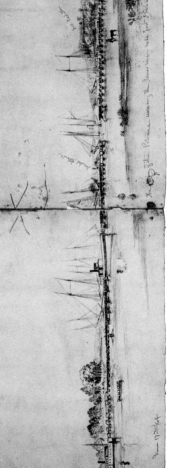

ROADS SOUTH: Army of the Potomac
crossing the James River (Forbes)

ever, were still celebrating victory. One exception was Theodore Lyman. "Some of Grant's staff were absurdly confident and were sure Lee was entirely beaten," he remembered. "My own experiences taught me a little more skepticism. Hancock presently sent to ask for a vigorous attack on his right, to cover and support his right flank. General Wright was accordingly ordered to attack with a part of the 6th Corps."

More Confederate battle lines emerged from the smoke, and more spiky files headed toward the last stretch of trenches held by Union troops. This time the soldiers were from Alabama, led by Brigadier General Abner Perrin. "Things looked desperate and there was a considerable show of excitement," one of Perrin's men remembered. The Alabamians had been posted on the Confederate left, and they came on the run. There was a pause while officers scouted the point of attack. Then it was time. "The sharp order 'Attention' rang out and the whole line sprang to its feet. Perrin spurred his horse to the front and the left flank of our regiment and, with the accustomed yell, our brigade drove at the enemy with a rushing step." Federal fire blasted the Alabama line. Abner Perrin was swept off his horse with seven bullet wounds, and killed; his men struggled and stalled. "We were being fired on from front, right flank and rear," declared one of the Alabama soldiers. Leaderless, Perrin's brigade fell back, out of range.

It was perhaps two and a half hours since Hancock had ordered the charge. Lee was feeding every unit he could find into the breach. Closing it, throwing the Federals out, obsessed him at this moment. Lee was, according to his nephew-biographer, Fitzhugh Lee, "very sensitive about his lines being broken. It made him more than ever personally pugnacious." Lee once more tried to lead troops in person — this time it was Nathaniel Harris's Mississippi brigade — into the fighting. For the second time today, and the fourth time in this campaign, Confederate soldiers shouted to him to go back.

Harris led his men in a desperate charge, losing half of his regimental commanders and a third of his men. But he had also taken a section of trenches on Ramseur's right, squeezing the Federals back that much closer to the apex. It was about 7:30 A.M.

The first Sixth Corps units had been fed into the salient between 6:00 and 6:30 A.M. For the most part these troops came into position west of Hancock. Other Sixth Corps units were held up until they were needed, and the men had to watch the slaughter, knowing that any moment they would get their orders to advance into the maelstrom. Captain Richard Rogers of the 93rd Pennsylvania paced his line nervously and exclaimed, "I would give my right arm if I had no need to go into battle this day."

At about 9:00 A.M., Robert E. Lee decided that another Confederate brigade was needed, and he sent for McGowan's South Carolina command. Lieutenant J. F. J. Caldwell took one look at the holocaust and thought to himself that they had arrived in the nick of time. "The demoralization of the troops that had been about this point was deplorable. They seemed to feel that Grant had all the hosts of hell in the assault upon us." McGowan's men raged forward and grappled onto more trenches west of the salient tip. Perhaps two hundred yards of the salient's defenses remained held by Federal troops.

Now the Union brigadier general Emory Upton led his men into the killing ground of the West Angle. "The rain was still falling in torrents and held the country about in obscurity," recalled a Pennsylvania soldier in Upton's leading regiment, the 95th. A Maine soldier remembered the bullets falling among the advancing lines: "The spurts of dirt were as constant as the pattering drops of a summer shower, while overhead the swish and hum of the passing bullets was like a swarm of bees." The bluecoats took a terrible volley from the Confederates, who had gotten to the trenches a few steps ahead of them. But driven by Upton's fierce determination, the Pennsylvanians, reinforced by men from the 5th Maine, 121st New York, and 96th Pennsylvania, held on. "It seemed impossible that troops could stand so severe a fire," remembered F. W. Morse, a New York staff officer. "I sat on my horse thinking that if I lived fifteen minutes I would do better than I could hope for."

Seeking to break what was shaping up as a bloody stalemate along the lines, Upton ordered a nearby battery to send some guns up to point-blank range. Twice the astonished artillery officer refused this suicidal order, and not until the Sixth Corps commander himself, Horatio Wright, delivered the directive were two guns brought up to the firing line. Edwin Mason, an officer in the 5th Maine, recalled, "One battery of the Fifth United States Artillery was in action close to the breastworks near where I stood, the muzzles of the guns protruding into the very faces of the enemy." Twenty-three enlisted men and one officer rode in with the battery. In the time it took to fire fourteen rounds, all but two of these were shot down. Sergeant William E. Lines, one of the surviving pair, remembered, "The effect of our canister upon the Confederates was terrible; they were evidently trying to strengthen their first line from the second when we opened on them, and you can imagine the execution at that distance."

Warren's Fifth Corps was under orders to threaten Lee's left in order to prevent the Confederate general from stripping it of troops to support his crumpled center. Warren dutifully began a long-range bombardment of the enemy line soon after daylight, but he was reluctant to commit his infantry. Starting at 8:00 A.M., Meade sent Warren a series of increasingly strident communications urging that a full-scale attack be launched. Warren's continued stalling prompted Meade to complain to Grant, who, at 10:40, wired a reply: "If Warren fails to attack promptly . . . relieve him."

By this time, however, Warren had his men moving across the corpse-littered face of Laurel Hill. The attacks failed. "Lost very heavily," Warren later reported. Young Henry B. James, who had defied his father to reenlist with the 32nd Massachusetts, remembered, "What a shower of death came down upon us!"

By midday Robert E. Lee realized that his counterattacks had stalled. As a precautionary measure on May 11, following Upton's briefly successful assault, Lee had had his engineers lay out a new defensive line across the salient base, one that would eliminate the bulge altogether. Now the Confederate army commander ordered that the line be completed quickly. Provost units spread out to catch unwounded stragglers and then herd them to the task, joining with pioneer units to clear fields of fire, dig trenches, and pile up new log fortifications. But until this new line was ready, the salient would have to be held.

In a tactical sense, the battle was over. Lee had invested as many men as he was willing in order to try to close the breach and had fallen short by two hundred yards. The Federals had probed in vain all along Lee's line and found no weakness, and were gaining no further advantage with the piece of the salient they already held. Tactically the battle was over, but the fighting had slipped beyond tactics, beyond winning or losing; it had slithered past whatever control rational men can have over something as irrational as organized slaughter. A pandora's box of hate and killing lust had been blown open, and seventeen more hours would go by before the exhausted men let

*it close again. Along those two hundred yards of mutually held
trenches, men now killed each other with zealous abandon. In a war
that had birthed its share of bloody angles, this day and the morning
of the next at Spotsylvania would give birth to the bloodiest of
them all.*

"I never expect to be fully believed when I tell what I saw of the
horrors of Spotsylvania," wrote Thomas Hyde, a Sixth Corps staff officer. A North Carolina soldier trying to find the words to describe
what he had seen to his "sweet darling wife" finally scribbled, "The
battle of thursday was one of the bloodiest that ever dyed God's foot-
stool with human gore."

Something of a pattern now emerged. Confederate squads huddled in their rain-filled trenches and bunkers, firing as accurately and
as quickly as they could. A fresh batch of Federals would appear on
the scene and lunge forward, at which time the scattered Confederates would swarm up from their holes to beat back the assault. Then,
as the Federals retreated, a brief lull might set in, during which the
living on both sides would lever bodies out of their way. Then the
firing would increase again, and the combat-weary Confederates
would hunch down to await the next attack. It went on all through
the afternoon, evening, and night, and into the next morning.

Robert Robertson (an aide to Nelson Miles): "The 'horseshoe'
was a boiling, bubbling and hissing caldron of death. . . . To advance was impossible, to retreat was death. . . . Clubbed muskets,
and bayonets were the modes of fighting for those who had used up
their cartridges, and frenzy seemed to possess the yelling, demonic
hordes on either side."

St. Clair A. Mulholland (116th Pennsylvania): "The drenching,
chilling rain that fell during the day had no effect on the incessant
fire. . . . Men fired into each other[']s faces, were shot through the
crevices of the logs, bayoneted over the top of the works."

G. W. Nichols (61st Georgia): "This battle was the worst slaughter I ever saw. . . . Such groans! such cries! and such pitiful calls for
water and other assistance; but none could go to them, for the enemy would not let us go and we would not let them go."

G. Norton Galloway (95th Pennsylvania): "A daring lieutenant
in one of our left companies leaped upon the breastwork, took a rifle
that was handed to him, and discharged it among the foe. In like

manner he discharged another, and was in the act of firing a third when his cap flew up in the air, and his body pitched headlong among the enemy."

Berry Benson (1st South Carolina): "Where the lines over-lapped, the men said they and the enemy both fired without show-ing their heads above the work, which was certain death. Guns were loaded, held up to the breastwork, depressed, and the trigger pulled with the thumb. One man . . . told me he several times took in his hand the barrel of a gun pointing down on him, held it up till it was fired and then let it go."

Anything to break the stalemate. At 1:00 P.M., Major Nathan Church of the 26th Michigan led a hundred men in a nerve-racking crawl along the outer base of the logworks, heading westward from the Union-held apex. His men got into position directly in front of the lines manned by McGowan's South Carolina brigade and, at a signal, jumped up to fire a volley in the faces of the surprised Confederates. Alerted by the signal, waves of Sixth Corps troops pressed forward to force the line, but in the end nothing was gained.

At different places along the embattled lines, at various times throughout the day and evening, white cloths suddenly fluttered in the air and men paused in their killing. In some cases there was treachery involved, and the first men on the other side to stand up in the clear were shot down. In other cases, one side implored the other to surrender and end the fighting. "To those who reflected a moment," noted a South Carolina soldier, "it should have been plain that we were deceiving ourselves. . . . So the two lines stood, bawl-ing, gesticulating, arguing, and what not. At length a gun was fired. . . . All of both lines joined in, and the roar of battle was renewed."

Anything to break the stalemate. At around 3:00 P.M., Federal artillerymen introduced a new weapon of war to the Eastern The-ater — the coehorn mortar. Weighing just under three hundred pounds when mounted into its woodblock base, the weapon was a bronze tube with a bore diameter of less than six inches, fixed to fire at a set elevation of forty-five degrees. It threw a seventeen-pound shot in a high, arching trajectory, enabling cannoneers to drop their rounds into the trenches and bunkers — something not possible with the flat trajectory fire of standard cannon. One observer from Maine claimed that "the mortar shells were dropped into that angle with fearful effect," though a Rhode Island man wrote home afterward that a few of the shells exploded prematurely, killing some Union soldiers.

Emory Upton was ready to try anything to break the impasse. If close-in artillery could not do the job, then perhaps the men might be *inspired* to fight harder. A member of his staff, sent to bring up the brigade band, found it about a mile to the rear. "We didn't enlist to play in a fight," one of the musicians protested as the group was herded forward. After some "skillful maneuvering," the staff officer tucked the band into a gully within sight of the brigade and went off to report his success to Upton. By now the brigadier had thought better of his idea, however, and countermanded the order. "The aide returned to the point where he had left his musicians, when lo! not a 'horn' was to be seen. On looking across the bare fields about a mile to the rear, the coat-tails of some two or three (the others were probably in advance of them) were seen flapping in the breeze as they disappeared below the horizon."

Even as he labored selflessly to save his army, Robert E. Lee was struck a tragic, personal blow. A Confederate captain, W. Gordon McCabe, watched as "a courier galloped up with the despatches announcing that ["Jeb"] Stuart had been mortally wounded and was dying. General Lee was evidently greatly affected, and said slowly, as he folded up the despatch, 'General Stuart has been mortally wounded; a most valuable and able officer.' Then, after a moment, he added in a voice of deep feeling, 'He never brought me a piece of false information' — turned and looked away."

O. B. Curtis (24th Michigan): "Standing in deep mud and keeping up a constant fire for hours and till after midnight, the men's muskets became so foul that details were made for cleaning the guns while their comrades kept up the fire. The men were so weary . . . that some lay down in the mud under the enemy's fire and slept soundly amid the thunders of battle."

John Gordon (Confederate officer): "As Confederates fell their bodies rolled into the ditch, and upon their bleeding forms their living comrades stood, beating back Grant's furiously charging columns. . . . The coming of the darkness failed to check the raging battle. It only served to increase the awful terror of the scene."

Henry Roback (152nd New York): "The dead, dying and wounded are lying literally in heaps, hideous to look at. The writhing of the wounded and dying who lay beneath the dead bodies, moved the whole mass. . . . It is long past midnight before the firing has ceased in front of the Second Corps."

Virginian John Casler worked with the soldiers who were toiling to finish Lee's new line of entrenchments across the base of the salient. He remembered, "Generals Lee and Ewell walked up and down the line all night encouraging the men to work, and telling us that 'the fate of the army depended on having that line done by daylight,' and I knew by the way they acted that it was a critical time."

> Robert Park (12th Alabama): "It was a night of unrest, of misery, of horror. The standing men would occasionally hear a comrade utter an exclamation as a stray bullet from the enemy pierced some part of his body. . . . And it was well that the men were kept standing, as I saw many of them walking first by the right flank and then by the left flank, and in a profound sleep, wholly unconscious of what they were doing. These were hours that tried men's souls."

Sometime after 2:00 A.M. on the morning of May 13, whispered orders came to the Confederates in the salient to pull back to the new line. "We quietly left with only a few stray bullets following," wrote Colonel Joseph Brown of South Carolina.

Even as Lee's men were withdrawing to safety, a courier brought the general the inevitable message. "Jeb" Stuart was dead. Lee sat silently in his tent, "communing with his own heart and memory. When one of his staff entered, and spoke of Stuart, General Lee said, in a low voice, 'I can scarcely think of him without weeping.'"

Weary Federals along the salient lines did not hear the Confederates leave. "We watched for the dawn and then cautiously peered over the earthworks," recalled Captain Mason Tyler of Massachusetts. "They had so quietly stolen away that we were not aware they had gone."

FRIDAY, MAY 13

Daylight came, and the living took stock. "What a tired, wet, dirty, hungry crowd the Regiment was on the morning of the 13th of May!" a member of the 19th Maine exclaimed. On the Confederate side, hungry survivors enjoyed feasts from captured Yankee haversacks.

"These luxuries contributed as much as any material agency to recover and sustain the spirits and physical energies of the men in a
campaign that had taxed both to their utmost limit," one of Lee's
sharpshooters proclaimed.

For the doctors working in the field hospitals, there was no rest
this day. "I am so exhausted and nervous, it is difficult to express
myself; am operating day and night," a Union surgeon wrote. Everywhere there were wounded men looking for help.

At first Grant thought Lee was retreating, and he worried about organizing a pursuit. But reports soon arrived indicating that Lee had
only taken up "a new position in rear of the works which had been
captured from him." Then, according to Horace Porter, "The general
busied himself principally with inquiries about the care of the
wounded and the burial of the killed." Grant also wrote to the secretary of war, proposing a number of promotions, among them one
for George Meade. This provoked a sharp reaction from some outspoken members of Grant's staff, who argued that Meade wielded no
true command authority and urged that Grant himself take up the
reins of the Army of the Potomac. Grant waved their arguments away.
"I am commanding all the armies," he said, "and I cannot neglect
others by giving my time exclusively to the Army of the Potomac."
Grant also found time to pen a letter to his wife, Julia. "The world
has never seen so bloody or so protracted a battle as the one being
fought and I hope never will again," he wrote. "The enemy were
really whipped yesterday but their situation is desperate beyond anything heretofore known. To lose this battle they lose their cause."

Robert E. Lee measured the damage and worked to refit his army.
Three local farmers offered two thousand bushels of corn to feed the
horses. Lee gratefully sent wagons and a North Carolina regiment to
fetch it. And there were reports to make. To War Secretary Seddon,
Lee wired, "The enemy today has apparently been engaged in burying his dead & caring for his wounded." To Jefferson Davis he sent a
request for more troops. "We are outnumbered & constant labor is
impairing the efficiency of the men," Lee warned. Then he had to
cope with the serious losses among his divisional and brigade officers.
Johnson and Steuart had been captured, Perrin was dead, and Junius
Daniel had been mortally wounded. Less seriously hurt were James
Walker, Samuel McGowan, R. D. Johnston, and Stephen Ramseur.

A. P. Hill was still sick, and the strain of the campaign was beginning to catch up with Richard Ewell. A credo that Lee had expressed earlier in the war helped carry him through this dark time: "There is a true glory and a true honor; the glory of duty done."

In the daylight, with the shooting over and the Confederates gone, Union men could walk about the salient. No one was quite prepared for what he saw. "Oh, God, what a sight," a Pennsylvanian wrote in his diary. A Vermont soldier noted, "On the slope in front of the angle lay dead bodies of men and horses so riddled with bullets that they flattened out on the ground. Not a blade of grass, twig or shrub left standing; the face of the gun carriages and caissons toward the enemy was sheeted with lead from striking bullets."

Then there was the tree. Located just behind the Confederate lines, approximately three hundred yards west of the salient's apex, the oak had stood tall with a base diameter of some twenty-two inches. Throughout the savage fighting of May 12, bullet after bullet had chewed into the bark of the tree. Sometime between midnight and 2:00 A.M., the tree had come crashing down, its trunk shredded away solely by rifle fire. The death of this tree touched the soldiers in a curiously personal way. Virtually every account of the Bloody Angle makes careful mention of it. In a campaign that was piling up the casualty statistics to the point where they no longer had any meaning, the death of this single tree was a way of measuring a scale of combat that surpassed understanding.

When the final count was made, it would be calculated that the May 12 fighting had cost Grant's army 6,820 killed, wounded, or missing. Among them was Lieutenant Colonel Waldo Merriam of Massachusetts, whose hand-drawn map had been all the guidance Francis Barlow could find to direct his charge. Barlow himself had survived, unwounded, and retrieved his personal belongings from the friend who was holding them for him. On the list of mortally wounded was Pennsylvania captain Richard Rogers, who had paced the waiting Sixth Corps lines, offering his right arm to avoid action that day. Gone and presumed dead was Colonel Richard Dale of the 116th Pennsylvania. At Chancellorsville on May 4, Dale's melancholy reverie on the unburied bones of the Union dead had touched many in his regiment. His own body was never identified. In the small 10th New York Battalion, old-timers noted that a number of recent recruits had not

made it through. "In some instances the time elapsing between joining the battalion and being killed or wounded in action was counted
by hours."

Richmond

Confederate officialdom turned out in force for the funeral of "Jeb"
Stuart when it got under way at 5:00 P.M. at Saint James's Church. A
Virginia officer who was present noted, "Both Houses of Congress
attended, and occupied either side of the central aisle, immediately
in rear of the seat taken by President Davis and his cabinet. . . .
Hundreds of sad-faced soldiers and citizens filled the part of the room
not occupied by the vast concourse of ladies."

Stuart's body lay in a closed metallic coffin "covered with white
flowers, surmounted by a cross of evergreen interspaced with lilies of
the valley and sprigs of laurel." There was no band or military escort
in the procession that drew up to the church, since all the able-bodied
males were manning Richmond's defenses. A portion of the Episcopal
service was read, followed by a hymn and a prayer. "As if to add to
the solemnity of the occasion," said John Reagan, the Confederate
postmaster general, "while the funeral services were going on the
noise of the enemy's cannon made it partially difficult to hear what
was said." Then the coffin was carried outside and borne off to the
Hollywood Cemetery. More words were spoken over the body, which
was then interred in a vault. As the funeral party left the cemetery,
rain began to fall again.

One official not present was War Clerk John Jones, who spent
part of this day preparing for the siege of Richmond, an event that
seemed highly likely, given Sheridan's force perched at the capital's
northern gate and Butler's army threatening the city from the south.
Remembered Jones, "I directed my wife to lay out all the money
about the house in provisions. . . . It is too late now for the evacuation of Richmond and a *desperate* defense will be made."

Washington

This evening everyone in Washington was talking about Grant's May
11 dispatch from Spotsylvania. One phrase, reworked slightly by a
newspaper editor to make for a better quotation, had such a defiant
ring to it that it struck a common chord. Headline after headline ban-
nered it: "I PROPOSE TO FIGHT IT OUT ON THIS LINE IF IT TAKES ALL
SUMMER." "In the evening of the day on which the letter was received," wrote one correspondent, Noah Brooks, "Washington had

broken loose with a tremendous demonstration of joy. . . . There was something like delirium in the air. Everybody seemed to think that the war was coming to an end right away."

Spotsylvania

Soon after 8:00 P.M., George Meade issued marching orders that substantially reoriented the Union forces at Spotsylvania. Warren and Wright were to pull their corps out of line on the Union right and move them to the rear and east in order to take up a new position on the Union left. Before this, the Federals had held a semicircular line north of Spotsylvania, with the order of the corps (from Union right to left) being Warren-Wright-Hancock-Burnside. The move resulted in the whole army's twisting its position to a line running roughly north to south and located *east* of Spotsylvania, in the new configuration Hancock-Burnside-Warren-Wright. As Meade's chief of staff, Andrew Humphreys, later explained, "A movement . . . by the left promised an opportunity of attacking Lee's right before it could be reinforced from his left or his intrenchments extended, and . . . at the same time it would cover our hospitals and communication with . . . Washington. General Warren was directed to move his corps immediately after dark on the 13th. . . . The Sixth Corps was directed to follow the Fifth. . . . General Hancock was directed to be prepared to attack at four A.M. on his front, but not to attack until ordered. General Burnside was instructed similarly to General Hancock."

Despite Warren's best efforts, it was not until 9:30 P.M. that the Fifth Corps began its march. Robert Tilney, a staff officer, remembered, "It was a terrible night." A Massachusetts soldier in the 22nd added, "The roads were miry and the rain and mist made the darkness impenetrable. Fires were built to guide the column, but were extinguished by the rain." Straggling was pervasive. Said a Pennsylvanian in the 118th, "On the slightest break in the column those in advance would disappear entirely and what was behind would be compelled to halt until somebody found them or by some accident they made connection with the advance."

Four A.M. — the time designated for the attack — came, and only pieces of Warren's corps were in position. Some twelve hundred "fagged out men" of Charles Griffin's division were on hand; three hours later, Lysander Cutler managed to round up thirteen hundred mud-caked soldiers from his division. As Andrew Humphreys later

summed it up, "It was not practicable to get the command in condition for offensive operations that day. The attack was therefore
cancelled."

SATURDAY, MAY 14

Dawn came, and the Confederate troops on the left of Lee's lines
realized that the Federals opposite them had departed during
the night. A gunner in the Bedford Light Artillery remembered,
"We . . . went over the breastworks and out on the field of battle.
Our men searched for watches, rings, money and hats." At 12:30
P.M., Lee responded to a scouting report received from Richard Ewell, the Second Corps commander, whose men held the center of the
Confederate position: "The enemy is making movements here which
are not yet to be fully understood. He seems to be extending to our
right."

Men found time to write letters. Young C. Seton Fleming, an officer
in the 2nd Florida who had helped draft the regiment's reenlistment
proclamation back in winter camp, wrote to his mother, "The fighting
has been most desperate. Each side seems to feel that this must be
the decisive fight of the war." A wounded Georgian named John Everett, from "Tige" Anderson's brigade, headed his letter "Brigade
Hospital" and echoed these sentiments: "So far we have given the
Yankees the worst whipping they have ever had in all the war, and it
is not over with yet."

     Faced with severe losses, Robert E. Lee reorganized his army.
Of Edward Johnson's division, which had manned the heart of the
"Mule Shoe," only fragments now remained. There were barely
enough men answering the roll call in the four brigades (Walker's
Stonewall, Witcher's, Monaghan's, and Steuart's) to make up one un-
dersized brigade, but it was done. This unit joined John Gordon's old
brigade to form a new division under Gordon's command. Everyone
could see that the fabric of the Army of Northern Virginia had been
sorely strained. In John Casler's company of the 33rd Virginia, only a
captain and three privates remained — and one of those was a cavalryman who had lost his horse.

During the day, Federals and Confederates scrapped over a bit of
high ground east of Spotsylvania, known as Myers Hill. Elements
from Warren's Fifth Corps secured the slope at 8:30 A.M. and then
turned the ground over to Emory Upton's Sixth Corps brigade. Lee

was promptly informed of this threat to his right, and he ordered his troops on that flank to dislodge the Yankees. A combined infantry-cavalry force pushed up the hill in the late afternoon, sending Upton's outnumbered command scurrying pell-mell back to the main Union lines. A few of the Sixth Corps soldiers quickly dubbed the whole affair "Upton's Run."

SUNDAY, MAY 15

"Rained again on the 15th," a Union soldier noted wearily. "Rain is becoming monotonous." On the Union left, Warren's Fifth Corps slopped the mud up into breastworks and tried to improve their position. "We pushed our intrenchments forward," remembered Abner Small, "and called them 'water works.'" "It looked," said George Neese, a Confederate gunner, "as if Heaven were trying to wash up the blood as fast as the civilized barbarians were spilling it."

Everywhere men were worn down. A Virginia officer returning to the front from sick leave observed, "Our men were looking very much fatigued in line." A lieutenant in the 15th New Jersey wrote in his journal that his men "are listless and feel doomed."

The troops posted along the Sixth Corps line knew that something was up when officers moved among them saying, "Don't cheer." A soldier in the 61st Pennsylvania described what happened next: "Gen. Grant, on a bay horse, came from the right, proceeding toward the left, riding slowly through the brush, keeping his eye on the breastwork. When . . . the general passed the 61st the men broke out into a tremendous cheer. . . . At the same instant rebel batteries opened, firing shells, one of which burst over Gen. Grant's head, sending a shower of debris down upon him. . . . Gen. Grant gave no evidence that he heard the cheering or the firing but proceeded quietly out of sight."

According to Horace Porter, this day brought some news from other fronts: "General Averell's cavalry had cut a portion of the East Tennessee Railroad and . . . [Benjamin] Butler reported that he had captured some works near Drewry's Bluff, on the James River."

Today Robert E. Lee twisted his army around to follow the shift of the Union army toward the east. Anderson's First Corps was moved from the left to the right of Lee's line to cover the road to Richmond.

While riding around the Confederate positions, Lee and his staff came under fire from a Union battery. The staff officers let their frightened horses open the pace to a gallop, but Lee forced Traveller to slow the group to a walk. "The General remarked that he did not wish to have the appearance of being nervous under fire in the presence of his men," one of the young aides later wrote.

MONDAY, MAY 16

Among the thousands of soldiers huddled in the mud and wet of Spotsylvania, at least two wrote their mothers today. Walt Whitman's brother George penned: "We have had the best of the fighting so far and its my opinion that Genl Grant has got Lee in a pretty tight spot." Some distance in the rear of the Confederate lines, a Georgia boy named Merrill Bowan scratched out a note that proudly claimed, "We . . . give old Grant a whipping."

Phil Sheridan's report of his expedition to "whip" "Jeb" Stuart's Confederate cavalry arrived at Grant's headquarters, and the lieutenant general learned for the first time of Stuart's death.

Sheridan's riders had swung east around Spotsylvania, then turned south on the Telegraph Road to the very gates of Richmond. They had destroyed a great deal of Confederate supplies, liberated a column of captured Federals on their way to Southern prisons, and met "Jeb" Stuart's cavalry on May 11 in a pitched battle just north of Richmond, near Yellow Tavern. In the fight, a Michigan soldier named John Huff had shot and mortally wounded the famous Confederate cavalry leader. Realizing that he lacked the strength to take Richmond, Sheridan had taken his men east through a fierce summer rainstorm, then slipped south to rest under the protective guns of Butler's Army of the James. "The loss of General Stuart was a severe blow to the enemy," Horace Porter noted. "He was their foremost cavalry leader, and one in whom Lee reposed great confidence."

Lee had cause to be reminded of his loss of Stuart this day. Poring over the fragmentary and often contradictory reports of Federal movements, Lee confessed to an aide, "If my poor friend Stuart were here I should know all about what those people are doing."

It was late in the afternoon, around 5:00 P.M., when John Gibbon's command swung *west* out of the Union lines on a mercy mission. As Gibbon later reported, "The division was moved several miles to the right for the purpose of bringing in some 600 or 700 of our wounded lying in temporary hospitals." Most belonged to the Sixth Corps and had been left behind during the rapid flank march on the night of the 13th. Gibbon made his temporary headquarters in a house on the hospital site, occupied by a pro-Union family named Couse. Young Katherine Couse, one of the few Spotsylvania civilians to write of the battle, recalled that Gibbon's staff officers "all took tea. The Gen. only took a cup of coffee from the window. Was too much engaged to eat. Every thing was hurry, and all excitement." The wounded Federals claimed that Confederate cavalrymen had rifled their possessions but left them otherwise unhurt. The evacuation was accomplished without incident.

At 7:00 P.M., Charles Dana, Lincoln's personal observer at Grant's headquarters, telegraphed Washington, "No rain here since daylight. Roads rapidly drying. If the good weather holds it will be possible to move to-morrow."

TUESDAY, MAY 17

Fatigue was taking its toll. Rufus Dawes, a Wisconsin officer, wrote to his wife, "Day after day we stupidly and drearily wait the order that summons us to the fearful work." A Massachusetts man writing home quickly scribbled, "A terrible accident occurred a few moments ago; a man in a regiment nearby carelessly discharged his gun, and killed one man, and wounded two severely in another regiment. Such occurrences are frequent."

It was now determined that the roads were dry enough to break the stalemate. At the urging of Horatio Wright and Andrew Humphreys, a battle plan was worked up to return Federal troops to the scene of the May 12 fighting. According to Horace Porter, "We knew that the enemy had depleted the troops on his left in order to strengthen his right wing, and on the night of the 17th Hancock and Wright were ordered to assault Lee's left the next morning, directing their attack against the second line he had taken up in rear of the 'angle,' or, as some of the troops now called it, 'Hell's Half-Acre.'" Added Humphreys, "General Burnside was directed to attack in conjunction with them, and General Warren to open his artillery at the same time and be prepared for the offensive."

WEDNESDAY, MAY 18

New York City–Washington

Beginning at around 3:00 A.M., the night editors of the major New York daily newspapers stopped the presses for an urgent rewrite and tried to make some sense out of the official presidential proclamation that had just been delivered to them. Written on authentic Associated Press manifold paper, the document made the startling announcement that Grant's Virginia campaign had failed disastrously. The offensive against Lee "has come to a virtual close," it read, and in light of the pessimistic state of Union military affairs, May 26 was to be set aside for a national "day of fasting, humiliation, and prayer." The message concluded with a call for an additional drafting of four hundred thousand men. The names at the bottom of the dispatch were Abraham Lincoln and William H. Seward. This was dramatic, catastrophic news.

The press crews at the *New York Herald* and the *New York World* immediately began to reset their front pages to make room for this terrible announcement. But at the *New York Times* the night editor, Lorenzo L. Crounse, was bothered by some minor details. The wording of the text seemed a bit peculiar, and the handwriting was new to him. Crounse sent a note to the nearby offices of the *New York Tribune*, asking if they had received the dispatch. When the *Tribune* replied "no," Crounse sent a runner over to the AP offices on Broadway. The messenger shot back with a terse note from the Associated Press night manager: "It is false as hell." Word spread among the newspaper offices that the presidential proclamation might be a hoax. The *Daily News* stopped its rewrite and the *Herald* destroyed the twenty thousand copies of the story issue that it had already run off, but the anti-Lincoln *World* refused to accept the retraction, and its presses whirred on. A smaller, equally rabid anti-administration paper, the *Journal of Commerce*, also ran with the story.

When the two papers hit the morning stands, things began to pop. In Washington, Secretary of State Seward learned of the story and reacted in a white heat. Orders clattered on the telegraph lines to Major General John Dix in New York to take over the two papers, stop the presses, and arrest the owners. The instructions were signed "A. Lincoln." On Wall Street, the price of gold shot up eight points, despite the disclaimers that appeared on the wire services. A special urgency drove War Secretary Stanton to demand the arrest of anyone who might even possibly be involved. Today was "steamer day," when newspapers were shipped abroad. If this tale reached Europe, the damage to the Union's financial standing could be irreparable. Stanton's suspicions centered on the AP's rival, the Independent Telegraph Company. Offices of the ITC were seized in five cities and the employees hauled in for interrogation. Among those swept up in the frantic dragnet was a reporter for the *Brooklyn Eagle*, Francis Mallison. Under questioning, he confessed to having forged the flimsies and overseen their distribution. He fingered the mastermind of the plot, one Joseph Howard, Jr., an unsavory, sensationalistic reporter who carried a deep grudge against the newspaper fraternity that had shut him off from the choice jobs. Howard had settled on this scheme to reap his revenge on the papers and make a killing in the gold market.

Mallison and Howard both wound up imprisoned in Fort Lafayette. Howard spent three months behind bars, while Mallison was released after only a month, thanks in part to the ceaseless lobbying of his "aged mother," who, Lincoln complained, was "making a handle of continued confinement." An open letter signed by many of the New York editors explained how the hoax had happened and concluded that it "was very liable to have succeeded in any daily newspaper." Lincoln's reply was to the point: editors were responsible for what their papers printed.

Spotsylvania

During the night, Federal soldiers from the Second and Sixth corps marched to what was revealed by dawn to be chillingly familiar ground. Union troops had returned to the "Mule Shoe" salient.

Only Confederate pickets now manned the salient's trenches. The main defensive line lay across the base of the bulge. This new position was screened by a heavy abatis and bristled with twenty-nine artillery pieces. The cannoneers manning these peered over their sights at broad fields of fire and were coldly confident that no "serious attempt would be made to assail such a line."

Federal attackers moved out soon after sunrise, scattered the skirmishers who were posted in the old trenches, and stalled at the abatis, trapped in an obvious killing ground. "The Artillery cut our men down in heaps," a Rhode Island soldier in Wright's corps remembered dazedly. The attack never had a chance.

At 10:00 A.M., George Meade ordered the assault stopped. In a letter to his wife, he wrote irascibly, "We found the enemy so strongly intrenched that even Grant thought it useless to knock our heads against a brick wall, and directed a suspension." As usual, the soldiers on the firing line saw it differently. Said Thomas Galwey, "We kept . . . holding position long enough for Mr. Grant, or his Lieutenant Meade, to become assured that Lee was not to be beaten by fighting here, either."

Grant and Meade watched the doomed assaults from a position near Battery A of the 1st Rhode Island Light Artillery. While riding over from army headquarters, newly located near Massaponax Church, Grant's party had passed a group of wounded soldiers lying by the roadside. One of the bloody figures had clearly been dying, yet, recalled Horace Porter, "there was something in his appealing look which could not fail to engage attention, even in the full tide of battle." As Grant had stared sadly at the soldier whose life was draining from him, a mounted courier had splashed past, his horse covering the helpless figure with a mass of black mud. Grant had been enraged. Porter continued, "He reined in his horse, and seeing from a motion he made that he was intending to dismount to bestow some care upon the young man, I sprang from my horse, ran to the side of the soldier, wiped his face with my handkerchief, spoke to him, and examined his wound; but in a few minutes . . . he had breathed his last. . . . There was a painfully sad look upon the general's face, and he did not speak for some time."

The news that greeted Grant when he returned to headquarters was all bad. Three spokes of his great war wheel were twisted askew. Horace Porter enumerated them: "[Franz] Sigel had been badly defeated at New Market[, Virginia], and was in retreat; [Benjamin] Butler had been driven from Drewry's Bluff . . . and [Nathaniel] Banks had suffered defeat in Louisiana." In his summary report of the campaign, Grant described Butler's situation this way: "[Butler] was forced back . . . into his intrenchments between the forks of the James and Appomattox Rivers, the enemy intrenching strongly in his front, thus covering . . . all that was valuable to him. [Butler's] army, therefore, though in a position of great security, was as completely shut off from further operations directly against Richmond as if it had been in a bottle strongly corked." According to Porter, Grant received the information "in a philosophic spirit" and took immediate action. Sigel was relieved, and another general was sent to replace

Banks. Butler was a tougher problem; his powerful political connections made him a hard man to remove. For the moment, Grant let him alone.

Turning to his staff, Grant said that he regretted the morale boost this news would give Lee's army. Grant also decided that there was nothing further to be gained by keeping the Army of the Potomac at Spotsylvania, and he resolved to set a trap. As he later wrote, "I believed that, if one corps of the army was exposed on the road to Richmond, and at a distance from the main army, Lee would come up; in which case the main army could follow Lee up and attack him before he had time to intrench." Grant's "first act," Porter recorded, "was to sit down at his field desk and write an order providing for a general movement by the left flank toward Richmond, to begin the next night, May 19." Hancock's Second Corps would be the bait, marching six miles east to the Richmond, Fredericksburg and Potomac Railroad, then down the far side of the Mattapony River to Milford Station. This would put Hancock and his men well in Lee's flank and rear. Grant was betting that Robert E. Lee would not pass up an opportunity to catch an isolated Union corps and attempt to destroy it.

Robert McAllister of New Jersey, writing to his wife and family, said, "I have been very tired and worn down by fatigue and exhaustion. . . . I expect a battle tomorrow. It may be a hard one. It is fight, fight, every day." Meade's aide Theodore Lyman was also writing that evening. "Lee is not retreating," he noted. "He is a brave and skillful soldier and will fight while he has a division or a day's rations left."

During the day, Robert E. Lee sent two messages to Jefferson Davis, both requesting more men. "If the changed circumstances as around Richmond will permit," he said in the first, "I recommend that such troops as can be spared be sent me at once." In the second, he argued that Grant was receiving reinforcements from Northern citadels. "The question is whether we shall fight the battle here or around Richmond. If the troops are obliged to be retained at Richmond I may be forced back."

It was around midnight, remembered Nelson Miles's aide Robert Robertson, when "the moon shone through a rift in the clouds, clearly outlining on the opposite clouds a beautiful rainbow."

THURSDAY, MAY 19

Harris Farm

Throughout the night of May 18, the Army of the Potomac was on the move. Elements of Winfield Scott Hancock's Second Corps and Horatio Wright's Sixth trudged wearily in the darkness along narrow country roads east of Spotsylvania Court House. The columns wound their way southward, moving past other Union encampments where freshly uniformed, untested regiments of heavy artillerymen sat around campfires, watching the troops shamble past and wondering what it all meant.

Many of the heavy regiments were a recent addition to the Army of the Potomac. They represented Ulysses Grant's total mobilization of Federal resources for what he expected to be the final Union drive of the war. These artillery regiments had originally been organized to man the heavy-caliber guns in the forts surrounding Washington, D.C. Given the lack of any direct, substantial Confederate threat against the capital, however, these units had soon found things to do other than fighting. Since they were so readily available to be shown off to visiting VIPs, the heavies had often been called upon for official inspections and morale-raising dress parades. Union combat veterans passing through town had looked derisively on these white-gloved outfits, dubbing them "bandbox regiments" and "paper-collar" soldiers.

Recruiting for an outfit that sported handsome uniforms, marched very little, and fought even less was easy. At a time when veteran combat regiments could barely muster three to five hundred men, the heavies enjoyed a roster numbering between eighteen and twenty-two hundred.

The first intimation that their days of white-glove service were numbered came in the spring of 1864, when the 4th New York Heavy Artillery received orders to report to the Army of the Potomac at Brandy Station, Virginia. As the newly arrived soldiers began to undergo intensive infantry drill, the suspicion arose, and was voiced by a disgruntled New Yorker, "that our *heavy* guns would be carried on our shoulders during the coming campaign." Augustus Brown, a captain in Company H of the 4th, added his bitter protest: "I shall never cease to condemn in the strongest terms the action of the Government in enlisting us for one branch of the service and then, without our consent, transferring us to another."

The welcome extended to these "bandbox" soldiers by the Army of the Potomac was something less than sympathetic. Theodore Lyman fairly chortled as he reported that the "latest joke is the heavy sell that has been practiced on some regiments of 'Heavy Artillery,' which had reenlisted and had been sent home to recruit. Now these gentry, having always been in fortifications, took it for granted they should continue. . . . Then they returned to the forts round Washington, with the slight difference that the cars kept on, till they got to Brandy Station; and now these mammoth legions are enjoying the best of air under shelter-tents! A favorite salutation now is, 'How are you, Heavy Artillery?'"

Once the campaign of 1864 began, the honeymoon also ended for other heavy regiments around Washington. In the wake of his staggering losses in the Wilderness and at Spotsylvania, Ulysses Grant called for additional reinforcements. More heavy regiments were marched out of their well-policed camps, put on steamers, deposited at Belle Plain, Virginia, and marched through Fredericksburg to the front. Fredericksburg, by this time, was one vast hospital. Its streets were filled with Union wounded, stragglers, and rear-echelon men, who enjoyed jeering the fresh faces from Washington. Remembered the soldier behind one of those faces, from the 1st Massachusetts Heavy Artillery, "The wounded seem to delight in making us as uncomfortable as possible. Our band was playing and one fellow said: 'Blow, you're blowing your last blast.'"

From Fredericksburg the heavies marched south to Spotsylvania. When the newcomers finally arrived during the early morning of May 18, they were grouped under two commands. Five regiments — 1st Maine, 1st Massachusetts, and 2nd, 7th, and 8th New York — formed a fourth division to Hancock's Second Corps, with Brigadier General Robert O. Tyler commanding.* Three others — 6th New York and portions of the 4th and 15th New York, which had been with the army since the start of the campaign — made up a brigade attached to the Fifth Corps, under Colonel J. Howard Kitching. Tyler's men saw some action on May 18, when they stood in support of the ill-conceived attack on Lee's new line across the base of the "Mule Shoe." The supporting heavies endured a few stray shells and the sight of horribly wounded survivors stumbling to the rear. When darkness came that night, the still-unbloodied soldiers returned to their camps. All through the night they heard the rumble of troops moving south.

---

*Hancock's previous 4th Division — Gershom Mott's — had been consolidated into David Birney's 3rd Division on May 13.

While the heavies slept, both Ulysses S. Grant and Robert E. Lee kept their staff aides busy with plans for the next day. The bloody repulse on May 18 convinced Grant that nothing further was to be gained around Spotsylvania. He now put plans in motion to disengage his army, slide it around Lee's right flank, and send it south. Lee, for his part, strongly suspected that such a move was in the offing. He called in his Second Corps commander, Richard S. Ewell, and asked him to push his troops forward on the nineteenth to find out exactly how heavily Grant's lines were manned. In lieu of a straight-ahead testing of the Federals' entrenchments, Ewell counterproposed a swing around Grant's right flank. Lee nodded his assent, and the quirky, unpredictable Ewell went off to plan his maneuver.

It was still dark when the men of the 4th New York Heavy Artillery were roused awake. This morning the regimental cooks finally got around to butchering an ox that had been plodding along with the outfit for several days; a few of the New Yorkers had made a pet of the animal and were sorry to see it go. The fresh meat was divided, cooked, and eaten. As it became light, companies D, H, and K were detailed for picket duty on the right flank of the army. The men marched quietly along the Fredericksburg Road, passing a Union wagon train heading the other way. Near where the Fredericksburg Road took a sharp turn to the east, the three companies veered west, passing along the idle rows of a large Federal ammunition and supply train parked to their right. The New Yorkers followed a rough country lane, moving by a pair of wood houses, crossing a small stream and swale, and going up a low ridge crowned by an abandoned log house. Here the picket detail spread out. Company K filed off to the left, Company D headed right, and Company H clustered around the log house as the picket reserve. "The picket posts were formed at intervals of five or six rods, with five men on a post." Hardly had Company K gotten its line established when a squad of Confederate riders suddenly dashed out of the nearby woods. Both sides were surprised and fired wildly. The horsemen got away without loss, but Jack Michael, of Company K, was hit in the hand. The scare over, the pickets settled down for some serious card playing.

Richard Ewell spent the morning organizing his reconnaissance force. For reasons that were never fully explained, he decided to take his whole corps on the expedition. Three weeks earlier that corps had numbered nearly twelve thousand muskets. This day, in the wake of the fearful execution of the Wilderness and Bloody Angle battles, Ewell could count on perhaps half that number. Few of these troops were in prime condition. Writing to his wife this morning, the fire-eating Colonel Bryan Grimes complained that his men "nearly all are fagged out and need rest." Ewell chose Stephen Ramseur's North Carolina brigade to lead the expedition. Behind it, and probably in this order, came the brigades of Cullen Battle and Bryan Grimes, John Gordon's cobbled-together division — formed from Gordon's old brigade, the consolidated Louisiana brigade, and the remnants of Edward Johnson's division — and John Pegram's brigade, which was under the temporary command of Colonel John Hoffman. Accompanying this infantry force were two of Wade Hampton's cavalry brigades. The long column set out on a roundabout route to the Union right flank at around noon. The Confederates first crossed a field where the departing Federals had hurriedly buried their dead. Steady rains had washed away the shallow coverings, and many of the bodies were exposed. "It was an awful sight," one Virginian remembered, "and the stench was horrible."

At this same time, things were starting to warm up for the pickets of the 4th New York Heavy Artillery. A squad of Company D men on the right of the line captured a civilian whom they assumed to be a Confederate scout. Corporal A. Eugene Cooley took the man back to the picket's headquarters in the empty log house. "As we passed down the skirmish line," Cooley recalled, "a few bullets were coming over, and the men were lying down, protecting themselves as best they could." Cooley turned the suspected scout over to his colonel and scuttled back to his post.

Richard Ewell's reconnaissance force barely got under way before things began to go wrong. The head of the column was little more than two or three miles from its starting point when Carter Braxton, in command of the six-gun artillery battery accompanying the force, reported that the muddy Ny River could not be crossed by his cannon. Ewell pondered the matter briefly before deciding to continue the advance without the heavy weapons. In the confusion of the moment, no one thought to send word of that decision back to Robert E. Lee.

Captain Augustus Brown of New York, still rankled over his reassignment to the infantry, led Company H out to relieve Company D on the right. Brown found the company spread along a fishhook-shaped line. As the Company D men headed back to the picket reserve to draw rations, Brown set his defenses. He had not quite finished his disposition when he heard "some scattering shots down toward the left." Leaving his first sergeant in charge, Brown ran across the curve of the fishhook, toward the center. On the left, the Company K picket posts were "startled by the sudden firing of our videttes, who came in in great haste." It was sometime after 3:30 P.M., but not yet 4:00.

At around 3:00 P.M., the head of Ewell's flanking column crossed the Ny River. Soon afterward, a heavy skirmish line backed by a strong column of troops was pushed forward. No one in the Confederate command was quite sure what the line was coming up against.

Before Captain Brown reached the center of the Union line, the source of the trouble became clear. "I saw a rebel picket line advancing across an open field in our front." Behind these skirmishers the New Yorker could make out a heavy column of enemy infantry. Even as the opposing voltigeurs began firing in earnest, the Confederate column deployed into a line of battle. "It was," Brown remembered, "a magnificent sight, for the lines moved as steadily as if on parade." Warren Works, a member of Company K, was cooking dinner when he heard someone yell, "There they come!" The time was approaching 4:00 P.M.

In his after-action report, Richard Ewell stated, "After a detour of several miles through roads impassable for my artillery I came on the enemy prepared to receive me." Dodson Ramseur, leading the Confederate advance, reported laconically that "the enemy discovered our movements."

The three picket companies of the 4th New York Heavy Artillery hustled into some semblance of battle order. Officers scrambled to the upper floors of the abandoned shack in the center of the line to scout the Confederate force. Almost as soon as their column deployed into line, the Southerners fired a volley at the house. "The balls came through as if the building were paper, and several men were struck." Warren Works thought that "it tore away the whole side of the building." His friend John Burns, standing nearby, was shot in the heart. Works "watched him a moment as he gasped his last breath." There was a piece of swampy ground in front of the center of the thin Union line; Captain Brown realized that it would help break up the Confederate formation, and he positioned his men to cover it. As the Rebel skirmishers struggled across the soft ground, Brown's riflemen peppered them mercilessly. The air in places was filled with tiny blizzards of white as cattails were exploded by the bullets. The Confederate skirmish line broke up and ran for cover. Behind it, the Rebel line of battle spread into the woods on either side of the field and prepared to advance.

Help was coming to the beleaguered New Yorkers. In the Union camps nearest to the action, men were falling into line and hurrying up the Fredericksburg Road through a passing shower. The Union army commanders were not expecting a major Confederate thrust at their right flank, so protection there was left to the untried regiments just in from Washington. Grant's aide Horace Porter was asleep at headquarters when he was shaken awake by his black servant, who cried, "Wake up, sah, fo' God's sake! De whole ob Lee's army am in our reah!" Porter hurried out of his tent and met Grant, who told him, "The enemy is detaching a large force to turn our rear." Porter was ordered to investigate and was assured by Grant that help was coming from both Warren's Fifth and Hancock's Second corps. Leading the rescue column were two heavy artillery regiments, the 1st Massachusetts and 1st Maine. Porter put the time at near 5:30 P.M.

The three companies of the 4th New York Heavy Artillery were hard-pressed. Companies D and K in the center fell back off the hill to a fence along the swale near its base. Confederates swarmed over the abandoned log house. Corporal Cooley, who had earlier escorted the captured scout to that house, now picked off a Confederate standing in the doorway of the building. Next to him, another New Yorker fired, and "a man rolled off from the roof." The Southern line steadied itself across the ridge and began clawing at the Union position with a vengeance. Cooley remembered, "The enemy's fire was simply terrible; the ground, which was brown and bare when we formed the line, was soon covered with a carpet of green leaves and foliage, cut from the limbs of the young pine-trees." Immediately behind the Union line, a bulldog belonging to Company D was running back and forth and yapping wildly. "Whenever a ball whizzed by him he would jump and snap as if trying to catch it." One shot clipped his tail, and the dog "went to the rear like a yellow streak."

The concentration of the two companies near the center of the old Union picket line effectively detached Company H on the right. Captain Brown ordered a withdrawal, and for a while Company H fought from tree to tree. But the enemy line overlapped his, so

Brown was helpless to stop Confederate parties from slipping past his flank and getting to the Union supply wagons in the rear. Panic set in among the noncombatant teamsters; horses were cut loose, and men fled in all directions. Brown began to fear that his company would be surrounded.

At about this time, Robert E. Lee learned that Ewell's cannon were coming back. Realizing that his Second Corps commander was risking disaster, Lee ordered Jubal Early to push his lines northward to try to cover Ewell's right flank. Out on the point of Ewell's advance, the spirited defense put up by the New York heavies convinced Stephen Ramseur that even though the object of the reconnaissance had been achieved, he could not disengage without risking a serious counterattack. Ramseur's solution was to attack, and he asked for permission to do so. It was granted. The Confederate officer ordered his whole brigade into line.

The 1st Massachusetts Heavy Artillery arrived on the scene sometime before 6:00 P.M. The struggling pickets of the 4th New York Heavy Artillery heard cheering behind them and "knew that help was coming." The Massachusetts soldiers turned off the road and then "wheeled to the left into a large open field near the Harris house, where we formed." True to their training, they dropped their well-stuffed knapsacks in long parade-ground rows. The 1st Massachusetts artillerymen took a line between the Alsop House on the right and the Harris House on the left. Behind them, the 1st Maine Heavy Artillery pushed up a country road past the panic-stricken teamsters. A portion of the regiment filed into line on the right of the 1st Massachusetts while another portion made a dash for the wagons. Joining the heavies in the sweep was the 1st Maryland Infantry. This Federal unit had been returning to Spotsylvania along the Fredericksburg Road when its commander had heard the rising roar of gunfire. He had promptly put his men into line and led them across the fields to help, arriving "just at the very moment the rebels first struck the road." The small squads of Southern troops that had slipped in among the supply trains dropped what they were doing and scrambled into the woods. Captain Brown's troubles were not solved by the arrival of reinforcements, however: the first Federal battle formation he saw was going the wrong way, parallel to the main axis of fighting. Brown grabbed the misguided colonel in charge and straightened him out. Then another Union line of battle appeared, this one proceeding in the right direction. Some of Brown's men joined up to this line and went in with it.

Things quieted down somewhat as Stephen Ramseur prepared his brigade for the assault. The 1st Massachusetts Heavy Artillery was deployed along the ridge of the Harris and Alsop farms, and Companies D and F were sent forward to relieve the pickets of the 4th New York Heavy Artillery. Behind the Federal skirmishers came the 360 riflemen of the First Battalion of the 1st Massachusetts. "As if on parade, we marched, touching elbows. . . . Into the wood we went in complete line, reserving fire." The Massachusetts line now collided head-on with Ramseur's determined advance. "It was like a stroke of lightning from clear skies," said one Bay State soldier. Remembered another, "The bullets striking the fence and pine trees about us came like hailstones, scattering splinters and the perfume of pine." Confederate fire ripped into the neatly dressed Federal ranks; the battalion commander was punched from his horse, hit by eleven bullets. Men were down everywhere, and the Union line milled in confusion. "With the most terrific yells on came Ramseur's brigade, crashing through us, firing as they came and wounding and killing our men at short range." The Massachusetts survivors broke and fell back to the Alsop House knoll. Among those retreating was Corporal Cooley of the 4th New York. As the 4th made its last stand along the fence bordering the swale, Cooley was hit in the right arm by a bullet that then glanced off his cartridge-box buckle and wounded him in the thigh. With "the most exquisite torture," Cooley staggered back to a Union aide station. It was the end of his military career. "I never saw Company D or the Fourth Heavy Artillery after that."

In his after-battle report, Stephen Ramseur wrote, "I advanced and drove the enemy rapidly and with severe loss." In the attack, Colonel Samuel Boyd, the popular commander of the 45th North Carolina, was shot and mortally wounded. Captured Federals were pointed to the rear and sent packing; they met the advancing columns of Pegram's Brigade and told the Confederates that the Union wagon train had been overrun. One soldier was asked, "How many men you got out there?" "Go out and see if you want to know," came the answer.

Ramseur's pursuing Confederates boiled up to the Alsop House line. Two guns of the 15th New York Independent Battery now came into play and blasted canister into the Confederate ranks. The two other battalions of the 1st Massachusetts held a position on the enemy's left flank and fired down the yelling lanes of men. Horace Porter arrived on the scene while "the contest was raging fiercely." He found General Tyler, who told him, "As you see my men are raw hands at this sort of work, but they are behaving like veterans."

Ramseur's report continued, "My flanks were both partially enveloped. I then retired about 200 yards and reformed my line, with Grimes' brigade on my left and Battle's on my right. At this moment the troops of Johnson's division, now under General Gordon, on Grimes' left, were flanked and retreated in disorder. This compelled our line to fall back to our first position. Here a heavy force attacked us. Fortunately Pegram's gallant brigade came in on my left in elegant style just as the enemy were about to turn me there." A Southern correspondent reported that "Jones' brigade, of Johnson's division, . . . fled incontinently." A Virginian in Pegram's Brigade was less charitable; the sight he remembered was that of "Johnson's division running like dogs." Pegram's men came on "yelling and making all the noise we could." They splashed across a knee-deep swamp, surged up a hill, and held that ground. "It rained all the time," one of Pegram's veterans recalled. At about this time, Ewell rode up close to the lines, and while he peered at the confused fighting, his horse was killed. A few members of Pegram's Brigade helped the shaken corps commander onto another horse and told him to move to the rear.

Now the inexperience of the heavies extracted a terrible price. Admitted one Maine officer, "We had not yet fully learned the habit of the old troops in digging themselves into a hole." Years later, one of the attacking Confederates chastised the survivors of the 1st Massachusetts Heavy Artillery: "Your men did not know how to protect themselves by taking advantage of the inequalities of the ground which they defended." Some Federals remembered this day with a fierce pride. "The men stood," recalled Major Charles House, and "fought just as you see them in pictures. . . . They loaded, took aim and fired, then would deliberately clear the smoke from the guns by half-cocking, throwing off the old cap and blowing into the muzzle. . . . Men were falling . . . but . . . the survivors were too much engaged with their work to notice."

Further Federal reinforcements began to arrive. They were the weary veterans of Hancock's Second Corps. With Birney's division in front, Hancock's men advanced, but by the time they arrived the worst of the fighting was already over. They were dissuaded from making any serious attempt to follow the Confederates by Wade Hampton's cavalrymen, who had managed to bring some cannon of their own along. Ramseur's fighting blood was up, and twice he yelled futilely into the gathering darkness, "Come on Yankees." To their last breath, many of Birney's men believed that their arrival saved the day. Clearly, though, by the time they showed up, the Confederates in front were more concerned with defensive matters than with offensive ones.

More heavy regiments also came up to help, but in the smoke and confusion of the fighting, they did more harm than good. The 2nd New York Heavy Artillery, supporting the 1st Massachusetts, fired one good volley that hit as many Federals as Confederates. Hart's 15th New York Battery added to the mess by dropping some shots in among the Bay Staters. Then too, one wing of the First Massachusetts overlapped the other and fired into its own line. This confusion, toward the end of the fighting, led to the most frequently quoted assessment of the whole affair, passed along in the diary of the Fifth Corps artillery chief, Charles Wainwright: "First there was Kitching's brigade firing at the enemy; then Tyler's men fired into his; up came Birney's division and fired into Tyler's; while the artillery fired at the whole d——d lot."

As night fell, the Confederates disengaged and slipped back to their entrenchments around Spotsylvania. By 10:00 P.M., the firing sputtered out. The withdrawal was not effectively executed, and many stragglers would be captured the next day. Captain Brown of New York prowled the dark woods, picking up survivors of Company H, and soon he and his squad were "asleep in a convenient little hollow." Along other parts of the Union line, weary "paper-collar" soldiers took stock of themselves. When the now-bloodied veterans of the 1st Massachusetts returned to the place where they had dropped their packs, they found that the pragmatic Second Corps troops coming up in support had helped themselves to the contents. Corpses lay everywhere across the gently undulating field of battle. One Maine officer accompanied a squad looking for the body of a popular lieutenant and found the dead of the various companies lying in neat lines, killed as they had stood in parade-ground order. The officer was struck by "how forcibly those rows of dead men reminded me of the gavels of reaped grain among which I had worked on my native hills, but here the reaper was the angel of death."

Ewell estimated his loss in this affair at nine hundred. Union casualties were later pegged at 1,535 killed, wounded, and missing — a costly initiation for the heavy regiments. The fighting had the practical effect of delaying for one day Grant's sidle away from Spotsylvania; then the wheels of war again creaked into motion, and both armies moved. The action of the heavy regiments on the Harris and Alsop farms near Spotsylvania became a mere footnote to a long, bloody campaign narrative.

In the immediate aftermath of the fighting, the heavy regiments chattered in nervous relief. One Union veteran reported, "It was most amusing to go through the 'First Heavy' after their fight. . . . They were very much excited, and were pleased beyond measure; they talked like wild men." Another old-timer came up to one of the heavies and admitted, "Well, you can fight [even] if you did come out of the forts." One Union light artilleryman, Frank Wilkeson, was carefully monitoring the progress of the heavies. He noted, "After Spotsylvania I never heard a word spoken against the heavy-artillery men." When the *New York Tribune* correspondent Charles Page asked a Union officer for his assessment of the whole affair, he got this reply: "Well, after a few minutes they got a little mixed and didn't fight very tactically, but they fought confounded plucky."

Ulysses Grant spent part of this day pondering his losses. The heavy regiments and other reinforcements arriving from the north represented the first substantial infusion of manpower he had received since the opening of the campaign. Only a few days earlier, taking into account the battle casualties and the absence of almost all of Sheridan's riders, Grant's nose count had come to 56,124* — fewer than half the number he had mustered three weeks before. According to Lincoln's man Charles Dana, "When Grant looked over the returns, he expressed great regret at the loss of so many men. Meade, who was with him, remarked, as I remember, 'Well, General, we can't do those little tricks without losses.'"

The closer Grant moved the Army of the Potomac to Richmond, the closer Lee was to his reinforcements, and the longer it took Grant to obtain his. "Lee could be reinforced largely," Grant later wrote, "and I had no doubt he would be." His grand plan had counted on Ben Butler's attack south of Richmond to tie up any reinforcements

---

*Omitted from this count were the thirty-six veteran regiments that were scheduled for discharge when their enlistments ended over the next few weeks.

intended for Lee's army. But with Butler corked, it was clear to Grant that "a comparatively small force of the enemy" could hold the Army of the James in place, while the freed-up units could move north to replace Lee's losses. And with Sigel having been repulsed in the Shenandoah Valley, it was likely that some of the Confederate troops there would also march to join Lee. Ewell's bloody testing of the heavy regiments had not stayed Grant in his purpose; it had only added a measure of caution to the gamble. Hancock would still be the bait, only now he would be dangled not quite so far away from the rest of the army.

It was a small action, hardly large enough to be glorified as a skirmish. It took place a few miles west of Salem Church, outside Fredericksburg. Brigadier General Edward Ferrero of the Ninth Corps put the time at 5:00 P.M. when "an attack was made on my lines . . . by a brigade or more of the enemy's cavalry." Three cavalry regiments detached from James Wilson's division were operating in concert with Ferrero's foot soldiers to cover the vital communication lanes from Spotsylvania to Fredericksburg. Two of the mounted regiments started the scrap; Lieutenant F. S. Bowley remembered that the first sprinkle of the little storm came when "the cavalry carbines began to crack at a furious pace." The call went back for infantry. The 30th U.S.C.T. (United States Colored Troops) came up on the run and was quickly spread into skirmishing order. The white major in charge sought to steady his men and yelled, "Just imagine you are hunting for coons, and keep your eyes open." A voice drawled out of the ranks, "'Pears like 'twas de coons doin' de huntin' dis time."

In his account Ferrero said only, "We held the enemy in check until dark." Other fragmentary references make it clear that a number of Union supply wagons — the figure ranges from twenty-five to thirty — were briefly held by Confederate riders, who were driven off by the appearance of the strong skirmish line. Some small-scale charges and countercharges doubtless occurred before the Confederate force — large enough to cause trouble for a pair of Federal cavalry regiments but probably not the full brigade that Ferrero estimated — rode off without the wagons.

Word soon spread along the army grapevine that the black troops had stood to the job and not run. "Their conduct was above criticism," was how one Pennsylvania soldier put it. By the time a history of the Army of the Potomac was written, the entry for this fight read: "When Ferrero's division was attacked, his colored troops fought most gallantly." Young Lieutenant Bowley had a smaller view of the affair. He recalled the bullets whizzing around him and the clear shot he had at a distant horseman who appeared to be an officer. "I aimed with great deliberation," Bowley said, "and fired. . . . The rifle . . . kicked spitefully, and gave me the impression that my shoulder had been almost dislocated. And the officer? He did not notice at all, but rode down his line perfectly unconcerned."

FRIDAY, MAY 20

Ulysses Grant overslept this morning and made a later than usual appearance before his staff. To Horace Porter he confided, "My chief anxiety now is to draw Lee out of his works and fight him in the open field, instead of assaulting him behind his intrenchments."

At 7:08 A.M. this morning, a Union soldier died at Spotsylvania. The man had been tried and found guilty of deserting his regiment under fire, and Brigadier General John Gibbon believed the execution was necessary to combat a "growing evil." If Gibbon had had his way, one out of every hundred stragglers picked up behind the lines after a fight would have been shot. However, the machinery of justice for the Army of the Potomac decided that this one individual would serve as an example.

Thomas Galwey of Ohio recalled, "The execution took place promptly and with none of the hitches which are usual in these terrible affairs." Whatever courage the condemned man may have lacked in battle, he made up for it by facing death with quiet dignity. According to Adjutant Charles Banes of the Philadelphia Brigade, "He walked unsupported in front of the firing party to the place appointed for the execution and stood with his back to the grave and his face to the provost guard. When the order to fire was given, he exclaimed, 'Oh, my poor mother!' and fell, an example of military severity."

John Gibbon closed his diary account of this matter with the entry, "He is just shot."

A North Carolina commissary officer, in a letter to his wife, confessed, "I am heartily sick of blood and the sound of artillery & small arms & the ghastly pale face of death and all the horrible sights & sounds of war." A Georgian in Gordon's division weighed the good and the bad in a letter to a friend: "The troops are as badly worn out as I ever saw them but still in good spirits. The Stonewall Brigade is played out — not worth a cent. . . . Prisoners we captured yesterday evening say that all the heavy Artillerists from Washington and New York have been brought to the front with muskets. If so, Grant is on his last legs."

Mail was at last coming through to the Union army from Belle Plain — so much of it that one observer in the Federal camps remarked that "the general appearance was one of an out-of-door reading expanse, rather than a vast army under fire from a vigilant foe, though the latter also appeared to be quite good natured, and the bands of both armies made the air resound with music."

In the camps of the Confederate First Corps, officers and men enjoyed a band concert followed by a "negro-show" presented by soldiers in blackface. One Confederate, Charles Blackford, reported, "The music and jokes were capital, the latter entirely confined to the army."

Beginning at around 11:00 P.M., Hancock's Second Corps set out on its march south. As usual, the destination was kept a secret from the marching soldiers. "None could tell where morning would find us," John Haley noted in his diary.

SATURDAY, MAY 21

The Army of the Potomac was leaving Spotsylvania. Grant's aide Horace Porter outlined the staggered departure schedule: "Hancock's corps . . . [reached] Guiney's Station . . . [this] morning after a night march of eight miles. Hancock's advance crossed the Mattapony at noon and intrenched its position. At ten o'clock that morning Warren had moved south, and that night he reached the vicinity of Guiney's Station. Burnside put his corps in motion as soon as the road was clear of Hancock's troops, and was followed by Wright."

As soon as the sun came up, Confederate patrols to the east of Spotsylvania spotted "dense columns of bluecoats . . . passing down the road leading to Bowling Green." Regular reports were forwarded to Robert E. Lee, who, one cavalryman noted, "was not satisfied as yet that Grant's whole army was moving." Lee had, however, alerted Ewell to have his corps ready to march at a moment's notice.

Lee was discussing the Federal movements with Jubal Early

when the wispy-haired officer burst out angrily, "I wish they were all dead." Lee seemed taken aback by the vehemence of Early's hatred. "How can you say so, General?" Lee responded. "Now, I wish they were all at home, attending to their own business, leaving us to do the same." Early maintained a grumpy silence until Lee moved out of earshot, then turned to an aide and said, "I would not say so before General Lee, but I wish they were not only all dead, but in hell."

According to Lee's topographer Jed Hotchkiss, who was riding with Ewell's corps this day, "About noon word came that the enemy was moving towards Hanover Junction, so we started down the Telegraph Road as hard as we could." Lee was not even nibbling at the dangling bait of Hancock's corps. His only concern now was to move his army along more direct routes to take up a new blocking position across the North Anna River, near Hanover Junction.

First, though, somebody had to find out if the Yankees had left their trenches, and at 5:00 P.M. battle lines pushed out from Lane's and Scales's brigades. The 13th North Carolina was out in front when one of its lieutenants declared to a friend, "I'll bet five dollars there isn't a Yankee in those works." Almost at that instant a poorly aimed volley erupted from the Union works, ripping the air well over the heads of most of the Tarheel soldiers. The Southerners charged the line, which proved to be held by Yankee skirmishers who abruptly fled back to the main works, stoutly manned by a rear guard from Thomas Neill's Sixth Corps division.* Both sides accepted a standoff and entrenched until nightfall, when the Federals drew off to the south.

As evening came on, Lee held his headquarters at the Southworth House, near the Po River, for final briefings. A. P. Hill (who was now well enough to resume command) was told to maintain his position in Spotsylvania until 9:00 P.M. unless the enemy in his front departed before that time. He was then to move to Hanover Junction by roads west of and parallel to the ones being used by Ewell. Richard Anderson was to move his First Corps behind Ewell's.

Then it was done, the orders all given. Lee was now alone, save for his staff and a few local guides. One last look around at the scene of so much fighting — Laurel Hill . . . Po River . . . Doles's Salient . . . the Bloody Angle . . . Myers Hill . . . Harris Farm — so much dying and suffering.

---

*George Getty had been wounded on May 6, and Neill now commanded his division.

Robert E. Lee mounted his horse, turned its head away from Spotsylvania, and "in his grave voice" said to his staff, "Come, gentlemen."

(A modern study, still in progress, of Lee's losses during the battles of Spotsylvania Court House suggests these figures as *minimums*: killed and wounded, 6,519; captured, 5,543; total, 12,062. Federal losses for the same period were: killed and wounded, 16,141; captured, 2,258; total, 18,399.)

★

Fredericksburg

From the report of Thomas A. McParlin, Medical Director, Army of the Potomac:

ON THE MORNING [OF MAY 7] . . . MAJOR-GENERAL MEADE ORDERED THAT ALL THE WOUNDED SHOULD BE SENT TO RAPPAHANNOCK STATION, BY WAY OF ELY'S FORD, TO BE SENT THENCE TO WASHINGTON. . . . THREE HUNDRED AND TWENTY WAGONS AND 488 AMBULANCES WERE USED . . . AND IT WAS FOUND ABSOLUTELY NECESSARY TO LEAVE BEHIND 960 WOUNDED ON ACCOUNT OF LACK OF TRANSPORTATION. . . . ON THE EVENING OF MAY 7 IT WAS DETERMINED TO ENTIRELY ABANDON THE LINE OF THE RAPIDAN. . . . THE TRAIN CON-TAINING THE WOUNDED WAS . . . ORDERED TO . . . ALRICH'S, ON THE FREDERICKSBURG PLANK ROAD, 2 MILES SOUTH OF CHANCELLORSVILLE.

According to William Howell Reed, a medical man with the US Sanitary Commission, "In the ambulances are concentrated probably more acute suffering than may be seen in the same space in all this world beside. The worst cases only have the privilege of transporta-tion; and what a privilege! A privilege of being violently tossed from side to side, of having one of the four who occupy the vehicle together thrown bodily, perhaps, upon a gaping wound; of being tortured, and racked, and jolted, when each jarring of the ambulance is enough to make the sympathetic brain burst with agony."

EARLY ON THE MORNING OF MAY 8 THE FOLLOWING ORDER WAS ISSUED: 'THE WOUNDED OF THE ARMY WILL BE IMME-DIATELY TRANSPORTED TO FREDERICKSBURG, AND THERE PUT IN HOSPITAL.' . . . THE ENTIRE TRAIN . . . ARRIVED AT ITS

DESTINATION BY 11 A.M. OF THE 9TH. . . . AT FIRST SOME OF
THE CITIZENS SEEMED INCLINED TO MAKE TROUBLE.

Nestled largely on the right bank of the Rappahannock River,
Fredericksburg had once been a small, charming Virginia town, but
its location had placed it in harm's way. During Burnside's action here
in December 1862, Fredericksburg had been bombarded and looted,
and portions of it had been wantonly razed.

The Federal ambulance train arrived with an armed escort. Said
one of the Union guards, "the citizens of Fredericksburg displayed
throughout extreme bitterness and hostility to the Union wounded
and those who ministered to them. . . ."

ALL THE CHURCHES, WAREHOUSES, AND CONVENIENT
DWELLING-HOUSES IN THE PLACE WERE IMMEDIATELY OC-
CUPIED AS HOSPITALS. . . . AS WOUNDED CONTINUED TO AR-
RIVE IN LARGE NUMBERS, CLOSER PACKING BECAME NECES-
SARY, AND THE USUAL RESULTS OF OVERCROWDING BEGAN
TO BE APPARENT.

Young nurse Cornelia Hancock* was in Philadelphia when she
heard the newsboys cry out the headlines: "The Battle of the Wilderness." Hancock hurried to Washington, where she found that "confusion and uncertainty marked everything." The sudden shift of ambulance routes from Rappahannock Station to Fredericksburg caught
the Army Medical Department unprepared, and supplies were slow
in getting down to the Virginia city. Hancock went immediately to
War Secretary Stanton to obtain a pass to the front, but her request
was refused, with the excuse that "things were in too much chaos to
grant it." Undaunted, she appointed herself assistant to her sister's
husband, Dr. Henry Child. "Every physician . . . [was] allowed one,"
she later explained, "and my being a *woman* was *not* noted on the
pass. . . . The steamboats on the Potomac were loaded with supplies
and dispatched to Belle Plain to return with the wounded."

SUPPLIES OF ALL KINDS ARRIVED AT BELLE PLAIN ON THE
10TH AND 11TH OF MAY, AND WERE BROUGHT TO FREDERICKS-
BURG AS RAPIDLY AS TRANSPORTATION COULD BE PROCURED.

Located on the Potomac River, thirteen miles from Fredericksburg, Belle Plain represented what the Navy felt was the closest spot

*no relation to the Federal Second Corps commander

it could safely land supplies. It began to rain on May 11, the day Cornelia Hancock arrived. "On going ashore at Belle Plain we were met with hundreds of wounded soldiers who had been able to walk from the Wilderness battlefield to this point. They were famished for food ard as I opened the remains of my lunch basket the soldiers behaved more like ravenous wolves than human beings, so I felt the very first thing to be done was to prepare food . . . with my past experience in arranging a fire where there seemed no possibility of one, I soon had a long pole hanging full of kettles of steaming hot coffee, and this, with soft bread, was dispensed all night to the tramping soldiers."

ON THE 11TH OF MAY ANOTHER TRAIN OF WOUNDED WAS OR-GANIZED AND SENT TO FREDERICKSBURG. . . .THIS TRAIN WAS 4 MILES LONG, AND HAD TO BE COLLECTED AND ORGANIZED IN THE MIDST OF A HEAVY RAINSTORM, WHICH BEGAN ABOUT 3 P.M., AND CONTINUED ALL NIGHT WITH BUT SHORT CESSA-TION. IT LEFT . . . ABOUT 9 P.M., BUT WHEN WITHIN FOUR MILES OF FREDERICKSBURG WAS HALTED AND COMPELLED TO WAIT FOUR HOURS UNTIL A GUARD COULD BE SENT, SO THAT IT DID NOT REACH ITS DESTINATION UNTIL 6 A.M. OF THE 12TH.

Cornelia Hancock reached Fredericksburg on May 12 — she later proudly claimed, "I was the first and only Union woman in the city" — and went at once to the churches that were being used as Second Corps hospitals. "On arriving here," she wrote, "the scenes beggared all description. . . .Rain had poured in through the bullet-riddled roofs . . . until our wounded lay in pools of water made bloody by their seriously wounded condition."

Clara Barton arrived at Belle Plain on May 12. She served as an independent nurse, fiercely unassociated with the US Medical Corps, the civilian Sanitary Commission, and the collection of well-meaning clerics and religious helpers known as the Christian Commission. Everything was chaotic when Barton showed up. She later recalled, "I shall never forget the scene. . . . Standing in the plain of mortar-mud were at least 700 6-mule army wagons, crowded full of wounded men waiting to be taken upon the boats for Washington. . . . Each driver had gotten his wagon as far as he could, for those in front of and about him had stopped.

"Of the depth of the mud, the best judgment was formed from

the fact that no entire hub of a wheel was in sight, and you saw nothing of any animal below its knees."

One of the young Christian Commission ministers, delivered here with little instruction and no warning of what to expect, turned to Barton helplessly and asked what should be done. "They are hungry and must be fed," she answered. By now she had filled her apron with crackers and set a firm course for the wagons holding the wounded. The clergyman stood on the edge of the mud sea and asked, "How are we to get to them?" "There is no way but to walk," Barton said, and she plunged into the goo. After struggling forward a few feet, she looked back. "I saw the good man tighten his grasp upon his apron and take his first step into military life. But thank God, it was not his last."

> BY THE 13TH THE CONDITION OF THE WOUNDED IN FRED-
> ERICKSBURG WAS COMPARATIVELY COMFORTABLE. . . . THE
> NUMBER OF WOUNDED AT THAT DATE WAS ABOUT 6,000. . . .
> NEARLY ALL THE . . . WOUNDED PASSED . . . THROUGH TO
> BELLE PLAIN, FROM WHICH PLACE THEY WERE SENT TO
> WASHINGTON.

One Sanitary Commission member, William Howell Reed, remembered that it was very early on the morning of May 10 when watchers along Washington's Sixth Street Wharf raised the cry, "Steamers in sight!" "It was as dark as a sepulcher — as silent as the grave. . . . The men were packed so closely that it was only with extreme caution that we could pass from stem to stern without jarring some shattered limb or suppurating stump."

A New Jersey soldier who was helping to protect the capital noted on May 14, "The wounded were arriving in large numbers from the late battles under Grant, and long lines of ambulances could be seen about every day, bearing them to the different hospitals in the city." A Washington woman named Emily Edison Briggs was struck by the strange quality of the noise the ambulances made: "We shall never forget that peculiar sound, unlike that produced by any other vehicle. Perhaps it was the zig-zag course the drivers took to avoid any little obstacle in the street. . . . The movements were always slower than a funeral march."

Abraham Lincoln was not unmoved. The painter E. B. Carpenter, who was working at the White House on a large-scale picture of Lincoln reading the first draft of the Emancipation Proclamation to

his cabinet, saw the President often. "The first week of the battles of
the Wilderness he scarcely slept at all. . . . One of those days I met
him clad in a long morning wrapper, pacing back and forth in a narrow passage leading to one of the windows, his hands behind him,
great black rings under his eyes, his head bent forward on his breast."

Of all the injured who passed under his care when he worked as
a volunteer hospital aide, Walt Whitman always remembered a
twenty-year-old Wisconsin boy named Stewart C. Glover, wounded
in the Wilderness on May 5. The poet wrote of the soldier as "a small
and beardless young man — a splendid soldier — in fact, almost an
ideal American, of common life, of his age. He had served nearly
three years, and would have been entitled to his discharge in a few
days. . . . He kept a diary. . . . On the day of his death, he wrote the
following in it: *Today, the doctor says I must die — all is over with
me — ah, so young to die.*"

FROM INFORMATION RECEIVED FROM SURG. R.O. ABBOTT,
U.S. ARMY, MEDICAL DEPARTMENT OF WASHINGTON, IT AP-
PEARS THAT 14,878 WOUNDED HAD BEEN RECEIVED INTO THE
WASHINGTON HOSPITALS BY THE EVENING OF THE 18TH OF
MAY.

George Stevens, a Sixth Corps surgeon, always recalled Fredericksburg as "one grand funeral; men were dropping away on every
side." Nurse Cornelia Hancock, writing to her sister on May 20, said,
"The groans go up from every building." A Massachusetts artilleryman passing through on his way to the front noted on the twenty-
first, "Every house in this city has wounded in it. . . . It is awful,
awful!" A Confederate prisoner marching through town was saddened
by what he saw. "No one, even though an enemy, could help feeling
emotions of pity and sorrow at the sight of so much suffering as was
here presented on every hand by the myriads of Federal wounded."

THE RAPPAHANNOCK WAS RENDERED PASSABLE BY GUN-
BOATS, WHICH WAS EFFECTED BY THE 20TH, AND THE RAIL-
ROAD TO AQUIA CREEK WAS PUT IN RUNNING ORDER, WHICH
WAS COMPLETED BY THE 22D. . . . THE REMOVAL OF THE
WOUNDED WENT ON WITH GREAT RAPIDITY AFTER THE OPEN-
ING OF THE RAILROAD, AND BY THE 27TH OF MAY ALL HAD
BEEN SENT OFF, EXCEPT 8 CONFEDERATES WHO WERE MOR-
IBUND. . . . THE TOTAL NUMBER OF WOUNDED SENT FROM
FREDERICKSBURG AND BELLE PLAIN IS . . . 26,191. . . . ALL

THE HOSPITAL TENTS AND STORES WERE PACKED IN BOATS
AND BARGES, AND ON THE 28TH THE ORGANIZATION STARTED
FOR WHITE HOUSE[, VIRGINIA].

The Army of the Potomac had moved farther south, so it no longer needed Fredericksburg or Belle Plain. Some days after the Federals left, a Confederate cavalry patrol passed through Fredericksburg. E. C. Moncure, a Virginian, reported that he "found the town 'a deserted village' indeed; it looked as if some giant pestilence had left the town nearly tenantless; it was sad to behold the deserted streets."

★

Roads South: 2

SATURDAY, MAY 21

─── ★ **GRANT** ★ ───

The evening on which the general met the Virginia lady was free of the sounds of war. Weary men talked quietly around campfires against a steady backdrop of insect chatter, broken occasionally by a distant animal cry. Only the methodically pacing shadows that marked the sentry posts suggested anything martial in the scene around Guinea Station.

The armies were in motion this night. To the west, Lee's men were dropping back from Spotsylvania to Hanover Junction, farther south. Ewell's corps, followed by Anderson's, marched on the Telegraph Road, while A. P. Hill's corps moved with the supply wagons on roads further to the west. For its part, the Union army was swinging east from Spotsylvania, then turning south to follow the R.F.& P. railroad tracks. This route would take most of the blue-coated soldiers through Guinea Station.

The headquarters staff bustled about, setting up tents and preparing supper. Grant strolled casually around the small railroad depot, finally sitting down on the porch of a brick house owned by Mr. Chandler. Horace Porter was close by when Mrs. Chandler came out and began chatting with the man who commanded the most powerful armed force in the world.

"This house has witnessed some sad scenes," she said. (Porter judged her "ladylike and polite" in her behavior.) Mrs. Chandler went on: "One of our greatest generals died here just a year ago . . . Stonewall Jackson of blessed memory."

"Indeed!" Grant remarked. "He and I were at West Point together for a year and we served in the same army in Mexico. . . . He was a gallant soldier and a Christian gentleman, and I can understand fully the admiration your people have for him."

"They brought him here the Monday after the battle of Chancellorsville," the Virginia lady continued, as if the general had not interrupted. "He had been wounded in the left arm . . . by his own men, who fired upon him accidentally in the night, and his arm had been amputated on the field. . . . The wound brought on pneumonia, and it was that which caused his death."

Here her story ended. As Porter related, "The lady . . . became very much affected, and almost broke down in recalling the sad event." Grant rose, promised the Virginia lady that her property would be respected, and walked into the night.

—— ★ **LEE** ★ ——

Robert E. Lee rode south this night in the company of the young Virginian cavalryman E. C. Moncure. The small party moved steadily along the Telegraph Road, passing various marching units of Ewell's corps. Soon after crossing the Matta River at Jerrell's Mill, Lee spotted some soldiers sprawled along the road, and he stopped to talk with them.

"I know you do not want to be taken prisoner," he said, "and I know you are tired and sleepy, but the enemy will be along before or by daylight and if you do not move on you will be taken."

In the light and shadows of the full moon, Lee was just another pushy officer; the men's replies were caustic and disrespectful. Lee waited silently and at last was recognized. "Marse Robert," the men whispered among themselves. "Immediately every man rose," recalled Moncure, "and I have never heard such a shout, and the voices saying, 'Yes, Marse Robert, we will move on and go anywhere you say, even to hell itself.'"

Lee rode on, finally reaching his field headquarters, located about four miles north of Mt. Carmel Church, at around 2:30 A.M. Some of Ewell's troops were resting nearby. Lee could count on one, perhaps two, hours of sleep before his army continued its move to Hanover Junction.

SUNDAY, MAY 22

—— ★ GRANT ★ ——

According to Horace Porter, "The next morning, May 22, [Grant's] headquarters moved south, following the line which had been taken by Hancock's troops. . . . The officers and men had never experienced a more sudden change of feelings and prospects. The weather was pleasant, the air was invigorating, the sun was shining brightly, and the roads were rapidly drying up. The men had been withdrawn from the scenes of their terrific struggles at Spottsylvania, . . . the deep gloom of the Wilderness had been left behind. . . . The roads were broad, the land was well cultivated, and the crops were abundant. The men seemed to breathe a new atmosphere, and were inspired with new hope."

—— ★ LEE ★ ——

The sun was barely up when Robert E. Lee, at his temporary headquarters near Dickinson's Mill on the Telegraph Road, dictated a message to Jefferson Davis. Lee began by thanking Davis for the reinforcements, largely from George Pickett's First Corps division, which had been hurried northward from Richmond. He then explained that he had decided not to interfere with Grant's march south because "in a wooded country like that in which we have been operating, where nothing is known beyond what can be ascertained by feeling, a day's march can always be gained." Also, Lee feared that Sheridan's cavalry, now prowling near the Confederate capital, might be hoping to link up with Grant's infantry. "I therefore thought it safest to move to the [North and South] Annas to intercept his march, and to be within easy reach of Richmond." Lest Davis fear that Lee was losing his belligerence, he assured the Confederate President, "I should have preferred contesting the enemy's approach inch by inch; but my solicitude for Richmond caused me to abandon that plan."

Lee then continued southward, and by 9:30 A.M. he had established his new headquarters at Hanover Junction. Staring out over the quiet countryside, Lee's aide Walter Taylor had an uneasy feeling that something was missing. He finally realized what it was. "For the first time since the 4th of the month," he noted, "we were . . . spared the sight of the enemy."

─── ★ GRANT ★ ───

Early in the afternoon, Grant and his party stopped to rest at a plantation that commanded a fine view of the Mattapony valley. Grant fell into conversation with the two women of the house, one of whom had a husband serving with Joseph E. Johnston in the west. Neither believed Grant's statement that Sherman's army was steadily pushing Johnston's men back toward Atlanta, but even as they were arguing, a courier arrived with dispatches that confirmed his words. Both women were shocked by the news.

The portly Ambrose Burnside rode up, made an exaggerated bow, and conversationally inquired as to whether the ladies had ever seen so many Yankee soldiers before.

"Not at liberty, sir," one of the women snapped back.

Remembered Horace Porter, "This was such a good shot that every one was greatly amused and General Grant joined heartily in the laugh that followed at Burnside's expense."

─── ★ LEE ★ ───

That Lee's plans were still unformed is strongly suggested by the one order he did *not* give to his corps commanders. Even though the bloody experience of Spotsylvania had made clear the value of building strong entrenchments, he issued no such instructions this day. At Lee's direction, his aide Charles Marshall told Richard Anderson to place his corps "in some good ground on . . . [the south side of the North] Anna, where they can get rest and refresh themselves. You will make every preparation to move at a moment's notice, and if necessary have rations cooked. The general wishes the men and horses to get all the rest they can."

The strain of the campaign was beginning to show. A Maryland soldier named George Wilson Booth saw Lee today and remembered that he "looked very much worn and troubled." Booth stood nearby while Lee met with Jubal Early, and he overheard the exasperated army commander exclaim, "General Early, you must not tell me those things, but when I give an order, see that it is executed." (Booth later learned that Early had tried to have his men excused from some duty on account of their wearied and weakened condition.) Early appeared at the tent flap, looked right at Booth, and muttered, "General Lee is much troubled and not well."

—— ★ **GRANT** ★ ——

Even as he gave overall direction to the movements of the Army of
the Potomac, Ulysses Grant wrestled with the problem of Ben Butler's Army of the James, now holding a peninsula-like loop called Bermuda Hundred. "I fear there is some difficulty with the forces . . .
which prevents their effective use," Grant had cabled Henry Halleck
on May 21. A series of strong Confederate earthworks across the four-
mile neck had "hermetically sealed" Butler's army, requiring only a
small Rebel force to hold him in place. The lieutenant general was
convinced that the Army of the James was no longer detaining reinforcements for Lee.

In a dispatch to Halleck, time-dated this evening at 8:00 P.M.,
Grant complained that prisoners taken by Meade's men had recently
joined the Army of Northern Virginia from Richmond, further bolstering Lee's force, which had already been augmented by troops
from the Shenandoah Valley under Major General John Breckinridge.
The manpower balance was slipping the wrong way, and Grant felt
that most of Butler's men could do more good north of the James than
south of it. His orders through Halleck were for Butler to detach as
many men as possible under the command of William F. "Baldy"
Smith and send them to join the Army of the Potomac.

Horace Porter spent part of this day watching some of Hancock's
men play a game called Jackknifing. The soldiers, as Porter recalled,
would "throw stones and chips past one another's heads and raise a
laugh at the active dodging" — or "jackknifing" — that took place.
Porter pronounced this pastime "a curious . . . effect which the constant exposure to fire had produced upon the nervous system of the
troops. . . . I have known, in my experience, only two men who
could remain absolutely immovable under a heavy fire, without even
the twitching of a muscle. One was a bugler in the cavalry, and the
other was General Grant."

MONDAY, MAY 23

—— ★ **LEE** ★ ——

Robert E. Lee sent a letter this morning to Jefferson Davis, providing
a general overview of the military situation. "This army is now lying
south of the North Anna," Lee explained, adding that General Breckinridge's Shenandoah Valley troops were protecting Hanover Court

House, further south. Lee guessed that the Federal army was advancing toward Richmond via the Telegraph Road. He believed that Grant's command was "very much shaken" and vowed, "Whatever route he pursues I am in a position to move against him, and shall endeavor to engage him while in motion."

Almost as if he and Grant had conferred beforehand, Lee pointed out that with Butler stoppered at Bermuda Hundred, "no more troops are necessary there than to retain the enemy in his entrenchments." Lee urged that General P. G. T. Beauregard, commanding the troops south of Richmond, bring as many of them as possible north to join with Lee's army. Referring to the Army of the Potomac, Lee declared that "it seems to me our best policy to unite upon it and endeavor to crush it."

—— ★ GRANT ★ ——

At Grant's direction, the Army of the Potomac approached the North Anna today on a wide front. Hancock came down the Telegraph Road and took up the Federal left in the east. Burnside moved to Hancock's right, and Warren completed the line to the west, with Wright close at hand.

"The purpose," said Horace Porter, "was to cross the North Anna River west of the Fredericksburg Railroad, and to strike Lee wherever he could be found."

—— ★ LEE ★ ——

It was midday when the Confederate videttes who had been posted north along the Telegraph Road came hurrying in with word that the Yankees were coming. Lee watched the Federal approach from the porch of Ellington House, the home of the Fox family, overlooking the North Anna where the Telegraph Road crossed it at the Chesterfield Bridge. The owner of the house, Mr. W. E. Fox, insisted that the Confederate general take a seat while he hurried off to find him some refreshments.

Even as Mr. Fox returned with a glass of buttermilk and a plate of bread, Federal gunners across the river set their range, sighted their gun, and fired.

The hissing ball smashed into a doorway frame only a few feet away from Lee, who finished his snack calmly, thanked his host, and then rode quickly away.

─── ★ **GRANT** ★ ───

A nagging problem dogged Union movements this day. "The country . . . was new to us," Grant later explained, "and we had neither guides nor maps to tell us where the roads were, or where they led to." Charles Dana, Lincoln's observer at Grant's headquarters, concurred: "The operations of . . . [this] day were much embarrassed by our ignorance of the roads and the entire incorrectness of our maps."

George Meade's aide Theodore Lyman was even less polite, declaring the map situation "almost ludicrous! Some places . . . are from one to two miles out of position, and the roads run everywhere except where laid down." Lyman's anger may have stemmed partially from his being put at personal risk by Grant's solution to the problem: "Engineer and staff officers were put to the dangerous duty of supplying the place of both maps and guides."

★

North Anna

Word that there were Federal troops upstream, along the north bank of the North Anna, touched a nerve in Lee. An unchallenged crossing there could flank his army out of its position.

Lee made a personal reconnaissance to check the reports. Feeling weary and unwell, he undertook the westward scout in a carriage. Gunner George Neese watched Lee clamber out of his vehicle to study the riverbank opposite. The old Lee magic was still there. Just seeing the Confederate general, Neese wrote afterward, made him feel "like a new man all over."

Lee completed his examination and turned to a courier. "Go back and tell General A. P. Hill to leave his men in camp, this is nothing but a feint, the enemy is preparing to cross below."

At 6:00 P.M., two brigades from David Birney's division moved forward through a passing rainstorm to clear a small Confederate fort on the north side of the Chesterfield Bridge, held by Colonel John Henagan's South Carolinians.

As Grant later recalled it, "The bridge was carried quickly, the enemy retreating over it so hastily that many were shoved into the river, and some of them were drowned." Horace Porter thought that Hancock's men carried off the assault "handsomely, some of the enemy being captured, and the rest driven over the bridge, followed closely by our men." On Grant's staff, only Cyrus Comstock was less than fully pleased, grumbling, "Some of the div[ision] commanders do not push very vigorously — too fearful of losing men."

Even as Grant and his staff were watching Hancock's attack,

Gouverneur Warren's corps was fighting for its life some five miles to the west.

Jericho Mill

The leading elements of Charles Griffin's division came into sight of the North Anna ford near Jericho Mill at around 1:00 P.M. It was not an easy point at which to bring a corps across. According to a soldier in the 9th Massachusetts, "The stream flowed between high, steep banks; the road was rough and rocky and the water all of four feet deep." Infantry might wade over, but it would require a pontoon bridge to get the artillery across. Until a bridgehead could be secured and Federal engineers given time to work, any force on the south side would be without support and open to attack.

The 22nd Massachusetts, deployed in widely spaced skirmishing order, splashed over to the other side first. "Gen. Warren was on hand," recalled one of the Bay State soldiers, "hurrying us across, and although cool, appeared exceedingly anxious."

Remembered Edwin Bennett, another soldier in the regiment, "As we emerged [from the river] we were confronted by a steep bank thirty feet high and covered with undergrowth. We climbed up it and found at the top a well tilled enclosure behind a small house. The ground was in well kept beds, about three feet wide, with paths between them. The men were eager to form line and to examine their muskets . . . and did not notice or care where they stood."

An elderly woman came bustling out of the small house to complain: "Gentlemen, why have you come? Mr. Lee is not here. You are spoiling my garden."

The combat-hardened squad laughed and ignored the woman's protest, but the regimental commander, Colonel William S. Tilton, was moved. "Boys," he admonished, "keep between the rows."

Three minutes later the skirmishers formed up and advanced across an open field toward a nearby tree line.

While most of A. P. Hill's Confederate Third Corps rested near Anderson's Station on the Virginia Central Railroad, McGowan's South Carolina Brigade, temporarily under the command of Colonel Joseph N. Brown, held up near Noel's Station, perhaps two miles back to the west along the line. "Great numbers of wagons and pieces of artillery passed us rapidly," one South Carolinian recalled.

Shortly after midday, riders came in from Rooney Lee's cavalry pickets, reporting "the advance of the enemy from Jericho Ford on the North Anna," a point a mile or so north and east of Noel's Station. Colonel Brown promptly detailed the 1st South Carolina Regiment, known as Orr's Rifles, to investigate.

The Palmetto State infantrymen filtered forward a short distance into some woods, moving through to the far side in time to see a strong force of Yankee skirmishers heading purposefully toward them.

As soon as the 22nd Massachusetts began moving inland from the Jericho Mill ford, Colonel Jacob Sweitzer hurried the remaining regiments of his brigade across the river. The 22nd, still out in front, advanced about a mile through mixed woods and fields, swung south on a dirt road, and ran right into Orr's Rifles.

The fight was brief but noisy. "We drove them back," recalled one Federal skirmisher, "and followed them to a rail fence, halted in full view of the Virginia Central Railroad." The regiment's commander, Colonel Tilton came up to the forward line to have a look: "The rebels were seen busy now hurrying off trains, both railroad and wagon." Tilton asked for, and received, reinforcements from the 32nd Massachusetts. By this time Sweitzer's men had been joined by Romeyn Ayres's command, and the two brigades began to fortify a line behind the skirmishers on either side of the country road that ran south toward Noel's Station and Hanover Junction.

The Fifth Corps commander, Gouverneur Warren, was worried. A South Carolina prisoner who was brought to him boasted that an entire Confederate division lay poised to attack the Federal pocket. At 3:20 P.M., when Warren reported this intelligence to Meade's headquarters, Federal engineers were toiling to put up the pontoon bridge needed for the artillery, and Samuel Crawford's division was wading across the ford.

Warren continued to fret. His corps, split on either side of the North Anna and lacking close-in artillery on the south bank, seemed terribly vulnerable.

The quick return of Orr's Rifles confirmed the cavalry report of a crossing at Jericho Mill. Brown's small South Carolina brigade boldly held its position along the Virginia Central Railroad until the last of the supply train had passed to the east, at which time it fell back slowly toward Anderson's Station.

Major General Cadmus Wilcox, a division commander in A. P. Hill's corps, had spent the early part of the day scouting potential crossing points along the North Anna near Quarles Mill. Some local residents mentioned a ford upstream at Jericho Mill that could be used by artillery and wagons, so Wilcox sent several staff officers to investigate. Then he rode his white horse back to Hill's headquarters to report. Even as he was briefing his corps commander, his aides galloped up with word that the Yanks were across in force at Jericho Mill. Hill at once sensed an opportunity. A portion of the Federal army was isolated on the south side of the river, where it could be trapped and destroyed. Advance and attack, Hill commanded.

Cadmus Wilcox moved quickly to organize his division, and at 4:30 P.M. his column marched west from Anderson's Station along the rail line toward Noel's Station.

Between 4:00 and 4:30 P.M., engineers from the 50th New York had finished building a bridge 160 feet long across the North Anna at Jericho Mill. The Fifth Corps artillery chief, Charles Wainwright, immediately ordered six of his twelve-pounder batteries to cross, for a total of twenty-four short-range, smooth-bore cannon.

Samuel Crawford's division was already over, and it completed the left extension of Griffin's line to the river. Behind Wainwright's guns, Brigadier General Lysander Cutler's division queued up, waiting to cross on the pontoon bridge. Once it was over, three quarters of Warren's corps would be settled into the beachhead. Each moment that passed without attack made the lodgment more secure.

Brown's South Carolinians had marched perhaps a mile toward Anderson's Station when they met "Gen. Hill and the rest of the division returning to us." The columns spread into lines of battle and advanced to Noel's Station, meeting no opposition. Once there, the division wheeled toward Jericho Mill, and the men were "ordered to throw down the rail fence in front. There was no longer any doubt of a battle. It was now about five o'clock."

As the afternoon passed without any serious challenge, the Fifth Corps soldiers on the south side of the North Anna confidently believed "that the enemy had vanished from the vicinity beyond all range possible for an encounter." It was drawing near sunset. "The men had their suppers cooked, and were engaged in eating, and noncombatants were peacefully bivouacked in the midst of the troops, not expecting battle."

Out on the Union picket line, Colonel Tilton was uneasy. The main Federal defensive position behind him was dangerously incomplete. It stretched in a loose semicircle across the fat neck of a loop in the North Anna River. The Union left was connected to the river by Crawford's line, and the center was well protected by Griffin's men, who were situated behind light breastworks in a stand of trees. But Griffin lacked the men necessary to stretch the right of the Union line fully across the neck and back to the river. Cutler's division was due to plug this gap, but amid the general air of complacency, the Union force was moving slowly.

One of Tilton's pickets remembered it as being "about half-past five P.M. [when] we discovered in the distance . . . rebel flankers coming from the south, parallel to our line, and back of them [we] could see the dust of a heavy column from the direction of Hanover Junction."

Even as Cadmus Wilcox set his battle lines, another of Rooney Lee's cavalrymen rode up with the encouraging news that the two brigades of Federals that had crossed the river were "cooking rations and making themselves comfortable." This was the kind of opening that Robert E. Lee's fighters had been seeking. As one eager South Carolinian put it, "To rout them would be no great work for a division of infantry."

Wilcox placed three of his four brigades in a single line perpendicular to the dirt road leading toward Jericho Mill. On the right of the division, its left moving along the road, was James Lane's North Carolina brigade. Brown's South Carolinians held the center, while Edward Thomas's Georgians were on the left. Once this front line was engaged, Scales's Brigade, commanded by William Lowrance, was to sweep around the left and catch the Yankees in the flank.

The weight of Wilcox's attack was directed against the Union right, where Cutler's division had yet to close the gap. To protect his right, Wilcox ordered Pegram's artillery battalion to sweep the open ground toward the river ford.

It was nearly 6:00 P.M. when the Confederate attack stepped confidently forward.

Cutler's division was still moving into position when the first Confederate attackers appeared and opened fire. The Yankees had been rousted from their camps near the river crossing, and "some of the men carried their coffee pails on sticks, others carried frying pans containing their partly cooked pork, just as they had snatched them from the fire."

Colonel William W. Robinson's brigade* had just gotten into place on Griffin's immediate right when "the enemy attacked both the front and flank." Steady volleys bit into the right of Robinson's line and began to chew it up. Compounding the confusion, "a bunch of cattle, some having bells on, happened to be between the contending lines. A number of them were hit by bullets and all frightened by the firing and noise of battle, they ran back and forth between the lines, bellowing madly, adding to the noise and din of battle." Robinson's brigade scattered. Its collapse spread panic to the other Union brigades moving on its right — Colonel Edward S. Bragg's and Colonel J. William Hoffman's.† Said one of Bragg's troopers, "Our whole force seemed a disorganized mass, pouring back toward the river."

In quick order, Wilcox's assault had shattered Warren's right and sent it whirling back to the North Anna. One Pennsylvanian in Griffin's division expressed it succinctly: "Warren was in a most hazardous position." Added a Massachusetts man in Crawford's reserve, "The Rebs calculated to turn our right flank and run us into the river."

General Edward Thomas set the mood for the left of Wilcox's attacking line by riding along behind his troops and "hollowing as if he was in a fox chase." But Thomas's Georgians were shakier than they looked. As his line of battle broke from cover, it was staggered by gunfire from a number of stubborn Union defenders. An amazed North Carolina soldier in Lowrance's command, swinging past Thomas's left, noted that "the whole of Georgia broke loose and ran for dear life." By now the Tarheel soldiers had completed their pivot and were advancing over a clover field on the extreme left of Wilcox's line, though the flight of the Georgians had opened a gap to their right. Lowrance's men instinctively sidled toward their comrades, shortened their sweep, and crashed more directly into Cutler's disorganized division. The North Carolinians were helped by two regiments from Brown's South Carolina brigade, which veered left from their advance to join them. Together they scattered Yankees "as fast as their legs could carry them."

---

*Robinson succeeded Cutler when the latter assumed command of Wadsworth's division.
†commanding the brigades formerly directed by James C. Rice and Roy Stone, respectively

In the center of the Union position, Charles Griffin's division buckled and bent but for the most part held. A portion of Sweitzer's right was swept back with Cutler's division, but the rest of his line hung on. Romeyn Ayres's brigade, the next one toward the river, was solid. Over the din of combat, the men of the 146th New York were steadied by Major James Grindlay, who prowled behind them, shouting, "Give 'em hell boys, give 'em hell!"

The two Confederate brigades carrying the right of Wilcox's assault were having a hard time of it. Brown's South Carolinians were initially encouraged by the sight of Cutler's men giving way "in great disorder on the left," but then their advance split, with two of the five regiments "bearing a little to the left, the other three about as much to the right." Brown's battle formation also drew away from James Lane's North Carolina line to its right, and in the confusion the normally phlegmatic Lane jumped to the conclusion that "a portion of the troops on our left gave way." He reported this to Wilcox, who "replied that it was not so, and ordered me to push on."

Lane was having other problems as well. For no apparent reason, the 37th North Carolina broke under fire and scattered back for cover. Earlier in the day the regiment had stirred up a commotion by foraging on a friendly farm and killing a sheep. Now, as the soldiers from the 37th scuttled rearward, their comrades bleated in derision.

All along the attacking line, the force of the Confederate assault was being spent. It was time for fresh troops to continue the momentum, but none were on hand. In his hasty assault dispositions, A. P. Hill had delayed in ordering the supports forward.

At the moment, though, Cadmus Wilcox saw only victory. He sent a staff officer back to Hill with the cocky assertion that the Yankees south of the North Anna "would soon be either captured or driven across the river."

Charles Wainwright never doubted that his Fifth Corps artillery had saved this day for Gouverneur Warren. Even as he observed Robinson's brigade disintegrating, Wainwright saw Charles Mink's New York battery trot confidently forward. "I could not help a glow of pleasure and pride as I watched the little guns moving straight through the fugitive infantry and forming on the very ground a whole brigade had abandoned," Wainwright wrote afterward.

Mink's gunners blasted canister into the faces of Lowrance's and Brown's men, stalling their advance. Working quickly, Wainwright had two additional batteries moved alongside Mink's pieces. This line of cannon also provided a nucleus for the retreating infantry, and portions of several regiments began to rally around the guns.

Confederate riflemen targeted the Federal gunners with a vengeance. The cannon fire slackened, and veteran Confederate shock troops were about to rush the pieces when a burst of rifle fire stunned them from the right.

Gouverneur Warren had not been idle. As fast as he could find them, he was sending fresh brigades into the fighting. The first soldiers to arrive were Brigadier General Joseph Bartlett's men, from Griffin's reserve. Three of Bartlett's regiments moved to help Sweitzer, while the rest backed up Ayres. Bursting out of the woods on Sweitzer's right, Bartlett's men fell on the flank of two South Carolina regiments. The counterattack was led by the 83rd Pennsylvania; recalled Amos Judson of that regiment, "We smashed in this flank at one blow, and this threw the rest of their brigade into such a panic that they turned and fled without firing over a dozen shots."

Brown's men ran rapidly to the rear, while Lowrance's North Carolina troops now found themselves isolated on the Confederate left, caught between the Yankee cannon fire in front and the rifle fire of Bartlett's men behind them. A hundred or so surrendered, and the rest scattered back toward Noel's Station.

Yet despite the fact that the Confederate sweep to the left had collapsed and the artillery posted on the right had been slowly beaten down by Federal counterfire, James Lane got his North Carolina regiments back into line for another attack at the center. Rebel officers yelled to their men, "Once more and we will drive them into the river." Again the 37th North Carolina broke under fire. James Lane had had enough. Even though his other regiments showed no signs of wavering, Lane ordered them all back.

Watching this last wave of Confederate attackers withdraw, Federal officers ordered their men to cheer. "We made some noise[,] I assure you," a Massachusetts soldier, George Fowler, wrote afterward.

The battle of Jericho Mill was over. It had lasted, by most estimates, about two hours. Southern losses were later pegged at between 650 and 700 men, while Warren's were estimated at 370. The South Carolinians, especially, had wounds to lick. Colonel Joseph Brown, their resourceful commander, had been captured, and the brigade as a whole had lost more than two hundred men, out of about one thousand engaged. But there was an even more bitter pill to swallow.

"The truth is," a soldier in the brigade later declared, "General Lee's scouts had been miserably deceived." Wilcox's six-thousand-man division had tackled more than fifteen thousand Yankees in three divisions. The South Carolina soldier continued, "It could hardly be expected that one small division, of four brigades, should rout those!"

As Wilcox's men fell back to Noel's Station, they met Heth's division coming up, but it was just too late in the day to do anything more. Wilcox later claimed that had Heth's men been ordered up sooner, Warren's force "would have been driven back across the river." It was also reported by Lieutenant George Mills of the 16th North Carolina that "General Wilcox cursed out Thomas and the others who failed to come up."

According to his aide Charles Venable, Robert E. Lee had "hoped much from an attack on Warren's corps, which, having crossed at Jericho ford . . . lay in a hazardous position, separated from the rest of the Federal army." Wilcox had failed in his mission, and Warren had been able to establish a strong position. One North Carolina soldier put the blame squarely on the shoulders of A. P. Hill, claiming that he "should have hurled his whole corps in one grand assault and accomplished Lee's purpose." It seems that Lee agreed with this assessment. Confronting Hill the next day, the admittedly ailing and irritable commander displayed a rare flash of anger and snapped, "Why did you not do as [Stonewall] Jackson would have done — thrown your whole force upon those people and driven them back?"

In a dispatch sent at 10:30 P.M., George Meade congratulated Warren and the Fifth Corps "for the handsome manner in which you repulsed the enemy's attack." Charles Wainwright was less charitable in his assessment. Cutler, the artillery chief noted, "lost his head entirely when his men behaved so badly." Wainwright also felt that his gunners had not gotten the credit they deserved. "General Warren has not given me one word of commendation for myself or my batteries," he grumbled. Some Yankee boys remembered this affair with a grim sort of satisfaction: "It was," a soldier in the 32nd Maine later wrote, "the only engagement in which we had the advantage of remaining under the cover of our works and receiving the attack of the enemy."

Abner Small, a Maine officer, had come across to the south bank with his regiment in Lyle's brigade. He managed to miss the fighting, but he remembered the evening: "We lay at length on the ground, or rested against the newly built works, some munching hard-tack, others whittling, and many improving the golden opportunity for writing letters; some peering into the sky through the trees overhead, as if to force the secrets of the morrow, and while all were in their own way busy, suddenly there came out of the silence a low moan, as if from the center of the earth. . . . The moan grew into a cadence, into a song, and from our whole front swelled in mighty voice that grand old [hymn] 'Old Hundred.'"

Night came, and according to Jed Hotchkiss, a Confederate topographer, "The General sent for all his staff and there was a consultation of Generals Lee, Ewell, Anderson, and others, under a large oak tree, near Mrs. Miller's." Whatever thoughts Lee may have had of contesting Grant's anticipated moves were now forgotten in light of Warren's successful upstream crossing of the North Anna. Hancock would surely force the Chesterfield Bridge the next day, and if Lee battled him along the riverbank, the Confederate force would be both outgunned by the Federal cannon posted on the higher northern bank and flanked by Warren as he moved eastward along the Virginia Central line. Lee was not prepared to abandon the vital rail center at Hanover Junction, so a withdrawal across the South Anna was ruled out. What then?

Lee listened as officers and engineers offered ideas. Out of the bits and pieces of the plans they put forward, he forged a solution. It was a novel, even — some would later say — a bold response. Lee's biographer-nephew, Fitzhugh Lee, later described the new plan as "an admirable one" that "showed the skill of the engineer."

For a time men bent over maps as fingers traced new lines to be laid out, new entrenchments to be built. Then the staff officers, engineers, and couriers rode off into the night to put the men into motion. Lee was setting a massive trap, and if he had learned anything at all in the last few weeks about Grant, it was that the pugnacious general would march into it with his eyes open. In a conversation he had with a local medical man around this time, Lee revealed something of the fierce competitiveness that burned within him. "If I can get one more pull at him," Lee said of Grant, "I will defeat him."

TUESDAY, MAY 24

The sun had been up for several hours before Winfield Hancock moved to force the Chesterfield Bridge crossing. During the night the enemy had successfully burned the railroad trestle a short distance east, failing in their attempt to do the same to the vehicular span. Now Hancock was pushing his men across the North Anna, on the bridge and on either side of it.

To everyone's surprise, the crossing was only lightly opposed. By midmorning, Hancock had several brigades established on the south bank. All the evidence seemed to confirm Grant's optimistic assessment of the situation, which he had sent off to Henry Halleck in Washington two hours earlier: "The enemy has fallen back from North Anna; we are in pursuit."

(Acting on his belief that Lee was retreating, Grant also suspended his orders for Benjamin Butler to detach a portion of the Army of the James under "Baldy" Smith as reinforcements for the Army of the Potomac. "Hold Smith in readiness to be moved," Grant commanded, "but to await further orders.")

Across the trampled-down fields and bullet-riddled forests on the plain south of Jericho Mill, Fifth Corps soldiers awoke to find "that the enemy had withdrawn from the battlefield of North Anna, leaving a large number of killed and wounded on the field." New York private August Seiser wandered out in front of the line held by his 140th regiment of Ayres's brigade and was "surprised at the results which our bullets have had; thirty dead, all shot through the breast and head, lie in all positions and distortions. . . . Miserably clad and dirty, resembling skeletons, the bodies look more like lumps of flesh than human beings. Oh mankind, why doest thou destroy thyself? . . . My heart is bleeding and yet perhaps I myself helped to kill."

During the night the first elements of Horatio Wright's Sixth Corps had come across the pontoon bridge and gone into bivouac nearby. Now Warren's skirmishers pushed out to Noel's Station, reached it without resistance, and began throwing up earthworks.

So far, so good, but when the Union vanguard turned east and began working along the Virginia Central line, it ran into clouds of skirmishers, who, in the proud words of one of them, "stubbornly contested every inch of the ground."

Still, Warren's advance, while not as spectacular as Hancock's, contributed to the optimistic fever infecting the Union army headquarters. At 1:00 P.M., Lincoln's man with Grant, Charles Dana, telegraphed Edwin Stanton, "Everything going on well. . . . Hancock and Warren will reach the South Anna by nightfall."

— ★ —

Only Ambrose Burnside, whose corps held the center of the arcing Union line, reported problems. His men were to cross the North Anna at Ox Ford, but the well-entrenched Confederates on the higher south bank showed no intention of falling back. Grant was anxious to have all of his troops south of the water barrier, and so Burnside was allowed to cross his men both above and below Ox Ford. "You must get over and camp to-night on the south side," Grant's chief of staff stressed.

Even as his columns marched off to their new crossing points, Ambrose Burnside engaged in puzzled reflection. If the enemy was falling back to the South Anna, why was he holding so tenaciously to Ox Ford?

At Grant and Meade's headquarters, plans were issued to continue the pursuit the next day. Hancock and Burnside would move south through Hanover Junction, while Warren and Wright would cross the South Anna west of the railroad intersection.

Other matters vied for the general's attention. Phil Sheridan arrived in advance of his cavalrymen and was, Horace Porter noted, "warmly greeted by General Grant." The well-tanned cavalry commander held everyone spellbound with his stories of the Richmond raid.

Meade's state of mind was not improved by Sheridan's presence. Grant had already taken the western officer's side in one argument, and now Meade, who had been forced to order the raid, had to endure Sheridan's glowing recitation. When a dispatch was received from Sherman proclaiming *his* success in the west and closing with the hope that Grant himself would similarly inspire the Army of the Potomac, Meade exploded. Theodore Lyman was there and later remembered, "The eyes of Major-General George Gordon Meade stood out about one inch as he said, in a voice like cutting an iron bar with a handsaw: 'Sir! I consider that despatch an insult to the army I command and to me personally. The Army of the Potomac does not require General Grant's inspiration or anybody's else inspiration to make it fight!'"

Meade, Lyman continued, "did not get over it all day."

Alarming reports began to come to Winfield Hancock, whose Second Corps was pushing southward along the Telegraph Road. Enemy resistance in that direction was stiffening, and the units that tried to link up to the west with Burnside's men were reporting that the way was blocked by strongly manned fortifications. Then, at around 4:00

P.M., Hancock learned from some prisoners that two Confederate corps — Ewell's and Anderson's — were on his front and right. If the report was true, its implications were chilling. Hancock's command, separated from the rest of the army, and with its back to the river, was facing two Confederate corps. If Lee chose this moment to attack, Hancock's fighters — the best in the Army of the Potomac — would be in serious trouble.

The critical moment had arrived; now was the time for Lee to strike a damaging blow against an isolated quarter of Grant's army. This movement was so important that Lee believed only he could coordinate it with the implacable resolution it required. None of his three corps commanders was taken into his confidence, as Lee found himself unable to trust any of them to carry out the assault. A. P. Hill's failure to move decisively against Warren had eliminated him from consideration; Dick Anderson was too inexperienced and Richard Ewell in too fragile a state of health to bear the stress. It was up to Lee to direct the eruption of two Confederate corps from their carefully prepared positions to crush Hancock's corps. According to his aide Charles Venable, "Lee would gladly have compelled battle in his position there. He was anxious now to strike a telling blow, as he was convinced that General Grant's men were dispirited by the bloody repulses of their repeated attacks on our lines."

But attack orders were never issued. At this vital moment, Lee's body betrayed him. "In the midst of these operations on the North Anna," reported Venable, "General Lee was taken sick and confined to his tent. As he lay prostrated by his sickness, he would often repeat: 'We must strike them a blow — we must never let them pass us again — we must strike them a blow.'"

In a private agony he shared with no one, the enfeebled Confederate commander realized that the chance for victory that he had been seeking for three bloody weeks was slipping from his grasp.

Brief, violent combat erupted at two points as groping Union forces stumbled through passing rainshowers and into Lee's trap.

Pushing eastward after crossing the North Anna upstream from Ox Ford, one of Burnside's brigades moved against some virtually impregnable entrenchments held by A. P. Hill's corps. The unauthorized Federal attack was directed by Brigadier General James H. Ledlie,* a man who owed his rise in the ranks to political pull rather

---

*Ledlie had taken command of Sumner Carruth's brigade on May 13.

than ability. And this day he owed his bellicosity to what one Massachusetts soldier described as "that artificial courage known throughout the army as 'Dutch courage.'"

Advancing without supports, Ledlie's men charged into a rainstorm and a storm of lead. The wavering Federal line was shattered by a Confederate counterattack, and "Every man became his own general," as one officer admitted afterward.

Ledlie, who had quickly lost all control over events, let his men fall back toward Quarles Mill, where the rest of the division had dug itself in. Lieutenant Colonel Stephen Weld of the 56th Massachusetts wrote in his diary this assessment of the whole affair: "General Ledlie made a botch of it. Had too much — on board, I think."

Although more than two hundred Federals were killed, wounded, or missing thanks to Ledlie's action, his immediate superior backed the brigadier, stating officially that he and his men had "behaved gallantly." Burnside, in turn, backed his division commander, and there the matter ended.

Even as Ledlie's men were advancing, Thomas Smyth's brigade was caught up in a fierce firefight a mile or so south of the North Anna, along the R.F.& P. railroad line.

Before long, John Gibbon's entire division was involved in a stubborn engagement with Ewell's corps, which crackled through a sudden thunderstorm and lasted well into the night before ending inconclusively.

At last Grant sensed the danger. He was still not certain what Lee was doing, but it was clear to him that his opponent had not fallen back behind the South Anna River. In an 8:20 P.M. message to Burnside, Grant confessed that the "situation of the enemy . . . [was] different from what I expected." The optimistic marching orders for May 25 were changed. Hancock was to entrench his position; Burnside was to halt the passage of his wagon train to the south bank of the North Anna and hold the connection between Warren and Hancock. Warren would probe forward at daylight and fix the Confederate position while Wright protected his right and rear.

Grant also decided to end the unwieldly dual-command structure that had maintained Burnside's Ninth Corps as an independent force. Under Special Order Number 25, the corps was made a part of the Army of the Potomac. Now Burnside would report directly to Meade. "It was found," noted Horace Porter, "that such a consolidation would be much better for purposes of administration, and give more unity to the movements."

WEDNESDAY, MAY 25

Soon after dawn, squads of Federals were scouting the extent of the fortified Confederate positions before them. By midday, a complete picture of Lee's defensive position had emerged. Horace Porter described it: "The lines were shaped something like the letter U, with the base resting on the [North Anna] river at Ox Ford. It had one face turned toward Hancock, and the other toward Warren." The western face of Lee's position stretched some two miles, from Ox Ford to Little River. The eastern face was longer, slanting southeast from Ox Ford, jogging directly east to shield Hanover Junction, and then spiking southward to anchor in swampy ground about a half mile away. While the distance between the tip ends of the position was only four or five miles, Federals from one wing needing to reinforce comrades on the other faced a march of fifteen to twenty miles.

One Confederate brigadier, Evander Law, later detailed Grant's predicament: "He had cut his army in two by running it upon the point of a wedge. He could not break the point, which rested upon the river, and the attempt to force it out of place by striking on its sides must of necessity be made without much concert of action between the two wings of his army, neither of which could reenforce the other without crossing the river twice; while his opponent could readily transfer his troops, as needed from one wing to the other, across the narrow space between them."

Grant decided *not* to press his attacks. "It now looks as if Lee's position were such that it would not be prudent to fight a battle in the narrow space between these two rivers," he told Horace Porter, adding, "I shall withdraw our army from its present position, and make another flank march to the left; but I want, while we are here, to destroy a portion of the Virginia Central Railroad, as that is the road by which Lee is receiving a large part of his supplies and reinforcements."

Early this morning, Robert E. Lee, operating from his sickbed, continued to monitor the situation. In a dispatch to Jefferson Davis in

Richmond, written at 4:45 A.M., Lee sent along a captured Union communication that gave some indication of the reinforcements Grant was receiving. "Every available man has been brought to the front," Lee lectured. "This makes it necessary for us to do likewise." Once again Lee hinted strongly that troops might readily be detached from Beauregard, south of Richmond, and sent to him.

Lee's sickness was straining his relationships even with his most trusted staff members. H. B. McClellan, an engineering officer, was standing near Lee's tent when Colonel Charles Venable emerged "in a state of flurry and excitement, full to bursting." Flashing a glance at McClellan, Venable blurted, "I have just told the old man that he is not fit to command this army, and that he had better send for Beauregard."

The wrecking of the railroads began this afternoon.

Horace Porter rode out along a portion of the Virginia Central line that was being torn up by men from Russell's division of Wright's Sixth Corps. The work here, as Porter described it, was orderly and thorough: "A brigade was extended along one side of the road in a single rank, and at a given signal the men took hold of the rails, lifted up the road, and turned it upside down. Then, breaking the rails loose, they used them as levers in prying off the cross-ties, which they piled up, . . . laid the rails across, . . . and set fire to. . . . Several miles of railway were thus destroyed."

A cavalryman returning this evening from a reconnaissance along the Little River took note of the destruction: "The fire of the ties, culverts and bridges makes a line of lurid light along the evening sky."

Sometime during the day, Robert E. Lee moved his headquarters from Hanover Junction to Taylorsville, three miles down the R. F. &P. railroad. His artillery chief, William Pendleton, read in Grant's reluctance to attack a softening of will among the Union soldiers. "[Grant's] men seem to have vastly less fight in them than when they first encountered us in the wilderness," Pendleton wrote in his diary this day, adding, "General Lee is quite unwell. . . . He expresses full assurance that the Judge of all the earth will do right."

This was Rebel country, and whatever compunction the Union soldiers may have had about destroying private property was quickly forgotten. The rear-echelon troops that had yet to see fighting seemed to be the most eagerly bent on vengeance. The fresh-from-Washington 2nd Connecticut Heavy Artillery was headquartered near the Fontaine House, located on Warren's Jericho Mill battle-field. "It was a lordly old mansion, enriched with libraries, antique furniture, pictures, coats of arms, and genealogical trees," recalled adjutant Theodore Vaill, who ended his description with a grim post-script: "If Mr. Fontaine ever returned to his domicile . . . he found that the army had left him, as a memento of their visit, a picture of *Ruin*, painted with the besom of destruction, on a scale as large as his domain." The Ellington House, where Lee had nearly been killed, received similar treatment.

During the night Grant convened a council of war at his headquarters near Quarles Mill, to discuss the next move. Assaulting any side of Lee's defensive position was out of the question. "To make a direct attack from either wing would cause a slaughter of our men that even success would not justify," Grant declared the next day. Lee's right was anchored in a swamp and thus unturnable. Some officers felt that a flanking march around the Confederate left held exciting possibili-ties. For one thing, Lee — who was now accustomed to Grant's con-stant sidling to the Confederate right — would not be expecting the move, and second, once they were across the South Anna, the Fed-erals would have a clear, direct run at Richmond. Also, a swing to the west would place the Union army squarely atop the Virginia Central line, thus denying Lee the use of his only rail connection with the fertile farms of the Shenandoah Valley. Both the Fifth Corps com-mander, Gouverneur Warren, and the Army of the Potomac's artillery chief, Henry Hunt, argued for such a move. Grant liked the idea and voted for it, overruling Meade, who was urging another march around Lee's right toward the Pamunkey River. This watercourse, formed by the joining of the North and South Anna rivers, would shield the right of a Union column marching southeast along its far side down to Hanovertown, where the column could cross over again. It was a less direct route, but it would allow them to maintain a con-nection to the important river ports, a necessity if the waterborne supply routes were to remain intact. There were other factors sup-porting Meade's argument, including the promise of quick access to reinforcements from Butler's Army of the James. But Grant stuck with the riskier plan to move around Lee's left, giving it his provi-sional approval.

THURSDAY, MAY 26

From his headquarters in Taylorsville, Robert E. Lee this morning reported the situation to War Secretary James Seddon in Richmond. "From present indication," Lee said of Grant, "he seems to contemplate a movement on our left flank." Noting that Sheridan's riders had rejoined Grant's command, Lee expressed his concern that the "enemy's superiority in cavalry will . . . enable him to do us much injury. . . . I hope that all the cavalry designated for this army may be sent to it at once."

If the Fifth Corps artillery chief, Charles Wainwright, had been hoping for a bold stroke, he was now bitterly disappointed. Camp rumor that morning held that Grant had decided to reverse the pattern of his previous two disengagements and push around Lee's left flank to get at Richmond. "But General Grant changed his mind this afternoon," Wainwright wrote in his diary, "and decided to try again to turn Lee's right. Can it be that this is the sum of our lieutenant-general's abilities? Has he no other reserve in tactics? Or is it sheer obstinacy?"

In a message sent to Washington this day, Grant defended his change of mind, pointing out that a move to turn Lee's left would require spanning three rivers, "all of them . . . presenting considerable obstructions to the movement of our army. . . . I have decided therefore to turn the enemy's right by crossing at or near Hanover Town. This crosses all three streams at once, and leaves us still where we can draw supplies."

Grant's headquarters aide Cyrus Comstock was pleased by the decision. He was also pleased that he and other close advisers had finally convinced their commander to rescind his previous communication on the subject and "to order a large part of the force under [Benjamin] Butler[,] now doing nothing, to join us via West Point [, Virginia]."

(At least one headquarters officer believed that the entire futile North Anna affair need never have happened at all. "Meade was opposed to our crossing the North Anna," Provost Marshal Marsena Patrick wrote in his diary this day, "but Grant ordered it, over his head.")

One of the more curious sidelights of this campaign was reported laconically by O. B. Curtis of the 24th Michigan: "During the day a woman was captured dressed as a Confederate soldier." Andrew Crossley, a Union engineer, provided more detail in a letter written on May 29: "She was mounted just like a man and belonged to cavalry though she was taken as a spy. She wore her hair long and did not like to have our men looking at her. Some men stopped to look at her as she went by us and she picked up rocks and threw at them."

The fact that Robert E. Lee had craftily maneuvered the Union army into a position of great danger and then *not* attacked started a great wave of confidence throughout the Yankee ranks. "One would naturally have supposed that General Lee would have . . . [taken] this opportunity to strike the Army of the Potomac a stunning blow," remarked John Day Smith, a corporal in the 19th Maine. The heady wine of assurance now became intoxicating as Grant and his staff began to believe that Lee had not attacked because he no longer *could* attack. "Lee's army is really whipped," Grant wired Washington today, adding, "I may be mistaken, but I feel that our success over Lee's army is already insured." Charles Dana, reporting to Lincoln through War Secretary Stanton, was even more sanguine. "Rebels have lost all confidence, and are already morally defeated," he declared. "This army has learned to believe that it is sure of victory. Even our officers have ceased to regard Lee as an invincible military genius. . . . Rely upon it, the end is near as well as sure."

The withdrawal of the Union army to the north bank of the North Anna River had begun on the night of May 25, when the supply trains and artillery posted on the Federal right had crossed back. Russell's Sixth Corps division had been marched over and moved behind Burnside, well out of sight of the enemy. Also on the twenty-fifth, James Wilson's cavalry division had swung around the Union right and staged a noisy diversion along the Little River. As soon as it was dark on the night of the twenty-sixth, the rest of the Army of the Potomac disengaged and withdrew.

Wright's Sixth Corps recrossed first, followed by Warren's Fifth. Said Horace Porter, "Burnside and Hancock next withdrew, and so cautiously that their movements entirely escaped detection by the enemy. All the corps left strong guards in their fronts, which were withdrawn at the last moment." Three of the last to pull back belonged to Company F of the 12th New Jersey. It was nearly morning, remembered a member of the regiment, when the trio "came in on a lively double-quick."

Horace Porter noted with some satisfaction, "The withdrawal from the North Anna had now been successfully accomplished."

(The officially reported Union casualties for operations around the North Anna were 1,973 killed or wounded and 165 captured, for a total of 2,138. Southern losses were estimated at 690 killed or wounded and 561 captured, totaling 1,251.)

★

Roads South: 3

── ★ LEE ★ ──

At 6:45 A.M., Lee wired the Confederate capital, "The enemy retired to the north side of the North Anna last night. . . . [Some of his] cavalry and infantry have crossed at Hanovertown. I have sent the cavalry in that direction to check the movement, and will move the army to Ashland."

Then Robert E. Lee, traveling with Ewell's corps, set out again on the road leading south.

── ★ GRANT ★ ──

Remembered a Pennsylvania cavalryman with Grant's escort, "On the 27th, Headquarters were up at 3 o'clock and off by 4." The Army of the Potomac was now moving through difficult country. As Grant recalled, "The streams were numerous, deep and sluggish, sometimes spreading out into swamps grown up with impenetrable growths of trees and underbrush. The banks were generally low and marshy, making the streams difficult to approach except where there were roads and bridges."

The plan of march was straightforward: the Army of the Potomac moved steadily to the southeast, along the eastern side of the Pamunkey River. Sheridan's cavalry, stiffened with one of Wright's divisions, was well out in front and already controlling a fordable stretch of the river near the almost deserted port of Hanovertown. The rest of the Sixth Corps moved close behind the advance on a track near the river. Behind Wright came Hancock. Moving on a parallel route farther east was Warren's Fifth Corps, followed by Burnside's Ninth. Grant's goal in this movement was, as he later said, "to turn the enemy's position by his right."

According to Horace Porter, "On the march the general-in-chief, as he rode by, was vociferously cheered, as usual, by the troops. Every movement directed by him inspired the men with new confidence in his ability and his watchfulness over their interests; and not only the officers, but the rank and file, understood fully that he had saved them on the North Anna from the slaughter which would probably have occurred if they had been thrown against Lee's formidable intrenchments . . . and that they were again making an advance movement."

─── ★ **LEE** ★ ───

Lee's headquarters tent was located this evening in the yard of the Jenkins House, near Hughes's Shop. The Confederate general was still uncertain whether Grant's intention was to turn his infantry westward and cross the Pamunkey River at Hanovertown or to continue southward. Until he could be sure, Lee gathered his army around Atlee's Station on the Virginia Central line, where it would be centrally positioned.

Lee also learned this evening that his Second Corps commander, Richard Ewell, was too ill to continue.* Jubal Early was put in temporary command.

SATURDAY, MAY 28

─── ★ **LEE** ★ ───

Robert E. Lee was still not well. Today he moved his headquarters closer to Richmond and set up shop in the Clarke House, near Atlee's Station. Lee disliked using private residences, fearing that they might be destroyed by Federal raiders in retaliation after he moved on, but his physical condition was such that this time, the offer of indoor space to transact army business was gratefully accepted.

Lee pondered reports that Federal cavalry had secured a position at Haw's Shop, a few miles west of Hanovertown. He had to know whether Grant had pushed his infantry across the Pamunkey as

───

*According to Ewell's official report, he stepped down "in consequence of a severe attack of diarrhea."

well. At his orders, a cavalry force commanded by Wade Hampton clattered eastward to investigate.

★ GRANT ★

"On the morning of the 28th," Grant later recalled, "the army made an early start and by noon all had crossed [the Pamunkey] except Burnside's Corps." There was optimism around Union headquarters. Noted Horace Porter, "In each of his three attempts to move close to Lee's troops and cross difficult rivers in his very face, Grant had been completely successful, and had manoeuvered so as to accomplish a most formidable task in warfare with insignificant loss."

"At the same time," continued Grant, "Sheridan was directed to reconnoitre towards Mechanicsville to find Lee's position."

From 10:00 A.M. to sunset, the probing cavalry fingers of the two armies locked in a noisy struggle around Enon Church, a short distance west of Haw's Shop. The cavalrymen fought dismounted for the most part, and the volume of rifle fire surprised even the hardened veterans. "The storm of shot and shell that howled madly over . . . was terrific," one Rebel trooper remembered. A New Jerseyman later called the affair "the severest cavalry fight of the war." Among the Federal dead was Private John Huff of Michigan, who had enjoyed the celebrity of having killed "Jeb" Stuart for just seventeen days.

★ LEE ★

At 6:00 P.M., Robert E. Lee reported his version of the battle to War Secretary James Seddon: "Genl Fitz Lee's division of cavalry engaged the enemy's cavalry near Haw's Shop about noon today and drove them back upon their infantry, which prisoners stated to be the 5th and 6th Corps."

Now that Grant had infantry across the Pamunkey, Lee reasoned, he had several options open to him. He might move northwest to cut the Virginia Central railroad above Richmond, or he might come directly west to strike at Lee, or he might try to slip southward to get past the Confederate right flank.

Lee acted to cover all contingencies. Hill's Third Corps was kept near the railroad to guard it, while Anderson's First Corps and Early's Second nestled eastward to take up a line behind the protective marshland of Totopotomoy Creek.

—— ★ **GRANT** ★ ——

According to Grant's recollection of the cavalry fight at Haw's Shop, "[Sheridan] encountered the Confederate cavalry dismounted and partially entrenched. [Brigadier General David] Gregg attacked with his division, but was unable to move the enemy. In the evening Custer came up with a brigade. The attack was now renewed. . . . This time the assault was successful, both sides losing a considerable number of men."

SUNDAY, MAY 29

—— ★ **LEE** ★ ——

Under Special Order Number 134, Jubal Early was today officially assigned to command the Second Corps. "Permission is granted to General Ewell to retire from the field that he may have the benefit of rest and medical treatment." It was further evidence that the leadership of the Army of Northern Virginia had been shuffled to a degree that would have been unimaginable one month earlier. Two of its three corps commanders had been replaced, three new major generals now commanded divisions, the leadership of fourteen brigades had changed, and no overall cavalry commander had yet been appointed by Lee to replace "Jeb" Stuart.

Jefferson Davis paid a brief call at headquarters this afternoon to provide moral support. Lee was unable, however, to wrangle any promises of reinforcements from the Confederate President, who remained frustratingly noncommittal about his priorities.

Amid these administrative matters, Lee found time for an affectionate note to his wife, Mary. "I have not been very sick," he wrote with forced cheerfulness, immediately contradicting himself by admitting, "but could not keep my horse for some days back." He continued, "I trust God will give me strength for all He wishes me to do."

—— ★ **GRANT** ★ ——

Ulysses Grant was very anxious to get an exact fix on the position of Lee's army. At his direction, "Wright's corps pushed to Hanover Court House. Hancock's corps pushed toward Totopotomoy Creek;

Warren's corps to the left on the Shady Grove Church Road, while Burnside was held in reserve."

These movements, according to Horace Porter, "disclosed the fact that all of Lee's troops were in position on the north side of the Chickahominy, and all were well intrenched."

──── ★ LEE ★ ────

Lee needed more men. Early this evening he met with the one person who might provide them: Pierre Gustave Toutant Beauregard.

Beauregard was a bundle of contradictions: quixotic and brilliant, selfless and petty, the just-turned-forty-six-year-old Creole had taken a prominent part in some of the early victories of the Confederacy. He had a penchant for heroic posturing and a knack for making enemies. Two of his most bitter foes were Jefferson Davis and his chief military adviser, Braxton Bragg.

Beauregard had been in command of the district south of Richmond when Benjamin Butler's army had landed there. To his credit, Beauregard had organized an effective defense and "bottled" Butler up in Bermuda Hundred. With matters south of Richmond seeming fairly stable, Lee wanted part of Beauregard's army transferred to his own. Beauregard, not so sure that Butler would remain harmless, was using army red tape to delay the troop transfers, so Lee decided to argue his case personally.

No written record of the meeting has survived, but at 9:00 P.M., Lee wired Jefferson Davis,

IN CONFERENCE WITH GENERAL BEAUREGARD. HE STATES THAT HE HAS ONLY TWELVE THOUSAND INFANTRY AND CAN SPARE NONE. IF GENERAL GRANT ADVANCES TOMORROW I WILL ENGAGE HIM WITH MY PRESENT FORCE.

Bethesda Church

MONDAY, MAY 30

Yankee soldiers belonging to Warren's Fifth Corps, camped in the fields south of Haw's Shop, shook the dew from their blankets, chewed a hasty morning meal, and fell into marching order. For the second time in as many days, Ulysses Grant had the entire Army of the Potomac probing for the main force of the enemy. "We will find out all about it to-day," he wired Henry Halleck.

From his headquarters in the Clarke family house, near Atlee's Station, Robert E. Lee looked for an opportunity to throw a wrench into the smoothly turning wheels of Grant's juggernaut.

Lee had positioned his army carefully to counter any Union moves west or south. For the moment it was wait and see. Lee's actions this day would depend upon Grant's.

Charles Griffin's division led the way for the Fifth Corps. Skirmishers from the 22nd Massachusetts filed out first; "We deployed . . . early in the morning," remembered Edwin Bennett, "in a thin line of one rank, with the men five paces apart." As the blue columns came to cross the Totopotomoy lowlands, scattered but obstinate resistance forced the Federals to deploy into lines of battle that struggled through the brambly swampland bordering the creek. "I shall never forget our march through Totopotomoy wood, keeping in line, over briers and fallen trees and stumps," recalled Henry B. James of the 32nd Massachusetts. The enemy stands slowed Griffin's advance to a crawl.

After pushing southward across the Totopotomoy, Griffin's battle line swung westward on the Shady Grove Church Road. Flankers spread the line out even further and kept contact with the Old

Church Road, which paralleled their route, about a mile to the south. This east-west thoroughfare led eventually to Mechanicsville, near Richmond, and was also called the Mechanicsville Pike.

Further to the north, Hancock's Second Corps was also pushing westward, with Wright's Sixth and Burnside's Ninth in close support.

By the time the sun was approaching its midday position, Robert E. Lee had a good picture of what was going on and a clear idea what it all meant. Two Yankee corps had crossed to the south of Totopotomoy Creek and were taking up positions on the near bank, facing west. At 11:00 A.M., the gray-haired commander explained things in a dispatch to Richard Anderson: "After fortifying this line they will probably make another move by their left flank over towards the Chickahominy. This is just a repetition of their former movements." Lee also saw opportunity beckoning. "[This movement] can only be arrested by striking at once at that part of their force which has crossed the Totopotomoi in Genl Early's front. I have desired him to do this if he thought it could be done advantageously."

Jubal Early did think it could be done advantageously. Anticipating having to follow the Yankees' next crablike shift to the south, Early had his men cut cross-country traces from their Shady Grove Church Road lines down to the Old Church Road. The cavalry reports indicated that the left flank of the Yankee thrust along the first of these roads only lightly brushed the second. That Union flank was ripe for turning, Early argued, and Lee agreed. By early afternoon the acting corps commander had assembled his strike force. Spearheaded by Robert Rodes's division, it was poised to sweep eastward along the Old Church Road, with Bethesda Church as its goal. Once that was secured, Early's men would be able to swing northward to slice in behind the forward elements of the Yankee Fifth Corps.

Something of Lee's thinking can be gleaned from his admonition to Richard Anderson later in the day: "Do everything for the grand object, the destruction of the enemy."

The farther west Griffin's men pushed, the more anxious Gouverneur Warren grew about his left flank. At about the same time that Robert E. Lee was explaining the situation to Richard Anderson, Warren was shunting Samuel Crawford's division south, down a farm road that left the Shady Grove Church Road near the Bowles House and angled into the Old Church Road a short distance west of Bethesda Church.

One of Crawford's three brigades consisted of two green heavy regiments commanded by Colonel J. Howard Kitching; the other two were made up of Pennsylvania Reserves. These veteran soldiers had an honorable history with the Army of the Potomac, though their fighting quality at this moment was very much open to question. The Pennsylvanians had only one day remaining in their term of enlistment. In fact, one regiment, the 13th Pennsylvania Reserves, was already eligible for discharge. Federals in other regiments who had, unlike the Pennsylvanians, re-upped for the duration harbored the suspicion that these once vaunted troops were no longer to be trusted in combat.

Crawford's men moved southward, cautiously. Around noon they came onto the Old Church Road west of Bethesda Church and almost immediately began throwing up breastworks near a house owned by a family named Tinsley. After a while, Colonel Martin Hardin's 1st Brigade of Pennsylvania Reserves ventured westward along the Old Church Road, a cloud of skirmishers spreading out before it.

Grant's all-out reconnaissance was having mixed results. Wright's Sixth Corps, on the right of the Union line, got bogged down in the lowlands along Crump's Creek, "a swamp and tangle of the worst character," and was stalled "until it was too late for it to effect anything against the enemy." Hancock, facing an enemy that was well entrenched across the broad Totopotomoy bottomlands, had to content himself with a long-range artillery duel.

Jubal Early's move brought his corps past the left flank of Charles Griffin's division, which was spread across the Shady Grove Church Road. The 22nd Massachusetts, still scouting in front of Griffin, spotted what was happening. "Several times our skirmishers when halting for a few moments in the openings in the woods, could see Early's heavy columns in the distance, moving to our left," recalled one Bay State soldier.

Rodes's Division formed at right angles to the Old Church Road and began a spirited advance eastward. An infantryman in the 43rd North Carolina recalled the moment of contact with Hardin's brigade of Pennsylvania Reserves: "Had not gone far before we came across the enemy. They were posted in a slender breastworks, we saw them out of this and they fled in . . . confusion." It was a little past 2:00 P.M.

Hardin's First Brigade was steamrollered. Hardin later described it: "[Rodes's] column, five or six times the strength of the First Brigade, came down the Mechanicsville Pike at a run, its left resting on the pike, and its front extended off to the right. . . . The volley or two delivered by our feeble force made no impression on the enemy; he ran over and around . . . [us], and his division headquarters arrived amidst the headquarters of the First Brigade before the latter could extricate itself. The enemy was so confident of his ultimate success, he did not stop to secure the First Brigade prisoners, but continued on his charge down the pike."

Rodes's battle lines smashed into Crawford's two remaining brigades near Bethesda Church. "We were attacked on both flanks with great fury," one dazed Pennsylvanian recalled. Charles Wainwright, the Fifth Corps artillery chief, figured that Hardin's line held for perhaps five minutes, and the two brigade lines near the church for a little longer, before everything was shoved to the north. In Wainwright's opinion, Crawford's men "were rather indiscriminately hurrying back to the Shady Grove Road." Some regiments fell apart completely. John Urban of the 1st Pennsylvania Reserves remembered the confusion as the troops tried to get over some marshy ground: "When we reached the swamp, the most available places for crossing were crowded and jammed with men. The rebels had advanced rapidly in pursuit, and were sending a shower of bullets into the struggling mass in the swamp. . . . I jumped for what I believed to be a firm spot of ground, but it proved to be anything but solid, for I sank into the mire almost to my knees. . . . I . . . lost considerable time in extricating myself from the mire; and . . . I found my retreat cut off, and was taken prisoner."

According to Colonel Hardin, the Confederate attackers were so keyed up that many of them pushed past the Yankees and went on to Bethesda Church. Hardin claimed, "They were moving in the wrong direction, to wit, parallel to the Union lines."

There now occurred one of those delays that would prove to be a boon for the defenders and a disaster for the attackers. Reflecting on it soon after the battle, Charles Wainwright was certain that had Rodes quickly followed his sweep to Bethesda Church with a strong thrust northward, the movement would have been successful. But the expected Confederate follow-up attack did not happen immediately, which gave Crawford time to re-form and Warren a chance to stiffen the supports on either side. A soldier in the 13th Massachusetts remembered how Gouverneur Warren moved his supports: "He seemed to think the urgency of the occasion great, as he called on 'Helen Damnation,' as if she could render assistance were she so disposed. You might call on 'Father Mars' until the cows come home without inspiring soldiers to fight; but the moment Helen's name was heard things began to move."

In the report he filed this evening, Jubal Early explained some of the causes of the delay. First, time was lost while Rodes extended the newly acquired Confederate position past Bethesda Church and "down the road toward Old Church." Then Early ordered his old division, now commanded by Stephen Ramseur, to come forward, and at the same time requested the First Corps commander, Richard Anderson, "to advance a division along the road to Old Church and take the enemy in the flank." Early's plan seemed to be to build up a strong line at right angles to the Union advance and roll the whole thing up all the way to the Pamunkey. Communication with Anderson was erratic, however, and the requested support did not materialize. Early had his men in position but was uncertain what to do until Stephen Ramseur took a hand in the matter.

Early was surveying the distant Union position as Ramseur brought his division up, with John Pegram's brigade — now commanded by a popular Georgia colonel named Edward Willis — in the van. The combative, high-strung Ramseur was consumed with impatience to attack. Lieutenant Colonel Charles B. Christian was standing near the head of Pegram's column when it came under fire from a lone Yankee cannon, posted well in front of the main enemy line. Christian remembered hearing Ramseur say to Early, "General, let me take that gun. . . ." According to Christian, "General Early vigorously advised and protested against it. Ramseur insisting, General Early finally acquiesced in the move."

Christian, commanding the 49th Virginia, had his own problems. Since the beginning of the current campaign, his regiment had lost nine color-bearers; it was now time to pick another. He went along the ranks and stopped in front of a "tall, lanky, beardless boy" named John William Orndorff. "Will you carry the colors?" Christian asked. The young Virginian nodded grimly and said, "Yes, Colonel, I will carry them. They killed my brother the other day, now damn them let them kill me too."

George Peyton in the 13th Virginia remembered the time as being "near 6 P.M. when we were suddenly ordered forward. . . . Brought guns to a trail, gave a yell and rushed forward."

At about this time, the crusty Charles Griffin came riding up, stopped where Colonel Hardin's men were furiously digging in, "and, as there was now no firing and no enemy in sight, . . . asked what we were making such preparations for." At Hardin's suggestion, the two of them rode a short distance forward, topping a small ridge, where they spotted Ramseur's advancing battle lines. "General Griffin called out, 'I'm satisfied,' and galloped off to prepare his own division to receive the attack."

"Now the enemy is seen advancing. Line after line . . . swung out. Shells come screaming over," recalled R. E. McBride of the 11th Pennsylvania Reserves. According to William Locke, also of that regiment, "The rebels come to the attack in double lines, exposing themselves with reckless daring to the unerring fire of our batteries, whose shot and shell made great and frequent gaps in their ranks." Adjutant E. M. Woodward of the nearby 2nd Pennsylvania Reserves never forgot the Confederate color-bearer Orndorff, who came up to point-blank range of the Federal cannon, where "he was struck by a shell and literally torn to pieces."

According to George Peyton of Virginia, "We were met by a hail of cannon and rifle balls although we could not see a single man." Lieutenant Colonel Christian of the 49th Virginia remembered the moment when the Yankees opened fire: "Our line melted away as if by magic — every brigade, staff and field officer was cut down, (mostly killed outright) in an incredibly short time."

Led by its young color-bearer, the 49th fought ahead on the right. "We crossed that field of carnage and mounted the parapet of the enemy's works and poured a volley in their faces. They gave way, but two lines of battle, close in their rear, rose and each delivered a volley into our ranks in rapid succession. . . . Our line already decimated was now almost annihilated." John Orndorff carried the regimental flag to within twenty feet of the Yankee cannon, where a battery blast caught him full in the body. "His little 'red-cap' flew up ten feet, one arm went up one way, the other another — fragments of his flesh were dashed in our faces."

The attack was over. As Jubal Early would report this evening, "The enemy was found in heavy force, intrenched. . . . Pegram's brigade was compelled to retire, sustaining considerable loss."

For the nine regiments of Pennsylvania Reserves, the end of this day marked the end of their service in the United States military. According to Josiah Sypher, who later compiled a history of the outfit, "To a succession of brilliant achievements from Dranesville to Gettysburg, without a blemish to mar the story of their greatness, without a defeat to tarnish their unsullied banners, or a blemish to detract from their fame, the battle of Bethesda Church . . . is a most proper ending."

Not every Union soldier agreed with Sypher's rosy assessment. According to one Massachusetts man in Griffin's division, "The Pennsylvania Reserves were to keep up with us, but they kept behind, were flanked, and ran like a flock of sheep . . . and we came near being cut off." When he tried to figure out the losses this evening, Wainwright, the Fifth Corps artillery chief, reckoned that the count for the Pennsylvania Reserves would be very inexact, since "many of Crawford's men now supposed to be missing will turn up; they always do after such a little stampede." Warren's own report on the action was noncommittal, noting only that "General Crawford . . . developed a force of the enemy near Bethesda Church, which forced him back."

In the Confederate ranks, the pain of loss was mixed with hot anger. Lieutenant Colonel Christian, wounded and captured in the engagement, remembered it as "the bloodiest fight of our Civil War considering the number engaged on our side. . . . The loss of officers was full ninety per cent of all engaged." Among them were the dashing Colonel Edward Willis and his aide, "the chivalrous young Lieutenant [Joseph] Randolph, of Richmond." The mortally wounded Willis passed away on May 31, using his last breath to declare, "I am no more afraid to die than I was to go into the battle."

The blame centered on the impetuous Stephen Ramseur, eager to prove himself in his first outing as a division commander. "A murder for ambition['s] sake," was how one soldier diarist put it. George Peyton was equally unforgiving. "Ramseur was to blame for the whole thing and ought to have [been] shot for the part he played in it," the Virginian declared. Jubal Early turned a blind eye to the matter, not even mentioning Ramseur's name in his report of the action. Ramseur himself engaged in no self-recrimination. His letters termed the combat at Bethesda Church a "hard fight" and contained no hint of guilt.

Charles Dana, Lincoln's representative at Grant's headquarters, summed up the results of the day's action: "There was no doubt that Lee's whole army . . . was close at hand and strongly entrenched again. Grant . . . declared emphatically he would not run his head against heavy works."

★

(Confederate and Federal losses in the fighting around Bethesda Church and the Totopotomoy are "light" when compared with those from the Wilderness and Spotsylvania. The cost to Lee's army, based on a current reexamination of Confederate casualty data, is now estimated at: killed and wounded, 811; captured, 348; total, 1,159. Grant's losses have been put at: killed and wounded, 679; captured, 52; total, 731.)

★ LEE ★

Aides around the Army of Northern Virginia's headquarters breathed a little easier today. While admitting to a friend that Lee "has been somewhat indisposed," Walter Taylor added with relief, "He is now improving." Another of Lee's officers asserted, "In fact, nothing but his own determined will kept him in the field; and it was then rendered more evident than ever that he was the head and front, the very life and soul of his army."

It was fortunate that Lee's health was on the mend, for the news he received today had the impact of a physical blow. The bits and pieces of information that dribbled in made it clear Grant was being massively reinforced from Butler's army. Worse yet, these fresh troops were landing at White House, fifteen miles down the Pamunkey from Hanovertown. The roads led west from that point like a dagger slipping in under Lee's right flank. An easy quick march by these Union troops would threaten his rear and possibly even cut him off from Richmond.

Where Lee had the resources to act, he now acted. Orders went out to Fitzhugh Lee to take his battered riders down past the end of the Confederate right and to hold on to a vital crossroads named Cold Harbor, three miles southeast of Bethesda Church, where Grant's left flank ended. But Lee knew that unsupported cavalry could not hold long against foot soldiers. He needed infantry down there too, but where would he find them? With Grant pressing all along the Totopotomoy line, it was impossible to pull Hill, Anderson, or Early out of their trenches. The answer was the one he had known all the while: Beauregard. Lee contacted the Creole officer, who again refused his request, claiming that it was up to Richmond to decide.

At 7:30 P.M., Lee played his final card. In a direct wire to Jefferson Davis, he noted Beauregard's delay in sending help and demanded that Hoke's Division, one of the two under Beauregard's command, be transferred north immediately. Warned Lee, "The result of this delay will be disaster."

── ★ GRANT ★ ──

"About noon," recalled Horace Porter, "Grant received word that transports bringing W. F. Smith's troops from Butler's army were beginning to arrive at White House; and they were ordered to move forward at once, and join the Army of the Potomac."

This time Grant was reading Lee's mind and guessing that the Southern commander would make some move to throw a force across Smith's path. At 6:40 P.M., Grant told Meade to order Sheridan, with at least half a brigade, to swing down from the Union left and clear the way for Smith.

Grant watched to see whether Lee would pull one of his corps out of the Totopotomoy line to block Smith. To Horace Porter, Grant said, "Nothing would please me better than to have the enemy make a movement around our left flank. I would in that case move the whole army to the right, and throw it between Lee and Richmond."

Lee's 7:30 P.M. cable to Jefferson Davis galvanized the Confederate bureaucracy. Davis called in his military adviser Braxton Bragg, who, at 10:30 P.M., wired Beauregard, "By direction of the President you will send Hoke's division . . . immediately to this point by railroad." But Beauregard, moved by a combination of devotion to the cause and political acumen, had reversed his previous decision and already acted. A wire sent by him to Bragg at 10:15 P.M. stated, "General Lee having called on me for reinforcements, . . . I have ordered Hoke's division to report to him."

The race was on: Smith's corps from White House, Hoke's from Bermuda Hundred.

Roads South: 4

TUESDAY, MAY 31

★ LEE ★

Lee felt well enough today to leave the Clarke House and move by carriage to his new field headquarters at Shady Grove Church. The time had come to gamble and beat Grant to the punch. "It being evident to General Lee that the enemy was moving [toward Cold Harbor]," noted his aide Walter Taylor, "he immediately ordered an extension of his own lines." Lee now saw the chance to deliver the kind of attack he had intended at North Anna. If he could send enough men down to Cold Harbor to link up with Hoke's Division as it came up from Richmond, he might just be able to double up that Yankee flank and pin Grant's army away from Richmond.

Accordingly, Richard Anderson was instructed at 3:00 P.M. to pull his corps out of the Totopotomoy line and march down to Cold Harbor. Anderson promptly got his men under way.

★ GRANT ★

Even as Lee was watching Grant shift his weight, Grant was watching Lee. According to Horace Porter, Grant now realized that Lee "was working his way southward by extending his right flank, with a view to securing Old Cold Harbor, and holding the roads running from that point toward the James River and White House. This would cut off Grant's short route to the James in case he should decide to cross that river, and would also command the principal line of communication with his base at White House. Old Cold Harbor was therefore a point much desired by both the contending generals, and the operations of the 31st were watched with much interest to see which army would secure the place."

── ★ LEE ★ ──

There was both good news and bad this evening. A rider sent by Fitzhugh Lee brought the disturbing information that his command and Clingman's brigade of Hoke's Division had been driven from their positions in Cold Harbor by Yankee cavalry and infantry. A few moments after receiving this information, Lee was handed a dispatch from Anderson announcing that he had successfully pulled his corps out of the Totopotomoy line and moved the head of his column to Beulah Church, perhaps a mile north of Cold Harbor. This put the First Corps in a perfect position to deliver a crushing blow.

Lee made certain that there would be no confusion. He placed Hoke under Anderson's command and worked to guarantee enough men to do the job. "[Hoke] has three brigades up, and the general wishes you to direct him to send back and try to get up the fourth," wrote Lee's aide Walter Taylor at his commander's direction.

The portents for the following day seemed excellent. Longstreet's corps, the finest offensive unit in Lee's army, the dependables who had smashed Hancock in the Wilderness and blunted Warren at Spotsylvania, would attack at first light.

── ★ GRANT ★ ──

Recalled Grant, "On the 31st Sheridan advanced to near Old Cold Harbor. He found it intrenched and occupied by cavalry and infantry. A hard fight ensued but the place was carried."

At Grant's direction, Horace Porter spent most of this day riding with Sheridan's command. As evening came, Sheridan's scouts brought word that Anderson was approaching from the direction of Beulah Church. "Finding no [friendly] troops advancing to his support," Porter remembered, "[Sheridan felt that] the only course which seemed open to him was to fall back."

Grant felt otherwise: "The enemy knew the importance of Cold Harbor to us and seemed determined that we should not hold it."

Orders were sent to Sheridan telling him "to hold the place at all hazards, until reinforcements could be sent."

Sheridan stopped his withdrawal and reoccupied Cold Harbor. Continued Porter, "In anticipation of a hard fight for the possession of Cold Harbor, General Grant had ordered Wright's corps to make a night march and move to Sheridan's relief."

Cold Harbor

WEDNESDAY, JUNE 1

It was a nerve-racking night for the Union cavalrymen around Cold Harbor. "Our position was anything but satisfactory," remembered a trooper in the 1st Maine Cavalry, "[and] we . . . began to dig for our lives." In some places the Federals were able to use the breastworks from which they had driven the Confederates during the day. In other places, the fence wood and brush barriers were moved "to suit the circumstances of the ground" and rebuilt.

Three roads led into Cold Harbor, from the north, west, and south, and Sheridan blocked them all. Even as his men made ready, Phil Sheridan recalled, all along their slim defensive positions "the enemy could be heard giving commands and making preparations to attack in the morning."

Confederate troops moving this night and morning did so with the confidence of history. Nearly two years earlier the newly named Army of Northern Virginia, under its new leader, Robert E. Lee, had gone on the offensive here against McClellan's army. Then the Federal force had been hammered back and stopped. Captain Dickert of Kershaw's Brigade spoke for many in the Southern ranks when he said, "Now Grant was tempting fate by moving his beaten troops to this ill-fated field, there to try conclusions with McClellan's old antagonist."

Captain Charles Sanders of Georgia limped along with his company, determined to keep up despite a painful blister on his heel. "I told the boys they did not have to run, because if they did the Yankees would get me with my boot off," Sanders remembered afterward. "They all laughed at the idea and told me not to worry."

— ★ —

Between midnight and 1:30 A.M., Federal soldiers belonging to Wright's Sixth Corps pulled out of their trenches on the extreme right of the line and began the forced march to Cold Harbor. "It was a most exhausting march," recalled a member of the 10th Vermont. "The night was dark and sultry, the way intricate and the road a part of the distance led through swamps."

Officers riding with the columns pulled out their watches and shook their heads. At the rate at which the troops were struggling along the choking, dusty Virginia roads, it would be well past daylight before the first of them got to Cold Harbor.

Some twelve thousand Confederate troops pressed against Sheridan's sixty-five hundred men around Cold Harbor. Major General Robert F. Hoke's seven-thousand-man division was dug in less than a mile west of Cold Harbor, across the road that led west through Gaines' Mill and then circuitously to Richmond.

Lee expected Hoke's men to take part in the Cold Harbor attack, but there was confusion surrounding his orders. Hoke, as Lee's aide Walter Taylor had explained to Anderson late on the thirty-first, "was directed to see you and arrange for co-operation to-morrow." But according to Brigadier General Johnson Hagood, Hoke's directions were to attack once Anderson's assault was fully developed. This was something quite different from a simultaneous assault by both Confederate forces.

Sunrise, June 1, came softly to Cold Harbor, Virginia. According to Captain Theodore Rodenbough, of Sheridan's command, "At 5 A.M., as things remained quiet in front, coffee was prepared and served to the men as they stood to horse. Officers' packs appeared in an adjoining field, and the mess-cooks managed to broil a bone, butter a hoecake, and boil more coffee, and although the command remained massed the surroundings seemed more peaceful. My fourth cup of coffee was in hand when a few shots were heard in front, causing a general pricking up of ears."

Brigadier General Joseph Kershaw's division was at the head of Anderson's column, closest to the enemy. Anderson decided to push ahead a strong reconnaissance force in order to determine the size, strength, and makeup of the Yankee troops holding on to Cold Harbor. Kershaw got the call and out of habit assigned the task to his old brigade. On paper, it was a good choice. The brigade's thinned ranks had been augmented recently by the 20th South Carolina, a fat reg-

iment fresh from garrison duty around Charleston. Numbering between "one thousand and one thousand two hundred strong," the
soldiers, remembered one of Kershaw's ragged veterans, "were as
healthy, well clad, and well fed [a] body of troops as anybody could
wish to see."

There were so many men in the regiment that Kershaw's old-
timers called it the "20th Army Corps." Marching proudly at its head
was a thirty-nine-year-old, well-educated, "silver-tongued" lawyer
and ex-congressman named Lawrence Massillon Keitt. Keitt had seniority over Colonel John Henagan of Kershaw's Brigade and so took
command of the whole unit.

There was an aura of past glory about Lawrence Keitt. He reminded one of Kershaw's jaded veterans of "a knight of old —
mounted upon his superb iron-gray, and looked the embodiment of
the true chevalier that he was." But Keitt was inexperienced in field
command, and there was delay and confusion as the men were
formed into lines of battle. Kershaw himself compounded the problem by allowing Keitt to put his own raw regiment into the front line;
a more prudent officer would have placed it in reserve.

Not until nearly 8:00 A.M. was Keitt's force ready. "Across a large
old field the brigade swept towards a densely timbered piece of oak-
land, studded with undergrowth, crowding and swaying in irregular
lines, the enemy's skirmishers pounding away at us as we advanced."

Sheridan's men facing Keitt numbered only six hundred, but they
were all armed with either Sharps breech-loading carbines or seven-
shot Spencer magazine carbines. As Kershaw's Brigade hove into
view, the dismounted cavalrymen allowed the yelling attackers to
come close, then loosed an awesome display of massed firepower.
Remembered Captain Rodenbough, "A sheet of flame came from the
cavalry line, and for three or four minutes the din was deafening. The
repeating carbines raked the flank of the hostile column while the
Sharps single-loaders kept up a steady rattle." "They were so badly
demoralized," added a trooper from the 1st Massachusetts Cavalry,
"that they took to their heels and skedaddled back to the woods from
which they had started on their charge."

Colonel Keitt was scythed off his horse by the first volley and killed.
His inexperienced regiment stood against the merciless leaden storm
for perhaps five minutes. Then the 20th South Carolina regiment
broke. Artilleryman Robert Stiles was appalled: "I have never seen

any body of troops in such a condition of utter demoralization; they actually grovelled upon the ground and attempted to burrow under each other in holes and depressions." Only the battle-hardened discipline of the other regiments prevented the rout from becoming a general one.

So quickly was Kershaw's advance repulsed that the fight was over before Hoke's men, on the right, realized it had started. "Hoke did not become engaged," noted the official diary of the First Corps.

The morning was well under way before Grant's headquarters staff realized that "Baldy" Smith's men had been marching the wrong way. Old orders directing the corps to move northwest to New Castle had not been corrected to turn the soldiers westward to Cold Harbor. The Eighteenth Corps commander had already suspected that something was wrong. A soldier in the 25th Massachusetts noted in his diary, "We can hear guns off to our left, at a distance, but get no report. Smith is very anxious and says he don't know what to do or where to go. He thinks there must be a mistake in his orders for there seems to be no good reason why we should be here."

Colonel Bowers of Grant's staff brought Smith his amended instructions late in the morning, but the damage was done. Smith's men, who should have been assisting Sheridan at Cold Harbor, were instead five to six miles from that place. "The command was therefore marched back to Old Church and thence to Cold Harbor," Smith later recalled. "The day was intensely hot, the dust stifling, and the progress slow, as the head of the column was behind the trains of the Sixth Corps. The ranks were consequently much thinned by the falling out of exhausted men."

A second, far less determined Confederate attack struggled forward before 10:00 A.M. Sheridan's riders met it with the same hurricane of fire that had shattered the first, and it was quickly stopped. "After the second failure," Thompson Snyder of the 1st Pennsylvania Cavalry recalled with weary gratitude, "they let us alone."

At 9:00 A.M., Sheridan reported the arrival of the Sixth Corps commander, Horatio Wright. By 10:00 A.M., the first dust-caked, footsore infantryman began to relieve Sheridan's riders.

Fifteen days earlier the 2nd Connecticut Heavy Artillery had been basking in the pleasures of garrison duty around Washington. Then came the orders for the front, orders that, as one member of the regiment recalled, "after such long immunity, it had almost ceased to expect." Since joining the Army of the Potomac, the Connecticut troops had yet to participate in a general assault.

The regiment, now part of Russell's division in Wright's Sixth Corps, halted at around noon near the Cold Harbor crossroads, which had been taken by Sheridan's men on May 31. Five dead enemy soldiers lay nearby. Some of the Connecticut boys carefully dug a set of shallow graves, rolled in the bodies, and covered them up.

Richard Anderson was still having problems. After his second repulse by Sheridan's rapid-firing carbineers, Anderson's only concern was defense. He let his battle line fall back to the west, taking a north-south direction from Hoke's position. Both George Pickett's and Charles Fields's men were up by this time and were busy entrenching.

By midafternoon the first elements of "Baldy" Smith's Eighteenth Corps finally began arriving at Cold Harbor and filing into position on Wright's right.

Grant was now more determined than ever to shift the weight of his line down to Cold Harbor. At 3:30 P.M., orders went to Hancock to prepare for a withdrawal from the right of the Union line "as soon as it is dark."

Lee was also shifting troops. They were spotted moving across the front held by Warren's Fifth Corps, and Grant wanted something done to halt them. "Warren fired his artillery at the enemy; but lost so much time in making ready that the enemy got by, and at 3 o'clock he reported the enemy was strongly intrenched in his front, and besides his lines were so long that he had no mass of troops to move with," Grant recalled later, adding sourly, "He seemed to have forgotten that lines in rear of an army hold themselves while their defenders are fighting in their front."

Then, surprisingly, Meade suggested that Wright and Smith go on the offensive. If Grant wanted a breakthrough the next day, Meade argued, the chances for success would be markedly improved if the Federals could grab positions closer to the Confederate lines. Grant agreed. There would be fighting yet today at Cold Harbor.

Meade's attack order came down the chain of command, and Colonel Elisha S. Kellogg called the eighteen hundred men of the 2nd Connecticut Heavy Artillery together to prepare them for their baptism of fire. The regiment was so large that it was subdivided into three battalions of six hundred men apiece. The troops massed in a hollow near their encampment and looked expectantly at Kellogg, who climbed up on a log breastwork and called the three battalion commanders to him. Recalled one of his staff officers, "He marked out on the ground the shape of the works to be taken — told the officers what dispositions to make of the different battalions — how the charge was to be made — spoke of our reputation as a band-box regiment, 'Now we are called on to show what we can do at fighting.'" Kellogg turned to Major Hubbard's First Battalion, which would lead the attack, and declared, "Now men, when you have the order to move, go in steady, keep cool, keep still until I give you the order to charge, and then go arms a-port, with a yell. Don't a man of you fire a shot until we are within the enemy's breastworks. I shall be with you."

Anderson finally connected with Hoke's Division during the afternoon. The lines came together near the Cold Harbor road. Clingman's brigade of Hoke's Division covered the road, while Brigadier General William T. Wofford's brigade of Kershaw's Division continued the line north. The adjoining flanks of the two brigades were separated by a stream and a gullied gap of fifty to seventy-five yards, which was thought to be impassable and was not covered by breastworks or troops. Clingman thought otherwise. "I rode over and expressed to the officer in command of the nearest regiment . . . a wish that he would extend his right to the branch, so as to unite with my command, but he declined to do so. I was about to extend my line across the branch, though contrary to the orders I had received, but soon after was informed by Major-General Hoke that this was unnecessary, as General Hagood's Brigade would be stationed in front of my left and cover this interval. . . . About 3 o'clock, however, this brigade, in obedience to Major-General Hoke's orders, was moved away to the right without my knowledge."

The Union assault began at around 5:00 P.M., when "Baldy" Smith ordered two of his divisions forward. The Federals had a long way to go. "The battle-field was broad, open, undulating, rising gently towards the front," recalled a New Yorker in the 98th. "A fourth of a mile distant, in the further edge of a wood, the Confederates had a line of rifle-pits and a low breastwork of logs and rails, thrown up during the day and the evening before. Behind this first line was an open field, and beyond the field about eighty rods . . . was another

wood, in the nearest edge of which was the enemy's second line."
"The noise, roar and crash of the musketry and artillery firing is tremendous," remembered a soldier in the 13th New Hampshire.

Smith watched his men go in. "Under a severe fire they crossed
the open field, and, entering the wood, made their way through
slashings and interlaced tree-tops, and carried the rifle-pits, capturing 250 prisoners. . . . Beyond the woods, in another open field, was
a second line of works, from which the troops received so heavy a fire
that they fell back under cover, and held the line of the captured rifle-
pits."

Now was the time for Wright's men to advance. Two full divisions and
portions of a third took part. The 2nd Connecticut Heavy Artillery,
in the front of Upton's division, stood poised to move. The men had
piled their knapsacks behind them and aligned themselves with the
Cold Harbor road to their left. Then Colonel Kellogg appeared in
front of the first battalion and gave the commands: "Forward! Guide
Center! March!"

Each of the three battalions was in its own line, the lines being
positioned one hundred paces apart. Recalled Theodore Vaill, an adjutant, "The 1st Battalion, with the colors in the center, moved directly forward through the scattering woods, crossed the open field
at a double quick, and entered another pine wood, of younger and
thicker growth, where it came upon the first line of the rebel rifle
pits." A New York soldier watching from the rear remembered that
as "soon as the heavies began to charge, the Rebel works were bordered with a fringe of smoke from the muskets and the men began to
fall very fast. . . . We could see them fall in all shapes. Some would
fall forward as if they had caught their feet and tripped and fell. Others would throw up their arms and fall backward. Others would stag-
ger about a few paces before they dropped."

A Connecticut soldier named States B. Flandreau later recollected that the Rebels "had cut the young pine trees down about
three feet from the ground, and let the tops fall over and form an
entanglement, all along the line for about fifty feet out. . . . Before
we reached the entanglement, our Colonel discovered the enemy was
about to give us a volley and he ordered us to 'lie down.' Down we
went on our faces, and the volley went over our heads. . . . How I
ever got through the tangled brush I do not know, all I know [is] that
I was on top of their works with the regiment right close to 'Old Flag'
and the 'Johnnies' running to beat the band."

The main Confederate breastwork lay beyond this line of rifle-pits and was screened by a heavier abatis. Here the enemy did not run but rather stood and delivered systematic volleys that stunned the raw heavies: "A sheet of flame, sudden as lightning, red as blood, and so near that it seemed to singe the men's faces, burst along the rebel breastwork; and the ground and trees close behind our line were ploughed and riddled with a thousand balls that just missed the heads of the men," remembered adjutant Vaill.

Kellogg's Connecticut troops had come face-to-face with Clingman's North Carolina brigade. As the Yankees surged up to the abatis, Clingman's aide Captain Fred R. Blake called out, "Here they are, as thick as they can be!" Clingman later recalled that the Federals "had on apparently new blue uniforms, and were marching at a quick step." Turning to his line, Clingman shouted, "Aim low and aim well." He later said, "The discharge from my line at once knocked down the front ranks of the column, while the oblique fire along the right and left cut down the men rapidly all along the column towards the rear. In a few minutes the whole column either acting under orders, or from panic, lay down."

With his men pinned down, Colonel Kellogg now realized that his regiment had advanced further than the supporting units on either side. "Our right was nobody's left, and our left nobody's right," one Connecticut soldier later observed. Suddenly a killing fire began to rip along the crouching lines from the left flank. Kellogg tried to order his men back but was shot in the head and killed. His body pitched into the abatis and lay dangling there, bloody and lifeless. According to Theodore Vaill, the first line of Connecticut soldiers was near panic: "Wild and blind with wounds, bruises, noise, smoke, and conflicting orders, the men staggered in every direction, some of them falling upon the very top of the rebel parapet, where they were completely riddled with bullets — others wandering off into the woods on the right and front, to find their way to death by starvation at Andersonville, or never to be heard from again." A New York officer who was watching from the supporting line later noted in his diary, "The enemy's fire being too severe for the 2nd Connecticut, they broke up in great confusion."

Remembered Brigadier General Clingman of North Carolina, "The men of my command continued to reload and discharge their pieces into the thick, dark mass. The officers fired their repeaters, while such as had none occasionally borrowed muskets from privates and discharged them at particular individuals. . . . After some fifteen or twenty rounds had been fired into the prostrate mass, I directed the firing to cease. Upon this occurring, a portion of the column . . . arose and fled to the rear; many of these, however, were shot down as they attempted to escape."

Like a mighty wind, Emory Upton came among the frantic Connecticut soldiers. "Lie down!" he yelled, and men all around tumbled to cover. Somehow he kneaded a defensive line out of the mob and prowled along it, beating out panic as a fireman might stamp out small flares in the wake of a brushfire. To a wide-eyed officer brandishing his sword, Upton snarled, "Put up your saber. I never draw mine until we get into closer quarters than this." Pointing to some Confederates who were running in to surrender, Upton yelled, "See the Johnnies! See the Johnnies! Boys, we'll have these fellows yet!"

By now the first battalion had become thoroughly intermingled with the second and third. Night was coming on, and with it, new waves of fear. Upton made a point of fearlessness. Standing behind a tree in the extreme front, he fired shot after shot at the enemy, as fast as loaded rifles were handed to him. Occasionally, sensing that a portion of the line was beginning to waver, he would pounce on it and bellow, "Men of Connecticut, stand by me! We MUST hold this line!"

Even as the right of Clingman's line was beating down the attack of the Connecticut heavies, other Federal troops were funneling into the gullied gap on his left. As the Confederate officer later remembered it, "Favored by the thick bushes and smoke, . . . [the Yankees] had gotten within fifty yards of the rear and left of . . . [my line], and suddenly, just as our men had ceased to cheer, they opened on them a heavy fire at short range against their backs and from their left simultaneously."

"Took the Rebs by surprise," a New Yorker later noted in his diary. A Pennsylvanian in the 87th claimed afterward that his outfit "was among the first to bound over the earth-works where in a few minutes they captured and sent to the rear a large part of Hoke's . . . North Carolina troops."

The Federal penetration also unhinged Wofford's Brigade, on Clingman's left. Up until that instant, the Georgian soldiers had been easily holding their own. Recalled the foot-blistered Captain Charles Sanders, "We were fighting away, when all at once a perfect shower of bullets came from behind. . . . There was only one thing to do [:] we all saw that we had to get out of that place, and that quick, too. . . . I always thought I could run pretty fast, but I didn't know until then how fast I could run."

Richard Anderson, whose actions so far this day had been several notches below his work at Spotsylvania on May 7, now rose to the moment. Promptly detaching Brigadier General John Gregg's brigade from Field's Division and Brigadier General Eppa Hunton's from Pickett's, he sent them forward in a counterattack. Portions of Kershaw's old South Carolina brigade and Brigadier General Alfred H. Colquitt's all-Georgia command also pitched in.

"It was a plucky fight," recalled a Vermont soldier in the gap. The sun was down by now, and the men fought in an eerie twilight. One of Hunton's soldiers remembered that "it was pitch dark, only the light of burning powder to shoot at." Hunton pushed part of his brigade across the gap and another portion along the left shoulder of the gully, while Gregg's men steadied Wofford's line. Hunton and Clingman had a testy exchange while attempting to coordinate their movements, but finally they were able to push the Federals out of the gap, even though, according to Artilleryman Robert Stiles, "we did not quite regain all we had lost, and our lines were left in very bad shape."

Major James Hubbard, who had taken command of the 2nd Connecticut Heavy Artillery after Colonel Kellogg's death, sent word to Emory Upton that his men were out of ammunition and might not be able to hold if attacked. Upton was hearing no talk of defeat. "If they come there," he growled, "catch them on your bayonets, and pitch them over your heads."

The intense firing finally died away by 10:00 P.M. Emory Upton later put the loss to the 2nd Connecticut Heavy Artillery at "53 killed, 187 wounded, 146 missing; total 386." He was bitter about the hasty decision to attack late in the day. Describing the affair to his sister as "a murderous engagement," Upton went on to explain, "I say *murderous,* because we were recklessly ordered to assault the enemy's intrenchments, knowing neither their strength nor position. Our loss was very heavy, and to no purpose. Our men are brave, but can not accomplish impossibilities."

(Andrew Humphreys later calculated that the "Sixth Corps lost in this engagement about 1,200 killed and wounded. . . . The loss of the Eighteenth Corps was about 1,000 killed and wounded.")

During the night, Major General Charles Field supervised a readjustment of the Confederate lines near the spot where the Yankees had penetrated the gap between Clingman and Wofford. Recalled Field, "I laid out and made a breastwork in the rear of the one taken from Kershaw . . . and connected it with the old one."

George Meade was feeling the pressure. Theodore Lyman remembered that the army commander "was in one of his irascible fits tonight." "Baldy" Smith was emerging as Meade's newest headache. Smith and Grant were old friends, and Meade may have suspected that the Eighteenth Corps leader was trying to bypass the chain of command. At 10:15 P.M., Meade was complaining to Grant, "I have heard nothing from Smith. . . . He is aware of the telegraph from Wright's headquarters, but does not report." When the reports finally did come in, they were filled with complaints and dire predictions of defeat should the enemy attack vigorously. The last straw came around midnight, when Captain Farquhar of Smith's staff found Meade and reported that the Eighteenth Corps commander had brought with him little ammunition and no supply wagons, and that "he considered his position precarious." Lyman was standing nearby when Meade roared, "Then, why in Hell did he come at all?"

Hancock's division commander John Gibbon put his finger on a problem that was moving along with the Army of the Potomac like a bothersome boil that might fester at any moment into something dangerous. As Gibbon later noted, "Gen. Meade occupied a peculiar position at the head of the army. He was a commander directly under a commander, a position at best and under the most favorable circumstances, not a very satisfactory one to fill. . . . With the best and most patriotic intentions on the part of both, clashings are almost certain to occur."

One was occurring at that moment. Meade was not happy with Grant's tactics. In a 10:10 P.M. dispatch to Horatio Wright, Meade complained about Grant's spreading the army too thin: "I do not like extending too much. It is the trouble we have had all along of occupying too long lines and not massing enough." Meade was also growing annoyed at the press coverage Grant was getting. In a letter written today to his wife, he groused, "The papers are giving Grant all the credit for what they call successes; I hope they will remember this if anything goes wrong."

A dangerous schism was yawning between the two generals, and Meade was perilously close to washing his hands of any responsibility for Grant's orders.

Whatever high hopes Robert E. Lee may have had for Richard Anderson were thoroughly dashed when he received his First Corps commander's 10:00 P.M. report on the action at Cold Harbor. Communication between Anderson and Hoke had been severed in the late-afternoon Federal attack and had not yet been reestablished; furthermore, Anderson felt that his men and Hoke's Division were not enough to secure the area. "Re-enforcements are necessary to enable us to hold the position," he warned.

Lee was already acting. General Breckinridge and his troops from the Shenandoah Valley were ordered to Cold Harbor to strengthen and extend the Confederate right.

Remembered Horace Porter, "The night of the First of June was a busy one for both officers and men. Grant, eager as usual to push the advance gained, set about making such dispositions of the troops as would best accomplish this purpose." The unit Grant was now counting upon to launch the decisive attack was Hancock's Second Corps. Grant wanted these dependable shock troops with Smith and Wright at Cold Harbor.

Nothing went right for Hancock's men this night. A soldier in the 116th Pennsylvania recalled it as being "one of the most trying experiences. It was very dark and very warm, the dust stifling and no water to be had. The road was unknown, and Captain Paine, of the Engineers, who was sent to lead the column and show the way, in his efforts to find a short cut, got the troops entangled in by-paths where artillery could not follow and much time was lost." The result of all of this, explained Francis Walker, a Second Corps adjutant, was enough to "put it out of General Hancock's power to reach Cold Harbor at daybreak of the 2d of June."

THURSDAY, JUNE 2

Morning

Dawn came to Cold Harbor, but not Breckinridge. Lee, recovering but still weak, mounted up and rode toward Mechanicsville. He covered the full distance before finding the former US Vice President. Breckinridge explained that his men had not been able to leave their trenches on the Confederate left before 10:00 P.M., and they had been so weary that he had felt compelled to let them rest every half hour. Major McClellan, a guide sent by Lee, had compounded the problem by leading the troops by a long route.

Lee gave orders for Breckinridge to hurry the march and rode back toward Cold Harbor, fully expecting to hear the sounds of Grant's guns signaling the attack.

Francis Barlow's division was the first of Hancock's corps to arrive at Cold Harbor. Behind it came John Gibbon's men, among them John S. Jones of Ohio, who recalled, "We were in a condition of almost utter physical exhaustion, to which was added the feeling of mortification and humiliation at being behind time." It was a hot, sultry day already, "the sun being very warm and Poring down its Heat in torrents," as a private in Company B of the 57th Pennsylvania wrote in his diary. Theodore Lyman noted, "Getting all the information, General Meade ordered a general assault at 4 P.M." This was soon changed to 5:00.

When the 12th New Jersey drew to a halt, it was quickly surrounded by smiling slaves, who told the sweat-streaked Federals that the place they had marched to was called Cold Harbor. A lot of Yankee boys wondered about the name. A private in the 2nd New York Heavy Artillery remarked that "'twas no harbor at all, and divil a drop of water to make 'un wid'." Theodore Lyman was not quite sure what its name was. He narrowed his choices to three: Coal Harbor, Cold Harbor, or Cool Arbor. Lyman finally decided he liked Cool Arbor best "because it is prettiest, and because it is so hideously inappropriate." Horace Porter also at first believed that Cool Arbor was the proper place name, "but it was ascertained afterward that the name Cold Harbor was correct, that it had been taken from the places frequently found along the highways of England, and means 'shelter without fire.'"

Afternoon

ULYSSES GRANT TO GEORGE MEADE — 2 P.M.

  IN VIEW OF THE WANT OF PREPARATION FOR AN ATTACK THIS EVENING, AND THE HEAT AND WANT OF ENERGY AMONG THE MEN FROM MOVING DURING THE NIGHT LAST NIGHT, I

THINK IT ADVISABLE TO POSTPONE ASSAULT UNTIL EARLY TO-
MORROW MORNING.

GEORGE MEADE TO ALL CORPS COMMANDERS — 2:30 P.M.
   THE ATTACK ORDERED FOR 5 P.M. THIS DAY IS POSTPONED
TO 4:30 A.M. TO-MORROW. CORPS COMMANDERS WILL EMPLOY
THE INTERIM IN MAKING EXAMINATION OF THE GROUND IN
THEIR FRONTS, AND PERFECTING THEIR ARRANGEMENTS FOR
THE ASSAULT.

It was afternoon before Breckinridge's men moved into position on
Hoke's right. By this time Lee had learned that the Federals appeared to be withdrawing strength from their right. Figuring that this
meant more Yankees on the roads to Cold Harbor, Lee ordered Mahone and Wilcox to march their divisions at once to extend Breckinridge's line to the Chickahominy.

   Lee also sent for the errant guide who had led Breckinridge's
men the long way around. Major Henry B. McClellan remembered,
"The General was seated on a camp stool in front of his tent, an open
map spread out on his knees. When I was in position before him, he
traced a road with his index finger, and quietly remarked, 'Major, this
is the road to Cold Harbor.'

   "'Yes, General,' I replied, 'I know it now.'

   "Not another word was spoken, but that quiet reproof sunk
deeper and cut more keenly than words of violent vituperation would
have done," young McClellan recalled afterward.

Attempts by Federal officers to scout the Confederate lines resulted
in no useful information. Adjutant Charles Cowtan of the 10th New
York noted that "little could be learned of the enemy's main works in
front of Gibbon's division, on account of the woods concealing them,
and, in front of [Barlow's] . . . Division, knowledge of the Confederate position was equally scant." Hancock's adjutant Francis Walker
later added his voice of complaint: "No opportunity had been afforded
to make an adequate reconnoissance of the enemy's line. . . . It was,
beyond question, the most unfortunate decision made during that
bloody campaign."

William Goldsborough, a Marylander in Lee's army, remembered
seeing some civilians fleeing the area: "There were a large number of
children among them who were suffering terribly from hunger, and
their appeals to the rough soldiers for a mouthful of food was distress-

ing indeed. Those shared their day's ration with them, and they eagerly devoured the coarse bacon raw."

During the afternoon, the Union army tightened up on its line near Cold Harbor. Grant later described the actions and counteractions: "Warren's corps was moved to the left to connect with Smith: Hancock's corps was got into position to the left of Wright's, and Burnside was moved to Bethesda Church in reserve. While Warren and Burnside were making these changes the enemy came out several times and attacked them, capturing several hundred prisoners. The attacks were repulsed, but not followed up as they should have been. I was so annoyed at this that I directed Meade to instruct his corps commanders that they should seize all such opportunities . . . and not wait for orders."

In the course of the day Robert E. Lee ordered actions on both Confederate flanks. Lee remembered this ground from 1862, especially a slight eminence near the Chickahominy known as Turkey Hill. Lee's June 1 orders to Hoke and Anderson had urged them to stretch their lines southward and cover this point, but that had not been done, and Yankee skirmishers now held the position. At 3:00 P.M., in response to Lee's orders, troops from Wilcox's and Breckinridge's commands moved forward and, in a sharp fight, cleared the hill. With this minor action, Lee's artillery now ranged the Chickahominy bottoms on the right, securing his forces against a move around that flank.

At about the same time, Lee unleashed Jubal Early's corps against the Federal right wing, which was slowly withdrawing. Early's men swept over a strong skirmish line and then came up against the main body of Union troops, where the response was more effective. "No sooner had the firing and yelling announced the proximity of the enemy," recalled a Pennsylvanian in the 45th Regiment, "than our massed troops began to deploy into shape for battle, reminding me instantly of a monstrous blue snake gracefully uncoiling itself after being disturbed. . . . The attack was easily repulsed with no great loss to us."

Most of the weary Union soldiers around Cold Harbor welcomed the delay in the attack orders, but a few felt otherwise. Theodore Lyman believed that every minute of postponement made the Confederate earthworks that much stronger. Lyman noted, "It is a rule that, when the Rebels halt, the first day gives them a good rifle-pit; the second, a regular infantry parapet with artillery in position; and the third a parapet with an abatis in front and entrenched batteries behind. Sometimes they put this three days' work into the first twenty-four hours."

John Gibbon, whose men had already charged their share of enemy positions, was even more definite: "A few hours were all that was necessary to render any position so strong by breastworks that the opposite party was unable to carry it and it became a recognized fact amongst the men themselves that when the enemy had occupied a position six or eight hours ahead of us, it was useless to attempt to take it."

Despite the delays and postponements, Grant remained determined to go ahead with the attack on the morning of June 3. "It was a nice question of judgment," said Horace Porter. "After discussing the matter thoroughly with his principal officers, and weighing all the chances, he decided to attack Lee's army in its present position. He had succeeded in breaking the enemy's line at . . . other places under circumstances which were not more favorable, and the results to be obtained would be so great in case of success that it seemed wise to make the attempt." Lincoln's observer, Charles Dana, agreed: "The breaking of Lee's lines meant his destruction and the collapse of the rebellion."

Union: Evening–Night

It began to rain at around 5:00 P.M.

Some Federal regiments, including the 116th Pennsylvania and others like it, "slept soundly" this night. In the 2nd New Hampshire the men "grouped in their comfortless bivouac, mid rocks and bushes wet with a sudden rain, [and] discussed their chances of battle." For some, the inexorable regimen of the army system went on no matter what. Around midnight, the men of the 19th Massachusetts were awakened, given two days' rations of hardtack, coffee, and sugar, and then allowed to go back to sleep.

It was also around midnight as the sweating, mud-streaked artillerymen of Captain J. Henry Sleeper's 10th Massachusetts Battery lugged and shoved their six rain-slicked cannon into the rifle-pits they had spent the evening enlarging and strengthening. Sleeper, when ordered to this position by Brigadier General John Gibbon, had protested the move, as it meant that other Union batteries would be firing directly over his. "Obey your orders, Captain," Gibbon snapped, and rode away.

Along another portion of the Federal line, cannoneer Frank Wilkeson passed the time talking with some of the boys from the 7th New York Heavy Artillery who were being used as infantry. Wilkeson found that "they were sad of heart. They knew that they were to go into the fight early in the morning and they dreaded the work."

Two Massachusetts officers in the Eighteenth Corps had bad feelings about the new day. Lieutenant James Graham turned to his friend Captain Foss and said, "Captain, I am induced to think that one or both of us will go up tomorrow morning, and if anything happens to me, I want you to take care of me, and if you are hurt and I am not, I will take care of you." Foss thought a moment and nodded, saying, "Yes, Jim, I will see to that. If you are hurt I will look out for you, if I'm alive."

Grant's aide Lieutenant Colonel Horace Porter saw something curious as he rode through the Federal camps this night. "I noticed that many of the soldiers had taken off their coats and seemed to be engaged in sewing up rents in them." Looking more closely, Porter found that "the men were calmly writing their names and home addresses on slips of paper and pinning them on the backs of their coats, so that their bodies might be recognized and their fate made known to their families at home."

Confederate: Evening–Night

The Confederates who were waiting in the trenches across from the Union lines were under no illusion. "The enemy was evidently concentrating in the woods in front," the Southern brigadier Evander Law wrote, "and every indication pointed to an early attack."

In John Haskell's battery, the Virginia cannoneers spent the night arguing about the merits of Grant's strategy and griping about the lack of food. Some stood the rain better than others. The situation was especially miserable on John Breckinridge's front, where one brigadier gave in to complaints by his troops and let most of the brigade withdraw a bit to higher ground. This left only a picket force to man the main trenches.

Along another portion of the line, Confederate engineers were bringing a new science to the point of perfection. Lieutenant Colonel William Willis Blackford, a cavalryman-turned-engineer, was seeing his first campaign in his new capacity. Blackford and his fellow engineers were spending the night laying out entrenchments with a hitherto unrealized accuracy. They used a long cord marked at intervals with small strips of white cotton cloth to mock up the trench lines along positions that had been sited and plotted during the day. The cord enabled the engineers to eye the line before the digging began, in order that any difficult-to-defend angles might be avoided. This night Blackford and his fellow engineers were to be successful beyond their wildest imaginings; through a combination of chance and design, Lee's men had created the perfect killing ground.

Colonel William Oates of Alabama, one of Evander Law's regimental commanders, had trouble getting a skirmish line to move out into the marshy area ranged by Federal pickets. Major Alexander Lowther, in charge of the skirmishers, declined to lead them out, claiming he was sick. Oates looked the man over, noted that he had presented no certificate from the surgeon, and ordered him to command the detail. It was still pitch-dark as the disgruntled officer made his way forward.

FRIDAY, JUNE 3

Union: Before Dawn

Brigadier General John Gibbon could not believe what he was not seeing. Gibbon's division was one of two from Hancock's Second Corps slated to attack at daylight. The brown-haired, serious-faced officer was on the move early, anxious to ensure that his troops were all in position and ready for the assault. Gibbon's four brigades would be advancing in two waves of two each; "Paddy" Owen's brigade was supposed to support the left. Years later Gibbon would still recall with incredulity how he found the "whole brigade and its commander sound asleep." Gibbon raised his voice angrily in the damp darkness. It was not an auspicious start.

"Baldy" Smith's Eighteenth Corps held the extreme right flank of the attacking line, so Smith was up early this morning to get his men set for the fight. He had serious reservations about his orders. Grant's plan called for a massive assault by three Union corps across a broad front, something that Smith felt was a bad idea. The goal of any attacking commander should be a concentration of force at a single point; spreading out went against military logic. Then, too, there was the question of coordination among the three corps that would be carrying the assault. To clarify things, Smith asked Horatio Wright, whose Sixth Corps would be advancing immediately on his left, about his attack plan. Wright's curt reply that he was "going to pitch in" helped not at all. In Smith's opinion, the assault plan "was simply an order to slaughter his best troops."

Sergeant William Chambers felt curiously exuberant as he opened his eyes in the darkness. All around him, thousands of Union soldiers were awakening to a morning that was chill, damp, and soured by swampy odors from the nearby Chickahominy River. Chambers was one of the lucky ones. He was among the few who had managed to hold on to a blanket through some pretty rugged marching, not quite twenty-four hours earlier. Chambers had shared his good fortune this night with two comrades who were grateful for the cover it had provided against the rain. As the two rubbed their eyes awake, Chambers stared at them, the grin on his face unseen in the dark. "This is my birthday," he announced. "I wonder what kind of present I will receive?" Five minutes later a Confederate rifle ball hit Chambers in the arm. It was not the kind of present he had been seeking. Chambers bound the wound as best he could in the predawn gloom, threw his precious blanket over his shoulder, and staggered off, looking for the Second Corps field hospital.

Low mists and fog still clung to the stunted pine thickets as blue-coated soldiers shuffled into formation all up and down the line. Some were learning for the first time that they were going to charge the Confederate entrenchments this day. When the 19th Maine got the news, there "was some hooting at the Brigade commanders by the soldiers but when it was ascertained that those officers themselves were going to lead the men there was no further hesitation." As the yet-untested 36th Wisconsin stood waiting, its quartermaster stepped up and calmly began issuing "some clothing, shoes and socks which had been called for." Most of the regiments still could not see what they were going to be attacking. One that could was the 25th Massachusetts in Smith's corps. The men were moved out of their bivouac, marched a short distance, and then told to lie down in a thin stand of woods. On the way everyone got a look at the Confederate position. "We knew it meant slaughter to make the attempt; and gloomy forebodings settled down over the whole regiment."

From bivouacs spread all across the scrubby countryside, thousands of blue-coated soldiers stumbled into companies that merged to create regiments that marched to form brigades that made up the divisions of a corps. There was a power in the very air, something palpable concocted out of the raw sounds of so many men — perhaps forty thousand — moving to a single purpose. "We're all right to-day, Dave, look there!" said William F. Daniels, a twenty-year-old sergeant from Massachusetts, to his friend David Wallis. "There are enough men ahead of us to go through to the Gulf of Mexico."

A young artilleryman in line in front of Brooke's advance remembered being passed by the 7th New York Heavies and being asked lots of questions: "What's ahead of us?" "Are the works strong?" "Is Longstreet's Corps in front of us?"

Recalled the youthful gunner, "And I, a boy 17 years old, answered as the whim took me."

Skirmishers began to filter forward from the waiting masses of men. One of these was Private William Haines, from the 12th New Jersey of Gibbon's division, who now worked his way through the thick brush toward the forward line of Union rifle-pits. His squad came upon a dead Rebel sitting against a tree; Haines guessed that the Johnny had been dead for a couple of days, probably killed by Sheridan's riders on June 1. Someone poked through the Confederate's knapsack and pulled out a small loaf of corn bread, stained at one end with the dead man's blood. "But as Johnny Cake was a great luxury to us," Haines recalled, "we cut off the damp end and breakfasted on the rest, first rolling him out so we could get back of the tree for a few minutes rest."

As dawn approached, Frank Wilkeson and his fellow cannoneers had been "leaning against the cool guns, or resting easily on the ponderous wheels" for quite some time, waiting nervously for daylight. Now Wilkeson became aware that the storm was about to break. "Indistinctly we saw moving figures. Some on foot rearward, cowards hunting for safety; others on horseback riding to and fro near where we supposed the battle-line to be; then orderlies and servants came in from out of the darkness leading horses, and we knew that the regimental and brigade commanders were going into action on foot." A bit forward from Wilkeson, the weary gunners of J. Henry Sleeper's 10th Massachusetts Battery had finished bolstering up their position only a few hours earlier. Now they were chosen to play a special role in the unfolding drama. "A few minutes after the time specified for the attack a staff officer rode up from General Gibbon and ordered our right piece fired as a signal gun. Then there was indeed a veritable tempest."

The Cannonade: 4:30–4:40 A.M.

Quartermaster Charles B. Peck of the 36th Wisconsin had not finished issuing his supplies when the cannonade thundered alive along the Union line. The Confederate response was quick in coming. One solid shot came whizzing by close to his supply wagon, and that was enough for Peck, who "picked up quickly and got to the rear." Closer to the front line, the 12th New Jersey came out of the tangled undergrowth and advanced to the edge of an open field. The officer commanding Company F of the regiment, seeking to inspire by example, struck a heroic pose, facing the nervous troops with one leg staggered forward. A Confederate shell screamed down the length of the blue line, about two feet from the ground and "so close," one private in the ranks remembered, "that it seemed to knock down almost every man in the regiment, just by the force of its wind." The impassive face of the posturing company officer turned to agony as the shell tore his forward leg completely off.

In Richmond, twelve miles away, residents were jarred out of bed as their windows rattled. War Clerk John B. Jones insisted that the sounds of the cannonade "could be heard distinctly in all parts of the city."

Along the Cold Harbor lines, dense clouds of acrid, burnt gunpowder billowed over the artillery emplacements. Cannoneer Frank Wilkeson recalled, "Out of the powder-smoke came an officer from the battle line of infantry. He told us to stop firing, as the soldiers were about to charge."

The Charge, First Wave, Second Corps: 4:40–4:50 A.M.

Francis Barlow's two leading brigades came surging out of the woods onto a broad and level field that ran in a smooth, even slope up to the enemy's works. The left of the advance, led by Colonel Nelson Miles, passed over a sunken road. The right, under Colonel John R. Brooke, crossed over the same road and hit a rail fence halfway up the hill. Brooke had placed his newest and biggest regiment, the sixteen-hundred-man-strong 7th New York Heavy Artillery, in the first line. Watching from the second line, a member of the 148th Pennsylvania remembered, "The brigade flag and its commander went forward with the first line of raw men through the damp, tall, wet grass and clinging bushes." In his artillery position, Frank Wilkeson saw a line of slouch hats pop up along the Confederate parapets, and then "the works glowed brightly with musketry, a storm of lead and iron struck the blue line, cutting gaps in it."

In Richmond, War Clerk John B. Jones, who had been awakened by the rumble of the cannonade, now noted "great crashes of musketry, as if whole divisions were firing at the word of command."

Both of Barlow's leading brigades enjoyed quick success. Nelson Miles's line, led by the 5th New Hampshire, poured across a row of Rebel rifle-pits, capturing two cannon and a number of prisoners, who were sent scuttling to the rear. John Brooke's first wave of yelling, freshly uniformed bluecoats struck the portion of Breckinridge's line where the considerate brigadier in charge had let most of his men rest on higher ground behind the main defensive position. The picket force that had been left to hold the trenches was overwhelmed, and before the main body could deploy to meet the attack, it was routed as well. "It was a hand-to-hand fight to the finish," recalled one of the heavies. "Clubbed muskets, bayonets, and swords got in their deadly work." Then John Brooke was down, hit by canister even as his exultant New Yorkers streamed over the Confederate battlements. "Tell Colonel Beaver he is in command and to push into the works," Brooke gasped to an aide as he was carried off the field.

The advance of John Gibbon's division was bedeviled almost at once. About two hundred yards from the starting point, his men hit a deep swamp that nobody had known about. The swamp, like a wedge, broke Gibbon's line into two bodies that flowed along either side and were forced farther apart as the swamp widened toward the Confederate line. Colonel Thomas Smyth's brigade veered left, with the 14th Connecticut leading the way. One Connecticut soldier remembered that when "mounting a ridge the men were exposed to a terrific fire from the enemy. For a time it was alive with fire. The men were dropping, wounded all along the line." The Connecticut soldiers pressed to within a hundred yards of the main enemy line and were stopped cold. Most of Robert Tyler's brigade split to the right and was stalled by "a deep ravine" close to the enemy's works; Tyler was quickly wounded, and Colonel James P. McIvor took command of the brigade. One of Tyler's regiments, the 164th New York, swerved left around the swamp, skirted the right flank of Smyth's stopped advance, and, goaded by the frenzied anger of its commander, Colonel James P. McMahon, stabbed into the main Confederate line.

The Charge, First Wave, Sixth Corps: 4:40–4:50 A.M.

On the Sixth Corps front, the attack by Russell's and Ricketts's divisions, advancing in one great line, was stopped quickly as a torrent of fire broke across the front and flanks of that line.

Not all of Russell's men took part. Emory Upton, for one, was not prepared to sacrifice his men in a hopeless gesture. He later phrased his official report this way: "June 3, another assault was ordered, but, being deemed impracticable along our front, was not made."

Most of Ricketts's men, on the other hand, did try it. "We never even reached the enemy's works," remembered Captain Lemuel Abbott of the 10th Vermont. "We advanced under a murderous fire in our front from the enemy's artillery, sharpshooters[,] and when in range of its main line of battle . . . were simply slaughtered."

The Charge, First Wave, Eighteenth Corps: 4:40–4:50 A.M.

The first indication Colonel William Oates had that trouble was coming was the sound of a volley of rifle fire in the woods in front of where his 15th Alabama was posted, on the left of Evander Law's brigade. Oates looked up and saw Major Lowther, the officer who had tried to avoid skirmish duty, running up a ravine toward Anderson's Brigade on the right. Behind the major came the skirmishers themselves, dodging and ducking, and behind them a column of Union troops ten lines deep, with arms at trail, yelling "Huzzah!" Oates ordered his men "to take arms and fix bayonets. Just then I remembered that not a gun in the regiment was loaded. I ordered the men to load and the officers each to take an ax and stand to the works. I was apprehensive that the enemy would be on our works before the men could load."

The bluecoats, advancing along a small stream with marshy sides that offered some flanking protection, were from "Baldy" Smith's Eighteenth Corps. They belonged to Colonel Griffin Stedman's brigade of Brigadier General John H. Martindale's division. The regiments advanced with the caps off their pieces and their bayonets fixed. Stedman was right in the thick of it, using a ramrod for a sword to wave his men on. "Forward! Forward!" he shouted. Stedman later described the enemy line as "a wicked red-green gash of piled up earth and felled pine trees." The 12th New Hampshire led the rush across an open plain that gradually narrowed toward the left. Rifle and cannon fire chewed at their flanks. A trooper in the 2nd New Hampshire, which brought up the tail of Stedman's brigade, remembered, "It was a straight dash of 400 yards to the enemy lines. As the column plunged forward it left an awful trail of the dead and wounded at every step of its progress."

The yelling New Hampshiremen of the 12th got close before Alabama colonel William Oates had matters in hand. "I thought of my piece of artillery. I called out, 'Sergeant, give them double charges of canister; fire, men, fire!' The order was obeyed with alacrity. The enemy were within thirty steps. They halted and began to dodge, lie down and recoil. The fire was terrific from my regiment, the 4th Alabama on my immediate right, and the 13th Mississippi on my left, while the piece of artillery was fired more rapidly and better handled than I ever saw before or since. The blaze of fire from it at each shot went right into the ranks of our assailants and made frightful gaps through the dense mass of men." Added another Alabamian, William McClendon, "it was hardly possible for a ball to pass through without hitting some one." Colonel Pickney Bowles, commanding the 4th Alabama, recalled, "Our artillery . . . was cutting wide swaths through their lines. . . . Heads, arms, legs, and muskets were seen flying high in the air at every discharge." A Massachusetts soldier who was watching from the reserve remembered the moment: "So intense was the fire . . . that the division in front seemed to melt away like snow falling on moist ground." According to a New Hampshireman in the midst of the carnage, "it seemed more like a volcanic blast than a battle."

The men of the 12th New Hampshire now stood through a nightmare. Sergeant Piper of Company B noted that "the men bent down as they pushed forward, as if trying, as they were, to breast a tempest, and the files of men went down like rows of blocks or bricks pushed over by striking against each other." Sergeant Tuttle of Company K "thought the order was to lie down and dropped myself among the dead, and did not discover my mistake until my living comrades had advanced some little distance beyond me." In Company H, Private A. J. Farrar looked on in horror. "I saw them all go down," he said.

As the leading ranks fell apart, the rearmost — the 2nd New Hampshire — was suddenly on the cutting edge. The men dived for cover and began trying to hold the advance position, taking heavy losses as they did so. One bullet struck close to the head of Lieutenant George T. Carter of Company I, throwing up a geyser of dirt.

"Carter's got it!" someone in the ranks yelled. "No, I guess not!" Carter shouted back, raising his head to show everyone that he was all right. At that instant "he did 'get it' from a bullet which inflicted an ugly wound." "In less than ten minutes from the word 'Forward,'" a 12th New Hampshire officer wrote afterward, "there was no brigade to be seen." Stedman's brigade finally reeled back "under the heavy front and cross fire, to the edge of the woods, but within short musket range of the line they had gallantly attempted to carry."

The Charge, Second Wave, Second Corps: 4:50–5:15 A.M.

The sudden success of Francis Barlow's two leading brigades was terribly short-lived. As Nelson Miles's lead outfit, the 5th New Hampshire, took stock of its situation, "It was now seen that the . . . regiment was . . . between the enemy's two lines without connections upon either flank. The colonel, upon ascertaining that no supports were at hand, gave orders to withdraw. So near was the regiment to the Confederates' second line that some of the men were captured before orders were given to retreat." It was the intention of the regiment's commander to fall back only to the front side of the Rebel works and to hold there until the supports came up. But many of the New Hampshiremen of the 5th were raw recruits, and once they started out of the inferno, they were not going to stop. The bluecoats flowed out of the rifle-pits they had taken and ebbed back to the sunken road. Colonel Richard Byrnes's brigade tried to support Miles, but "no sooner had the attacking party begun moving than the enemy opened fire and a terrible and destructive fire it was, sweeping the ground in all directions." "Our men fell in heaps," the battle report of the 28th Massachusetts later noted.

A vicious Confederate crossfire ripped the ground between the supporting brigades and the works held by the 7th New York Heavy Artillery. By now the New Yorkers, who were holding a small portion of the main Confederate line, were being hit by a counterattack. Joseph Finegan's Florida brigade, reinforced by the 1st Maryland, came boiling forward. "A most desperate and sanguinary hand-to-hand struggle then ensued," recalled William Goldsborough, a Marylander, "in which the bayonet and short swords of the officers were used with dreadful effect."

"We had lost all semblance of organization," remembered one dazed New Yorker. "Green soldiers though we were, our short experience had taught us to know just when to run, and run we did, I assure you."

John Gibbon's two supporting brigades were also stunned by the awesome enemy fire. The same swamp that had split Gibbon's first wave now did equal damage to the second. His attack plan called for the first to press on until it was stopped, at which point the second wave was to push *through* the first to continue the advance. But instead of pushing through Smyth's stalled brigade, "Paddy" Owen moved his men past Smyth and formed on his left. Owen's brigade, "massed in solid square by order of General Owen, rushed parallel with the enemy's works through the cleared field which was swept by shot and shell," said one Irishman. He continued, "We turn and rush toward the front, crossing the sunken road and swamp. Ascending the hill, we madly charge across the level space, and are met with a cyclone of bullets." "The moment the troops begin to pass over our advanced rifle-pits, and encounter the severe fire of the enemy," a member of the Philadelphia Brigade recalled, "the order 'Forward to the works!' took the place of all attempts at preserving relative formation." On Owen's right, Colonel Henry McKeen's brigade underwent the same storm of lead and iron as they moved toward the main Confederate line, where "the red clay soil of the enemy's entrenchments soon showed in the distance." This shell-swept arena may have seemed the last place for Yankee opportunism to flourish, but flourish it did. As the 19th Massachusetts entered the storm, its color-bearer was shot down. The regimental commander turned to Corporal Mike Scannel and told him to pick up the flag and carry it. "Too many corporals have already been killed carrying colors," Mike shouted back. The commander, knowing a hard bargain when he heard one, yelled, "I'll make you a sergeant on the spot." "That's business," Scannel answered. "I'll carry the colors."

"We could see no men to shoot at," a member of McKeen's brigade complained bitterly. McKeen himself received an agonizing mortal wound, so command passed to young Colonel Frank Haskell of the 36th Wisconsin. The regiment was a new one, and its commander a Gettysburg hero whose star was on the ascent. As the leading regiments either fell apart or flopped down, the 36th Wisconsin, which had begun the charge in the rear ranks of the brigade, was suddenly in the advance. Then it too slowed to a stop while Haskell surveyed the situation. He recognized the futility of trying to go forward in the face of such fire and gave the order, "Lie down, men." "The order had hardly been carried out," remembered the regiment's historian, "when a bullet struck him in the head, killing him instantly."

Up at the Confederate main line, the gallant rush made by the 164th New York had disintegrated when its colonel was shot down on the parapet of the enemy's works, clutching the regiment's colors.

The Charge, Second Wave, Sixth Corps: 4:50–5:15 A.M.

On Wright's Sixth Corps front, with the two leading divisions having been bogged down by ravines and gunfire, Brigadier General Thomas Neill's reserve division was ordered in on the right. Neill moved his men forward in column, like a great battering ram, but he hit an unopenable door. Wheaton's brigade overran a line of rifle-pits and was stopped; its advance had put it ahead of Ricketts's brigade on the left and Brooks's Eighteenth Corps division on the right. Wheaton's men were hit from the front and both sides as alert Confederates hustled into flanking trenches and shot down the length of Neill's front line. The Federal approach was tracked by Southerners belonging to Kershaw's Brigade, whose officers had difficulty in keeping their troops from firing too soon as the Yankee line swept closer. "But when close enough, the word 'fire' was given, and the men behind the works raised deliberately, resting their guns upon the works, and fired volley after volley. . . . The result was telling — men falling on top of men, rear rank pushing forward the first rank, only to be swept away like chaff."

The Charge, Second Wave, Eighteenth Corps: 4:50–5:15 A.M.

Even as Griffin Stedman's shattered brigade reeled back, "Baldy" Smith was riding forward to take personal control of matters. As he and his staff advanced, "they saw dead men behind them, dead men to the right and left — wounded men creeping to the rear or trying to find shelter from other wounds." Smith found his division commander Martindale readying his supporting line, George Stannard's brigade, to attack. Smith quickly realized that any advance by Martindale in the center would be disastrous unless it was coordinated with an advance by Brooks's division to the left. Yelling for Martindale to keep his troops under cover until Brooks got moving, Smith rode over to see what was holding up his 1st Division commander. Shortly after Smith left, Martindale heard the swelling roar of gunfire and cheering from his left, guessed that it was Brooks advancing, and ordered Stannard in. The firing was not Brooks advancing, however, but rather Neill's battering ram being stopped. Stannard's brigade dutifully attacked without support on either side and was gnawed all around. According to a soldier in the 27th Massachusetts, "The surface of the field seemed like a boiling cauldron from the incessant pattering and ploughing of shot, which raised the dirt in geysers and spitting sands." A member of the 25th Massachusetts remembered, "We moved slowly up the slight elevation beyond which a thousand deaths awaited us. . . . We were at once under a murderous fire. . . . Colonel Pickett . . . waved his sword over his head, and shouted orders: 'Come on, boys; forward, double-quick CHARGE!'" Lieutenant Graham and Captain Foss of Company F, who had promised to watch out for each other, were together when Foss fell, shot in the thigh. "Go on, Jim," Foss yelled to Graham, "I have one of them!" Graham rushed to find the next in command. On the way, he was hit and killed. As the regiment pushed near the main Confederate line, it was literally shredded.

The only worry that Stannard's advance caused the Confederate brigadier Evander Law was the fear that his fast-firing men would run out of cartridges before the attack was over. The battle-hardened Alabama colonel William Oates was appalled by what he saw: "The charging column . . . received the most destructive fire I ever saw. . . . I could see the dust fog out of a man's clothing in two or three places at once where as many balls would strike him at the same moment." One Massachusetts soldier, driven mad by the destruction, jumped up and raced to the rear toward cover but "was completely riddled in less time than it takes to write it."

Three times Stannard's brigade rose to rush forward, and three times it was beaten back. In the process, all of George Stannard's staff officers were put out of action — two killed and four wounded. By the time "Baldy" Smith got matters organized in Brooks's division, it was all over for Martindale's.

WILLIAM F. SMITH TO GEORGE MEADE:

GENERAL: . . . MY TROOPS ARE VERY MUCH CUT UP, AND HAVE NO HOPE OF BEING ABLE TO CARRY THE WORKS IN MY FRONT UNLESS A MOVEMENT OF THE SIXTH CORPS ON MY LEFT MAY RELIEVE AT LEAST ONE OF MY FLANKS FROM THIS GALLING FIRE.

HORATIO WRIGHT TO ANDREW HUMPHREYS:

. . . I AM IN ADVANCE OF EVERYTHING ELSE. IF I ADVANCE MY RIGHT FURTHER, WITHOUT A CORRESPONDING ADVANCE BY THE EIGHTEENTH CORPS, I AM, FROM THE FORM OF THE ENEMY'S LINES, TAKEN IN FLANK AND REVERSE. MY LEFT CANNOT WELL BE ADVANCED FOR THE SAME REASON; . . . I THINK I CAN CARRY THE ENEMY'S MAIN LINE OPPOSITE MY CENTER, AND HAVE ORDERED THE ATTACK, BUT . . . MY FLANKS CANNOT MOVE WITHOUT A CORRESPONDING MOVE-MENT OF THE CORPS ON MY RIGHT AND LEFT. MY LOSSES WILL SHOW THAT THERE HAS BEEN NO HANGING BACK ON THE PART OF THE SIXTH CORPS. . . . I MAY BE PARDONED FOR SUGGESTING THAT THE IMPORTANT ATTACK FOR OUR SUCCESS IS BY THE EIGHTEENTH CORPS.

At Grant's headquarters, the steady clicking of the field telegraph and the constant arrival of new dispatches was posing its own problem. "Some of the messages were rather contradictory," Grant's aide Horace Porter admitted, adding that they "became still more conflicting as the attack proceeded."

Sitting at his headquarters, George Meade was curiously isolated from the battle. "There has been no fight of which I have seen so little as this," his aide Theodore Lyman wrote. "The woods were so placed that the sound, even, of the musketry was much kept away, and the fighting, though near us, was completely shut from view."

At about this time the first of Lee's messengers returned from A. P. Hill. The Third Corps commander had shown the courier the Federal dead lying on top of one another. "Tell General Lee," Hill said, "it is the same all along my front."

Defeat
Union: 5:15–8:00 A.M.

All along the bleeding front a few, final, convulsive lunges were taking place. Even though Martindale's advance was by now shattered beyond hope of repair, William Brooks tried to move his division forward on the left. It never had a chance. "The bullets did not whistle, they came with a rush like lightning," a dazed Connecticut soldier recalled. In a battle where horrible woundings were only too common, one of Brooks's brigadiers, Gilman Marston, had the dubious distinction of being knocked out of action by a tree limb that was clipped by a solid shot. A couple of enterprising New York soldiers, seeing an instant opportunity to retire from the field with honors, grabbed the stunned general and began hustling him to the rear. Marston regained his senses and yelled at the New Yorkers to put him down. In a short while he was back along the firing line.

Confederate: 5:15–8:00 A.M.

In front of Evander Law's Alabama brigade, one Federal regiment simply melted away — save for its color-bearer, who, unaware that there was no longer anyone behind him, steadily advanced with the flag. "Go back! Go back! we'll kill you!" some of the Alabamians shouted. But still the Union soldier came on. When he got close enough, a few Confederates even stood up and waved him away. Then, remembered an officer in the 4th Alabama, "he finally stopped, and taking the staff from its socket, rested it on the ground. He then deliberately looked, first to the right rear, and then his left rear, and then seemingly for the first time taking in the situation, with the same moderation gathered in the flag, right-shoulder-shifted his charge, came to an about face as deliberately, and walked back amid the cheers of Law's men, who never saw anything equal to it before or since."

Confederate: After 8:00 A.M.

With the fighting so close to the Confederate capital, it was inevitable that some VIP's would come out to see the action firsthand. At around noon, Postmaster General John Reagan showed up with a couple of lawyer friends. They quizzed Robert E. Lee about the condition of the Southern army, giving the gray-haired commander another chance to repeat his pleas for more troops. One of the visitors asked Lee if the cannon fire was especially heavy this day. Lee nodded but gestured toward the battle lines, where the musketry was firing in such volume that the postmaster likened it to the tearing of a sheet. "It is that," Lee said with no emotion, "that kills men."

Union: After 8:00 A.M.

Everywhere, the battered Federals were entrenching at the point where they had been stopped. On Hancock's front, the 152nd New York reported, "We fell back . . . an average distance of 100 feet from the rebel works, and began to throw up breastworks, using case knives and tin plates." The men of the 19th Massachusetts found a rail fence just to their rear and immediately began to pass the rails forward to bolster their cover. Horatio Wright's soldiers dug in, "improvising all sorts of implements for this purpose." Along "Baldy" Smith's bloody line, the troops used material that was suddenly available in abundance. "We piled up bodies in front of us and covering them with earth, made them serve as a defense. The dirt would sometimes sift down and expose a hand or foot, or the blackened face of the dead."

George Place, one of Stedman's hard-hit soldiers, was stumbling back to the cover of the woods after being struck under the left eye by a ricocheting rock and in the arm by a Confederate bullet. Just as he reentered the woods, he was grazed in the small of his back. "As I received the third blow," he remembered, "that old familiar expression 'hit 'im again, bluejacket, he's got no friends,' passed across my mind."

The orders to renew the assault met a varied fate.

Along John Gibbon's line, recalled a member of the Philadelphia Brigade, no such command ever "reached the front of the Second Division." On other portions of the line, when the word to advance came, the soldiers just stepped up their rate of rifle fire without leaving the shallow trenches they had scooped out. When staff officers brought the orders to Stedman's mangled brigade, one New Hampshire officer exploded. He "denounced in righteous wrath the general, high or low, who was guilty of ordering such a murderous charge as that . . . [and] declared with an oath that he would not take his regiment into another such charge, if Jesus Christ himself should order it."

Not surprisingly, the victors of this battle were less than eager to present themselves as targets. One member of the Philadelphia Brigade reported hearing Confederate officers urging their own men to "advance and capture the few hundred Yankees," but no counterattack came out of the entrenchments.

Some concerted effort seems to have been made among the reserve troops to ready a new assault. In the Eighteenth Corps, a large body of infantry, mostly from Brooks's division, was formed into a column thirty-two ranks deep, "a solid body of men literally covering the ground." At the same time, "over the Sixth Corps — a large part of that corps, about 15,000 men, [were] similarly massed."

But the commanders in the field had had enough. Both Barlow and Gibbon told Hancock that any further attack was "inadvisable." "Baldy" Smith got a verbal order from Meade to renew the assault, but he refused to obey it. Wright repeatedly said that he would attack, but only if Smith and Hancock did as well.

It was all over.

HEADQUARTERS ARMY OF THE POTOMAC
JUNE 3, 1864 — 1:30 P.M.
ORDERS
FOR THE PRESENT ALL FURTHER OFFENSIVE OPERATIONS
WILL BE SUSPENDED. . . .

In his diary, the Fifth Corps artillery chief, Charles Wainwright, made note of the actions of the two other Union corps at Cold Harbor: "The Fifth Corps being strung out on a line some five miles long could do nothing save demonstrate and fire artillery. . . . Burnside was to have attacked with his whole corps at daylight, as a diversion to the attack on the left, but as usual was not ready until the matter there had been decided."

Confederate: Afternoon

The dead were everywhere and in every conceivable posture. "Men lay in places like hogs in a pen," a Southerner in Kershaw's Brigade recalled, "some side by side, across each other, some two deep, while others with their legs lying across the head and body of their dead comrades." John Haskell, an artilleryman whose battery had repeatedly enfiladed "Baldy" Smith's corps, could see that "the ground in front of our works was covered black with the dead." A Virginia cavalryman named Charles Minor Blackford struggled to describe the scene in a letter to his wife, finally having to content himself with the comment, "I never saw anything like it." A young Georgian in Hoke's Division concurred: "I have been upon some twenty battlefields, but the enemy's loss was greater on this field than I ever saw before."

At some points, squads of Northerners found themselves trapped too close to the Confederate lines to make their way back. Most tried to lie low, but as soon as they were spotted they were captured. One wounded Federal stumbled into the portion of the line being held by William Oates's Alabamians and gasped that there were more unwounded bluecoats nearby. Oates sent out a company, and it brought in a hundred Yankees, including a colonel. "He said he had been in many places," Oates remembered, "but that this was the worst."

Union: Afternoon

"The man who moved, even an arm, was remorselessly shot," a Massachusetts soldier recalled angrily.

Samuel Evans of Company D lay badly wounded in front of his regiment, the 140th Pennsylvania. His friend John Hathaway saw him move slightly to indicate that he was still alive. Armed only with a canteen of water, Hathaway "deliberately stepped out and in full view of a strong Confederate line walked to where his friend was lying." Not a shot was fired as Hathaway made Evans comfortable and gave him some water. But as Hathaway turned to go back to the Union lines, nearly a hundred riflemen opened up on him. Hathaway was hit and knocked down, finally crawling to safety "in fainting condition." Evans was dragged in later but died a few days afterward. On the portion of the line held by the 25th Massachusetts, unwounded survivors of the charge watched in helpless horror as a terribly mangled man lying between the lines cut his own throat with a jackknife to end his agony.

Confederate: Night

After dark, troops on the Confederate left learned of events on the opposite flank. The word came by means of what one soldier called "an improvised telegraphy." As he later explained, "[It] was nothing more than passing word from man to man and on this occasion came, 'Pass it along the line that we have whipped the enemy on the right.'"

Confederates were surprised at how light their losses had been this day. "In fact," wrote Dr. LeGrand Wilson of Mississippi, "so few wounded had been brought in by dark, that the regimental surgeons were ordered to visit their commands in person and see that the wounded had all been brought off."

Some small-scale operations took place after dark as Confederate officers moved to smooth out irregularities in their lines. One was in front of Breckinridge's position, where the Federals had temporarily breached the line. General Finegan ordered a raiding party to clear the Yankee pocket that was still holding on nearby. The Florida soldiers chosen for the assignment grumbled about charging out into the open for such a small action. Young Captain C. Seton Fleming, chosen to lead the raid, "made a little speech to his men — told them he was ordered to go — was going — and called upon them to . . . follow him. . . ." The Florida boys trusted Fleming, who had helped draft their reenlistment resolution earlier in the year.

Fleming had his own doubts about the wisdom of the orders, but he led his men forward. Almost at once gunfire rippled from the Federal works and sent the Confederate party reeling back. Left behind in the scrambling retreat was the body of the young captain.

At 8:45 P.M., Robert E. Lee wired Jefferson Davis in nearby Richmond, "Our loss today has been small, and our success, under the blessing of God, all that we could expect."

A young North Carolinian writing home this evening said, "I think this will be one of the most awful battles that has ever been fought in this war."

Union: Night

By the time night fell, most of the wounded who were to survive had crawled or been brought in. Those who still lived and lay in the no-man's land knew what their fate would be. Among the papers gathered by the burial parties several days later was a bloodstained diary with this final entry: "June 3. Cold Harbor. I was killed."

Federal losses reached high into the ranks. In Hancock's corps, three young colonels — H. Boyd McKeen, Frank Haskell, and James McMahon — were mourned by their fellow colonel Nelson Miles, who recalled that the three had "bivouacked that night together and slept under the same blanket; they were laughing and speculating as to the results of the morrow. When dawn came they all gallantly led their regiments and were all dead in fifteen minutes."

Once again Federal doctors labored through a nightmare. Recalled a soldier in the 81st New York, "Our surgeons worked nobly, looking like so many butchers; many were bareheaded, with sleeves rolled up to their arm pits, some of them spotted all over with blood; they really looked horrifying."

A few Southern combat patrols ventured out into the darkness, but they roused such a furious reaction that they quickly scuttled back, without much loss. Many of the vengeance-hungry Federals remembered these probes as full-scale attacks that were smashed back with great loss to the enemy. "Come on! Come on! Bring up some more Johnnies," a few screamed. "You haven't got enough!"

Frank Wilkeson watched the 7th New York Heavy Artillery come back. "They seemed to be dazed and utterly discouraged," he remembered.

A returning member of the 36th Wisconsin was struck by the curious appearance of the trees near the jump-off point. They "looked as if there had been a storm of large, heavy, wet flakes of snow sticking to the trunks." Examining the trees more closely, the Wisconsin soldier realized that the effect "was done by the balls of the enemy knocking off the bark, showing the white wood."

When the 12th New Jersey finally took up its line for the night, Private William Haines found himself behind the same tree from which he and his fellow skirmishers had rolled away the dead Confederate before feasting on his johnnycake.

Sergeant William Chambers, whose birthday was today, finally stumbled upon a field hospital and had his wounded arm treated. Chambers had spent the whole day looking for help, stopping every now and then to pour water on the wound in an attempt to keep down the inflammation. "When he finally found a heap of straw to lie down on," related the regiment's historian, "he was astonished to find on each side his two comrades of the night before, both wounded, and the same blanket covered the three again."

In the years after the war, Ulysses Grant confessed, "I have always regretted that the last assault at Cold Harbor was ever made."

There was never an accurate accounting of Union losses for this day. A surgeon in Hancock's corps guessed the casualties to be "not much less than 5,000." The Confederate First Corps artillery chief, E. P. Alexander, later estimated the number to be seventy-three hundred, while Provost Marshal Marsena Patrick of the Army of the Potomac was told by General Meade that their losses exceeded eight thousand. Drawing upon hospital records, Meade's chief of staff, Andrew Humphreys, put the June 3 totals at 4,517 wounded and "at least 1,100" killed.

Whatever the final determination, from this day on the Army of the Potomac's headquarters ceased to ask for morning reports from its company commanders. The numbers of lost men were potentially too explosive an issue for the staff to allow that data to be easily assembled.

This night, Charles Dana reported to Edwin M. Stanton, the secretary of war:

OUR FORCES ATTACKED THE ENEMY ALONG THE WHOLE LINE THIS MORNING, OPENING AT 4.30 O'CLOCK. . . . THE FIGHTING WAS PRETTY FAIR ALONG THE WHOLE FRONT. WE GAINED ADVANTAGES HERE AND THERE. . . . AT NOON WE HAD FULLY DEVELOPED THE REBEL LINES, AND COULD SEE WHAT WAS NECESSARY IN ORDER TO GET THROUGH THEM. HANCOCK REPORTED THAT IN HIS FRONT IT COULD NOT BE DONE. WRIGHT WAS DECIDEDLY OF OPINION . . . IT WOULD BE DIFFICULT TO MAKE MUCH . . . UNLESS HANCOCK AND SMITH COULD ALSO ADVANCE. SMITH . . . WAS NOT SANGUINE. . . . IN THIS STATE OF THINGS GENERAL GRANT ORDERED THE ATTACK SUSPENDED. . . . THE WEATHER IS COOL AND PLEASANT. SHOWERS HAVE LAID THE DUST.*

---

*A personal note: Among the Union soldiers wounded this day was one Andre Napoleon Trudeau, a sergeant in the 10th Massachusetts. A recent, albeit casual, inquiry has failed to establish any direct relationship to the author, but the Trudeau clan had been spreading with determination out of Canada for more than two hundred years by that time, so some kinship is possible. One trait that this distant forebear clearly had in common with his possible descendant was made clear in an account of Trudeau's wounding, published in the history of the 10th Massachusetts. According to the historian, Sergeant Trudeau "was hit in the back of the head by a solid twelve pound shot which rolled over the riflepits. Although knocked senseless, his head was too hard for the shot, and the wound was not dangerous."

Cold Harbor to the James

SATURDAY, JUNE 4

The rain ended during the night, taking most of the heat with it. The weather this morning was cool and pleasant.

Along the opposing lines near Cold Harbor, soldiers looked out on a field of dead and dying men. Never before in this war had battlefield death seemed so inevitable. Since the beginning of the campaign, the Army of the Potomac had lost, on average, two thousand men per day. Survivors of the earlier battles faced this new day fatalistically. Said one New Jerseyman in the 15th, "Men . . . who at sunrise helped to bury a comrade, felt that they might need others to perform the same office for them before the day closed." Another soldier apologized for writing letters that dwelled on gory detail. "Yet what else can we write?" he asked. "Our duties, our daily and nightly business, are with the dead, the dying and the tortured sufferer."

The lines were so close that any visible object became an instant target. In the 12th New Jersey, two men detailed to go to the rear for water were both shot. One of the pair died, and his passing was marked by another in the regiment, who made note of "the shortest service of any man in the company. A new recruit, he spent but one night in our ranks, and received his death-wound in the morning."

Lieutenant Randolph Shotwell of Virginia remembered that he and a fellow officer "were shaking out a blanket at sunrise, each holding one end of it, when whiz-z-z! and a well-aimed shell from a small cannon that the Yankees had brought to the edge of the woods along the right split the blanket between us, and killed a man several hundred yards to the rear."

★

Both commanding generals found time this day for personal letters.

Ulysses S. Grant wrote to his daughter, Nelly: "I received your pretty well written letter more than a week ago. You do not know how happy it made me feel to see how well my little girl not yet nine years old could write. . . . We have been fighting now for thirty days and have every prospect of still more fighting to do before we get into Richmond. . . . Be a good little girl as you have always been, study your lessons, and you will be contented and happy."

Robert E. Lee wrote to his wife, Mary: "On returning to camp last evening dear Mary I found your note & basket. Thank Mrs. Stannard for the bread which is a great comfort to me. . . . We are all in the hands of our Merciful God, whom I know will order all things for our good, but we do not know what that is or what He may determine, & it behooves us to use the perception & judgement He has given us for our guidance & well being. . . . I trust & believe He will save us in His own good time, & upon Him is my whole faith & reliance."

Things were too quiet for Robert E. Lee. At 6:00 P.M., he informed his First Corps commander, Richard Anderson, "I . . . [believe] the enemy . . . is preparing to leave us tonight, and I fear will cross the Chickahominy. In that event the best course for us to pursue[,] in my opinion, would be to move down and attack him with our whole force, provided we could catch him in the act of crossing."

At 7:00 P.M. this evening, Charles Dana telegraphed Washington, "No fighting of any account to-day. Our troops have been busy . . . making regular siege approaches to rebel works. . . . Before moving from Culpeper . . . [Grant] expected . . . he would have a chance to crush Lee's army by fair fighting. . . . This expectation has been foiled by Lee's success in avoiding battle upon any equal terms."

The strain on staff officers was intense. Meade's chief of staff, Andrew Humphreys, admitted, "For three nights prior to last night I had not two hours sleep for each night, and that broken. . . . As each successive dispatch comes in with a scratch at the tent, instead of ripping out as I feel inclined to do, it is simply 'Come in; What is it? Light the candle on the table; you will find matches there.'"

The most high-strung of the Union corps commanders was Gouverneur Warren. Theodore Lyman remembered hearing the Fifth

Corps general exclaim around this time, "For thirty days now, it has been one funeral procession, past me; and it is too much!"

SUNDAY, JUNE 5

"I think that Mr. Grant has got tired a charging our men and has gone to work with the spade," a Confederate artilleryman wrote at Cold Harbor. "Maybe he thinks that he can dig in to Richmond as he did at Vicksburg but he has not got Gen. Pemberton to contend with here, but he has got Mars Robert to contend with."

Life in the front lines was no picnic, as Andrew Humphreys noted: "The men in the advanced part of the lines . . . had to lie close in narrow trenches with no water, except a little to drink, and that of the worst kind, being from surface drainage; they were exposed to great heat during the day; they had but little sleep; their cooking was of the rudest character."

Many of the bodies between the lines had been fetidly corrupting for almost two days, and a few had been rotting since June 1. "The air was foul with the stenches," a Massachusetts soldier complained. Added Horace Porter, "In some places the stench became sickening."

Winfield Hancock could stand it no more. At 1:00 P.M. he wired Meade's headquarters, "Can any arrangements be made by which the wounded in front . . . can be removed? I understand men wounded on the 3d are still lying there."

Meade prodded Grant, who penned a personal note to Robert E. Lee. Grant was loath to ask Lee for a truce. As a Federal staff officer later explained, "An impression prevails . . . that a commander who sends a flag of truce asking permission to bury his dead and bring in his wounded has lost the field of battle." Rather, Grant tried to finesse the request. He mentioned the wounded — "probably of both armies" — lying exposed and cited humanitarian reasons for his note. Grant never mentioned a truce; what he proposed instead was more informal: "When no battle is raging [along a portion of the lines, that] either party be authorized to send . . . unarmed men . . . to pick up their dead or wounded."

It fell to George Meade to deliver Grant's note to Lee. At 3:00 P.M., Theodore Lyman was called to headquarters and given the errand. Lyman considered it "quite an episode in my military experiences." He carried the message off to the far left of the Federal lines, where he made contact with Confederate pickets. The young aide passed the note along, waited some time for a reply, and then was told to return empty-handed. The answer, when it came, would be sent across by picket officers.

Cyrus Comstock of Grant's staff was anxious for action. "It seems to me that we are wasting time here," he noted in his diary. Horace Porter also knew that something would have to happen to break the stalemate at Cold Harbor. "The general-in-chief realized that he was in a swampy and sickly portion of the country," Porter observed.

Grant agreed. In a long letter he sent to Henry Halleck today, he stated that "it would not be practicable to hold a line northeast of Richmond." Also, in order to maintain his present position, he would have to expend strength to protect his supply line via the R. F. &P. railroad. Since Lee had not come into the open to fight, as Grant had hoped he would, the Union general now decided on a new plan. First, Sheridan's cavalry would be cut loose again to disrupt Lee's supply chain by means of a raid on the Virginia Central railroad near Beaver Dam Station. "When this is effected," Grant continued, "I will move the army to the south side of the James River."

During the night, the Army of the Potomac shortened its line by abandoning its trenches around Bethesda Church. Warren's Fifth Corps, which had been on "Baldy" Smith's right, massed in reserve, while Burnside's troops filled the gap and bent the Union flank protectively back toward the east. In the move, a portion of the 16th Maine that was picketing near Bethesda Church was left behind. Some of the men were captured, and a few eventually worked their way to the new Federal position.

MONDAY, JUNE 6

Lee's reply passed through the Union lines after midnight: he was not buying Grant's proposal for informal humanitarian efforts. "I fear that such an arrangement will lead to misunderstanding and difficulty," Lee wrote. The Confederate commander insisted that strict protocol be observed and that "a flag of truce be sent, as is customary."

Hancock's chief of staff, Charles Morgan, later marveled ironically at the way the truce request was delayed "by something akin to points of etiquette."

The unburied dead continued to be a problem. "The air was laden with insufferable putrescence," said a trooper in Smith's corps. "We breathed it in every breath, tasted it in the food we ate and water we drank." In Richmond, War Clerk Jones reported that a "deserter says Grant intends to *stink* Lee out of his position."

Grant still resisted the thought of asking for a truce. His reply to Lee's note tried to bluff through this point. "I will send immediately, as you propose," he wrote, "to collect the dead and wounded between the lines of the two armies. . . . I propose that the time for doing this be between the hours of 12 M. and 3 P.M. to-day."

During this afternoon, as Horace Porter later recalled, Grant "called Colonel Comstock and me into his tent." Grant quickly explained that he had a special mission in mind for the two. They were to serve as an advance party for his planned movement south of the James, traveling to Bermuda Hundred to meet with Butler and, once there, obtaining what topographical information they could to help coordinate the move. Both officers had served with McClellan during the ill-fated Peninsula Campaign in 1862, and they were familiar with the region to be traversed.

The two young aides nodded in agreement and left to prepare for their departure on June 7.

Walter Taylor, of Lee's staff, felt that Grant's word games on the truce issue were "disingenuous." Lee firmly rejected the other's proposal. "I . . . regret to find that I did not make myself understood . . . ," he now wrote. "I could not consent to the burial of the dead and the removal of the wounded between the armies in the way you propose, but that when either party desire such permission it shall be asked for by flag of truce in the usual way."

During this day, James H. Wilson, who commanded a division in Sheridan's corps and was one of the western officers who had served previously with Grant, paid a call on headquarters. It was a disturbing visit. First Wilson met Meade, who was pacing the ground in front of his tent, "flecking his top-boots nervously with his riding whip." Spotting the cavalryman and knowing full well of his "intimacy with Grant," Meade exclaimed, "Wilson, when is Grant going to take Richmond?"

Wilson found Grant's staff aides feuding. In conversations that continued into the next day, both Rawlins and Dana complained that

Cyrus Comstock had achieved a strange dominance over Grant. "That officer," Rawlins asserted (with what Wilson remembered as "blanched lips, glittering teeth, and flashing eyes"), "having won Grant's confidence, was now leading him and his army to ruin by senselessly advocating the direct attack, and driving it home by the deadly reiteration of 'Smash 'em up! Smash 'em up.'"

Grant did raise the white flag this afternoon. He wrote Lee, "The knowledge that wounded men are now suffering from want of attention . . . compels me to ask a suspension of hostilities for sufficient time to collect them in, say two hours."

It was very late, around 7:00 P.M., when Lee received Grant's note. The Confederate general quickly suggested that the hours between 8:00 and 10:00 P.M. be used to gather in the suffering men, and he indicated that Southern parties would emerge from their trenches "to collect any of its wounded that may remain upon the field."

Confederate reverses in other areas now became a matter of concern for Lee. A new Union force was causing problems in the Shenandoah Valley. On June 5 the Federals, led by Major General David Hunter, had routed a brigade-sized Confederate command near the town of Piedmont and killed the officer in charge, General William E. "Grumble" Jones.

A Union army could not be allowed to control the verdant farmlands of the Shenandoah. Lee anticipated that Richmond would want to send men out there to counter Hunter's move, and he wrote two letters today on the subject. He warned War Secretary James Seddon, "If we can defeat Grant here, the Valley can easily be recovered, but if we cannot defeat Grant I am afraid we will be unable to hold the Valley." To Jefferson Davis, Lee pleaded poverty: "The only assistance I can give from this army . . . would be to send back . . . [Breckinridge's force], numbering now about twenty one hundred muskets."

During this day, Jubal Early's troops on the left pushed forward to locate the new Union line. Stephen Ramseur's men moved eastward from Bethesda Church and then swung south, looking for the Yankee flank. What they found was a well-defended shoulder manned by Burnside's Ninth Corps.

The point of contact was briefly violent. "The firing was heavy and rapid while it lasted," recalled one of Burnside's men, "but the attack was soon repelled, and the charging column driven back to the works from whence they had advanced."

George Peyton of Virginia was one of the soldiers who spent this day marching about on the dusty roads. "Whenever the enemy moves," he noted in his diary, "Old Jube will not be satisfied until he finds out where he has gone, so he keeps us on the run until he finds him. He don't know that I have no shoes and but little breeches, torn from pockets to bottom."

TUESDAY, JUNE 7

Lee's 7:00 P.M. note setting aside the hours between 8:00 and 10:00 for the truce had not arrived at Grant's headquarters until almost midnight. As a result, as Grant explained to Lee in a communication timed at 10:30 A.M. this morning, "two officers and six men of the 8th and 25th North Carolina Regiments, who were out in search of the bodies of officers of their respective regiments, were captured." Grant promised to have the men returned, and closed his note, "Regretting that all my efforts for alleviating the sufferings of wounded men left upon the battlefield have been rendered nugatory."

Major Mitchell of Hancock's staff carried the note across to the Confederate side at around noon.

Both commanders at Cold Harbor sent troops off today to other areas of conflict.

As Lee had suspected, Richmond was anxious to feed reinforcements into the Shenandoah Valley, so Breckinridge's command left for there.

Also moving out today was Phil Sheridan and most of his riders. The Federals were under orders to head north and cross the Pamunkey, then press on to the northwest along the North Anna to the vicinity of Louisa Courthouse, where they would destroy the Virginia Central rail lines. That accomplished, the force would push on into the Valley and link up with Hunter's men.

Young Oliver Wendell Holmes, Jr., hated the enemy snipers. "You show your nose anywhere and sizzle come the bullets at it in less than the twinkling of a bedpost," he complained.

Holmes had come to a difficult personal decision. He had been offered a promotion to line officer in the 20th Massachusetts, but he had decided to turn it down. He candidly explained in a letter to his mother, "The ostensible and sufficient reason is my honest belief that I cannot now endure the labors & hardship of the line." He also felt that he had worked hard to earn a position of trust and responsibility as an aide, and claimed, "I honestly think the duty of fighting has ceased for me."

Oliver Wendell Holmes, Jr., said all this with a new, quiet confidence in himself. "I started this thing as a boy," he said. "I am now a man."

The Army of the Potomac was changing. With each passing day it lost a bit more of its veteran fighting ability. On June 5 the 4th Ohio mustered out. As the men left the trenches for the last time, one Ohioan remembered it as "a feeling of relief — a very strange feeling that is indescribable." Other regiments mustering out in this period included the 14th Indiana, the 3rd Maine, and the 2nd Rhode Island.

There was also fresh blood coming in. The 187th Pennsylvania had assembled at Harrisburg on May 17, arrived at Port Royal on May 29, and joined the army of the Potomac on June 5.

On this day, Henry Halleck wrote Grant from Washington to warn him that the bottom of the manpower barrel was in sight. "Old Brains" carefully itemized the reinforcements that had been hungrily absorbed by Grant's army since the beginning of the campaign. By Halleck's careful reckoning, this came to 48,265 men. "I shall send you a few regiments more," Halleck said in closing, "when all resources will be exhausted till another draft is made."

Lee received Grant's 10:30 A.M. message at 2:00 P.M. In his reply, he suggested that they try again, picking the hours between 6:00 and 8:00 P.M. for the new truce. "If this will answer your purpose," Lee wrote, "and you will send parties from your lines at the hour designated with white flags, I will direct that they be recognized."

CIRCULAR

CORPS COMMANDERS ARE NOTIFIED THAT A FLAG OF TRUCE EXISTS FROM 6 TO 8 P.M. TO-DAY, AND THEY WILL IMMEDIATELY SEND OUT, UNDER A WHITE FLAG, MEDICAL OFFICERS WITH STRETCHER-BEARERS TO BRING IN THE DEAD AND WOUNDED. NO OTHER OFFICERS OR MEN WILL BE PERMITTED TO LEAVE THE LINES, AND NO INTERCOURSE OF ANY KIND WILL BE HELD WITH THE ENEMY.

J. W. Muffly (148th Pennsylvania): "When the time for the commencement of the truce began, a flag was put up on each side and, in a minute, the men from both sides were over their respective works and, notwithstanding the orders to the contrary, it was impossible to restrain them."

William Jefferson Mosely (10th Georgia Battalion): "All of us on both sides felt like I imagine a bird feels when let out of a cage. . . . We would see Yankees on the halfway ground and exchange all sorts of things. . . . We met and talked with them as if we were old friends."

John Billings (10th Massachusetts Battery): "Then ensued a scene so anomalous in the prosecution of war! . . . Now 'Yank' and 'Johnny' could barter, trade, or jest fearlessly with each other; for the more confident went outside the works from both sides, and stood in friendly converse together."

Grant Davis Carter (2nd Georgia Battalion): "We had a good time for a while as Gen. Lee gave Grant permishion . . . to bury the dead. . . . We traded for coffee and knives. I got a little black handel, three bladed not mutch account."

Johnson Hagood (Confederate brigadier): "The burial parties were in most instances unable to handle the dead, corruption had extended so far, and [they] contented themselves with covering as it lay each body with a slight mound of earth."

W. P. Derby (27th Massachusetts): "As the sepulchral work progressed, the notes of a dirge unutterably mournful and sad, came floating over the field from the bands within our lines. This requiem was our only service for the dead."

James Madison Drake (9th New Jersey): "What a task! . . . It was nauseating to those who handled the disfigured corpses, while those to whom the duty of removing the wounded had been delegated performed their task with tender hands and bleeding hearts."

Francis Walker (Second Corps adjutant): "One man was brought into our lines who had survived the dreadful ordeal. . . . He had quenched his thirst by sucking the dew from such grass as he could pull at his side, and had allayed the pangs of hunger in the same way."

John G. B. Adams (19th Massachusetts): "We found one man wounded many times, but yet alive. He was first shot in the leg, and being unable to move had taken shots from both sides; had been without food or water four days. . . . He had lost all trace of time, but said that he had suffered little, being unconscious most of the time."

F. W. Morse (121st New York): "As the burial parties were engaged in this sad duty, both armies stood on their respective works, and commenced shaking their blankets, the first opportunity they had had for a week to perform any job of this kind. . . . Clouds of dust arose from the plain by this needed operation of putting things in order."

Charles Cowtan (10th New York): "This promiscuous mingling, however, became obviously perilous . . . ; the almost unnatural . . . quiet . . . [was] suddenly terminated by a shot from a battery towards the left of the Second Corps, which acted much the same as a magician's wand, causing the soldiers between the lines to scurry like rabbits to their respective works. . . ."

Alanson Haines (15th New Jersey): "Although the truce was only to last, by agreement, for two hours, scarcely any shots were fired all night long, and the unusual stillness seemed very strange to ears so long accustomed to the roar and sounds of conflict."

The truce did not extend along the whole of the battle lines. "The enemy in front of the Ninth Corps did not appear to notice it," wrote a postwar historian, "and even fired upon those who were assumed to be under its protection."

WEDNESDAY, JUNE 8

Robert E. Lee reacted today to the news from outpost scouts that Sheridan and his riders were heading toward the Shenandoah Valley. A movement this large could not be ignored, and the Confederate general had no choice but to send out his own cavalry in pursuit. Major General Wade Hampton and two divisions, representing five sevenths of Lee's total cavalry strength, were ordered to cut Sheridan off.

"I have just witnessed a scene," wrote Robert Tilney, a Fifth Corps staff officer. "A mounted bugler, a man bearing the official flag of the Provost Marshal-General, three cavalry guards, a civilian, supposed to be a reporter, who has been convicted of some offense, mounted on a horse with two boards suspended round his neck, the words 'Libeller of the Press' written on each, more guards, and a whole rabble of spectators following the procession, as, to the sound of the bugle, it winds its way in and out of the corps around here."

The civilian was Edward Crapsey of the *Philadelphia Inquirer.* He had written an article stating that immediately after the fighting in the Wilderness, General Meade had opted for retreat, and that only Grant's determination to continue had "saved the army and the nation, too." The piece was not signed, but it had not taken much detective work for Meade to find out who had written it. Crapsey was brought before Meade and admitted that he had based his story on rumors in the camp at the time. Meade exploded. He ordered the reporter expelled in a manner designed to teach the other members of the Bohemian brigade a lesson.

The boys in the ranks applauded Meade's action. One Sixth Corps chaplain declared, "It is time to stop such writers, and all those who, for speculating or sensational reasons, get up 'Bogus Drafts and Bogus Proclamations.' The soldiers are indignant." Officers also agreed. "It will be a warning to his tribe," Provost Marshal Marsena Patrick growled.

The correspondents saw things differently, however. According to Sylvanus Cadwallader of the *New York Herald,* reporters hereafter began to leave Meade's name out of their dispatches. From now on, this was to be the story of *Grant's* army.

The armies were growing used to one another. Said a Massachusetts man in Smith's corps, "At night the military bands of both armies played, the Union bands sending out the patriotic strains of 'The Star Spangled Banner' and 'Yankee Doodle,' while the rebels responded with 'The Bonnie Blue Flag' and 'Dixie.'"

THURSDAY, JUNE 9

Wade Hampton's cavalrymen clattered out of camp on their way to intercept Sheridan. In a long letter to Jefferson Davis, Robert E. Lee mentioned that Grant's army was otherwise unusually quiet. This induced Lee "to believe that he is awaiting the effect of movements in some other quarter to make us change our position." Officers who were less perceptive than Lee read Grant's relative inactivity to mean something else. "Old U.S. Grant is pretty tired of it — at least it appears so," wrote Lee's aide Walter Taylor.

On another front, Beauregard was again clamoring for attention. A mixed force of enemy infantry, cavalry, and artillery had appeared outside the Petersburg defenses, and Beauregard was certain that an attack was imminent. "The return soon as practicable of my troops sent to General Lee is again urged on War Department," he wired Richmond.

Lee guessed that the Union action was a nuisance raid, nothing more, and simply ignored the subject in his communications with Richmond.

Preparations began today to move the massive Army of the Potomac south across the James River. In a 7:30 A.M. dispatch to Henry Halleck, Grant directed, "All re-enforcements sent hereafter please send to City Point." Special orders came down from Meade's headquarters, prohibiting all communication "with the enemy unless especially authorized." In addition, the engineer corps was put to work constructing a reserve line of entrenchments to cover the Federal left once the withdrawal got under way.

Staff officers were busy working out the detailed schedules needed to move a hundred thousand men and their supplies from close contact with an alert and aggressive foe. It was a daunting task: to disengage along an almost ten-mile front, march fifty miles across swampy, ravine-rippled ground, and cross a tidal river at a point where it was half a mile wide and ninety feet deep. To complicate matters even further, the crossing place was well within reach of the armored Confederate gunboats that were protecting Richmond.

A Confederate artilleryman named Creed Thomas Davis noted in his diary entry for this day, "The south side of the James is now said to be . . . [Grant's] destination." Davis also mentioned an act of charity: "Our regiment agreed to-day to give one ration in the next seven days to the suffering poor of Richmond. What will the Richmond extortioners say to that?"

Another side of the Confederate soldier was seen by a trooper in Mahone's Brigade named Westfield Todd: "Before our army moved out from its lines at Cold Harbor, a negro soldier was captured on the picket line, and brought to the rear. The men were very much inflamed at seeing a negro in arms. It was the first I had ever seen, and

I must confess I was considerably stirred. The poor creature was almost frightened to death as he looked around on the scowling faces
of the curious crowd. He was ashy pale. I do not remember now how
the guard happened to give him up, but some non-combatant officer
. . . who did not belong to our division, took charge of him and . . .
carried him off. I soon after heard the report of a gun, and was told
that the negro had been shot in the woods."

FRIDAY, JUNE 10

More Union veterans left army service today. "The Ninth Massachusetts went home this morning, they were the happiest lot of men you
ever saw," a comrade in the 22nd Massachusetts noted, adding, "How
I wish I were among the number."

In a letter to James Seddon, the Confederate war secretary, Robert
E. Lee repeated his speculation that the purpose of Sheridan's movement "was to cooperate with the forces under General Hunter in the
Valley." Lee also thanked Seddon for his efforts to provide the army
with fresh vegetables. "It greatly promotes the health and conflict of
the men," he wrote.

SATURDAY, JUNE 11

Grant had hoped that Cyrus Comstock and Horace Porter would have
returned by now from their mission south of the James. They had
not, but Grant felt he could wait no longer to put the wheels into
motion. In a dispatch to Meade, Grant ordered "that all preparation
may be made for the move to-morrow night."

In not-so-far-away Richmond, War Clerk Jones remarked, "There is
a calm in military matters, but a storm is gathering in the Valley of
Virginia."

Lee was mulling over a strong hint from Jefferson Davis that he
ought to send an even stronger force into the Shenandoah Valley. It
was clear from all reports that the Yankees under Hunter had joined
with two smaller Federal columns to form a combined force that was
more than double the number of rifles in Breckinridge's little command. "The only difficulty with me is the means," Lee wrote to Davis
today. "It would [take] one corps of this army. If it is deemed prudent
to hazard the defense of Richmond, the interests involved by thus

diminishing the force here, I will do so." But he was careful to add, "I think this is what the enemy would desire."

The sniper war had not abated. This morning a Massachusetts soldier in the 37th was shot "while drawing rations nearly a mile from the enemy's line in a position of supposed safety. . . ."

Along another portion of the front, the Confederate commander A. P. Hill thought that there seemed to be fewer Yankees in the trenches, so he ordered Brigadier General William Mahone to make a division-strength reconnaissance. Mahone disagreed with Hill. He believed that the Federals had just straightened out their defenses and would be waiting to blast any force foolish enough to step out into the open. On his own authority, Mahone scaled down Hill's order to a reinforced company of two hundred men. Captain Chappel of the 41st Virginia was ordered to advance and check out the situation. The small force of soldiers from the 41st and 12th Virginia moved out of cover, was hit with a furnace-blast of fire, and scrambled back. "General," Chappel said upon his return, "your orders have been obeyed."

The Federal preparations were just too massive to be missed. "We are bound for the James River, south side," noted Charles Wainwright, the Fifth Corps artillery chief. "At least so says rumour. . . ."

Orders issued this day also said so. The movement was laid out in this way: James Wilson's cavalry division would head out first, cross the Chickahominy, and clear away the Confederate pickets and patrols posted along the routes leading toward Charles City. Wilson would be followed by Warren, who was charged with protecting the vulnerable west flank of the marching columns. At the same time, "Baldy" Smith was to pull back the way he had come in, returning to White House, where he and his men would reboard transports and be taken back to Bermuda Hundred. Once Smith had cleared the roads, Burnside was to swing east and then south to Jones Bridge, taking up a position on the east flank of the multipronged movement to the James. Wright and Hancock would drop back to entrenched lines in the rear, holding them until the roads were clear, and would then follow the columns heading south, with Hancock crossing the Chickahominy after Warren and Wright taking his lead from Burnside. Once across the Chickahominy, the winding columns would push through the slightly wooded flatlands beyond, toward Wilcox's Landing on the James.

Everything was timed to start on the evening of June 12.

SUNDAY, JUNE 12

Cyrus Comstock and Horace Porter returned to Grant's headquarters between 1:00 and 2:00 A.M. this morning. "We went at once to his tent," recalled Porter, "and were closeted with him for nearly an hour discussing the contemplated operation." Grant listened to their report with impatient interjections of "Yes, yes." "We could barely get the words out of our mouths fast enough to suit him," Porter continued. "It was evident that he was wrought up to an intensity of thought and action which he seldom displayed."

Remembered the Confederate Second Corps commander, Jubal Early, "On the 12th of June . . . I received verbal orders from General Lee to hold the corps . . . in readiness to move to the Shenandoah Valley."

Lee was detaching more than eight thousand men from his hard-pressed army. It was a high-risk move, but he felt he had no alternative. Word from the Valley was that Hunter, the Yankee general, was continuing his advance and had occupied Lexington.

Lee did not make this move lightly, and he hoped for a solid return on his investment of nearly twenty percent of his total manpower. His expectation was that Early would defeat Hunter and then move down the Shenandoah Valley to threaten both Baltimore and Washington. This, Lee hoped, would force Grant to weaken his army in order to counter Early's moves.

"June 12," wrote a soldier in the 45th Pennsylvania, "there seemed to be a hum of preparation in camp that told us something important was brewing." "Baggage was packed, teams were loaded, rations were issued and cooked," added a Massachusetts man in the 36th.

Richard Ewell was a problem.

The ailing, erratic lieutenant general wanted his Second Corps back. On June 1 he had informed Lee that he was "as able for duty to-day as at any time since the campaign commenced."

Lee sat on the message for eleven days, watching Jubal Early take aggressive, confident control of Ewell's corps, and realized that the Army of Northern Virginia would be better served if "Old Bald Head" did not return.

He made his feelings known in a message to Samuel Cooper, the Confederate inspector general. Lee was not satisfied that Ewell's recovery was anything but temporary. "I think the labor and exposure to which he would be inevitably exposed would at this time again incapacitate him for field service," Lee wrote. "I therefore propose that he be placed on some duty attended with less labor and exposure. It has occurred to me that the command of the defenses of Richmond would be more in accordance with his state of health."

It was 7:00 P.M., noted a soldier in the 152nd New York, when "the music from the brass bands resounded along the whole line of eight miles." As he had done at Spotsylvania, on the night of May 11, Grant now had the musicians work to help cover the sounds of his march.

"We received orders to evacuate as slyly as possible," was how a New Yorker in the 117th put it.

A Massachusetts soldier in Warren's corps recalled that it was about ten o'clock in the evening when the men "withdrew from their breastworks . . . and marched to the left. It was bright moonlight, and the utmost caution was observed that the enemy should not discover their intentions."

The route planned for Smith's corps took it back through a dusty cavalry battlefield. Remembered George Buck of the 40th Massachusetts, "Rapid travelling in the sultry heat induced profuse perspiration, which forming a combination with the dense, suffocating dust, literally encased the men in an earthen armor, and the horrible odors from the dead mules and horses scattered along the road was such to make an occasional breath of fresh air a heavenly luxury."

The movement was already well under way when Grant joined it. Horace Porter noted, "Although there was moonlight, the dust rose in such dense clouds that it was difficult to see more than a short distance, and the march was exceedingly tedious and uncomfortable."

(The intensity of the Cold Harbor fighting can be gauged by its casualty figures. Confederate losses, newly tabulated by means of contemporary newspapers and service records, are: killed and wounded, 3,765; captured, 1,082; total, 4,847. The damage done to the Union army is clearly reflected in its losses: killed and wounded, 12,475; captured, 2,456; total, 14,931.)

MONDAY, JUNE 13

Long columns of men shuffled forward in the early-morning darkness. Jubal Early's troops were on the march — not to the south to head off Grant, as some had suspected, but north. "What does this mean?" the soldiers wondered aloud. The topographer Jed Hotchkiss shrugged and, with the fatalism of a soldier, remarked in his diary that they were off "for some distant expedition."

With his thoughts and plans turned now toward the Shenandoah Valley, Jubal Early stopped thinking about Grant. "This [move-ment]," Early later recalled, "closed my connection with the cam-paign from the Rapidan to James River."

"When a great army moves, it fills all the roads," wrote one corre-spondent, Charles Page. "It seeks every country cross-road, every farm by-road and uses it, no matter how circuitous the road, no mat-ter what direction it pursues; so that it intersects some road that does make toward the right point, it must be used. Troops often march ten or fifteen miles, and the point reached shall not be five from that of starting."

At daybreak, Robert E. Lee learned that Grant's army had slipped away during the night. According to Eppa Hunton, one of George Pickett's brigadiers, "It was said that General Lee was in a furious passion — one of the few times during the war. When he did get mad he was mad all over."

Robert Stiles, an artilleryman, put it this way: "When we waked on the morning of the 13th and found no enemy in our front we re-alized that a new element had entered into this move — the element of uncertainty. . . . [Even] Marse Robert, who knew everything knowable, did not appear to know just what his old enemy proposed to do."

Nevertheless, Lee had his men in motion quickly. A Georgia soldier named Joseph Fuller scribbled in his diary, "At 8 o'clock A.M. we received orders to march immediately." The Army of Northern Virginia, now reduced to just Anderson's First Corps and A. P. Hill's Third, crossed the Chickahominy, moved onto the Charles City road, and headed down to Riddell's Shop. Remembered J. F. J. Caldwell of McGowan's Brigade, "The day was intensely hot, so that it re-quired unusual vigilance in officers, and unusual exertion in the men, to execute the frequently repeated order to close up and keep in four ranks. As it was, a good many straggled." Stiles recalled the march as being "a slow, stupid affair." South Carolina private Frank Mixson agreed: "It is strange that I cannot recall anything from Cold Harbor to Petersburg."

Lee was calm enough by evening, when he informed War Secretary John Seddon of the facts. In the same message, he also passed along good news. Wade Hampton's cavalrymen had caught up with Sheridan's column near a place called Trevilian Station, and Hampton was claiming that he had "defeated the enemy's cavalry . . . with heavy loss."

(Grant's report on the Trevilian fight was very different from Lee's. According to Grant, the combat of June 11–12 had resulted in a repulse of the Confederate attackers and the successful completion of Sheridan's primary mission, the destruction of the Virginia Central railroad. Sheridan, Grant said, had then determined that a link-up with Hunter in the Shenandoah would not be possible, and on June 12 had started back for the Army of the Potomac.)

According to Horace Porter, on the morning of the thirteenth, Grant "made a halt at Long Bridge, where the head of Hancock's corps had arrived. . . . That evening he reached Wilcox's Landing, and went into camp on the north bank of the James, at the point where the crossing was to take place."

The scene of all the Union activity on the James was impressive. A Pennsylvanian riding with Grant's cavalry escort remembered, "The sight of that grand river — it was a splendid day — the gunboats, steamers and sailing vessels, was a novel sensation. We gazed upon the scene with as much joy and eagerness as if for the first time in our lives." Another member of the headquarters' escort, this one from the infantry, recalled, "It was really a treat, a transformation of things generally, to see this river, with its steamboats and gunboats steaming up and down, and the Stars and Stripes streaming above them."

The *New York Tribune* reporter Charles Page sketched the scene this evening: "Grant and Meade are engaged in conversation upon indifferent topics apparently. . . . Mr. Dana strides up and down as though the day had not afforded sufficient exercise. . . . It is reported that the [supply] train will be [delayed]. . . . In crossing a stream . . . one or two wagons had been capsized. . . . Mr. Dana remarks that it was 'evidently a piece of dam(n) folly.' Grant rises, steps toward the fire and says, 'If we have nothing worse than this —' The sentence was never finished."

The Yankee boys marched away from Cold Harbor with a new grimness in their souls. In the days since May 4, they had seen the full panoply of war in its most brutal manifestations. The small, courteous gestures that had always formed a humanizing backdrop to the campaign seemed less and less important to these hard-faced men.

Samuel Chase belonged to the 86th New York in Hancock's corps. Chase still held on to his humanity, but it was getting harder all the time. He later recalled an incident from this evening: "Just before dark we crossed the finest wheat field I ever looked upon, just fit for harvest, and why we crossed that beautiful field in the manner in which we did I have never been able to understand, for all day we had been in columns, the right in front, but when we came to this field we moved by the file right along the edge of the field and then moved by the left flank, our line extending beyond the field to the right and left and consequently every foot of this beautiful wheat field was trodden down. . . . Whether it was right or wrong, I have never felt it was the right thing to do, but so it was, and on we marched."

★

Epilogue

The goal of the Army of the Potomac was now the vital rail hub at Petersburg. Hopes were high. "The capture of Petersburg," wrote Andrew Humphreys, "would leave but one railroad in the hands of the Confederates. . . . Following the possession of Petersburg would be the turning of Beauregard's intrenchments in front of Butler and an advance toward Richmond." On June 14, Grant took a steamer up to Bermuda Hundred to coordinate attack plans with Benjamin Butler.

A few miles east of Wilcox's Landing, Horace Porter marveled at the work of the Federal engineers, who had begun to construct a great pontoon bridge across the James at 4:00 P.M. on the thirteenth, finishing it seven hours later. "It was twenty-one hundred feet in length, and required one hundred and one pontoons," Porter noted, adding that "Admiral Lee's fleet took position in the river and assisted in covering the passage of the troops." Most of Grant's infantry were shipped to the south bank of the James in navy transports; the bridge was used principally for wheeled vehicles and animals.

The transfer of the army began on the morning of the fourteenth. A nurse named Anna Holstein sailed near the crossing point around this time. She recalled, "The roads leading to the river could be traced by clouds of dust which hung heavily over them. . . . In the evening signal lights were seen flashing upon the hilltops and from their camp grounds; the shipping was beautifully illuminated with various colored lanterns; and though in the midst of war, the river with its numerous lights, had a gay, holiday look."

Ulysses Grant stood on the north bank of the James on the evening of the fifteenth, watching, as Horace Porter observed, "with unusual interest the busy scene spread out before him. . . . His cigar had been thrown aside, his hands were clasped behind him, and he

seemed lost in the contemplation of the spectacle. . . . The bright
sun, shining through a clear sky upon the scene, cast its sheen upon
the water, and was reflected from the burnished gun-barrels and glittering cannon, and brought out with increased brilliancy the gay
colors of the waving banners. . . . It was a matchless pageant that
could not fail to inspire all beholders with the grandeur of achievement and the majesty of military power. The man whose genius had
conceived and whose skill had executed this masterly movement
stood watching the spectacle in profound silence. . . . After a time he
woke from his reverie, mounted his horse, and gave orders to have
headquarters ferried across to the south bank of the river."

In two messages he wrote to Jefferson Davis on the fourteenth, Lee
summed up what he knew and did not know about Grant's intentions.

At 12:10 P.M., Lee mused, "I think the enemy must be preparing
to move south of James River." A portion of Hill's corps had bumped
into Federal infantry and cavalry — Warren and Wilson — near Riddell's Shop on the thirteenth, but the covering force had "disappeared
from before us during the night." Lee's problem was that there was
too much information, too many reports of Union movements in too
many directions. "Still I apprehend that he may be sending troops up
the James River with the view of getting possession of Petersburg
before we can reinforce it."

At 3:45 P.M., Lee was more certain of where Grant's army was
located — along the James River, near Wilcox's Landing. He was also
more certain of its goal: "As his facilities for crossing the river and
taking possession of Petersburg are great, . . . I think it will more
probably be his plan."

John Jones, the Confederate war clerk, penned this assessment of the
campaign that had begun on May 5 in the Wilderness: "Grant has
failed, after doing his utmost to take Richmond. He has shattered a
great army to no purpose; while Lee's army is as strong as ever."

Southern hopes now lay in a battle of wills — North versus
South. Brigadier General Evander Law put it this way: "The question
with us (and one often asked at the time) was, 'How long will the
people of the North, and the army itself, stand it?' We heard much
about the demoralization of Grant's army, and of the mutterings of
discontent at home with the conduct of the campaign, and we verily
believed that their patience would soon come to an end."

In his heart, Robert E. Lee knew that Grant's move across the

James marked the beginning of the end for the Confederacy. Only a week earlier, he had made this point to Jubal Early: "We must destroy this Army of Grant's before he gets to the James River. If he gets there it will become a siege, and then it will be a mere question of time."

In the loneliness of his White House office, Abraham Lincoln sat holding a War Department telegram. It had arrived yesterday from Grant, who, in typical understatement, was reporting that his army would be crossing the James shortly and that he had hopes of quickly capturing Petersburg. Grant closed with the comment that his movement to the James "has been made with great celerity and so far without loss or accident."

Forty-seven days before, Lincoln had wished Grant well and asked "that any great disaster, or the capture of our men in great numbers, shall be avoided." What Grant had provided for Lincoln was a succession of nightmares: the Wilderness, Spotsylvania, Cold Harbor. His strategy had resulted in massive casualty lists, and the piteously groaning evidence of the slaughter wheeled almost daily through the streets of the capital. No longer was Grant hailed as the savior of the Union. The tag applied to him more and more often now was "butcher."

In the deepest, darkest part of his heart, Lincoln knew that the war had had to come to this — a mutual butchery in which the strongest would live and the weakest die. The Confederacy could not be defeated in a normal sense — no loss of arms or land could make it recant its defiant secession. Defeat would have to be total, overwhelming. More men would have to die, more wives would have to be widowed, and more mothers would have to mourn their lost sons. Lincoln and the country had traveled too far down the bloody path of war to stop now that the end was in sight.

It would take cold, hard resolution to see the combat through to its inevitable conclusion, but Lincoln knew now that he had found his man. Throughout all the horrors — Wilderness, Spotsylvania, Cold Harbor — Grant had not once wavered, not once asked that he be allowed to pass on the cup of responsibility. The hopes and plans with which he had begun the campaign were now only so many might-have-beens in the dust of long Virginia roads. The Army of the Potomac went on; Grant went on; the war would continue. It was as Lincoln knew it must be. He would make a speech the next day in Philadelphia in which he would say, "War, at best, is terrible, and this war of ours, in its magnitude and in its duration, is one of the most terrible, . . . it having destroyed property, and ruined homes. . . . We accepted this war for an object, a worthy object, and the war will end when the object is attained. Under God, I hope it never will until that time. Speaking of the present campaign, General Grant is reported to have said, 'I am going through on this line if it takes all summer.' I say we are going through on this line if it takes three years more."

Before leaving for Philadelphia, Lincoln would send Grant this message:

HAVE JUST READ YOUR DISPATCH OF 1 P.M. YESTERDAY. I BE- GIN TO SEE IT. YOU WILL SUCCEED. GOD BLESS YOU ALL.

Notes

The main sources for each chapter are listed below with a few brief comments. Further bibliographical information may be found in the bibliography. A few books proved to be of value throughout and, in lieu of repeated listings, are acknowledged here: George Agassiz, ed., *Meade's Headquarters 1863–1865: Letters of Theodore Lyman*; Clifford Dowdey, *Lee's Last Campaign*; Douglas Southall Freeman, *R. E. Lee*; Ulysses Grant, *Personal Memoirs*; Andrew Humphreys, *The Virginia Campaign of 1864 and 1865*; Horace Porter, *Campaigning with Grant*.

Prologue

The observations of the Confederate war clerk John B. Jones may be found in *Rebel War Clerk's Diary*. I used the edition edited by Earl Schenck Miers. The best single-volume study of Lincoln and the commanders of the Army of the Potomac is T. Harry Williams, *Lincoln and His Generals*.

Preparation

John Casler's utterly unromanticized memoirs of the Civil War were published as *Four Years in the Stonewall Brigade*. A more comprehensive exploration of the "Virginia mentality" among Union officers is made by Michael C. C. Adams in *Our Masters the Rebels*. The march of the Ninth Corps through Washington is well described by Charles Coffin in his *Four Years of Fighting*.

Decision

Aspects of the relationship between Robert E. Lee and James Longstreet are touched upon in Thomas Connelly's *The Marble Man*.

The Wilderness

After more than twenty years, the basic tactical and strategic study of the Wilderness fighting remains Edward Steere's *The Wilderness Campaign*. Morris Schaff's overly poetic recollections, published as *The Battle of the Wilderness*, contain many gems. The saga of the fight of the 140th New York at Saunders Field is derived from reminiscences by Henry Cribben, Porter Farley, and August Seiser. The adventures of the cub reporter Henry Wing are expansively told in his memoir, *When Lincoln Kissed Me*. There are so many different accounts of the "Lee to the Rear" episode near the Tapp Farm that one diligent author was able to create a sizable book out of them.

I have opted for one of the least romantic accounts, believing (along with Edward Steere) that it represents a version that "is most consistent with military psychology." Also controversial is Gordon's flank attack. John Gordon's oft-quoted memoirs represent, in places, the way he wanted things to be remembered and not necessarily the way they happened. Gordon's account includes a dramatic, last-minute intervention by Robert E. Lee, overriding the hesitancy of Ewell and Early with a direct command in favor of Gordon. No other significant account mentions this visit by Lee, and it seems utterly unlike the punctilious Southern commander to so clearly violate the chain of command. Early's own memoirs have an agenda of their own and are not fully trustworthy. I have fashioned what is to me a plausible sequence of events, based on a number of little-known accounts by staff officers who were also present.

Roads South: 1

The experience of black troops in this campaign has not yet been fully explored. Freeman S. Bowley's memoir, *A Boy Lieutenant*, though overwritten in places, contains some moving moments. John Haley's cockeyed views of the war are a fairly recent discovery, thanks to their editor Ruth L. Silliker, who published them as *The Rebel Yell and the Yankee Hurrah*. My conclusion that Robert E. Lee believed on May 7 that he had beaten the Union army goes against the grain of the traditional image of him as being always one step ahead of his adversaries. However, Edward Steere, in the closing pages of his Wilderness study, makes a (to me) persuasive case for this.

Spotsylvania

By all accounts, William Matter's detailed study of the battles of Spotsylvania Court House, *If It Takes All Summer*, will be the definitive work on the subject. It had not yet been published as this book was completed. The details of Upton's May 10 charge come largely from Isaac Best's *History of the 121st New York* and Francis W. Morse's *Personal Experiences in the War*. Concerning the fighting at the Bloody Angle, A. Wilson Greene's battle study was invaluable. The tale of the heavy regiments at Harris Farm may be found in Augustus Brown, *The Diary of a Line Officer*; Hyland Kirk, *Heavy Guns and Light*; and Alfred Roe, *History of the First Regiment Heavy Artillery, Massachusetts Volunteers*.

Fredericksburg

The determined Cornelia Hancock tells her story in *South after Gettysburg*. William Barton's *The Life of Clara Barton* and William Reed's *War Papers of Frank B. Fay* helped complete the story of an overwhelmed Union medical corps.

Roads South: 2

Ned Moncure's remarkable ride south with Robert E. Lee was organized by the editor H. R. McIlwaine into a pamphlet titled *Moncure Reminiscences.*

North Anna

The basic study of this battle and standoff is Joseph Miller's hitherto unpublished thesis, "The North Anna River Campaign." Also helpful was Cadmus Wilcox's "Notes on the North Anna Campaign," which can be found among his papers at the Library of Congress. Only fragments of Lee's great earthworks remain, and none is currently protected from commercial development.

Roads South: 3

In addition to the basic Lee books mentioned above, T. Harry Williams's *Beauregard: Napoleon in Gray,* of 1955, provides a perspective from south of the James. Some measure of Beauregard's achievement there can be found in William Glenn Robertson's full-scale study of the Bermuda Hundred Campaign, titled *Back Door to Richmond.*

Bethesda Church

The last fight of the Pennsylvania Reserves is based on accounts found in Josiah Sypher, *History of the Pennsylvania Reserve Corps*; M.D. Hardin, *History of the Twelfth Regiment Pennsylvania Reserve Volunteer Corps*; and Evan Woodward, *Our Campaigns.*

Cold Harbor

The story of the 2nd Connecticut Heavies is told by Theodore Vaill in his *Second Connecticut Volunteer Heavy Artillery.* Also helpful was John Niven, *Connecticut for the Union.* The account of the June 3 charge represents the first detailed study of this tragic episode in the history of the Army of the Potomac.

Cold Harbor to the James

None of Grant's many biographers has managed a satisfactory explanation for his refusal to treat with Lee in order to rescue the Union wounded (and they were all *Union* wounded) lying between the lines.

Bibliography

Nearly a thousand sources, most of them firsthand accounts, were used to create this informal history of the campaign from the Wilderness to Cold Harbor. Many were of value for small things — a dash of color, confirmation of another source — or contributed to the overall impression of a moment. The bibliography below is limited to those items that were of primary use to me. Since this book is, for the most part, a story of people, the bibliography is organized along those lines.

Ulysses S. Grant

Badeau, Adam. *Military History of Ulysses Grant.* 1881.
Catton, Bruce. *Grant Takes Command.* 1968.
Dana, Charles. *Recollections of the Civil War.* 1898.
Grant, Ulysses S. *Personal Memoirs.* 1885.
Macartney, Clarence. *Grant and His Generals.* 1953.
Porter, Horace. *Campaigning with Grant.* 1897.
Simon, John, ed. *Papers of U. S. Grant.* 1982–1984.
Sumner, Merl, ed. *The Diary of Cyrus B. Comstock.* 1987.
Tenney, Luman Harris. *War Diary.* 1914.
Wilson, James H. *Life of John A. Rawlins.* 1916.

Robert E. Lee

Connelly, Thomas L. *The Marble Man.* 1977.
Cooke, John Esten. *A Life of General Robert E. Lee.* 1871.
Dowdey, Clifford. *Wartime Papers of Robert E. Lee.* 1961.
———. *Lee.* 1965.
Freeman, Douglas Southall. *R. E. Lee.* 1944.
Lee, Fitzhugh. *General Lee.* 1894.
Long, A. L. *Memoirs of Robert E. Lee.* 1886.
R.C. "Gen. Lee at the Wilderness." *Land We Love,* 1868.
Taylor, Walter. *Four Years with General Lee.* 1877.
———. *General Lee.* 1906.

The Soldiers: Autobiographies, Biographies, Diaries, Letters, Memoirs, and Personal Narratives

Abbott, Lemuel. *Personal Recollections.* 1908.
Agassiz, George. *Meade's Headquarters 1863–1865: Letters of Theodore Lyman.* 1922.
Alexander, E. P. *Military Memoirs of a Confederate.* 1907.

Baxter, Nancy, ed. *Hoosier Farm Boy in Lincoln's Army.* 1971.

Bennett, Edwin C. *Musket and Sword.* 1900.

Benson, Susan, ed. *Berry Benson's Civil War.* 1962.

Bernard, George, ed. *War Talks of Confederate Veterans.* 1892.

Black, John. "Reminiscences of the Bloody Angle." Minnesota MOLLUS, 1896.

Blackford, Susan, ed. *Letters from Lee's Army.* 1947.

Blackford, W. W. *War Years with Jeb Stuart.* 1945.

Blake, Henry. *Three Years in the Army of the Potomac.* 1865.

Bloodgood, J. D. *Personal Reminiscences of the War.* 1893.

Bond, Natalie, ed. *The South Carolinians.* 1968.

Booth, George. *Personal Reminiscences of a Maryland Soldier.* 1898.

Bowley, Freeman S. *A Boy Lieutenant.* 1906.

Brown, Augustus. *The Diary of a Line Officer.* 1906.

Brown, Campbell. "Memoranda — Campaign of 1864." Manuscript, n.d. (Tennessee State Library)

Brown, Varina. *A Colonel at Gettysburg and Spotsylvania.* 1931.

Brown Papers. Southern Historical Society.

Buck, Samuel. *With the Old Confeds.* 1925.

Buel, Clarence, and Robert Johnson. *Battles and Leaders of the Civil War.* 1884.

Burr, Frank. *Life and Achievements of James Addams Beaver.* 1882.

Carter, Grant Davis. Letter dated 6/11/1864.

Carter, Robert. *Four Brothers in Blue.* 1913.

Casler, John O. *Four Years in the Stonewall Brigade.* 1951.

Chase, Stephen. Memoirs, n.d.

Confederate Veteran (Nashville). Various issues, 1893–1933.

Corby, William. *Memoirs of Chaplain Life.* 1893.

Cowper, Pulaski, ed. *Extracts from Letters of Major General Bryan Grimes.* 1884.

Crossley, Andrew Jackson. Letters, 1864.

Crotty, D. G. *Four Years' Campaigning in the Army of the Potomac.* 1874.

Dame, William. *From the Rapidan to Richmond.* 1920.

Davis, Burke. *Jeb Stuart — The Last Cavalier.* 1957.

Davis, Creed Thomas. Diary, 1864.

Donald, David, ed. *Gone for a Soldier.* 1975.

Douglas, Henry Kyd. *I Rode with Stonewall.* 1940.

Doyle, Thomas. Memoir, n.d.

Early, Jubal. *Memoir of Last Year of the War for Independence.* 1866.

Eggleston, George Cary. *A Rebel's Recollections.* 1874.

Ewell Papers. Southern Historical Society.

Farley, Porter. "Reminiscences of the 140th Regiment New York Volunteer Infantry." Rochester Historical Society Publications XXII, 1944.

Favill, Josiah. *Diary of a Young Officer.* 1909.

Flandreau, States. Letters, n.d.

Fleming, Francis. *Memoir of Captain C. Seton Fleming.* 1884.

Fuller, Joseph Pryor. Diary, 1864.

Fulton, William. *War Reminiscences.* 1986.

Gallagher, Gary. *Stephen Dodson Ramseur.* 1985.

Galwey, Thomas. *The Valiant Hours.* 1961.

Gerrish, Theodore. *Army Life — A Private's Reminiscences of the Civil War.* 1882.

Gibbon, John. *Personal Recollections of the Civil War.* 1928.

Gordon, John B. *Reminiscences of the Civil War.* 1905.

Goss, Warren Lee. *Recollections of a Private.* 1890.

Hagood, Johnson. *Memoirs of the War of Secession.* 1910.

Hall, George Washington. Diary, 1864.

Hamilton, J. G., ed. *Papers of Randolph Shotwell.* 1931.

Hamlin, Percy Gatling. *Old Bald Head.* 1940.

Hancock, Winfield. Letter to Francis Walker, 1886.

Haskell, John Cheves. *The Haskell Memoirs.* 1960.

Hoole, Stanley, ed. "Letters of Joab Goodson." *Alabama Review* 10, 1957.

Hotchkiss, Jed. "Virginia." In *Confederate Military History.* Series edited by Clement Evans. 1899.

Howard, McHenry. *Recollections of a Maryland Confederate.* 1914.

Howe, Mark, ed. *Touched with Fire: Oliver Wendell Holmes Jr. Letters.* 1946.

Hudgins, F. L. Memoir, n.d.

Humphreys, Henry H. *Andrew Atkinson Humphreys.* 1924.

Hunton, Eppa. *Autobiography of Eppa Hunton.* 1933.

Hyde, Thomas. *Following the Greek Cross.* 1894.

Jackson, Asbury Hill. Letter dated 5/11/1864.

Jackson, Harry, and Thomas O'Donnell, eds. *Back Home in Oneida.* 1965.

James, Henry B. *Memories of the Civil War.* 1898.

Jones, John. "From North Anna to Cold Harbor." Ohio MOLLUS, 1893.

Jones, Melvin, ed. *Give God Glory.* 1979.

Jones, Thomas. Letters to John W. Daniel, 1904.

Justice, Benjamin Wesley. Letters, 1864.

King, John. *My Experience in the Confederate Army.* 1917.

King, W. C., and W. P. Derby. *Camp-Fire Sketches, Battlefield Echoes.* 1890.

Lee, Susan, ed. *Memoirs of William Nelson Pendleton.* 1893.

Lewis, Richard. *Camp Life of a Confederate Boy.* 1883.

Longstreet, James. *From Manassas to Appomattox.* 1896.

Loving, Jerome, ed. *Civil War Letters of George Washington Whitman.* 1975.

Martin, Thomas. Memoirs, n.d.

McBride, R. E. *In the Ranks — From the Wilderness to Appomatox Court House.* 1881.

McClellan, Henry Brainerd. *I Rode with Jeb Stuart.* 1958.

————. Letter dated 1/26/1878.

McClendon, William. *Recollections of War Times*. 1909.

McDonald, Archie, ed. *Make Me a Map of the Valley*. 1973.

McDonald, Carlos. "Extracts from the Diary of a Boy Cavalryman." Forty-sixth Reunion of the 6th Ohio Cavalry, 1911.

McIlwaine, H. R., ed. *Diary of H. W. Wingfield*. 1927.

————. *Moncure Reminiscences*. 1927.

McMurran, Joseph. Diary, 1864.

Meade, George. *Life and Letters of George Gordon Meade*. 1913.

Michie, Peter S. *Life and Letters of Emory Upton*. 1885.

Miller, Delavan. *Drum Taps in Dixie*. 1905.

Mixson, Frank. *Reminiscences of a Private*. 1910.

Morrison, James L. *Memoirs of Henry Heth*. 1975.

Morse, F. W. *Personal Experiences*. 1866.

Mull, Oscar. Diary, 1864.

Neese, George. *Three Years in the Confederate Horse Artillery*. 1911.

Nevins, Allan, ed. *A Diary of Battle*. 1962.

Nichols, G. W. *A Soldier's Story of His Regiment*. 1898.

Oates, William. *The War between the Union and the Confederacy*. 1905.

Pearson, Henry Greenleaf. *James S. Wadsworth of Genesco*. 1913.

Pennypacker, Isaac. *General Meade*. 1901.

Peyton, George. Diary, 1864.

Polk Papers. Southern Historical Collection.

Rhodes, Robert, ed. *All for the Union*. 1985.

Robertson, James. *General A. P. Hill*. 1987.

Robertson, Robert. *Personal Recollections of the War*. 1895.

Rockwell, A. D. *Rambling Recollections*. 1920.

Roemer, Jacob. *Reminiscences of the War*. 1897.

Royall, William. *Some Reminiscences*. 1909.

Runge, W., ed. *Four Years in the Confederate Artillery*. 1961.

Seiser, August. "Short Sketches of a Four Weeks Campaign with the Potomac Army." Rochester Historical Society Publications XXII, 1944.

Seymour, William. Journal, n.d.

Sheridan, Philip H. *Memoirs*. 1888.

Silliker, Ruth L., ed. *The Rebel Yell and the Yankee Hurrah*. 1985.

Sketches of War History 1861–1865: Ohio MOLLUS Papers. 1888.

Small, Abner. *The Road to Richmond*. 1939.

Smith, William Farrar. *From Chattanooga to Petersburg*. 1893.

Sorrel, G. Moxley. *Recollections of a Confederate Staff Officer*. 1905.

Southern Historical Society Papers. 50 volumes. 1876–1953.

Sparks, David, ed. *Inside Lincoln's Army*. 1964.

Stevens, Cyrenus. Diary, 1864.

Stevens, George T. *Three Years in the Sixth Corps*. 1866.

Stiles, Robert. *Four Years under Marse Robert*. 1903.

Stone, James Madison. *Personal Recollections of Civil War*. 1918.

Summers, Festus S., ed. *A Borderland Confederate*. 1962.

Taylor, Emerson. *Gouverneur Kemble Warren*. 1932.

Tilney, Robert. *My Life in the Army*. 1912.

Todd, Westfield. Reminiscences, n.d.

Toney, Marcus. *Privations of a Private*. 1905.

Tyler, Mason Whiting. *Recollections of the Civil War*. 1912.

Urban, John W. *My Experiences Mid Shot and Shell*. 1892.

Walker, Cornelius. *A Life of Lieutenant-General Richard Heron Anderson*. 1917.

Walker, Francis. *General Hancock*. 1895.

Walkup, Samuel. Diary and letters, 1864.

Weld, Stephen M. *War Diary and Letters*. 1979.

Whitaker, Cary. Diary, 1864.

Wilcox, Cadmus. "Lee and Grant in the Wilderness." In *Annals of the War*. 1879.

————. Notes on the North Anna Campaign, n.d.

Wilkeson, Frank. *Recollections of a Private Soldier in the Army of the Potomac*. 1887.

Wilson, James H. *Under the Old Flag*. 1912.

Wilson, LeGrand. *The Confederate Soldier*. Edited by James W. Silver. 1973.

Winslow, Richard. *General John Sedgwick*. 1982.

Wood, James H. *The War*. 1910.

Worsham, John. *One of Jackson's Foot Cavalry*. 1915.

Yeary, Mamie. *Reminiscences of the Boys in Gray*. 1912.

Youker, J., ed. *The Military Memoirs of Captain Henry Cribben*. 1911.

Unit Histories

Adams, John G. B. *Reminiscences of the Nineteenth Massachusetts Regiment*. 1899.

Albert, Allen. *History of the Forty-fifth Regiment Pennsylvania Veteran Volunteer Infantry*. 1912.

Anderson, John. *The Fifty-seventh Regiment Massachusetts Volunteers*. 1896.

Andrews, H. F. *Company D, 16th Maine Volunteers*. 1906.

Aubery, James. *The Thirty-sixth Wisconsin Volunteer Infantry*. 1900.

Baker, Levi. *History of the Ninth Massachusetts Battery*. 1888.

Banes, Charles. *History of the Philadelphia Brigade*. 1876.

Barrett, Orvey. *Reminiscences, Incidents, Battles, Marches and Camp Life*. 1888.

Bartlett, Asa W. *History of the Twelfth Regiment New Hampshire Volunteers*. 1897.

Bates, Samuel. *History of Pennsylvania Volunteers*. 5 volumes. 1869–1871.

Bean, William. *The Liberty Hall Volunteers*. 1964.

Bell, Robert. *11th Virginia Infantry*. 1985.

Best, Isaac. *History of the 121st New York State Infantry.* 1921.

Bicknell, George. *History of the Fifth Regiment Maine Volunteers.* 1871.

Bidwell, Frederick. *History of the Forty-ninth New York Volunteers.* 1916.

Billings, John D. *The History of the Tenth Massachusetts Battery.* 1909.

Bosbyshell, Oliver. *The 48th in the War.* 1893.

Bowen, James. *History of the Thirty-seventh Regiment Massachusetts Volunteers.* 1884.

Brainard, Mary, ed. *Campaigns of 146th Regiment New York State Volunteers.* 1915.

Brewer, A. T. *History Sixty-first Regiment Pennsylvania Volunteers.* 1911.

Brown, Maud. *The University Greys.* 1940.

Bruce, George. *The Twentieth Regiment of Massachusetts Volunteer Infantry.* 1906.

Burford, Thomas. *Lamar Rifles.* 1902.

Caldwell, J. F. J. *History of a Brigade of South Carolinians.* 1866.

Camper, Charles, and J. W. Kirkley, eds. *Historical Record of the First Regiment Maryland Infantry.* 1871.

Chamberlin, Thomas. *History of the 150th Regiment.* 1905.

Chapla, John. *42nd Virginia Infantry.* 1983.

Cheek, Philip, and Mair Pointon. *History of the Sauk County Riflemen.* 1909.

Child, William. *A History of the 5th Regiment New Hampshire Volunteers.* 1893.

Clark, Walter. *Histories of the Several Regiments and Battalions from North Carolina.* 5 Volumes. 1901.

Cogswell, Leander. *A History of the Eleventh New Hampshire Regiment Volunteer Infantry.* 1891.

Coker, James. *History of . . . Company E 6th South Carolina.* 1899.

Conyngham, D. P. *The Irish Brigade and Its Campaigns.* 1867.

Cook, Benjamin. *History of the Twelfth Massachusetts Volunteers.* 1882.

Corn Exchange Regiment: Antietam to Appomattox with 118th Pennsylvania Volunteers. 1892.

Cowtan, Charles. *Services of the Tenth New York Volunteers.* 1882.

Craft, David. *History of the One Hundred Forty-first Regiment Pennsylvania Volunteers.* 1885.

Cudworth, Warren. *History of First Regiment Massachusetts Infantry.* 1866.

Cuffel, Charles. *Durell's Battery in the Civil War.* 1900.

Cunningham, John. *Three Years with the Adirondack Regiment.* 1920.

Curtis, Orson. *History of the Twenty-fourth Michigan of the Iron Brigade.* 1891.

Cutcheon, Byron. *The Story of the Twentieth Michigan Infantry.* 1904.

Davis, Charles. *Three Years in the Army — The Story of the Thirteenth Massachusetts Volunteers.* 1894.

Dawes, Rufus. *Service with the 6th Wisconsin Volunteers.* 1890.

Denny, J. Waldo. *Wearing the Blue in the Twenty-fifth Massachusetts Volunteer Infantry.* 1879.

Derby, W. P. *Bearing Arms in the Twenty-seventh Massachusetts Regiment.* 1883.

Dickert, D. Augustus. *History of Kershaw's Brigade.* 1899.

Drake, James. *The History of the Ninth New Jersey Veteran Volunteers.* 1889.

Driver, Robert. *52nd Virginia Infantry.* 1986.

Dunlop, W. S. *Lee's Sharpshooters.* 1899.

Dusseault, John. *Company E Thirty-ninth Infantry.* 1908.

Emmerton, James. *A Record of the Twenty-third Regiment Massachusetts Volunteer Infantry.* 1886.

Fields, Frank. *28th Virginia Infantry.* 1985.

Floyd, Fred. *History of the Fortieth (Mozart) Regiment New York Volunteers.* 1909.

Ford, Andrew. *The Story of the Fifteenth Regiment Massachusetts Volunteer Infantry.* 1898.

Frederick, Gilbert. *The Story of a Regiment.* 1895.

Frye, Dennis. *2nd Virginia Infantry.* 1984.

Fuller, Edward. *Battles of the Seventy-seventh New York State Foot Volunteers.* 1901.

Galloway, G. Norton. *The Ninety-fifth Pennsylvania Volunteers in the Sixth Corps.* 1884.

Goldsborough, William. *The Maryland Line in the Confederate States Army.* 1869.

Gould, Joseph. *Story of the Forty-eighth.* 1908.

Haines, Alanson. *History of the Fifteenth Regiment New Jersey Volunteers.* 1883.

Haines, William. *History of the Men of Company F.* 1897.

Hardin, M. D. *History of the Twelfth Regiment Pennsylvania Reserve Volunteer Corps.* 1890.

Haynes, E. M. *A History of the Tenth Regiment, Vermont Volunteers.* 1894.

Haynes, Martin. *History of the Second Regiment New Hampshire Volunteers.* 1865.

Hays, Gilbert. *Under the Red Patch.* 1908.

Henderson, William D. *12th Virginia Infantry.* 1984.

Historical Sketch of the Quitman Guards. 1866.

History of the Fifth Massachusetts Battery. 1902.

History of the Nineteenth Regiment Massachusetts Volunteer Infantry. 1906.

History of the 121st Regiment Pennsylvania Volunteers. 1893.

History of the Third Pennsylvania Cavalry. 1905.

Hopkins, William. *The Seventh Regiment Rhode Island Volunteers.* 1903.

Houghton, Edwin. *The Campaigns of the Seventeenth Maine.* 1866.

House, Charles. "How First Maine Heavy Artillery Lost 1,179 men in 30 days." In *Maine Bugle.* 1895.

Houston, Henry. *The Thirty-second Maine Regiment of Infantry Volunteers*. 1903.

Howell, Helena, comp. *Chronicles of the One Hundred Fifty-first Regiment New York State Volunteer Infantry*. 1911.

Hussey, George. *History of the Ninth Regiment*. 1889.

Jackman, Lyman. *History of the Sixth New Hampshire Regiment*. 1891.

Jones, Terry L. *Lee's Tigers — Louisiana Infantry in the Army of Northern Virginia*. 1987.

Judson, Amos M. *History of the 83d Regiment Pennsylvania Volunteers*. 1865.

Kent, Arthur, ed. *Three Years with Company K*. 1976.

Kepler, William. *History of Three Months and Three Years' Service*. 1886.

King, David. *History of the Ninety-third Regiment New York Volunteer Infantry*. 1895.

Kirk, Hyland. *Heavy Guns and Light*. 1890.

Kreutzer, William. *Notes and Observations*. 1878.

Krick, Robert E. L. *40th Virginia Infantry*. 1985.

Krick, Robert K. *30th Virginia Infantry*. 1985.

———. *The Fredericksburg Artillery*. 1986.

———. *Parker's Virginia Battery C.S.A.* 1975.

Lewis, Osceola. *History of the One Hundred and Thirty-eighth Regiment Pennsylvania Volunteer Infantry*. 1866.

Locke, William. *The Story of the Regiment*. 1868.

Lord, Edward. *History of the Ninth Regiment New Hampshire Volunteers*. 1895.

Love, David. *The Prairie Guards*. 1890.

Macnamara, Daniel G. *The History of Ninth Regiment Massachusetts Volunteer Infantry*. 1899.

Marbaker, Thomas. *History of the Eleventh New Jersey Volunteers*. 1898.

Mark, Penrose. *Red, White and Blue Badge*. 1911.

Muffly, J. W. *The Story of Our Regiment*. 1904.

Mulholland, St. Clair. *The Story of the 116th Regiment Pennsylvania Infantry*. 1899.

Nash, Eugene. *A History of the Forty-fourth Regiment New York Volunteer Infantry*. 1911.

Newell, Joseph. *"Ours": Annals of 10th Regiment*. 1875.

Nichols, James. *Perry's Saints*. 1886.

Osborne, William. *The History of the Twenty-ninth Regiment Massachusetts Volunteer Infantry*. 1877.

Page, Charles. *History of the Fourteenth Regiment Connecticut Volunteer Infantry*. 1906.

Palmer, Abraham. *The History of the Forty-eighth Regiment New York State Volunteers*. 1885.

Parker, Francis. *The Story of the Thirty-second Regiment Massachusetts Infantry*. 1880.

Parker, John. *Henry Wilson's Regiment.* 1887.

Phillips, S., and L. Hale. *History of the 49th Virginia Infantry.* 1981.

Polley, J. B. *Hood's Texas Brigade.* 1910.

Powell, William H. *The Fifth Army Corps.* 1896.

Powelson, B. F. *History of Company K of the 140th Regiment Pennsylvania Volunteers.* 1906.

Prowell, George. *History of the Eighty-seventh Regiment Pennsylvania Volunteers.* 1901.

Putnam, Samuel. *Story of Company A, Twenty-fifth Regiment Massachusetts Volunteers.* 1886.

Rankin, Thomas. *23rd Virginia Infantry.* 1985.

Rauscher, Frank. *Music on the March.* 1892.

Reidenbaugh, Lowell. *33rd Virginia Infantry.* 1987.

Rhodes, John. *The History of Battery B.* 1894.

Riggs, David. *7th Virginia Infantry.* 1982.

Ripley, William. *Vermont Riflemen in the War.* 1883.

Roback, Henry. *The Veteran Volunteers of Herkimer and Otsego Counties.* 1888.

Robertson, James. *4th Virginia Infantry.* 1982.

———. *18th Virginia Infantry.* 1984.

———. *The Stonewall Brigade.* 1963.

Robertson, James, ed. *Civil War Letters of General Robert McAllister.* 1965.

Roe, Alfred. *History of the First Regiment Heavy Artillery Massachusetts Volunteers.* 1917.

———. *The Ninth New York Heavy Artillery.* 1899.

———. *The Thirty-ninth Regiment Massachusetts Volunteers.* 1914.

Santvoord, C. Van. *One Hundred and Twentieth New York State Volunteers.* 1894.

Sawyer, Franklin. *A Military History of the 8th Regiment Ohio Volunteer Infantry.* 1881.

Scott, Kate. *History of the One Hundred and Fifth Regiment of Pennsylvania Volunteers.* 1877.

Shaw, Horace. *First Maine Heavy Artillery.* 1903.

"Side Lights on the Battle of the First Maine Heavy Artillery on May 19th." *Maine Bugle.* 1894.

Simons, Ezra. *A Regimental History: One Hundred and Twenty-fifth New York Volunteers.* 1888.

Smith, John Day. *The History of the Nineteenth Regiment of Maine Volunteer Infantry.* 1909.

Smith, W. A. *Anson Guards.* 1914.

Stephenson, Luther. *A Sketch Giving Some Incidents during the Service of the Thirty-second Regiment Massachusetts.* 1900.

Stevens, C. A. *Berdan's United States Sharpshooters.* 1892.

Stewart, A. M. *Camp, March and Battlefield.* 1865.

Stewart, Robert L. *History of the One Hundred and Fortieth Regiment Pennsylvania Volunteers.* 1912.

Sublett, Charles. *57th Virginia Infantry.* 1985.

Swinfen, David B. *Ruggles' Regiment: The 122nd New York Volunteers in the American Civil War.* 1982.

Sypher, Josiah. *History of the Pennsylvania Reserve Corps.* 1865.

Terrill, J. Newton. *Campaign of the Fourteenth Regiment New Jersey Volunteers.* 1884.

Thomas, Henry. *History of the Doles-Cook Brigade.* 1903.

Thompson, S. Millett. *Thirteenth Regiment of New Hampshire Volunteer Infantry.* 1888.

Thomson, O. R. Howard. *History of the Bucktails.* 1906.

Under the Maltese Cross . . . Campaigns of the 155th Pennsylvania Regiment. 1910.

Vaill, Dudley. *County Regiment — A Sketch of the Second Regiment Connecticut Heavy Artillery.* 1908.

Vaill, Theodore. *History of the Second Connecticut Volunteer Heavy Artillery.* 1868.

Valentine, Herbert. *Story of Company F, 23d Massachusetts Volunteers.* 1896.

Vautier, John. *History of the 88th Pennsylvania Volunteers.* 1894.

Walker, Francis. *History of the Second Army Corps.* 1887.

Ward, Joseph. *History of the One Hundred and Sixth Pennsylvania Volunteers.* 1906.

Washburn, George. *Military History and Record of the 108th Regiment New York Volunteers.* 1894.

Westbrook, Robert. *History of the 49th Pennsylvania Volunteers.* 1898.

Weygant, Charles. *History of the One Hundred and Twenty-fourth Regiment New York State Volunteers.* 1877.

Willson, Arabella. *Disaster, Struggle, Triumph.* 1870.

Woodbury, Augustus. *The Second Rhode Island Regiment.* 1875.

Woodward, E. M. *Our Campaigns.* 1865.

Campaign/Battle Studies

Cullen, Joseph. "The Wilderness Campaign" and "Spotsylvania." In *Civil War Times Illustrated: Great Battles of the Civil War.* 1984.

———. "When Grant Faced Lee across the North Anna." In *Civil War Times Illustrated.* February 1965.

———. "Cold Harbor." In *Civil War Times Illustrated.* November 1963.

Dowdey, Clifford. *Lee's Last Campaign.* 1960.

Dwight, T. F., ed. "The Wilderness Campaign." Massachusetts MOLLUS, Military Historical Society of Massachusetts. 1905.

Frassanito, William. *Grant & Lee: The Virginia Campaigns.* 1983.

Greene, A. Wilson. "One Hideous Golgotha: The Bloody Angle of Spotsylvania." Unpublished battle study, n.d.

Humphreys, Andrew. *The Virginia Campaign of 1864 and 1865.* 1883.

Jaynes, Gregory. *The Killing Ground: Wilderness to Cold Harbor.* 1986.

Krick, Robert K. "Into the Wilderness." In *Image of War, Volume V.* Edited by William C. Davis. 1983.

Martin, Samuel. "Gordon's Flank Attack." *The Kepi,* Oct.–Nov. 1983.

Miller, Joseph. "The North Anna River Campaign." Thesis, Virginia Polytechnic Institute, 1981.

Monteith, Robert. "Battle of the Wilderness, Death of General Wadsworth." Wisconsin MOLLUS, 1891.

Schaff, Morris. *The Battle of the Wilderness.* 1910.

Scott, Robert Garth. *Into the Wilderness with the Army of the Potomac.* 1985.

Steere, Edward. *The Wilderness Campaign.* 1960.

Civilian Accounts

Beale, Howard, ed. *Diary of Gideon Welles.* 1960.

Brooks, Noah. *Washington in Lincoln's Time.* 1971.

Carpenter, F. B. *Six Months at the White House.* 1961.

Couse, Katherine. Letter in Diary Form, 5/4–5/20/1864.

Davis, Varina. *Jefferson Davis — A Memoir.* 1890.

Jones, John B. *Rebel War Clerk's Diary.* Edited by E. Miers. 1958.

Powell, C. Percy. *Lincoln Day by Day.* 1960.

Reagan, John H. *Memoirs.* 1906.

Newspapers/Reporters

Cadwallader, Sylvanus. *Three Years with Grant.* 1956.

Coffin, Charles. *Four Years of Fighting.* 1866.

Forbes, Edwin. *30 Years After — An Artist's Story of the Great War.* 1891.

Page, Charles. *Letters of a War Correspondent.* 1899.

Starr, Louis M. *Reporting the Civil War.* 1962.

Swinton, William. *Campaigns of the Army of the Potomac.* 1882.

Wing, Henry E. *When Lincoln Kissed Me.* 1913.

Medical/Hospital/Sanitary Commission

Barton, William. *The Life of Clara Barton.* 1922.

Basler, Roy, ed. *Walt Whitman's Memoranda during the War.* 1962.

Hancock, Cornelia. *South after Gettysburg.* 1956.

Holstein, Anna. *Three Years in the Field Hospitals of the Army of the Potomac.* 1867.

Locke, E. W. *Three Years in Camp and Hospital.* 1870.

Reed, William, ed. *War Papers of Frank B. Fay.* 1911.

Official Documents

War of the Rebellion: Official Records of the Union and Confederate Armies.
1880–1901.

Secondary Material

Adams, Michael C. C. *Our Masters the Rebels.* 1978.
Bill, Alfred Hoyt. *Beleaguered City — Richmond 1861–1865.* 1946.
Catton, Bruce. *A Stillness at Appomattox.* 1954.
Foote, Shelby. *The Civil War: A Narrative.* 1974.
Freeman, Douglas Southall. *Lee's Lieutenants.* 1944.
Leech, Margaret. *Reveille in Washington 1860–1865.* 1949.
Naisawald, L. van Loan. *Grape and Canister.* 1960.
Niven, John. *Connecticut for the Union.* 1965.
Starr, Stephen Z. *The Union Cavalry in the Civil War.* 1981.
Whitman, William, and Charles True. *Maine in the War.* 1865.
Williams, T. Harry. *Lincoln and His Generals.* 1952.
Wilmer, L. Allison, et al. *History and Roster of Maryland Volunteers.* 1898.
Wilson, Joseph T. *The Black Phalanx.* 1892.

Maps

Cowles, Calvin, comp. *The Official Military Atlas of the Civil War.* 1978.
Fredericksburg and Spotsylvania National Military Park: Troop Movement
    Maps of the Battle of the Wilderness, May 5–6, 1864. Prepared by
    Ralph Happel, January 1962. Five maps.
Fredericksburg and Spotsylvania National Military Park: Troop Movement
    Maps of the Battle of Spotsylvania Court House, May 8–21, 1864. Pre-
    pared by Ralph Happel, n.d. Twelve maps.
Richmond Civil War Centennial Committee: Troop Movement Maps of the
    Battle of Cold Harbor, May 30–June 13, 1864. Prepared by the De-
    partment of Public Works, City of Richmond, Virginia, and Richmond
    Civil War Centennial Committee, 1964. Sixteen maps.

Acknowledgments

Writers of history have heroes; historical books have models. I have long admired those popular historians who found ways of turning complicated events into engrossing narratives. In the non–Civil War vein, I owe a debt of spirit to Cornelius Ryan and Walter Lord, while in the realm of the War Between the States I cheerfully acknowledge the masterful work of Burke Davis and salute the book that served as a model for this one: *To Appomattox: Nine April Days, 1865.*

I owe a great deal to the courteous, professional, and at times downright friendly assistance provided by the staffs at the following institutions: the Library of Congress, the National Archives, the Virginia State Library, the Virginia Historical Association, the Museum of the Confederacy, the North Carolina Department of Archives and History, Duke University, the Southern Historical Collection at the University of North Carolina, the Georgia Department of Archives and History, and the Robert W. Woodruff Library at Emory University. The historian Richard J. Sommers was especially gracious and helpful to this researcher, as was the rest of the staff at the US Army Military History Institute at the War College, Carlisle Barracks, Pennsylvania.

William D. Matter, whose definitive study of the battle of Spotsylvania Court House was in preparation as I completed this manuscript, took time to read that section of my text and make comments. Robert Younger of the Morningside Bookshop saved me much headache-inducing work by generously providing galleys of the Cyrus Comstock diary well in advance of its publication.

The archives and expertise that I found at the three national battlefield parks that embrace this campaign were invaluable. In Richmond, historian Mike Andrus kindly reviewed the North Anna and Cold Harbor portions of my manuscript and made helpful suggestions. From Petersburg, historian Donald Pfanz went above and beyond the call to provide important materials concerning Richard S. Ewell. In Fredericksburg, Chief Historian Robert K. Krick allowed me free run of his impressively organized and bound collection of primary and secondary materials, while historian A. Wilson Greene pored over the main portion of my manuscript, catching errors of fact, questioning hasty conclusions, and reining in my tendency to "Cattonize" the text. All this was done within a framework of encouragement and support. Thanks, Will.

Finally, a salute to an unsung hero, Christine Malesky, who spent many hours proofreading the text and, with quiet determination, corrected grammar and spelling, made certain that verbs and subjects were in agreement, and provided well-thought-out alternatives for clumsy passages or phrases.

The text of this book represents a succession of choices made. I have not argued the relative merits of various firsthand recollections that are in disagreement on certain points, nor have I attempted to reconcile minor conflicts in testimony. Instead, I have created my narrative from those accounts that make the most sense to me. For all questions of interpretation, and all other matters where I chose to accept or ignore the advice offered by those individuals listed above, I take full responsibility.

Acknowledgment is made for permission to quote from the following copyrighted works:

Howard Beale, ed., *The Diary of Gideon Welles*, copyright 1960 by Harper & Row.

W. G. Bean, ed., *The Liberty Hall Volunteers*, copyright 1964 by University Press of Virginia.

Sylvanus Cadwallader, *Three Years with Grant*, Benjamin P. Thomas, ed., copyright 1956 by Alfred A. Knopf, Inc.

Mark DeWolfe Howe, ed., *Touched with Fire: Civil War Letters and Diary of Oliver Wendell Holmes, Jr.*, copyright 1946 by Harvard University Press.

James L. Morrison, Jr., ed., *The Memoirs of Henry Heth*, copyright 1974 by James L. Morrison, Jr. Reprinted with permission of the editor and Greenwood Press.

Wilbur S. Nye, ed., *The Valiant Hours*, copyright 1961 by Stackpole Books. Reprinted with permission of Stackpole Books.

James I. Robertson, ed., *The Civil War Letters of General Robert McAllister*, copyright 1965 by Rutgers, The State University. Reprinted by permission of Rutgers University Press.

Ruth L. Silliker, ed., *The Rebel Yell and the Yankee Hurrah: The Civil War Journal of a Maine Volunteer*, copyright 1985 by Ruth L. Silliker, published by Down East Books.

James W. Silver, ed., *The Confederate Soldier* by LeGrand J. Wilson, copyright 1973 by Memphis State University Press.

Festus S. Summers, ed., *A Borderland Confederate*, copyright 1962 by University of Pittsburgh Press.

David B. Swinfen, *Ruggles' Regiment: The 122nd New York Volunteers in the American Civil War*, copyright 1982 by Trustees of Dartmouth College. Reprinted by permission of University Press of New England.

I am grateful to the following for making available for study materials in their collections:

The Library of Congress, Manuscript Division, for the diary of George Washington Hall, the diary of Henry F. Gray, the memoirs of Thomas S. Doyle, and the diary of Cyrus Comstock.

The Robert W. Woodruff Library of Emory University for the letters of Benjamin Wesley Justice and the letter of John A. Everett.

The Rochester Historical Society for the diary of August Seiser and the reminiscences of Porter Farley.

The Southern Historical Collection, Library of the University of North Carolina at Chapel Hill, for the diary of Cary Whitaker, the reminiscences of Westfield Todd, and the Polk, Brown, and Ewell papers.

The US Army Military History Institute at Carlisle Barracks, Pennsylvania, for the postwar letters of States B. Flandreau and the memoirs of Stephen P. Chase.

The University of Virginia Library, Manuscripts Department, for the Katherine Couse Letter (#10441).

The Virginia Historical Society for the diaries of Buckner Magill Randolph and Creed Thomas Davis.

The William R. Perkins Library, Manuscript Department, Duke University, for the diary of William E. Ardrey, the letters of Andrew Jackson Crossley, the letter of V. E. Lucas, the letters of Thomas Jones, and the letters of Asbury Jackson.

Casualties

UNION FORCES: May 5–June 12, 1864

(Computed by Bryce Suderow, using Frederick H. Dyer's *Compendium of the War of the Rebellion* and tables contained in *The War of the Rebellion: The Official Records of the Union and Confederate Armies*)

	Killed or Wounded	Captured	Total
Wilderness (May 5–7)	14,283	3,383	17,666
Spotsylvania (May 8–21)	16,141	2,258	18,399
North Anna (May 22–26)	1,973	165	2,138
Totopotomoy/Bethesda Church (May 28–31)	679	52	731
Cold Harbor (June 1–12)	12,475	2,456	14,931
TOTAL	45,551	8,314	53,865
GRAND TOTAL*	45,917	8,342	54,259

*Includes campaign losses outside above-noted battles

CONFEDERATE FORCES: May 5–June 12, 1864

(These figures have been newly computed by Alfred Young and are based in part on casualty lists found in contemporary Confederate newspapers and on service records of Lee's soldiers. Also used in the computations were Frederick H. Dyer's *Compendium of the War of the Rebellion* and tables contained in *The War of the Rebellion: The Official Records of the Union and Confederate Armies*)

	Killed or Wounded	Captured	Total
Wilderness (May 5–7)	8,949	1,881	10,830
Spotsylvania (May 8–21)	6,519	5,543	12,062
North Anna (May 22–26)	690	561	1,251
Totopotomoy/Bethesda Church (May 28–31)	811	348	1,159
Cold Harbor (June 1–12)	3,765	1,082	4,847
TOTAL	20,734	9,415	30,149
GRAND TOTAL*	21,979	9,784	31,763

*Includes campaign losses outside above-noted battles

Organization of Forces (May 4, 1864)

THE ARMY OF THE POTOMAC

Lieutenant General Ulysses S. Grant
(Commanding US Armies in the Field)

Major General George Gordon Meade
Provost Guard: Brigadier General Marsena R. Patrick
Engineer Brigade: Brigadier General Henry W. Benham
Artillery: Brigadier General Henry J. Hunt

Second Army Corps

Major General Winfield S. Hancock

1st Division: Brigadier General Francis C. Barlow
  1st Brigade: Colonel Nelson A. Miles
  2nd Brigade: Colonel Thomas A. Smyth
  3rd Brigade: Colonel Paul Frank
  4th Brigade: Colonel John R. Brooke†

2nd Division: Brigadier General John Gibbon
  1st Brigade: Brigadier General Alexander Webb†
  2nd Brigade: Brigadier General Joshua T. Owen
  3rd Brigade: Colonel Samuel S. Carroll†

3rd Division: Major General David B. Birney
  1st Brigade: Brigadier General J. H. Hobart Ward‡
  2nd Brigade: Brigadier General Alexander Hays*

4th Division: Brigadier General Gershom Mott
  1st Brigade: Colonel Robert McAllister
  2nd Brigade: Colonel William R. Brewster

Artillery Brigade: Colonel John C. Tidball

Fifth Army Corps

Major General Gouverneur K. Warren

1st Division: Brigadier General Charles Griffin
  1st Brigade: Brigadier General Romeyn B. Ayres
  2nd Brigade: Colonel Jacob B. Sweitzer
  3rd Brigade: Brigadier General Joseph J. Bartlett

2nd Division: Brigadier General John C. Robinson†
  1st Brigade: Colonel Samuel H. Leonard

---

*Killed in the course of the campaign
†Wounded, incapacitated, or captured in the course of the campaign
‡Removed from command on May 12 for "misbehavior and intoxication"

2nd Brigade: Brigadier General Henry Baxter†
3rd Brigade: Colonel Andrew W. Denison†

3rd Division: Brigadier General Samuel W. Crawford
1st Brigade: Colonel William McCandless†
3rd Brigade: Colonel Joseph W. Fisher

4th Division: Brigadier General James S. Wadsworth*
1st Brigade: Brigadier General Lysander Cutler
2nd Brigade: Brigadier General James C. Rice*
3rd Brigade: Colonel Roy Stone†

Artillery Brigade: Colonel Charles S. Wainwright

Sixth Army Corps

Major General John Sedgwick*

1st Division: Brigadier General Horatio G. Wright
1st Brigade: Colonel Henry W. Brown
2nd Brigade: Colonel Emory Upton
3rd Brigade: Brigadier General David A. Russell
4th Brigade: Brigadier General Alexander Shaler†

2nd Division: Brigadier General George W. Getty†
1st Brigade: Brigadier General Frank Wheaton
2nd Brigade. Colonel Lewis A. Grant
3rd Brigade: Brigadier General Thomas H. Neill
4th Brigade: Brigadier General Henry L. Eustis

3rd Division: Brigadier General James B. Ricketts
1st Brigade: Brigadier General William H. Morris†
2nd Brigade: Brigadier General Truman Seymour†

Artillery Brigade: Colonel Charles H. Tompkins

Ninth Army Corps

Major General Ambrose E. Burnside
(This corps was under the direct orders of Lieutenant General Grant until May 24,
1864, when it was put under Major General Meade)

1st Division: Brigadier General Thomas G. Stevenson*
1st Brigade: Colonel Sumner Carruth†
2nd Brigade: Colonel Daniel Leasure†

2nd Division: Brigadier General Robert B. Potter
1st Brigade: Colonel Zenas R. Bliss†
2nd Brigade: Colonel Simon G. Griffin

3rd Division: Brigadier General Orlando B. Willcox
1st Brigade: Colonel John F. Hartranft
2nd Brigade: Colonel Benjamin C. Christ

4th Division: Brigadier General Edward Ferrero
1st Brigade: Colonel Joshua K. Sigfried
2nd Brigade: Colonel Henry G. Thomas

---

*Killed in the course of the campaign
†Wounded, incapacitated, or captured in the course of the campaign

Cavalry Corps

Major General Philip H. Sheridan

1st Division: Brigadier General Alfred T. A. Torbert†
  1st Brigade: Brigadier General George A. Custer
  2nd Brigade: Colonel Thomas C. Devin
  3rd Brigade: Brigadier General Wesley Merritt

2nd Division: Brigadier General David McM. Gregg
  1st Brigade: Brigadier General Henry E. Davies, Jr.
  2nd Brigade: Colonel J. Irvin Gregg

3rd Division: Brigadier General James H. Wilson
  1st Brigade: Colonel John B. McIntosh
  2nd Brigade: Colonel George H. Chapman

THE ARMY OF NORTHERN VIRGINIA

General Robert E. Lee

First Army Corps

Lieutenant General James Longstreet†

Kershaw's Division: Brigadier General Joseph B. Kershaw
  Kershaw's Brigade: Colonel John W. Henagan
  Wofford's Brigade: Brigadier General William T. Wofford
  Humphreys's Brigade: Brigadier General Benjamin G. Humphreys
  Bryan's Brigade: Brigadier General Goode Bryan

Field's Division: Major General Charles W. Field
  Jenkins's Brigade: Brigadier General Micah Jenkins*
  Law's Brigade: Colonel William F. Perry
  Anderson's Brigade: Brigadier General George T. Anderson
  Gregg's Brigade: Brigadier General John Gregg
  Benning's Brigade: Brigadier General Henry L. Benning

(Although assigned to the corps, Major General George E. Pickett's division was on detached duty, assigned to the defenses of Richmond. Individual brigades rejoined the army at North Anna.)

Artillery Brigade: Brigadier General E. Porter Alexander

Second Army Corps

Lieutenant General Richard S. Ewell

Early's Division: Major General Jubal A. Early
  Hays's Brigade: Brigadier General Harry T. Hays†
  Pegram's Brigade: Brigadier General John Pegram
  Gordon's Brigade: Brigadier General John B. Gordon

Johnson's Division: Major General Edward Johnson†
  Stonewall Brigade: Brigadier General James A. Walker†
  Jones's Brigade: Brigadier General John M. Jones*
  Steuart's Brigade: Brigadier General George H. Steuart†
  Stafford's Brigade: Brigadier General Leroy A. Stafford*

---

*Killed in the course of the campaign
†Wounded, incapacitated, or captured in the course of the campaign

Rodes's Division: Major General Robert E. Rodes
  Daniel's Brigade: Brigadier General Junius Daniel*
  Doles's Brigade: Brigadier General George Doles*
  Ramseur's Brigade: Brigadier General Stephen D. Ramseur†
  Battle's Brigade: Brigadier General Cullen A. Battle
  Johnston's Brigade: Brigadier General Robert D. Johnston†
Artillery Brigade: Brigadier General Armistead L. Long

Third Army Corps

Lieutenant General Ambrose P. Hill

Anderson's Division: Major General Richard H. Anderson
  Perrin's Brigade: Brigadier General Abner Perrin*
  Harris's Brigade: Brigadier General Nathaniel H. Harris
  Mahone's Brigade: Brigadier General William Mahone
  Wright's Brigade: Brigadier General Ambrose R. Wright
  Perry's Brigade: Brigadier General Edward A. Perry†

Heth's Division: Major General Henry Heth
  Davis's Brigade: Brigadier General Joseph R. Davis
  Cooke's Brigade: Brigadier General John R. Cooke
  Kirkland's Brigade: Brigadier General William W. Kirkland†
  Walker's Brigade:
  Archer's Brigade. Brigadier General Henry H. Walker†

Wilcox's Division: Major General Cadmus M. Wilcox
  Lane's Brigade: Brigadier General James H. Lane
  Scales's Brigade: Brigadier General Alfred M. Scales
  McGowan's Brigade: Brigadier General Samuel McGowan
  Thomas's Brigade: Brigadier General Edward L. Thomas
Artillery Brigade: Colonel R. Lindsay Walker

Cavalry Corps

Major General James E. B. Stuart*

Hampton's Division: Major General Wade Hampton
  Young's Brigade: Brigadier General Pierce M. B. Young
  Rosser's Brigade: Brigadier General Thomas L. Rosser
  Butler's Brigade: Brigadier General Matthew C. Butler‡

Fitzhugh Lee's Division: Major General Fitzhugh Lee
  Lomax's Brigade: Brigadier General Lunsford L. Lomax
  Wickham's Brigade: Brigadier General Williams C. Wickham

William H. F. Lee's Division: Major General William H. F. Lee
  Chambliss's Brigade: Brigadier General John R. Chambliss
  Gordon's Brigade: Brigadier General James B. Gordon*
Artillery Brigade: Major R. P. Chew

---

*Killed in the course of the campaign
†Wounded or captured in the course of the campaign
‡Did not join the Army of Northern Virginia until May 28

Index